Sustainable Resource Use

Sustainable Resource Use

Institutional Dynamics and Economics

Edited by
Alex Smajgl and Silva Larson

London • Sterling, VA

First published by Earthscan in the UK and USA in 2007

ISBN: 978-1-84407-459-4

Typeset by FiSH Books, Enfield, Middx.
Printed and bound in the UK by Cromwell Press, Trowbridge
Cover design by Susanne Harris

For a full list of publications please contact:

Earthscan
8–12 Camden High Street
London, NW1 0JH, UK
Tel: +44 (0)20 7387 8558
Fax: +44 (0)20 7387 8998
Email: earthinfo@earthscan.co.uk
Web: **www.earthscan.co.uk**

22883 Quicksilver Drive, Sterling, VA 20166–2012, USA

Earthscan is an imprint of James and James (Science Publishers) Ltd and publishes
in association with the International Institute for Environment and Development

A catalogue record for this book is available from the British Library

Library of Congress Cataloging-in-Publication Data

Sustainable resource use : institutional dynamics and economics / edited by Alex
Smajgl and Silva Larson.
    p. cm.
  Includes bibliographical references and index.
  ISBN-13: 978-1-84407-459-4 (alk. paper)
  ISBN-10: 1-84407-459-5 (alk. paper)
  1. Natural resources—Management. 2. Sustainable development. I. Smajgl,
Alex. II. Larson, Silva.
  HC79.E5S8688 2007
  333.7—dc22

                                                                2006101243   •

Mixed Sources
Product group from well-managed
forests and other controlled sources
www.fsc.org Cert no. TT-TOC-2082
© 1996 Forest Stewardship Council

Contents

List of Figures and Tables

Figures

Tables

Preface

This book summarizes papers presented at an international workshop, 'Property rights: The key to achieving ecologically sustainable development in Outback regions', held in early March 2005 at Undara, Australia. This workshop was a part of the project 'Opportunities for the Australia Outback: Researching institutional arrangements in the North', which focused on analysing the existing institutional arrangements in the region using different case studies. The underlying workshop approach was to bring together the international experience and explore together potential learnings for the use of natural resources.

The workshop was conceptualized around two perspectives relevant to Australia's outback: the natural resource perspective and the Indigenous perspective. We would like to thank all presenters for their excellent presentations and the efficient process of improving papers through intense reviewing by each workshop participant.

Furthermore, we would like to thank the emerging science area Social-Economic Integration (SEI) of CSIRO for funding this publication and the three parties that funded the broader research project: CSIRO, Desert Knowledge Corporate Research Centre and Tropical Savannah Corporate Research Centre. We received excellent support from all three funding agencies during the research process.

We are very grateful for the contributions from the core team members Romy Greiner, Karen Vella, Melissa Nursey-Bray and Alexander Herr. Additionally, we acknowledge administrative support by Sally Way and Rosemary Schultz. We are also very grateful for the reviewing work Liz Tynan did under very tight timelines. Special thanks belong to Beau Hug for his great effort in bringing this book together.

Alex Smajgl and Silva Larson
Townsville
May 2006

Part I

The Context

Institutional Dynamics and Natural Resource Management

Alex Smajgl and Silva Larson

The Context

One of the fundamental characteristics of a social system is the development of shared concepts. Those shared concepts can enable and/or constrain the behaviour of individuals in the system as formal and informal rules and sets of norms. The rules and norms developed within the social system are often defined in theoretical discussions as *institutional arrangements* (Dietz et al, 2003). Institutions are 'the shared concepts used by humans in repetitive situations organized by rules, norms, and strategies' (Ostrom, 1999).

Agrawal (2002) argues that institutions have to be analysed within their context, as the same rule can have different impacts in different contexts. Conversely, a change of context can create a different impact even in long-existing institutions. We argue that, in addition, changing an institution is likely to lead to a modification of the wider set of institutions. This institutional change has a potential to lead to *evolution of context*; that is, a change in a wider social, economic and ecological context. And conversely, *evolution of wider context* has a potential to lead to *evolution of institutional context*. Depending on the direction of the change, this *institutional ripple effect* might be either beneficial or negative.

In the context of natural resources, the way humans organize both resource access and resource use is of crucial importance to the management of that natural resource. The rules of the relevant institutional arrangement potentially become levers by which human behaviours can be modified and the goals of natural resource management can be steered towards. This book focuses on institutional dynamics from the perspective of natural resources management.

This chapter first discusses the ecological perspective of the system, in order to identify the demands current ecological theory places on institutional arrangements. We discuss how the ecological perspective has changed over the past three decades and argue that the current paradigm of adaptive governance often ignores the complexity of social systems. Institutional changes forced by adaptive governance can lead to situations where the ability of institutions to adapt to changing conditions decreases, and reversal to former institutional arrangements becomes impossible.

In order to further analyse social and institutional complexity, the following section presents the system from the institutional dynamics perspective. Here, we start with principal property rights regimes and the underlying assumptions of institutional theory. We argue that the institutional perspective under-represents the complexity and dynamics of the system and propose elements in order to advance our understanding of *institutional dynamics*, the core focus of this book.

Following from there is an explanation of how this book provides approaches to understanding institutional dynamics and presents the storyline of the book.

Finally, this chapter synthesizes the discussion and points out future research needs.

Paradigms of Natural Resource Management

This section discusses complex social-ecological systems in the context of natural resource management.

The theory and principles of complex ecological systems have introduced the requirement for institutional arrangements, related to natural resource systems, to be adaptive. The ecological imperative for adaptive institutions governing resource use is a step beyond strong or weak criteria for sustainability; however, it lacks appreciation of the complexity of the social side of the system. Furthermore, depending on the direction adaptation takes, the institutional ripple effect of change might create either positive or negative impacts on the natural resource and its stakeholders.

Sustainability is a concept that has fundamentally changed societies and many research disciplines. While between the 1950s and the 1980s the vast majority of environmental economics focused on the identification of optimal usage or extraction rates of resources (often based on Gordon, 1953; Schaefer, 1954; also Clark, 1976; Dasgupta, 1982), sustainability-based research has changed the perception of the interdependency of ecological, social and economic variables (Sayer and Campbell, 2004; Smajgl et al, 2005).

Thus, triple-bottom-line research requires analysing how ecological, social and economic variables interact. The increasingly perceived complexity makes it difficult for researchers to give policy recommendations based on a few isolated system variables. Whole-of-system approaches define social-ecological systems as having critical boundaries, broadening research agendas and often linking and merging disciplines in order to operationalize sustainability (Mitchell, 1996; Sayer and Campbell, 2004; Smajgl and Hajkowicz, 2005). While historical models aimed at simulating a variable for a long period of time, for instance, fish stock with its impacts on economic returns subject to management options (Silvert and Smith, 1977), an integrated set of indicators is crucial to providing information about sustainability (Larson and Smajgl, 2006).

When a set of required indicators is broadened, theoretical frameworks developed within disciplinary isolation become problematic. Additionally, new insights about the critical interactions driving a social-ecological system are likely to change demands for governance and institutional arrangements. What is required, then, is an approach that can operate within the scope of a whole social-ecological system and have a strong focus on the dynamics of system variables. Increasingly, the resilience approach offers a promising set of theories that could potentially do just that. Unfortunately, the concept is mainly developed from an ecological perspective and other disciplines are mainly add-ons instead of integrated components. Similar to the long domination of economics in natural resource management, ecology dominates the resilience discussion. Hopefully, resilience discussions of the future will be more inclusive and will come back to the main integration idea of sustainability research.

One of the key assumptions of resilience theory is that 'ecosystems are complex, adaptive systems that are characterized by historical dependency, non-linear dynamics, multiple basins of attraction and limited predictability'. (Folke, 2003). A key concept for the application of resilience approach is that a system can exist in several different states, each of which is controlled by a different set of processes, and some of which are more stable and possibly more desirable than others. Resilience can thus be defined as 'the magnitude of disturbance that can be tolerated before a socioecological system moves to a different region of state space controlled by a different set of processes'. (Carpenter et al, 2001)

While many aspects remain problematic – for instance, the specification and identification of attractor basins and the quantification of resilience in an applied context – one important feature of social-ecological systems is much better understood: the ever-changing nature of ecological components and the need for adaptive management that frames any resource use or allocation problem. In other words, natural resource management has to consider the complexity of ecosystems and adapt to environmental changes (Folke, 2003; Holling, 2004).

Resilience theory provides a step towards defining institutions that are more capable of responding to ecosystem dynamics. But at the same time, its view captures only part of the system complexity as it does not acknowledge the complexity of the social system and the likelihood of institutional ripple effects triggered by changes in management regulations (institutions). To better understand these co-evolutionary dynamics, practitioners of the resilience approach are turning to the study of social complexity. Similar to the thresholds of ecological variables that indicate potentially undesirable or catastrophic conditions, institutions and social variables have positions and states that may not be conducive to the broader goals of society. Once an institution has changed, thresholds may be crossed prohibiting a reversal of such a change. The following section will argue that the creation of the *institutional footprint* impacts upon perceptions, motivations and the behaviour of individuals and groups.

The ability to understand institutional dynamics, therefore, becomes crucial. Capturing the context specific structure of a resource use situation, which links social dynamics that define how rules change to the perception of ecological change, is a major challenge. This challenge will have to be overcome in order to enable the development of a natural resource governance approach that takes social and economic adaptation into consideration. Accruing learning and knowledge about participants, strategies, ecological conditions, changes in technologies and economic relations, over time, might lead towards crafting sustainable institutions (Ostrom, 2005). Institutional dynamics are further discussed in the next section.

Institutional Dynamics

Progress in institutional research has aided our understanding of many structural components of any resource use situation. Individual decision-making is constrained by institutional arrangements, of which property rights are a fundamental part. *Property* 'is a claim to a benefit or income stream, and a *property right* is a claim to a benefit stream that some higher body – usually the state – will agree to protect through the assignment of duty to others who may covet, or somehow interfere with the benefit stream' (Bromley, 1992, p4). Property rights can therefore be defined as some of the individual components of relationships comprising institutions, as discussed in Chapter 10.

In principle, property rights can be found on the level of single entities like individuals (*res privatae*), on the group level (*res communes*), on the level of a government (*res publica*), or are not specified at all, which leads to an open-access regime (*res nullius*). Hardin (1968) articulated a strong position supporting the environmental discussion that questioned the ability of humans to govern natural resources sustainably. He argued that individually perceived incentives always lead to an overuse of resources, which he described as the tragedy of the commons. From Hardin's point of view, humans are selfish and, together with the incentive to behave as free riders within a community governed resource, this will always shift the status quo of the resource to overuse. The only way to overcome this problem would be to change incentive schemes through privatizing (*res privatae*) or centralizing property rights (*res publica*).

While Hardin's intention was to enhance the protection of natural resources, his work provides a strong argument for privatization or centralization of the commons. Both strategies entail a radical change of incentives. Privatization is often coupled with market incentives that can exclude some social externalities of certain activities, while centralization can often result in inflexible bureaucratic behaviour (Holling and Meffe, 1996). Therefore, both strategies tend not to enhance the sustainability of a system.

Ostrom (1990) shows that Hardin's view is oversimplified. Generally, the assumption of purely selfish behaviour is increasingly criticized. Field experiments emphasise that the general assumption of selfish behaviour for *homo oeconomicus* does not hold (Henrich et al, 2005). Sober and Wilson (1998) show how relevant altruistic behaviour is in the real-world context.

This means that the *res communes* systems of property rights are a potential option for natural resource management (Ostrom, 1990, 1992; Bromley,

1992). Chapter 2 and Ostrom et al, (1993) go a step further and argue that in various situations natural resources should be governed by direct users, since adaptive capacity requires their knowledge. Often, privatized and centralized governance structures do not lead to sustainable outcomes (Ostrom et al, 1993; Holling and Meffe, 1996).

Simulation models can be used to explore institutional change. For those models that seek to endogenize institutional change, the definition of institutional building blocks and how they combine to build institutional structures is crucial. Understanding the structural features of institutions requires identification of, first, a typology of rules (Ostrom, 1990, 1992), and second, the elements that constitute rules (Crawford and Ostrom, 1995).

The recent work of Ostrom (2005, Chapter 2), improves our understanding of institutional dynamics as, instead of analysing institutional snap shots, the structural components are analysed in order to contextualize change.

We put forward the notion that it would be insightful for understanding institutional dynamics to develop, similar to static building blocks of typology and elements of rules, types of *processes* of institutional change. A generic institutional process could take the following format:

1   Perception of change: Individuals perceive a change or perturbation in conditions they operate in, which includes environmental, social, economic or institutional conditions.
2   Identification of causality: Depending on their behavioural tendencies and attitudes, some individuals compare the perceived change with their mental models of why it might have happened and what its impacts could be and come up with their own explanation of these causal relationships.
3   Communication of the opinion on change: Depending on their behavioural tendencies and attitudes, some individuals communicate their opinion of causal relationships within their social network; this communication might create diffusion processes, depending on the individual's position/power relations within the network, as well as perceived relevance of the change.
4   Alignment of opinions: Individuals align themselves, based on their opinion of causal relationships and motivation factors.
5   Decrease of fitness of the existing institution.
6   Formation of new institutions.
7   Replacement or modification of existing institutions.

To understand the structure and resulting dynamics of any resource use situation, all relevant institutions, resource users, their values and their connection in a social network would need to be identified. Crucial for understanding institutional changes is knowledge of the thresholds responsible for ripple effects. These thresholds have to be identified at each level. On the individual level, a crucial threshold is defined between the states of *accepting/not accepting* and *communicating opinion/not communicating opinion*, in other words, how much tolerance do individuals have before demanding a change in constraints they face. This threshold can be defined as a function of perceived incentives, values and attitudes. On the social level the crucial threshold divides the states *accepting institution* and *not accepting institution*. This threshold can also be described as a function of power relations within social networks (Brown, 2003), social cohesion (Friedkin, 2004), and institutional consistency.

Individual decision-making is often explained by the fact that a certain strategy is expected to lead to a higher benefit for the individual decision-maker. Since Simon (1955), this monetary-based position has steadily lost ground (Sober and Wilson, 1998; Henrich et al, 2005). Unfortunately, while research developed a significant focus on valuation (Adamowicz, 2004), the debate was mainly focused on valuation techniques like choice modelling or multi-criteria analysis instead of on capturing values and their role in defining thresholds.

Recent research into subjective well-being provides an opportunity to capture and prioritize individual values (Cummins, 1996; Diener and Suh, 1997; Headey and Wearing, 1998; Irwin, 2001; Fray and Stutzer, 2002). Furthermore, there is an increasing recognition that individuals in many cultures do not perceive individual benefits as primary drivers of their strategy choice (Diener and Suh, 1997; Larson et al, 2006). In this case, individual decision-making is explained by group benefits and cognitive processes prioritizing strategies according to group level outcomes. This would mean that individual thresholds can be grouped and defined as functions of individually perceived states of the social system (Larson, 2005, forthcoming). Such an understanding could allow for an improved conceptual base linking individual and group level dynamics and could lead to the ability to simulate how shared concepts evolve in a dynamic environment.

Equally important for the analysis of institutional dynamics is the understanding of decisions and dynamics at the scale of social thresholds.

The consistency of institutions is a major component for social thresholds. Brown (1998, 2003) employs the concept of institutional fit (Hanna et al, 1997; Berkes and Folke, 1998) to explain that institutional change can lead to a misfit between institutions. Institutional changes can reduce social resilience by:

- creating conflicts between different users and user groups;
- modifying power relationships between different stakeholders (see also Agrawal and Verughese, 2000);
- communicating conflicting management objectives;
- impacting resource access for various stakeholders differently.

Such a reduction in social resilience can enhance the sustainability of the system if the system was in a resilient but unsustainable state. Conversely, such impacts can reduce not only social resilience but also sustainability.

Additionally, social thresholds themselves can be defined as functions of institutional change. Experimental evidence shows that the introduction of a certain rule set has an impact on behaviour and reinstalling the prior rule set does not restore the prior behaviour (Reeson, forthcoming). If, for instance, a market for tradeable water rights is introduced, the perception of the nature of property rights for water is permanently changed. Returning to the previous management regime does not result in return to a prior behaviour. Rather, an *institutional footprint* is created in the mental models of water users.

Knowledge and learning underlie the concept of social thresholds (Bandura, 1977; Young, 1998; Fudenberg and Levine, 1998). They go some way to explaining how individual experiences can be linked with institutional designs to result in institutional footprints. Included within this are the cognitive processes involved with evaluating the effectiveness of institutions in terms of individual and/or social criteria. Explaining linkages between the individual and social processes that form institutional change requires an improved understanding of social thresholds.

As discussed earlier, from an ecological perspective, governance and institutions have to be adaptive as ecological systems are ever-changing. It was argued that such a view has to be broadened by implementing social complexity and that dynamics of institutions are crucial. While the previous sections were able just to touch on some of the key points and suggest potential pathways for approaching institutional dynamics, the following section presents aspects of adapting the rules this book discusses in further depth.

Overview of this Book

The main argument presented in this book is that institutional arrangements cannot be perceived as a set of parameters that can be optimized and locked in for the most efficient functioning of a system. Nor can institutions be evaluated outside the context in which they were developed. The chapters of this book develop and provide evidence for this argument.

Part II – Institutional diversity and contextual change

In Chapter 2, Elinor Ostrom provides an overview of the Institutional Analysis and Development (IAD) framework, the framework used by many scholars to study the outcomes in diversely structured common-pool resource regimes. The chapter explores some of the core foundations of contemporary policy analysis and specifically provides a description of types of rules used by resource users for governing and managing common-pool resources.

Ostrom challenges the assumption that designing rules is a simple process that can be accomplished by skilled analysts working for a central government. The number of rules actually used in field settings is far greater than generally recognized. Furthermore, the type of rules is also different from those most frequently recommended in the textbooks on policy analysis. The chapter is fittingly entitled 'Multiple Institutions for Multiple Outcomes', recognizing the need for institutions to fit context, current circumstances and objectives for future outcomes.

Not only can institutions not easily be copied from one context to the other, the institutional arrangements might become ineffective over time as context, circumstances and desired outcomes change.

In Chapter 3, Katrina Brown investigates the historically enduring

common property regimes of Western Europe. The formal and informal governance structures of those commons are in varying states, depending on the
response made to the pressures of contemporary rural change. Two particular
challenges recognized are the growing difficulty of gaining sufficient livelihood
contributions from traditional agriculturally based activities, and the increasing heterogeneity of rights holders. Brown's chapter discusses the implications
of these challenges for Scottish common land institutions. Brown explores the
dynamics of introducing new users or rights holders with potentially different
ideas, values and norms, and how this affects the way values are attached to
and captured from commons, in particular land.

Part II of the book sets the scene for the discussion on institutional dynamics. We argue that institutional arrangements are both spatially and temporally
specific. Institutions may become ineffective over time as context, circumstances and desired outcomes change. Furthermore, a change of institutions
based on experiences in other geographical contexts can have a devastating
outcome. This notion is further considered in Part III.

Part III – Institutional misfit

Part III provides insights into the situations where institutions appropriate to
one (geographic and social) context were transplanted into the new context.
This transplantation of the institutional arrangements was a key driver in the
colonization process. However, many of the arrangements introduced during
the colonization era are still in place and act today as a main institutional layer
over-riding Indigenous institutions and organizing essential parts of Indigenous
life. Chapters of Part III look into various aspects of institutional arrangements
as they affect contemporary Indigenous peoples. The first chapters provide
discussions on international legislative provisions and their potential impacts for
Indigenous peoples. The on-ground outcomes of the dynamic created through
the overlap of Indigenous and enforced arrangements are then investigated in
the context of land rights in the Pacific, fishing rights in New Zealand, and
water and forestry rights and informal institutional arrangements in Australia.
The Part III discussions indicate that furthering the compatibility of Indigenous
and non-Indigenous institutions, both in an Australian and international
context, warrants additional research and discussion.

Part III starts with the discussion by Alex Amankwah (Chapter 4) on traditional and customary land tenure. In western cultural systems, land constitutes
an economic asset easily convertible into cash. Land therefore is just one
species of property, where commercialization has reduced land to the level of
chattel. Amankwah argues that, in the world's predominantly non-western
cultures, however, land is considered an ancestral trust left to the living by their
ancestors for the use of the present generation, and to be transmitted to generations yet unborn. Land is, therefore, communal property and inalienable
except between members of the community. Limitations imposed on the alienability of traditional land might ensure its sustainability and prevent its misuse.
Therefore, if properly structured, traditional interests and rights in land could
complement rather than detract from institutional efforts to promote a sustain-

able environment. However, western legal systems tend to dismiss traditional land tenure as nothing more than a relic of the 'Arcadian fantasy'. For the traditional systems to be able to express their full potential for sustainable management, a dramatic shift in the current and dominant property law paradigm would need to occur.

A detailed investigation of the role that intellectual property, as it applies to the traditional knowledge, plays in the sustainable natural resources management is presented by Michael Jeffery in Chapter 5. Jeffery focuses on recent developments in the area of intellectual property rights and discusses their appropriateness and ability to provide adequate protection of Indigenous knowledge and practices. The contextual platform on which discussion takes place are international efforts to protect and conserve biological diversity, particularly biological diversity associated with genetic resources. This chapter argues that, to achieve equitable and sustainable use of essential resources in the future, we need to move towards the creation of new forms of property rights protection that link conventional property rights, environmental principles and human rights.

There is no property in nature – the concept of property and property rights is a human construct – argues Spike Boydell in Chapter 6. Boydell presents a case study from the Pacific, where confusion and conflict between constitutional and customary law are common. The traditional concept of communalism, which is accepted practice in many Pacific island countries, clouds and confuses attitudes to natural resources ownership, set in constitutional law. The chapter presents two stories, one investigating challenges of spiritual materialism; and one investigating land property rights from the customary and a western, formal and informal, perspective.

The importance of understanding the spiritual and cultural connection that Indigenous people have with their land and waters is further discussed by Donna Craig in Chapter 7. This chapter presents an overview of the international legislative development in the field of Indigenous water rights, and specifically investigates water-related rights of Aboriginal people of Australia and presents a case for fishing rights of the Maori people of New Zealand. Modern Australian water management institutions rarely recognize the traditions, customs and laws of Aboriginal people as related to water and access to water. This lack of legal recognition flows from a deeper lack of recognition and understanding of Indigenous spiritual values and cultures (ATSIC and Lingiari Foundation, 2002). However, Craig argues, there are many sources of international and domestic law that support the right of Aboriginal peoples to have their customary relationships to water recognized and respected, such as International Human Rights law, particularly the emerging discourse of a human right to water; or the Australian federal government strategy of Ecologically Sustainable Development. This chapter suggests a 'rights based approach', where international human rights and environmental law support the wider recognition of Indigenous rights to water.

Following the story of the New Zealand Maori fishing rights, Tyron Venn investigates the rights of Wik people to use and develop forestry resources. In Chapter 8, Venn presents the case of the Wik people of Cape York Peninsula,

Queensland, who see commercial processing of native forest timbers as a culturally appropriate engine for economic development. However, much uncertainty surrounds their property rights to native forest timber. Some economists have argued that the inalienable and communal nature of the land title granted to Indigenous communities, including Wik people, is an obstacle to development. An assessment of Wik property rights to timber resources reveals that a commercial forestry industry is consistent with their rights. Venn further points out that, in comparison with social and cultural factors, the inalienable and communal characteristics of native title are but a second-order development constraint for Wik people.

Social and cultural factors, and in particular capacity issues as they relate to Indigenous development, have been brought up in discussions by Craig and Venn. In Chapter 9, Rolf Gerritsen and Anna Straton continue the discussion on specificities of social and cultural factors of Aboriginal peoples. Gerritsen and Straton present an essay on norms, values and cultural rules of Aboriginal people and settlements in northern and central Australia. They argue that conditions for Aboriginal people in those settlements are much worse than for non-Aboriginal people in the same regions. Various reasons are conventionally advanced to explain this phenomenon, including levels of government expenditure, lack of access of Aboriginal people to conventional labour markets and mutual cultural incomprehension. Gerritsen and Straton propose an interesting alternative reason: governments' misunderstanding of the 'community'. They argue that the official policy assumption that Aboriginal people living on these settlements are 'communities', and therefore share common norms, values and purpose, might be at the root cause of the failure of social government programmes.

Throughout Part III we are presented with discussions stressing the importance of understanding the context of interweaving formal and informal arrangements and the overlap of traditional (Indigenous) institutions with constitutional ('western') institutions. The chapters provide discussions on international legislative provisions and examples from the Pacific, New Zealand and Australia that explore aspects of traditional and constitutional rights related to land, fishing, water and forestry. The Part III discussions indicate that furthering the compatibility of Indigenous and non-Indigenous institutions, in both Australian and international contexts, warrant additional research and discussion.

Chapters in Parts II and III support the notion that institutions develop in a context-specific way, and that context is both spatially and temporally specific. Furthermore, in order to maintain relevance and applicability, the institutions need to be dynamic and capable of adapting to changing context. Examples of the issues and aspects of relevance to institutional dynamics, investigated in practice, are presented in Part IV.

Part IV – Experiences in dealing with institutional dynamics

Institutional dynamics are complex and entail a complex set of issues. Some of those issues are discussed in Part IV of the book: examples of business structures that allow formalization of commons in the 'modern' world; administrative frameworks and processes required to support effective functioning of formal institutions; the role of informal institutions in stimulating progress; and the use of market-based instruments in management of natural resources. The discussions offered in Part IV highlight some of the range of issues that would need to be taken into account when discussing the design of adaptable institutions; as well as different points of view that would inevitably enter that discussion.

In Chapter 10, Brunckhorst and Marshall discuss potential business structures for cross-property collaboration and present some of the lessons learnt in the process of designing some of the modern, robust, common property regimes in Australia. Brunckhorst and Marshall discuss the failure of property rights to facilitate adaptation of rural land uses in response to the declining economic, environmental and social sustainability of rural communities. Many individual rural properties, whether under freehold or leasehold, are too small to be sustainable. There is, therefore, an increasing necessity to explore innovative property arrangements for rural lands and resources. In this chapter, Brunckhorst and Marshall propose that attempts at innovation can benefit considerably from the lessons drawn from international experiences with robust common property regimes, and that much practical knowledge is to be gained from elaborating these lessons through 'on-ground' experimentation in contemporary rural land-use contexts. The authors further argue that contemporary business structures supported by legislation or government administration can be used creatively in translating these lessons to existing rural settings, and present three such examples from Australia.

The administration of property rights and restrictions is explored by Lyons, Davies and Cottrell in Chapter 11. The authors suggest that the introduction of environmental legislation has unbundled property rights historically implicit within a land title, and therefore has created a need for modification of the historic land title administration systems. This chapter reports on studies carried out into the efficiency of the administration of property rights and restrictions in Australia. Lyons, Davies and Cottrell continue with suggestions on areas for improvement and 'good practice' for administration of property rights, obligations and restrictions.

Smajgl, Nursey-Bray, Vella and Herr look into the role of informal institutions through their case study presented in Chapter 12. The research found that (lack of) informal institutional arrangements resulted in weak social cohesion, triggering out-migration dynamics that contradict governmental aspirations for economic development. The quantitative model developed for the region tested hypothetical adaptation of the rules in the informal dimension of institutional arrangements. The model investigates the opportunities, such as tourism and external investment in road infrastructure, that could be used as a vehicle for strengthening social cohesion.

In Chapter 13, John Rolfe explores the potential role of market mechanisms, through the investigation of their potential role in achieving vegetation protection in the rangelands area of central-western Queensland, Australia. Vegetation clearing for development and intensive grazing and introduction of new pastures have improved production of the region, but have also created negative environmental consequences. While regulation has been used by the Queensland Government to address environmental issues, the use of regulatory mechanisms comes at a cost. These include administration, compliance, transaction and opportunity costs, as well as the impacts on existing property rights. In this chapter, Rolfe puts forward the case for market-based instruments as an alternative. He argues that market-based instruments work well in the existing framework of property rights and that outcomes are often more efficient because both production and conservation goals can be pursued together. He reports on a series of field experiments that evaluate the use of conservation auctions for purchasing environmental services, with particular focus on establishing corridor linkage zones.

In the final chapter of the book, Chapter 14, Garrick Small takes us on a journey exploring metaphysical grounding for ecologically sustainable property rights. He argues that a narrow economic view of property suggests that property rights are irrelevant to sustainable ecological outcomes. Small further argues that this position rests on problematic premises, inherited from the larger framework of modernity. The chapter therefore investigates realism as a philosophical system capable of supporting the environmental goal of sustainable resource management. Small argues that the classic methodological organization of science is best suited to the needs of environmentalism, and points out the significance of classical metaphysics and their location within the classical organization of the sciences. The institution of property is then reviewed within this framework to demonstrate its validity.

The discussions in Part IV present experiences in dealing with some aspects of institutional dynamics. Brunckhorst and Marshall discuss the potential for using current business structures to create robust and legally defensible commons sufficiently large to enable economic and ecologically sustainable management. Lyons et al point out the importance of improving administration and processes so that they can support a dynamic property rights system. Smajgl et al look into informal institutional arrangements and the critical role they might be playing in the remote localities in particular. Rolfe explores the potential benefits of market mechanisms, while Small points at the narrowness of the current economic view. Part IV of the book therefore presents different approaches and proposes potential changes to the system that could create beneficial solutions for Australia.

Future Research

This chapter presents discussion on the dynamics of institutions in the context of temporal and spatial changes. We argue not only that institutions cannot easily be copied from one context to the other, but that institutional arrangements may become ineffective over time as context, circumstances and desired outcomes change. Additionally, we argue that institutions themselves determine essential parts of the context. Introducing, for instance, a new formal rule on managing natural resources is likely to impact the effectiveness of existing set of institutions. Therefore, in order to maintain relevance and applicability, the institutions need not only to be dynamic and capable of adapting to a changing context but also have to be designed against the background of potential institutional ripple effects.

We argue furthermore that 'context' is often wider then typically appreciated. The relationship between an institution and a resource can not be studied in isolation. Figure 1.1 shows how institutional system components (I_1–I_3) could be embedded in a whole-of-system approach, linked to economic (E), environmental (R) and social (S) system components. Changing an institution I_1 in order to regulate the access and use of resource R_1 can have flow-on effects that impact how I_3 regulates R_2 and also how I_2 affects S_1. These ripple effects can change the effectiveness of existing institutions. Ripple effect feedback processes might also change the evolutionary effectiveness of the newly introduced institution.

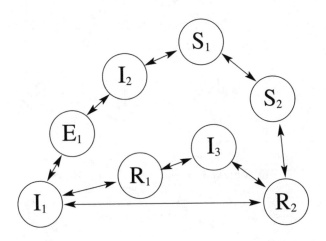

Figure 1.1 Conceptual system with components and links

Research often isolates the different layers of a system, as shown in Figure 1.2, and then analyses the impact of one institution regarding one natural resource in order to enhance the condition of this specific resource. The findings of this institutional research enhanced our understanding of the impact institutions can have and if an institution might be suitable for governing a certain natural resource. However, the institution also needs to be studied as a part of the institutional layer it is embodied in, as well as a part of, the economic, ecological and social layers it might impact on or be impacted by.

Institutional arrangements might become ineffective on the temporal scale as context, circumstances or desired outcomes change, and the institutions remain inflexible (Figure 1.3a). Decreasing suitability of existing institutions creates the demand for adaptive governance. Such a demand defines balancing out a co-evolution of institutions and the natural resources it attempts to govern.

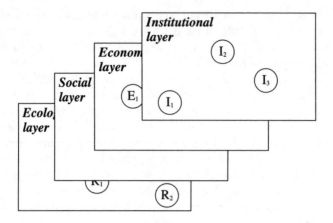

Figure 1.2. Multiple layers of the conceptual system

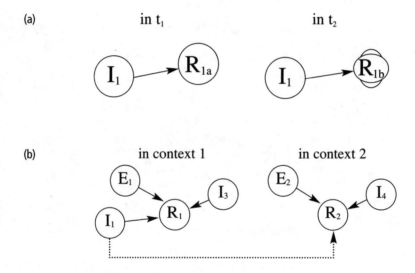

Figure 1.3 Temporal (a) and spatial (b) change of institutional context

Several chapters of this book also provide insights into the changes in spatial context, where institutions appropriate to one geographic and social context were transplanted into a new context (Figure 1.3b).

Many arrangements introduced during the colonization era are still in place and provide the main institutional layer over-riding Indigenous institutions. However, over time, Indigenous institutions, values and desired outcomes have evolved, as the result of both the institutional footprint and the social, ecological and economic evolution of the system. Therefore, we argue for the need for future investigations into the dynamics of Indigenous institutions, and the compatibility of Indigenous and non-Indigenous institutions.

In conclusion, one dimension we deem interesting for further investigations is the spatial and temporal dynamic of the institutional layer and the relevant dynamics of the ecosystems, society and economy. This dimension broadens the scope of analysis and links institutions to other system components.

The second dimension we deem interesting for further investigation concerns the dynamics of links and relationships between 'traditional' or Indigenous and 'western' or 'non-Indigenous' institutional arrangements. The third dimension is the study of the dynamics of formal versus informal arrangements. Both dimensions aim at enhancing the understanding of perception-related and motivational elements of institutional effectiveness.

We also see the potential for investigating further the variety of arrangements existing in relation to commons in Australia. Commons in Australia are experiencing a rather dynamic phase, with several recent, current or upcoming legislative, operational and management changes. We will therefore aim at furthering our work in the area of institutional dynamics of Australian commons.

Overall, we put forward the notion that types of *processes* of institutional change need to be better understood. The focus of future research would therefore need to shift from the components of the system (circles in Figure 1.1) to the links, dynamics and drivers between the components (arrows between system components in Figure 1.1).

Crucial for the development of a holistic, adaptive management approach is the implementation of institutional dynamics and social complexity. This requires the identification of processes that explain institutional dynamics and thresholds within social systems. Institutional changes made as a consequence of perceived and undesired states of ecological variables can push the institutional arrangement and the wider social system into a state with undesirable social impacts.

References

Adamowicz, W. L. (2004). 'What's it worth? An examination of historical trends and future direction in environmental valuation'. *The Australian Journal of Agricultural and Resource Economics*, 48, 419–444.

Agrawal, A. (2002). 'Common Resources and Institutional Sustainability'. In Ostrom, E.; Dietz, T.; Dolsak, N.; Stern, PC.; Stovitch, S. and Weber, E. U. (eds.). *The Drama of the Commons*. Washington, DC: National Academy Press.

Agrawal, A. and Varughese, G. (2000). 'Conservation's visions: Poverty, participation and protected area management in Nepal's Terai'. Paper presented at the 8th Biennial meeting of the IASCP. Bloomington, Indiana, May 28, 2000.

ATSIC and Lingiari Foundation Partnership (2002). *Indigenous Rights to Waters: Report and Recommendations*. Canberra: ATSIC.

Bandura, A. (1977). *Social Learning Theory*. Englewood: Prentice-Hall.

Berkes, F. and Folke C. (eds.) (1998). *Linking Social and Ecological Knowledge and Resource Management*. Philadelphia, PA: Taylor and Francis.

Bromley, D. W. (1992). *Making the Commons Work*. San Francisco, California: Institute for Contemporary Studies.

Brown, K. (1998). 'The political ecology of biodiversity, conservation and development in Nepal's Terai: Confused meanings, means and ends'. *Ecological Economics*, 24, 73–88.

Brown, K. (2003). 'Integrating conservation and development: a case of institutional misfit'. *Frontiers in Ecology and the Environment*, 9, 479–487.

Carpenter, S.; Walker, B.; Andries, J. M. and Abel, N. (2001). 'From metaphor to measurement: Resilience of what to what?' *Ecosystems*, 4, 765–781.

Clark, C. W. (1976). *Mathematical Bioeconomics: The Optimal Management of Renewable Resources.* New York: John Wiley (2nd edition 1990).

Crawford, S. E. S. and Ostrom, E. (1995). 'A grammar of institutions'. *American Political Science Review*, 89, 582–600. Also in Ostrom, E. (2005) *Understanding Institutional Diversity.* (pp. 137–74). Princeton, NJ: Princeton University Press.

Cummins, R. A (1996). 'Domains of life satisfaction: An attempt to order chaos'. *Social Indicators Research*, 38(3), 303–328.

Dasgupta, P. (1982). *The Control of Resources.* Oxford: Basil Blackwell.

Diener, E. and Suh, E. (1997). 'Measuring quality of life: economic, social, and subjective indicators'. *Social Indicators Research*, 40, 189–216.

Dietz, T.; Ostrom, E. and Stern, P. C. (2003). 'The struggle to govern the commons'. *Science*, 302, 1907–1912.

Folke, C. (2003). 'Freshwater for resilience: A shift in thinking'. *Philosophical Transactions of the Royal Society of London*, 358, 2027–2036.

Fray, B. S. and Stutzer, A. (2002). *Happiness and Economics: How the Economy and Institutions Affect Wellbeing.* Princeton: Princeton University Press.

Friedkin, N. E. (2004). 'Social cohesion'. *Annual Review of Sociology*, 30, 409–425.

Fudenberg, D. and Levine, K. D. (1998). *The Theory of Learning in Games.* Cambridge: MIT Press.

Gordon, H. S. (1953). 'An economic approach to optimum utilization of fishery resources'. *Journal of the Fisheries Research Board of Canada*, 10, 442–457.

Hanna, S. S.; Folke, C. and Mahler, K. G. (eds.) (1997). *Rights to Nature: Ecological, Economic, Cultural and Political Principles of Institutions for Environment.* Washington, DC: Island Press.

Hardin, G. (1968). 'The tragedy of the commons'. *Science*, 162, 1243–1248.

Headey, B. and Wearing, A. (1998). 'Who enjoys life and why: Measuring subjective wellbeing'. In Eckersley, R. (ed.). *Measuring Progress: Is life Getting Better?* (pp. 169–182). Collingwood: CSIRO Publishing.

Henrich, J.; R. Boyd, S.; Bowles, H.; Gintis, E.; Fehr, C.; Camerer, R. et al. (2005). '"Economic Man" in cross-cultural perspective: Ethnography and experiments from 15 small-scale societies'. *Behavioral and Brain Sciences*, 28, 795–855.

Holling, C. S. (2004). 'From complex regions to complex worlds'. *Ecology and Society*, 9. Online: www.ecologyandsociety.org/vol9/iss1/art11.

Holling, C. S. and Meffe, G. K. (1996). 'Command and control and the pathology of natural resource management'. *Conservation Biology*, 10, 328–337.

Irwin, A. (2001). *Sociology and the Environment. A Critical Introduction to Society, Nature and Knowledge.* Cambridge, UK: Polity Press.

Larson, S. (2005). *Can Wellbeing Function Assist in the Assessment of Policy Impacts on Regions?* James Cook University School of Business. Townsville, December 2005.

Larson, S. (forthcoming). 'Communicating stakeholder priorities in the Great Barrier Reef region'. *Socio-Economic Planning Sciences Journal* (forthcoming).

Larson, S. and Smajgl, A. (2006). 'Conceptual framework for the water use benefit index in the Great Barrier Reef region'. *International Journal of Sustainable Planning and Development*, 1; 2,1–13.

Larson, S.; Herr, A. and Greiner, R. (2006). 'Human wellbeing and natural environments: An indigenous perspective'. *International Journal of Environmental, Cultural, Economic and Social Sustainability*, 2; 3, 39–50.

Mitchell, G. (1996). 'Problems and fundamentals of sustainable development indicators'. *Sustainable Development*, 4, 1–11.

Ostrom, E. (1990). *Governing the Commons*. Cambridge: Combridge University Press.

Ostrom, E. (1992). *Crafting Institutions for Self-Governing Irrigation Systems*. San Francisco, CA: ICS Press.

Ostrom, E. (1999). 'Institutional rational choice: An assessment of the institutional analysis and design framework'. In Sabatier, P. A. (ed.). *Theories of the Policy Process*. (pp35–71). Boulder, Colorado: Westview Press.

Ostrom, E. (2005). *Understanding Institutional Diversity*. Princeton: Princeton University Press.

Ostrom, E.; Schroeder, L. and Wynne, S. (1993). *Institutional Incentives and Sustainable Development: Infrastructure Policies in Perspective*. Boulder, Colorado: Westview Press.

Reeson, A. (forthcoming). 'Institutions, motivation and framing'. In Smajgl, A.; Hatfield-Dodds, S. and Ward, J. (eds.). *Understanding Human Behaviour in Complex Adaptive Systems: Building Foundations for Promoting Adaptive Governance*. (forthcoming).

Sayer, J. and Campbell, B. (2004). *The Science of Sustainable Development: Local Livelihoods and the Global Environment*. Cambridge: Cambridge University Press.

Schaefer, M. B. (1954). 'Some aspects of the dynamics of populations important to the management of commercial marine fisheries'. *Inter-American Tropical Tuna Commission Bulletin*, 1, 25–56.

Silvert, W. and Smith, W. R. (1977). 'Optimal exploitation of a multi-species community'. *Mathematical Biosciences*, 33, 121–134.

Simon, H. A. (1955). 'A behavioural model of rational choice'. *The Quarterly Journal of Economics*, 69, 99–118.

Smajgl, A. and Hajkowicz, S. (2005). 'Integrated modelling of water policy scenarios in the Great Barrier Reef region'. *Australian Journal of Economic Papers*, 24, 215–228.

Smajgl, A.; Morris, S. and Heckbert, S. (2005). 'Water policy impact assessment: Combining modelling techniques in the Great Barrier Reef region'. *ModSim 2005 Conference Proceedings*.

Sober, E. and Wilson, D. S. (1998). *Unto Others: The Evolution and Psychology of Unselfish Behaviour*. Cambridge, Massachusetts: Harvard University Press.

Young, H. P. (1998). *Individual Strategy and Social Structure: An evolutionary Theory of Institutions*. Princeton: Princeton University Press.

Part II

Institutional Diversity and Contextual Change

2

Multiple Institutions
for Multiple Outcomes

Elinor Ostrom

Multiple Institutions for Multiple Outcomes

Australia's diverse ecological zones include multiple common-pool resources among them. The most world renowned are the coral reefs of Great Barrier Reef in Queensland (Hughes et al, 2005) and the salinization problems resulting from overgrazing in the Murray Darling basin (Marshall, 2004; Janssen et al, 2004). Less known outside of Australia is the outback, a vast arid and semi-arid region where extending pastoralism has also led to some difficult ecological problems. Further, pastoralists in southern Australia have organized the Tilbuster Commons and other innovative efforts to create new enterprises to manage large parcels of land owned by multiple ranchers as a commons at this larger scale (Williamson et al, 2003; Brunckhurst et al, 2004; and Brunckhurst and Marshall, Chapter 10).

Whenever ecological systems are large and extensive, the resource system has attributes of a common-pool resource (Smajgl and Larson, Chapter 1). Such resources can be managed by many diverse property-rights systems (including private property, government property or communal property) or remain as open access where no one has rights to use. No matter what general type of property rights exist, however, managing such resources is always a struggle (Dietz et al, 2003). We do not have easy packaged solutions.

What we now know from extended research is that, under some conditions, those directly involved may be able to develop effective rules that enable them to manage a resource sustainably over time. This is, however, only partially good news. Instead of the total pessimism that dominated in the 1970s and 1980s, we can only now move to a moderate and reasoned level of optimism. Of course, anything is more optimistic than an impossibility! We are, however, still struggling to understand why there are so many cases where the individuals most directly involved do not make any investment in changing the governance of resources they are using, or are thwarted in their efforts to undertake such efforts (NRC, 2002). Further, we are only just now beginning to understand why some efforts tend to be more successful than others (Dietz et al, 2003).

In a semi-arid region, water rights are extremely valuable and the short- and long-term storage facilities of a groundwater basin are even more valuable. Water producers are motivated to get as many rights as they can, and to pay as low a cost as feasible. Conducting my dissertation work with the West Basin Water Association users in California, I have witnessed development of a remarkably efficient and fair set of institutions by resource users themselves. One could not call the final set of institutions a market, a government or any other named form of property rights. It gives me great respect for the ingenuity of resource users to design rules and for the incredible diversity of rules that are related to the governance of a complex resource.

At the same time, I witnessed State of California officials designing an overly expensive and inefficient state aqueduct to bring water from the north of the state to the south. Thus, I gained a deep understanding of the importance of institutions to create incentives that increased or decreased the efficiency and fairness of resource allocations.

The Institutional Analysis and Development (IAD) Framework[1]

For scholars interested in how institutions affect resource conditions, five actions are particularly important as they are the object of many institutional rules that potentially affect resource use, distribution of benefits and long-term sustainability. The five actions are:

1   Entering a resource (or access). This is the least intrusive thing that an individual may decide to do – if rules permit – in relation to a resource. An example: driving through or hiking in a forest.
2   Appropriating (or harvesting) resource units. Since it is assumed that appropriators will overharvest fish, water or trees from a natural resource, considerable policy analysis has focused on how to set limits by an external authority on the total quantity of resource units harvested. It has been assumed that the appropriators themselves will not limit their own harvesting.
3   Managing the physical system by changing the biophysical structure in order to improve its generative capacity over time. An example: building an irrigation system or improving fishing grounds.
4   Deciding who can be excluded or included in the set of authorized appropriators. An example: the issuance of a fishing licence or making rules about who in a community has a right to fish.
5   Alienating an individual's rights to take the above actions.

In the resource economics literature, it has generally been assumed that rules affecting the fifth type of action – in other words, the possession of private, transferable property rights – were the only 'well-defined' property rights and were essential before appropriators would take responsibility for managing a resource responsibly. In our field studies, we have found that there are multiple 'well-defined property rules' related to all five of these core actions and that one should expect to find 'bundles of rights' with different consequences rather than a single right that is essential in any and all settings (Schlager and Ostrom, 1992). We have identified multiple groups that lacked the authority to alienate their rights and that have managed resources responsibly for long eras (E. Ostrom, 1990; Schlager, 1994). Other scholars have found that resource users with at least the first four rights have also engaged in robust institutional development that has sustained natural resources (Grafton, 2000).

As someone who has frequently observed and tried to measure the complexity of institutions and the resources to which they were linked, I found many of the models used to analyse resource situations fascinating – but frustrating. How could a researcher go back and forth between studying field settings, using formal models and conducting experiments? That challenge led to the development, over more than two decades, of a framework that would help us organize multiple research modes (Kiser and Ostrom, 1982; E. Ostrom, 2005).

At the core of this framework is an action situation. The action situation can be analysed as a common-pool resource game, a market or a bureaucratic structure. We have gained more and more confidence over time that most relatively stable patterns of interaction among individuals and groups can be disaggregated into one (or more) action situations affected by exogenous variables and leading to incentives, patterns of interaction, and outcomes (see Figure 2.1).

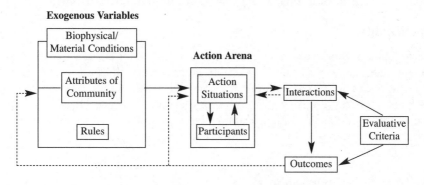

Figure 2.1 A framework for Institutional Analysis

Source: Adapted from Ostrom et al (1994, p.37)

Below I provide a brief sketch of the working parts of an action situation in the Institutional Analysis and Development (IAD) framework. The structure of an action situation is affected by exogenous variables including:

- the biophysical world to which it is linked (the fishery, groundwater basin, or forest when studying resource situations);
- the rules used to specify aspects of each of these components (e.g. entry rules specifying who is authorized, required, or forbidden to be a participant in the situation); and

- the community surrounding the situation (e.g. how large and heterogeneous it is, what kinds of norms are shared, etc.).

In these operational situations, actions may directly affect appropriation of resource flows and management of the biophysical system. One can also analyse collective-choice situations where the rules to be used in operational situations are chosen, or constitutional situations where the rules to be used in collective-choice situations are chosen.

This framework has been a very useful meta-theoretical language enabling scholars associated with the Workshop in Political Theory and Policy Analysis to study multiple types of resources. Even more important, it has enabled us to undertake cumulative empirical research based on in-depth case studies (Yandle, 2001; Yandle and Dewees, 2003) as well as to design protocols for collecting data from a larger set of field sets (in irrigation and forest resources) and to undertake meta-analysis of the case studies prepared by other scholars related to inshore fisheries (Schlager, 1994) and irrigation (Tang, 1994). Without a common framework, it is extremely difficult to achieve cumulation across multiple resource types and multiple research methodologies.

Let us now turn to the elements – or working parts – of an action situation.

The Basic Working Parts of Action Situations

Participants

Participants in an action situation are decision-making entities assigned to a position and capable of selecting actions from a set of alternatives made available at nodes in a decision process. Several attributes of participants are relevant when representing and analysing specific situations. These include (1) the number of participants, (2) their status as individuals or as a team or composite actor, and (3) various individual attributes, such as age, education, gender, and experience.

The number of participants
Interdependent action situations require at least two participants where the actions of each affect the outcomes for both. The dividing line between major types of games is between two-person and N-person games, where N is defined as any number greater than two. The *specific* number of participants is frequently overtly specified in real-world settings (or in formal theories about these settings) such as legislatures, juries, and most sports. Some descriptions of a situation, however, specify the number of participants in a looser fashion, such as a small or large group, or face-to-face relationships versus impersonal relationships.

The individual or team status of participants
Participants in many action situations are individual persons, or the participants may represent a team or composite actor such as a household or a firm.

A group of individuals may be considered as *one* participant (a team) in a particular action situation. A fully organized market with well-defined property rights, for example, may include buyers and sellers who are organized as firms as well as individual participants. Firms are composed of many individuals. Each firm is treated as if it were a single participant, but this is a 'short-hand' way of viewing the lattice of internal action situations within a particular firm that leads to external decisions to be taken in market settings.

Attributes of participants

Participants bring a diversity of ascribed or acquired characteristics to any situation. These characteristics may or may not influence their actions in one situation while having a major impact on another. Whether drivers passing one another on a busy highway are both of the same social or ethnic background is unlikely to affect their actions. A young, inexperienced driver of any background, however, may approach passing another car with great hesitation and not pass when most adult drivers would do so. The same two adults might hesitate a long time before extending trust and reciprocity to each other if facing an opportunity to enter a long-term contract in a community that has recently faced racial or ethnic conflict.

The action situation

Seven working parts characterize the action situation in which participants decide how to act. These are: positions, actions, potential outcomes, action-outcome linkages, control, information about the action situation, and benefits and costs.

Positions

Another element of an action situation is the set of positions or '*anonymous slots*' into and out of which participants move. Examples of positions include voters, judges, buyers, sellers, legislators, police officers, etc. Positions and participants are separate elements in a situation even though they may not be clearly so identified in practice. In many formal games, the distinction between a participant and the position that a participant holds is blurred. If players make simultaneous moves and receive the same pay-offs given their strategies and those of others, the definition of player and position is the same. In sequential games, however, one player holds the position of first mover and, frequently, there are first mover advantages or disadvantages.

Positions are thus the connecting link between participants and actions. In some situations, any participant in any position may be authorized to take any of the allowable actions in that situation. However, in most 'organized' situations, the capability to take particular actions is assigned to a specific position and not to all positions. The nature of a position assigned to participants in an action situation defines the 'standing' of the individual in that situation. The standing of a position is the set of authorized actions and limits on actions that the holder of the position can take at particular choice sets in the situation.

Actions

Participants assigned to a position in an action situation must choose from a set of authorized actions at any particular stage in a decision process. An action can be thought of as a selection of a setting or a value on a control variable that a participant hopes will affect an outcome or variable. In game theory, the set of actions available to a participant at a specific sequence in a game – a decision point – is called a move. The specific action selected by a participant from the set of authorized actions is called a choice. The types of variables included within the concept of a set of authorized actions are vast. The term 'action' includes both overt acts as well as the choice not to act in some situations. Both voting for one or another candidate and abstaining from voting are included in a voter's action set, for example. Both can be conceptualized as a setting on a control variable.

Potential outcomes

In the analysis of formal games, the standard practice is to report the outcomes of joint decisions as the analyst assumes they are ranked in utility to the participants in particular positions. When the purpose of analysing a situation is focused entirely on understanding the result of a particular structure and the analyst is certain about the ordinal ranking of participant's values over outcomes, then this abbreviated process of representing outcomes in utility space is an effective means of analysing a situation. When the analyst has a longer-run interest in understanding how rules (or attributes of the biophysical world or the community) change an action situation, greater precision is obtained by initially focusing on the physical outcomes of a situation rather than on utility outcomes. Then it is possible to understand how rules affect incentives leading to different physical outcomes and to the assignment of specific benefits and costs to that outcome.

If there were a market where commodities were exchanged at known prices, one could assign a monetary value to the commodities. If there were taxes imposed on the exchange of commodities (a sales tax), one could represent the outcomes in a monetary unit representing the market price minus the tax. If one wanted to examine the profitability of growing chickens as contrasted to potatoes or other crops, one would represent the outcomes in terms of the monetary value of the realized sales value minus the monetary value of the inputs (land, labour and other variable inputs).

Combining all physical outcomes, external valuation and participants' intrinsic valuation into one measure – utility – does not enable an analyst to clearly identify how rules affect the structure of a situation. The set of physically possible actions and resulting transformations is the same in two situations that differ only in regards to monetary pay-offs. What is affected by a change in pay-off rules is the net level of benefits or costs assigned to a particular path of actions and physical results. Thus, to examine the effect of rules in a careful and systematic manner, one needs to consider the underlying physical transformations separately from the material rewards assigned to a chain of actions and results.

Action–outcome linkages

Action–outcome linkages can be investigated through investigation of the 'control' and 'state' variables. A setting on a control variable is considered 'linked' to a state variable when it is possible to use that setting to cause the state variable (1) to come into being, (2) disappear, or (3) change in degree. A light switch, for example, is a control variable with two positions – on and off. It is linked to some source of light that shines or does not shine. By turning the switch to off, one can make the light disappear.

A state variable may be linked to many control variables. One might think of a situation in which three switches jointly control a light – at least two of them must be in the 'on' position for the light to appear. A person authorized to set one of the switches to on or off can potentially affect whether the light is on or off but cannot totally control the presence or absence of light. If only one other switch is turned on, a person assigned to one of the other two switches can either make the light appear (by turning their switch on) or can produce darkness (by turning their switch off). If one person's switch is already off, the other person can allow darkness to continue by refraining from changing her control switch. It is in this sense that a 'non-action' may affect an outcome variable.

Control

The extent of control over the linkage of the action to outcomes that a participant has varies from absolute to almost none. An individual has total control (omnipotence) over an outcome variable, which we may call o_i in the situation where for each value o_i potentially affected within that situation there is an action a_i, such that the conditional probability of o_i given a_i equals one. For two-dimensional outcomes, an individual has total control if for each combination of outcome variable values $o_i o_j$ there is an a_i, such that the conditional probability of $o_i o_j$ given a_i equals one (Coleman, 1973, p61).

An individual has partial control over a state variable if the conditional probability of a change in the value o_i of the state variable given an action a_i available to the individual is greater than zero and less than one. Partial control can, thus, vary from an extremely small chance of affecting an outcome to a high probability of affecting the outcome. A participant can be said to be impotent with respect to an outcome when he or she has no control over the values of a state variable (see von Wright, 1966, pp129–31 for a discussion of control that is similar to that of Coleman).

Information about the action situation

Participants in an action situation may have access to complete or incomplete information. Almost all formal representations of action situations assume that participants have access to complete information by which is meant that each participant could know the number of other participants, the positions, the outcomes, the actions available, how actions are linked to outcomes (and thus the certainty, risk or uncertainty of the linkage), the information available to other players and the pay-offs of the same. In other words, complete information is an assumption that each participant could know the full structure of an action situation as defined here. When participants are assumed to have access to complete information, a further distinction is made in formal theory between perfect and imperfect information. When a participant has access to perfect information, they cannot only know all of their own past actions; they can also know the actions of all other players before they make any move. In other words, they can know the exact decision node at which they are making a choice. Under imperfect but complete information, the individual is assumed to have access to knowledge of the full structure of the situation, but may not have access to knowledge about all the moves that other participants have taken prior to a particular move. The participants could know all the possible nodes at which he or she could be, but is unable to distinguish the exact node for the current move.

When information is less than complete, the question of who knows what at what juncture becomes very important. With incomplete information, how much any one individual contributes to a joint undertaking is often difficult for others to judge. When joint outcomes depend on multiple actors contributing inputs that are costly and difficult to measure, incentives exist for individuals to behave opportunistically (Williamson, 1975).

Benefits and costs

The discussion of outcomes, and of action–outcome linkages presented above, relies on the relationships between control variables and state variables. In addition to the physical actions and outcomes that are involved in a situation, rewards and/or sanctions may be distributed to participants in positions dependent upon the path taken to achieve a particular outcome. Benefits and costs are cumulative external rewards or sanctions assigned to outcomes including the rewards (financial returns) or sanctions (fines) assigned to actions taken along a path to an outcome. For simplicity, it is frequently assumed that acts are costly and outcomes are beneficial. Participants are then viewed as weighing the costs of an action against the benefits of an outcome. Actions may, however, have associated benefits and outcomes may be 'bads' instead of 'goods'.

For institutional analysis, a distinction needs to be made between a physical outcome, an external reward or sanction, and the valuation that a participant assigns to the physical transformation and external rewards and/or sanctions. So long as the linkage between actions and outcomes remains the same, the outcome remains the same. The external or extrinsic values are the set of 'reward' variables affected by the path of actions and outcomes. Examples of extrinsic rewards include the financial returns assigned a worker in a principal-agent contract. The reward may be assigned strictly on action variables (e.g. how many hours the worker clocks in), strictly on outcome variables (e.g. how much of a particular final or intermediate product is produced), or on some combination of action and outcome variables (a wage plus a production bonus). Extrinsic benefits and costs are frequently assigned through the operation of a rule system and thus do not rely only on biophysical processes.

If the primary interest is to predict what will happen in a particular situation, and not how to change the situation, the only value that a researcher needs to use is the value assigned by participants to the achievement of an outcome. This value is referred to as utility in economics and game theory. In economics, theorists normally assume that utility is monotonically associated with profits, which is a reasonable assumption to make in many but not all situations. Some individuals may assign a positive or negative intrinsic value to actions or outcomes. The *intrinsic valuation* attached to an external reward or sanction is the internal value that individuals associate with the components of the objective transformations and rewards (Deci, 1975; Frey, 1997). If the person evaluates an action as being improper, they may assign a negative intrinsic value. If the person is proud of an action, they may assign it a positive intrinsic value.

The number of times the action situation will be repeated

In addition to the internal components of an action situation, it is also important to know whether the situation is a one-shot interaction or a repeated interaction. Analysts usually agree, for example, that the outcome that individuals will obtain in a social dilemma game will depend, among other factors, on whether the participants are engaged in a one-time encounter or will be engaged over an indefinitely long sequence of plays. If a game is repeated a finite number of times, most game theorists would predict the same equilibrium as for a single-round game due to backward induction.

When participants in a social dilemma game are placed into an indefinite series of rounds, however, the disadvantage of continued lack of cooperation can lead them to adopt a conditional cooperative strategy so long as other participants also cooperate. The well-known folk theorem of game theory establishes that full cooperation is one (out of many) feasible equilibria that participants in an infinitely repeated (or, even an indefinitely repeated) situation may achieve if they use one of several conditional cooperative strategies (Kreps et al, 1982). It is, however, only one of many equilibria. Thus, participants face a challenging coordination problem in reaching this outcome.

Studying Common-Pool Resources in the Field

We have done extensive research on common-pool resources in field settings using the IAD framework. An extraordinary number of field studies have found that local groups of resource users, sometimes by themselves and sometimes with the assistance of external institutional arrangements, have created a wide diversity of institutional arrangements for cooperation in use and management of common-pool resources where they have not been prevented from doing so by central authorities (McCay and Acheson, 1987; Fortmann and Bruce, 1988; Berkes, 1989; Bromley et al, 1992; V. Ostrom et al, 1993; Netting, 1993; Berkes et al, 2001).

These empirical studies document successful self-organized resource governance systems in diverse sectors in all parts of the world where cooperative strategies have been successful. It must also be stressed that examples exist of commons dilemmas that have continued unabated and of common-property institutions that have collapsed (Seixas and Berkes, 2003). One conclusion that can firmly be made, in light of extensive empirical evidence, is that overuse and destruction of common-pool resources is not a determinant and inescapable outcome when multiple users face a commons dilemma. An automatic process to solve these problems is also not an appropriate assumption. Instead, one should conclude that overcoming commons dilemmas is always a struggle (Dietz et al, 2003). Many officials and users fail in their efforts to do so.

Scholars have begun to identify the conditions of a resource and the attributes of users of a resource that are most conducive to local users self-organizing to find solutions to commons dilemmas (see Berkes et al, 1989; Baland and Platteau, 1996; E. Ostrom, 1998). And, broad design principles that characterize robust self-organized resource governance systems resolving commons dilemmas for long periods of time have been identified (E. Ostrom, 1990).

Another important set of findings is that national governmental agencies have been notably unsuccessful in their efforts to design effective and uniform sets of rules to regulate important common-pool resources across a broad domain (Ascher, 1995). Many developing countries nationalized all land and water resources during the 1950s and 1960s. The institutional arrangements that local resource users had devised to limit entry and use lost their legal standing. The national governments that were assigned these new and difficult tasks lacked adequate funds and personnel to monitor the use of these resources effectively. In these countries, common-pool resources were converted to a de jure government-property regime, but reverted to a de facto open-access regime (Arnold, 1998; Arnold and Stewart, 1991). The perverse incentives of an open-access commons were accentuated since local users had specifically been told that they would not receive the long-term benefits of their own costly stewardship efforts.

When resources that were previously controlled by local participants have been nationalized, state control has usually proved to be less effective and efficient than control by those directly affected, if not disastrous in its consequences (Curtis, 1991; Panayotou and Ashton, 1992). The harmful effects of nationalizing forests that had earlier been governed by local user groups have been well documented for Thailand (Feeny, 1988), Africa (Thomson, 1977; Shepherd, 1992; Thomson et al, 1992), Nepal (Arnold and Campbell, 1986), and India (Gadgil and Iyer, 1989; Jodha, 1990, 1996). Similar results have occurred in regard to inshore fisheries taken over by state or national agencies from local control by the inshore fishermen themselves (Dasgupta, 1982; Cruz, 1986; Pinkerton, 1989; Cordell and McKean, 1992; Higgs, 1996).

Tang (1992), Lam (1998) and Joshi et al, (2000) have all found that large-scale government irrigation systems do not tend to perform at the same level as smaller-scale, farmer-managed systems (see also Levine, 1980; Mehra, 1981; Bromley, 1982; Hilton, 1992). In a study of over 100 irrigation systems in Nepal, Lam (1998) found that the cropping intensity and agricultural yield of crudely constructed irrigation systems using mud, rock, timbers and sticks is significantly higher than the performance of systems built with modern concrete and iron headworks operated by national agencies. Considerable disjunctures thus exist between textbook recommendations and evidence from the field (Holling et al, 2001).

Evidence challenges three important theoretical foundations of contemporary policy analysis. The first foundation is the model of the human actor that is frequently used in textbooks. Resource users are explicitly thought of as rational egoists. Government officials are implicitly depicted, on the other hand, as seeking the more general public interest and capable of designing optimal policies. The rational egoist used in conventional non-cooperative game theory is appropriate in modelling behaviour in open competitive markets, but not in dilemma settings in which individuals can communicate and come to know and potentially trust one another. Assuming a multiplicity of orientations is more appropriate in these settings. Rational egoists may come to dominate in any situation in which conflicts are left unresolved and participants lose trust in one another. One should not, however, presume that all government officials are 'saints' while assuming that all resource users are 'sinners'.

A second foundational belief of contemporary policy is that designing rules to change the incentives of participants is a relatively simple analytical task best done by objective analysts not specifically related to any specific resource. A third foundation is the view that organization itself requires *central direction*. Consequently, the multitude of self-organized resource governance systems are viewed as mere collections of individual agents each out to maximize their own short-term returns. The groups who have actually organized themselves are invisible to those who cannot imagine organization without rules and regulations issued by a central authority (see, for example, Lansing, 1991).

These simple, foundational assumptions are an inadequate foundation for public policy recommendations related to common-pool resources. Instead of one type of actor present everywhere, we need to assume heterogeneity of norms and preferences and that institutions themselves are a selection mechanism affecting the distribution of participants holding diverse values and norms.

In the next section of this chapter, I will explore the second and third foundations related to the simplicity of designing rules and the efficacy of central direction. An examination of the types of rules used in the field yields several important findings. First, the number of rules actually used in field settings is far greater than generally recognized. Second, the type of rules is also different. Boundary rules tend to include as co-appropriators of a resource those who are more likely to be trustworthy because they live permanently nearby and have a long-term stake in keeping a resource sustainable. Choice rules define rights and duties that are easy to understand, directly related to sustaining the biophysical structure of the resource, and easy to monitor and enforce. Some rules recommended in the policy literature are *not* found among the rules used in self-organized systems.

Given the complexity of the process of designing rules to regulate the use of common-pool resources, I will argue that all public policies should be considered as experiments (Campbell, 1969). No one can possibly know whether a proposed change in rules is among the optimal rule changes or even whether a rule change will lead to an improvement. All policy experiments have a positive probability of failing.

Experimenting with Rules in the Field

When we study rules used by appropriators from common-pool resources in the field, we can think of appropriators trying to understand the biophysical structure of their resource and how they can develop a set of rules consistent with the norms shared in their community. One of their first challenges will be convincing those who doubt that the resource is limited, and thus that they need to constrain use in a manner that they agree is workable and fair. Instead of being given a set of instructions with the transformation function fully specified (as subjects are given to them in the experimental lab), appropriators in the field have to explore and discover the biophysical structure of a particular resource. It will usually differ on key parameters from similar resources in the same region. Further, they have to cope with considerable uncertainty related to the weather, complicated growth patterns of biological systems that may at times be chaotic in nature, and external price fluctuations affecting the costs of inputs and value of outcomes (see Wilson et al, 1994; Wilson, 2002; Baker, 2005). Therefore, institutional tools they can use to change the structure of the action situations they face consist of the seven clusters of rules that directly affect the seven working parts of an action situation. They need to agree on rules listing specific attributes and conditions rather than using a generic rule.

Given the nonlinearity and complexity of many action situations, it is challenging to predict the precise effect a change in a particular rule will produce. For example, a change in a boundary rule to restrict who is authorized to enter and harvest from a resource reduces the number of individuals who are tempted to break choice rules. It also reduces the number of individuals who monitor what is happening or contribute funds toward hiring a guard (Agrawal, 2000). Thus, the opportunities for rule breaking may increase. Further, the cost of a rule infraction will be spread over a smaller group of appropriators. Thus, the harm to any individual may be greater. Assessing the overall effects of a change in boundary rules is a nontrivial analytical task (for examples, see Weissing and Ostrom, 1991a, 1991b). Instead of conducting such a complete analysis, appropriators are more apt to use their intuitive understanding of the resource and of each other's norms and preferences to experiment with different rule changes until they find a combination that seems to work in their setting.

In discussing how appropriators in the field may attempt to craft rules to solve commons dilemmas, I draw on the extensive case study literature written about local common-pool resources by anthropologists, agricultural economists, ecologists, historians, political scientists and sociologists, as well as our own field research. Colleagues at the Workshop in Political Theory and Policy Analysis have collected an immense archive of original case studies written by many scholars on all resource sectors in all parts of the world (Hess, 1999). Using the IAD framework, we developed structured coding forms to help us identify the specific kinds of action situations faced in the field as well as the types of rules that users have evolved over time to try to govern and manage their resource effectively (Ostrom et al, 1989). In order to develop standardized coding forms, we read hundreds of cases describing how local common-pool resources were or were not regulated by a government agency, by the users themselves or by a nongovernmental organization (NGO).

Using Rules to Cope with the Commons

To understand the tools that appropriators use in the field, we will examine in some detail the kinds of boundary, position, choice, and pay-off rules used in field settings. These four clusters of rules are the major tools used everywhere to affect commons dilemmas while information, scope and aggregation rules are additional tools used to complement changes induced by these four rules.

Affecting the attributes of users through boundary rules

Boundary rules define the attributes and conditions required of those who enter a position in an action situation. In field settings, many action situations are involved, but I will focus attention on the appropriation situation: Who appropriates (harvests) how many resource units from which common-pool resource? Boundary rules, thus, define who has a right to enter and use a resource as an 'authorized appropriator' – the term we will use for this most general position that exists in multiple settings. Boundary rules affect the types of participants with whom other participants will be interacting related to a particular resource.

If contingent cooperation is perceived to be a possibility, then an important way to enhance the likelihood of using reciprocity norms is to increase the proportion of appropriators who are well known in a community. These participants have a long-term stake in that community and would find it costly to have their reputation for trustworthiness harmed in that community. Reducing the number of users, but opening the resource to strangers willing to pay a licence fee, as is frequently recommended in the policy literature, introduces appropriators who lack a long-term interest in the sustainability of a particular resource. Using licences to regulate entry increases the number of strangers using the resource and may reduce the level of trust among participants and their willingness to use reciprocity and thus increase enforcement costs substantially.

From our initial reading and our own fieldwork, we expected to find boundary rules that focused on local residency as a way of increasing the opportunity for reciprocity and that these rules were used extensively. What amazed us, however, as we read the extensive number of case studies describing field settings, was the variety of attributes and conditions used to define who could be an authorized appropriator from diverse inshore fisheries, irrigation systems, and forests. As shown in Table 2.1, we identified 23 attributes of individuals and 13 conditions described by case-study authors as having been used in at least one common-pool resource somewhere in the world

Table 2.1 *Attributes and conditions used in boundary rules to define who is authorized to appropriate from a common-pool resource*

Attributes		Conditions
Residency or Membership	Personal Characteristics	Relationship with Resource
National	Ascribed	Use of specified technology
Regional	Age	Continued use of resource
Local community	Caste	Long-term rights based on:
Organization	Clan	Ownership of a proportion of annual flow
(e.g. co-op)	Class	of resource units
	Ethnicity	Ownership of land
	Gender	Ownership of nonland asset (e.g., berth)
	Race	Ownership of shares in a private
	Acquired	organization
	Education level	Ownership of a share of the resource system
	Skill test	Temporary use-rights acquired through:
		Auction
		Per-use fee
		Licenses
		Lottery
		Registration
		Seasonal fees

Source: E. Ostrom (2005, p224)

(Ostrom et al, 1989). While some systems use only a single attribute or condition, many use two or three of these rules in combination.

Boundary rules that are used in the field can be broadly grouped in three general classes related to how individuals gain authority to enter and appropriate resource units from a common-pool resource. The first type of boundary rule focuses on generally acquired attributes of an individual such as an individual's citizenship, residency or membership in a particular organization. Many forestry and fishing user groups require members to have been born in a particular location. A second broad group of attributes relates to individual ascribed or acquired personal attributes. User groups may require that appropriation depends on age, ethnicity, clan or caste. A third group of boundary rules relates to the conditions of use relating an appropriator with the resource itself. Using a particular technology or acquiring appropriation rights through an auction or a lottery are examples of this type of condition.

In a systematic coding of those case studies for which sufficient information existed about rules related to inshore fisheries in many parts of the world, Schlager (1990, 1994) coded 33 user groups out of the 44 groups identified as having at least one boundary rule regarding the use of the resource. All 33 groups depended on some combination of 14 attributes or conditions (Schlager, 1994, p.258). None of these groups relied on a single attribute or condition. Thirty out of 33 groups (91 per cent) limited fishing to those individuals who lived in a nearby community, while 13 groups also required membership in a local organization. Consequently, most inshore fisheries organized by the users themselves restrict fishing to those individuals who are well known to each other, have a relatively long-term time horizon and are connected to one another in multiple ways (see Taylor, 1982; Singleton and Taylor, 1992; Berkes et al, 2001).

After residency, the next most frequent attribute or condition, used in two-thirds of the organized subgroups, involves the condition that the appropriator would use a particular type of technology. These rules are often criticized by policy analysts, since gear restrictions tend to reduce the 'efficiency' of fishing. Gear restrictions have many consequences, however. Used in combination with choice rules that assign fishers using one type of gear to one area of the fishing groups and fishers using another type of gear to a second area, they solve conflicts among noncompatible technologies. Many gear restrictions also place a reduced load on the fishery itself and thus help to sustain longer-term use of the resource (Acheson, 2003).

Other rules were also used. A scattering of groups used ascribed characteristics (age – two groups; ethnicity – three groups; race – five groups). Three types of temporary use rights included government licences (three groups), lottery (five groups), and registration (four groups). Seven groups required participants to have purchased an asset such as a fishing berth, while three groups required ownership of nearby land as a condition of appropriation. Schlager (1994) did not find that any particular attribute or condition was correlated with higher performance levels, but she did find that the 33 groups who had at least one boundary rule tended to be able to solve common-pool problems more effectively than the 11 groups who had not crafted boundary rules.

In a study of 43 small- to medium-sized irrigation systems managed by farmers or by government agencies, Tang (1992) found that the variety of attributes or conditions used in irrigation was smaller than among inshore fisheries. The single most frequently used boundary rule, used in 32 of the 43 systems (74 per cent), was that an irrigator must own land in the service area of an irrigation system (ibid. pp84–5). All of the government-owned and operated irrigation systems relied on this attribute and *only* this attribute. Many of the user-organized systems relied on other attributes and conditions or land ownership combined with other rules. Among the other rules used were ownership of a proportion of the flow of the resource, membership in a local organization and a per-use fee.

Tang found a strong negative relationship between reliance on land as the *sole* boundary requirement and performance (ibid. p87). Over 90 per cent of the systems using other boundary rules or a combination of rules including land ownership, were rated positively in the level of maintenance achieved and in the level of rule conformance, while less than 40 per cent of those systems relying solely on land ownership were rated at a higher performance level (p = .001).

This puzzling result can be understood by a deeper analysis of the incentives facing engineers who plan irrigation systems. Many government systems are designed on paper to serve an area larger than they are actually able to serve when in operation, due to a variety of factors including the need to show as many posited beneficiaries as possible to justify the cost of construction (see Palanisami, 1982; Repetto, 1986; Shivakoti and Ostrom, 2002). The government then uses ownership in the authorized service area as the criterion for possessing a right to water. After construction, authorized irrigators find water to be very scarce because of the unrealiztic plans. Frequently, farmers are then unwilling to limit the amount of water they take or to contribute to the maintenance of the system.

Thus, many of the rich diversity of boundary rules used by appropriators in the field attempt to ensure that the appropriators will be interacting with others who live nearby and have a long-term interest in sustaining the productivity of the resource. One way of coping with commons dilemmas is thus to change the composition of who uses a common-pool resource to increase the proportion of participants who have a long-term interest, who are more likely to use reciprocity and who can be trusted. Central governments tend to use a smaller set of rules and some of these may open up a resource to strangers without a long-term commitment to the resource, generate conflict among users and lead to an unwillingness to abide by any rules.

Position rules creating monitors

In the above discussion of boundary rules, we focused on the general position of authorized appropriator. In some self-organized resource governance systems, they also create a second position of guard or monitor. Many different names are used.

Among self-organizing forest governance systems, creating and supporting a position as guard is frequently essential since resource units are highly valuable and a few hours of stealth can generate substantial illicit income. Monitoring rule conformance among forest users by officially designated and paid guards may make the difference between a resource in good condition and one that has become degraded. In a study of 279 forest *panchayats* in the Kumaon region of India, Agrawal and Yadama (1997) found that the number of months a guard was hired was the most important variable affecting forest conditions. The other variables that affected forest conditions included the number of meetings held by the forest council (a time when infractions are discussed) and the number of residents in the village.

It is evident from the analysis that the capacity of a forest council to monitor and impose sanctions on rule breakers is paramount to maintaining the forest in good condition. Nor should the presence of a guard be taken simply as a formal mechanism that ensures greater protection. It is also an indication of the informal commitment of the *panchayat* and the village community to protect their forests. Hiring a guard costs money. The funds have to be generated within the village and earmarked for protection of the resource. If there was scant interest in protecting the forest, villagers would have little interest in setting aside the money necessary to hire a guard (Agrawal and Yadama, 1997, p.455).

Whether irrigation systems create a formal position as guard depends both on the type of governance of the system and on its size. Of the 15 government-owned irrigation systems included in Tang (1992), 12 (80 per cent) have established a position of guard. Stealing water was a problem on most government-owned systems, but it was endemic on the three government systems without guard. Of the 28 farmer-organized systems, 17 (61 per cent) utilize the position of water distributor or guard. Of the 11 farmer-organized systems that do not employ a guard, farmers are vigilant enough in monitoring each other's activities on five systems (45 per cent) that rule conformance is high. That means, of course, that self-monitoring is not high enough on the other six systems to support routine conformance with their own rules. An earlier study by Romana de los Reyes (1980) of 51 communal irrigation systems in the Philippines illustrates the effect of size. Of the 30 systems that were less than 50 hectares, only six (20 per cent) had established a position as guard; of the 11 systems that served between 50 to 100 hectares, five (45 per cent) had established guards; and of the ten systems over 100 hectares, seven (70 per cent) had created guards. In a survey of over 600 farmers served by these communal irrigation systems, she also found that most farmers also patrolled their own canals even when they were patrolled by guards accountable to the farmers for distributing water. Further, the proportion of farmers who reported patrolling the canals serving their farms increases to 80 per cent on the largest self-organized systems compared with 60 per cent on the smallest systems.

Many self-organized fisheries rely on self-monitoring more than the creation of a formal position of guard. Most inshore fishers now use short-wave radios as a routine part of their day-to-day operations, allowing a form of instant monitoring to occur. An official of a West Coast Indian tribe reports, for example, that 'it is not uncommon to hear messages such as *Did you see so-and-so flying all that net?* over the short-wave frequency – a clear reference to a violation of specified gear limits' (cited in Singleton, 1998, p. 134). Given that most fishers will be listening to their short-wave radio, 'such publicity is tantamount to creating a flashing neon sign over the boat of the offender. Such treatment might be preceded or followed by a direct approach to the rule violator, advising him to resolve the problem. In some tribes, a group of fishermen might delegate themselves to speak to the person' (ibid.).

Affecting the set of allowable actions through choice rules

Choice rules are also a major type of rule used to regulate common-pool resources. In the CPR coding manual (Ostrom et al, 1989), we identified a diversity of choice rules used in field settings. Some rules involve a simple formula as a way of devising how many resource units appropriators may obtain. Others simply chose the resource for a defined period(s) and then allowed harvesting during a particular season. Many forest resources, for example, are closed to all forms of harvesting during one portion of the year and open for extraction by all who meet the boundary rules during an open season. Most choice rules, however, have two components.

In Table 2.2, the eight allocation formulas used in the field are shown in the left column. A fisher might be assigned to a fixed location (a fishing spot) or to a fixed rotational schedule, a member of the founding clan may be authorized to cut timber anywhere in a forest, while an irrigator might be assigned to a fixed percentage of the total water available during a season or to a fixed time slot. In addition to the formula used in a choice rule, most also attach a condition as a basis for the assignment. For example, a fisher might be assigned to a fixed location based on a number drawn in a lottery, on the purchase of that spot in an auction or on the basis of his or her historical use. An irrigator might be assigned to a fixed rotation based on the amount of land owned, the amount of water used historically or the specific location of the irrigator.

Table 2.2 *Choice rules used to allocate common-pool resources*

Allocation Formula for Appropriation Rights	Basis for Allocation Formula
Percentage of total available units per period	Amount of land held
Quantity of resource units per period	Amount of historical use
Appropriate only from a specific location	Location of appropriator
Appropriate only from a specific time slot	Quantity of shares of resource owned
Rotate in time or space	Proportion of resource flow owned
Appropriate only during open seasons	Purchase of periodic rights at auction
Appropriate only resource units meeting criteria	Rights acquired through periodic lottery
Appropriate whenever and wherever	Technology used
	License issued by a governmental authority
	Equal division to all appropriators
	Needs of appropriators (e.g., type of crop)
	Ascribed characteristic of appropriator
	Membership in organization
	Assessment of resource condition

Source: E. Ostrom (2005, p.229)

If all of the conditions were equally likely to be combined with all of the formula, there would be 112 different choice rules (eight allocation formulas x 14 bases). A further complication is that the rules for one product may differ from those of another product harvested from the same resource. In regard to forest resources, for example, children may be authorized to pick fruit from any tree located in a forest so long as it is for their own consumption, women may be authorized to collect so many head-loads of dead wood for domestic firewood and certain plants for making crafts, while *shaman* are the only ones authorized to collect medicinal plants from a particular location in a forest (Fortmann and Bruce, 1988). Appropriation rights to fish are frequently related to a specific species. A still further complication is that the rules may regularly change over the course of a year depending on resource conditions. Thus, the exact number of rules that are actually used in the field is difficult to compute.

Schlager (1994, p259–260) found that user groups included in her study frequently assigned fishers to fixed locations using a diversity of bases including technology, lottery or historical use. Seven groups allocated fishers to fishing spots using a rotation system, and seven other groups allowed fishing locations to be used only during a specific season. Four groups allocated fishing spots for a particular time period (a fishing day or a fishing season). On the other hand, nine user groups required fishers to limit their harvest to fish that met a specific size requirement.

An important finding – given the puzzles addressed in this chapter – is that the choice rule most frequently recommended by policy analysts (see Anderson, 1986, 1995; Copes, 1986) was not used in any of the coastal fisheries included in Schlager's study. Thus, no attempt was made by the fishers using an inshore fishery coded by Schlager to regulate the quantity of fish harvested per year based on an estimate of the yield. 'This is particularly surprising given that the most frequently recommended policy prescription made by fishery economists is the use of individual transferable quotas based on estimates on the economically optimal quantity of fish to be harvested over the long run' (Schlager, 1994, p. 265).

In an independent study of 30 traditional fishery societies, Acheson et al, (1998) also noted the surprising absence of quota rules:

All of the rules and practices we found in these 30 societies regulate how fishing is done. That is, they limit the times fish may be caught, the locations where fishing is allowed, the technology permitted, and the stage of the life cycle during which fish may be taken. None of these societies limits the amount of various species that can be caught. Quotas – the single most important concept and tools of scientific management – is conspicuous by its absence. (1998, p. 397; see Wilson et al. 1994)

Local inshore fishers, when allowed to manage a riparian area, thus use rules that differ substantially from those recommended by advocates of scientific management. Fishers have to know a great deal about the ecology of their inshore region including spawning areas, nursery areas, the migration routes of different species and seasonable patterns just in order to succeed as fishers. Over time, they learn how 'to maintain these critical life-cycle processes with rules controlling technology, fishing locations, and fishing times. Such rules in their view are based on biological reality' (ibid. 405). Lobe and Berkes (2004) also illustrate how a combination of these three types of rules sustains contemporary coastal shrimp fisheries in Kerala, India.

Tang (1992) found that many irrigation systems use different sets of rules depending on the availability of water. During the most abundant season, for example, irrigators may be authorized to take water whenever they need it. During a season when water is moderately available, farmers may use a rotation system where every farmer is authorized to take water for a fixed amount of time during the week based on the amount of land to be irrigated. During scarcity, the irrigation system may employ a special water distributor who is authorized to allocate water to those farmers who are growing crops authorized by the irrigation system and are most in need.

In addition to devising choice rules specifying how resource units may be harvested, many systems also have to devise rules for how resources will be mobilized. These types of choice rules specify duties as contrasted to rights.

Robust common-property regimes tend to rely on a close match between the formulae used for harvesting and the formulae used for input requirements. In regard to irrigation, farmers may even craft different rules related to maintenance according to the part of the canal needing attention – such as the headworks, the main canal, secondary canals or for emergency repair. In Chitwan, most systems tend to rely on mobilizing labour for repairing the headworks on an irrigation system on a per household basis (also for emergency repair anywhere on the system), but use the amount of land owned and served by a particular part of a canal in regard to repairing the main or secondary canals (see summary of these findings in Shivakoti and Ostrom 2002, pp14–15). In Tanahun – where the systems tend to be much smaller than in Chitwan, and thus smaller differences between farmers located at the head and the tail – different rules tend to be used. About half of the 160 systems for which Shukla, Poudel and colleagues gathered data (see Shukla et al, 1993; Poudel et al, 1994) relied on landholding anywhere in the system and a per household basis for mobilizing regular repairs on all parts of the systems.

The diversity of rules devised by users greatly exceeds the few rules recommended in textbook treatments of this problem. Appropriators thus cope with the commons by crafting a wide variety of rules affecting the actions available to participants and thus their basic set of strategies. Given this wide diversity of rules, it is particularly noteworthy that rules assigning appropriators a right to a specific quantity of a resource are used so infrequently in inshore fisheries and irrigation systems. (They are used more frequently when allocating forest products, where the quantity available, as well as the quantity harvested is much easier to measure (Agrawal, 1994).) To assign an appropriator a specific quantity of a resource unit requires that those making the assignment know the total available units. In water resources, only when water is stored from one season to another in a groundwater basin or dam, and reliable information about the quantity of water is available, are rules that allocate a quantity of water to an authorized appropriator utilized (Blomquist, 1992; Schlager et al, 1994).

Affecting outcomes through pay-off rules

One way to reduce or redirect the appropriations made from a common-pool resource is to change pay-off rules so as to add a penalty to actions that are prohibited. Many user groups also adopt norms that those who are rule breakers should be socially ostracized or shunned and individual appropriators tend to monitor each other's behaviour rather intensively. Three broad types of pay-off rules are used extensively in the field:

1   the imposition of a fine,
2   the loss of appropriation rights, and
3   incarceration.

The severity of each of these types of sanctions can range from very low to very high and tends to start out on the low end of the scale.

Inshore fisheries studied by Schlager (1990) relied heavily on shunning and other social norms and less on formal sanctions. Thirty-six of the 43 irrigation systems studied by Tang used one of these three rules and also relied on vigorous monitoring of each other's behaviour and shunning of rule breakers. The seven systems that did not self-consciously punish rule infractions were all rated as having poor performance. Fines were most typically used (in 21 cases) and incarceration the least (in only two cases). Fines tend to be graduated depending on the seriousness of the infractions and the number of prior infractions. The fines used for a first or second offence tend to be very low.

Once a position of a paid guard is created, pay-off rules must also change so as to be able to remunerate a guard. Several formulas are used. On government-owned irrigation systems, guards are normally paid a monthly wage that is not dependent on the performance of a system or farmers' satisfaction. In South India, Wade (1994) describes self-organized systems where the water distributor-guard is paid in kind as the harvest is reaped by going to each farmer to collect his share based on the amount of land owned by the farmer. Sengupta (1991, p.104) describes another system where immediately after appointment the guards 'are taken to the temple for oath taking to remain impartial. With this vow, they break a coconut. They are paid in cash at the rate of Rs ten per acres ... per month by the cultivators. The *neerpaichys* themselves collect the money.' Having the farmers pay the guards enables the farmers to 'monitor' the monitor more effectively.

Boundary and choice rules also affect how easy or difficult it is to monitor activities and impose sanctions on rule infractions. Closing a forest or an inshore fishery for a substantial amount of time, for example, has multiple impacts. It protects particular plants or fish during critical growing periods and allows the entire system time to regenerate without disturbance. Further, during the closed season, rule infractions are highly obvious. *Any* person in the resource during the closed season is almost certainly breaking the rules. Similarly, requiring appropriators to use a particular technology may reduce the pressure on the resource, help to solve conflicts among users of incompatible technologies and also make it very easy to ascertain if rules are being followed. Many irrigation systems set up rotation systems so that only two persons need to monitor actions at any one time. The farmers whose 'turn' it is watches to be sure the next farmer does not start a turn early, and the next farmer watches to be sure the turn-taker stops at the specified time. This keeps monitoring costs low.

Affecting outcomes through changes in information, scope and aggregation rules

These rules tend to be used in ways that complement changes in boundary, position, choice and pay-off rules. Individual systems vary radically in regard to the mandatory information that they require. Many smaller and informal systems rely entirely on a voluntary exchange of information and on mutual monitoring. Where resource units are very valuable and the size of the group is larger, more and more requirements are added regarding the information that must be kept by appropriators or their officials. Scope rules are used to limit harvesting activities in some regions that are being treated as refugia. By not allowing any appropriation from these locations, the regenerative capacity of a system can be enhanced. Aggregation rules are used extensively in collective-choice processes and less extensively in operational settings, but one aggregation rule that is found in diverse systems is a requirement that harvesting activities be done in teams. This increases the opportunity for mutual monitoring and reduces the need to hire special guards.

It is important to note that we have not yet found any *particular* rules to have a statistically positive relationship to performance across resource types, ecological zones and communities. On the other hand, the absence of *any* boundary or choice rule is consistently associated with poor performance. Relying on only a single type of rule for an entire set of common-pool resources in a large region is also negatively related.

Experimenting with Rules

In addition to the type of exchange of information that those involved in self-governing entities can undertake on their own, it is important to find ways of undertaking rigorous, comparative research that controls for the many confounding variables that simultaneously affect performance (Hayes and Ostrom, 2005; Gibson et al, 2005). In the field of medicine, folk medicine has frequently been based on unknown foundations that turned out to be relatively sound, but some folk medicine continued for centuries, doing more harm to patients than good. The commons that are governed by users and the institutions they use are complex and sometimes difficult to understand. It is important to blend knowledge and information obtained in many different ways as we try to build a more effective knowledge base about what works and why. The recent study of Theesfeld (2004) is an outstanding example of such a blend. It is a rigorous study drawing on theory, in-depth fieldwork and quantitative survey research to understand the constraints facing Bulgarian farmers in their efforts to engage in collective action in the Bulgarian transitional economy.

It should now be obvious that the search for rules that improve the outcomes obtained in commons dilemmas is an incredibly complex task involving a potentially infinite combination of specific rules that could be adopted. To ascertain whether one has found an optimal set of rules to improve the outcomes achieved in a single situation, one would need to analyse how diverse rules affect each of the seven components of such a situation and as a result, the likely effect of a reformed structure on incentives, strategies and outcomes. Since multiple rules directly or indirectly affect each of the seven components of action situations, conducting a full analysis is impossible. Thus, instead of proposing an optimal set of rules (such as Individual Transferable Quotas) as has been the tendency of academics, we need to find ways of helping those users and officials involved in using and managing common-pool resources to experiment and learn from their experiments (Folke et al, 2002; Berkes, Colding et al, 2003). Instead of proposing one set of rules for large terrains, the need exists to authorize users to organize themselves, select rules that they think will fit their local circumstances, and adapt these over time as they learn from experience. Then, creating larger-scale government entities that generate accurate information and provide effective and fair conflict resolution mechanisms has frequently been a more important investment of national governments than trying to manage the vast variety of local ecological systems that exist in any large country, as in Australia.

Acknowledgements

The author is appreciative of funding from the National Science Foundation, the Ford Foundation, and the MacArthur Foundation. Work with colleagues in the Resilience Alliance (supported by the McDonnell Foundation) has proved important during recent years.

Note

1　Parts of this section draw on the work published in Understanding Institutional Diversity (E. Ostrom, Princeton University Press, 2005).

References

Acheson, J. M. (2003). *Capturing the Commons: Devising Institutions to Manage the Maine Lobster Industry*. Hanover, NH: University Press of New England.

Acheson, J. M., Wilson, J. A., and Steneck, R. S. (1998). 'Managing chaotic fisheries.' In Berkes, F. and Folke, C. (eds.), *Linking Social and Ecological Systems: Management Practices and Social Mechanisms for Building Resilience.* (pp. 390–413). New York: Cambridge University Press.

Agrawal, A. (1994). 'Rules, rule making, and rule breaking: Examining the fit between rule systems and resource use'. In Ostrom, E., Gardner, R., and Walker, J. (eds.), *Rules, Games, and Common-Pool Resources.* (pp. 267–82). Ann Arbor: University of Michigan Press.

Agrawal, A. (2000). 'Small is beautiful, but is larger better? Forest-management institutions in the Kumaon Himalaya, India'. In Gibson, C., McKean, M., and Ostrom, E. (eds.), *People and Forests: Communities, Institutions, and Governance.* (pp. 57–85). Cambridge, MA: MIT Press.

Agrawal, A., and Yadama, G. N. (1997). 'How do local institutions mediate market and population pressures on resources? Forest Panchayats in Kumaon, India'. *Development and Change*, 28 (3), 435–65.

Anderson, L. G. (1986). *The Economics of Fisheries Management*. Revised edition. Baltimore, MD: Johns Hopkins University Press.

Anderson, L. G. (1995). 'Privatizing open access fisheries: Individual transferable quotas'. In Bromley, D. W. (ed.), *The Handbook of Environmental Economics.* (pp. 453–474). Oxford: Blackwell.

Arnold, J.E.M. (1998). *Managing Forests as Common Property*. FAO Forestry paper no. 136. Rome, Italy: Food and Agriculture Organization of the United Nations.

Arnold, J.E.M., and Campbell, J. G. (1986). *Collective Management of Hill Forests in*

Nepal: The Community Forestry Development Project. In Proceedings of the Conference on Common Property Resource Management, National Research Council, (pp. 425–54). Washington, DC: National Academy Press.

Arnold, J.E.M., and Stewart, W. C. (1991). *Common Property Resource Management in India.* Tropical Forestry papers no. 24. Oxford: Oxford Forestry Institute.

Ascher, W. (1995). *Communities and Sustainable Forestry in Developing Countries.* San Francisco, CA: ICS Press.

Baker, M. (2005). *The Kuhls of Kangra: Community Managed Irrigation in the Western Himalaya.* Seattle: University of Washington Press.

Baland, J.-M., and Platteau, J.-P. (1996). *Halting Degradation of Natural Resources: Is There a Role for Rural Communities?* Oxford: Clarendon Press.

Berkes, F. (ed.). (1989). *Common Property Resources: Ecology and Community-Based Sustainable Development.* London: Belhaven Press.

Berkes, F., Colding, J., and Folke, C. (2003). *Navigating Social-Ecological Systems: Building Resilience for Complexity and Change.* Cambridge: Cambridge University Press.

Berkes, F., Feeny, D., McCay, B. J., and Acheson, J. M. (1989). 'The benefits of the commons'. *Nature,* 340 (6229), 91–93.

Berkes, F., Mahon, R., McConney, P., Pollnac, R., and Pomeroy, R. (2001). *Managing Small-Scale Fisheries: Alternative Directions and Methods.* Ottawa: International Development Research Centre.

Blomquist, W. (1992). *Dividing the Waters: Governing Groundwater in Southern California.* Oakland, CA: ICS Press.

Bromley, D. W. (1982). *Improving Irrigated Agriculture: Institutional Reform and the Small Farmer.* Working Paper no. 531. Washington, DC: World Bank.

Bromley, D. W., Feeny, D., McKean, M., Peters, P., Gilles, J., Oakerson, R., Runge, C. F., and Thomson, J., (eds). (1992). *Making the Commons Work: Theory, Practice, and Policy.* San Francisco, CA: ICS Press.

Brunckhorst, D., Coop, P., and Reeve, I. (2004). *An Eco-Civic Regionalization for Rural New South Wales: Final Report to the NSW Government.* Armidale, NSW: Institute for Rural Futures and Centre for Bioregional Resource Management.

Campbell, D. T. (1969). 'Reforms as experiments'. *American Psychologist* 24(4),409–429.

Coleman, J. (1973). *The Mathematics of Collective Action.* Chicago: Aldine.

Copes, P. (1986). 'A critical review of the individual quota as a device in fisheries management'. *Land Economics,* 62 (3), 278–291.

Cordell, J. C., and McKean, M. (1992). 'Sea tenure in Bahia, Brazil'. In Bromley, D. W., et al. (eds.), *Making the Commons Work: Theory, Practice, and Policy.* (pp. 183–205). San Francisco, CA: ICS Press.

Cruz, W. D. (1986). *Overfishing and Conflict in a Traditional Fishery: San Miguel Bay, Philippines.* In National Research Council, Proceedings of the Conference on Common Property Resource Management. (pp. 115–135). Washington, DC: National Academy Press.

Curtis, D. (1991). *Beyond Government: Organizations for Common Benefit.* London: Macmillan.

Dasgupta, P. (1982). *The Control of Resources.* Cambridge, MA: Harvard University Press.

Deci, E. L. (1975). *Intrinsic Motivation.* New York: Plenum Press.

de los Reyes, R. P. (1980). *Managing Communal Gravity Systems: Farmers' Approaches and Implications for Program Planning.* Quezon City, Philippines: Ateneo de Manila University, Institute of Philippine Culture.

Dietz, T., Ostrom, E., and Stern, P. (2003). 'The struggle to govern the commons.' *Science,* 302 (5652), 1907–1912.

Feeny, D. (1988). 'Agricultural expansion and forest depletion in Thailand,

1900–1975'. In Richards, J. F., and Tucker, R. P. (eds.), *World Deforestation in the Twentieth Century.* (pp. 112–43). Durham, NC: Duke University Press.

Folke, C., Carpenter, S., Elmqvist, T., Hunderson, L., Holling, C. S., and Walker, B. (2002). 'Resilience and sustainable development: Building adaptive capacity in a world of transformations'. *Ambio,* 31 (5), 437–440.

Fortmann, L., and Bruce, J. W. (1988). *Whose Trees? Proprietary Dimensions of Forestry.* Boulder, CO: Westview Press.

Frey, B. (1997). *Not Just for the Money: An Economic Theory of Personal Motivation.* Cheltenham, England: Edward Elgar.

Gadgil, M., and Iyer, P. (1989). 'On the diversification of common-property resource use by Indian society'. In Berkes, F. (ed.), *Common Property Resources: Ecology and Community-Based Sustainable Development.* (pp. 240–272), London: Belhaven Press.

Gibson, C., Williams, J. T., and Ostrom, E. (2005). 'Local enforcement and better forests'. *World Development,* 33 (2), 273–284.

Grafton, R. Q. (2000). 'Governance of the commons: A role for the state? *Land Economics,* 76 (4), 504–517.

Hayes, T. M., and Ostrom, E. (2005). 'Conserving the world's forests: Are protected areas the only way?' *Indiana Law Review,* 38, 595–617.

Hess, C. (1999). *A Comprehensive Bibliography of Common Pool Resources.* (CD-ROM) Bloomington: Indiana University, Workshop in Political Theory and Policy Analysis. Online www.indiana.edu/~workshop/wsl/wsl.html

Higgs, R. (1996). 'Legally induced technical regress in the Washington salmon fishery'. In Alston, L. J., Eggertsson, T., and North, D. C. (eds.), *Empirical Studies in Institutional Change.* New York: Cambridge University Press, 247–279.

Hilton, R. (1992). 'Institutional incentives for resource mobilization: An analysis of irrigation schemes in Nepal'. *Journal of Theoretical Politics,* 4(3), 283–308.

Holling, C. S., Gunderson, L. H., and Ludwig, D. (2001). 'In quest of a theory of adaptive change'. In Gunderson, L. H., and Holling, C. S. (eds.), *Panarchy: Understanding Transformations in Human and Natural Systems.* (pp. 3–24). Washington, DC: Island Press.

Hughes, T. P., Bellwood, D. R., Folke, C., Steneck, R. S., and Wilson, J. (2005). 'New paradigms for supporting the resilience of marine ecosystems.' *TRENDS in Ecology and Evolution,* 20(7), 380–386.

Janssen, M. A., Anderies, J. M., and Walker, B. H. (2004). 'Robust strategies for managing rangelands with multiple stable attractors'. *Journal of Environmental Economics and Management,* 47, 140–162.

Jodha, N. S. (1990). 'Depletion of common property resources in India: Micro-level evidence'. In McNicoll, G., and Cain, M. (eds.), *Rural Development and Population: Institutions and Policy.* (pp. 261–283). Oxford: Oxford University Press.

Jodha, N. S. (1996). 'Property rights and development'. In Hanna, S., Folke, C., and Mäler, K.-G. (eds.), *Rights to Nature.* (pp. 205–222). Washington, DC: Island Press.

Joshi, N. N., Ostrom, E., Shivakoti, G., and Lam, W. F. (2000). 'Institutional opportunities and constraints in the performance of farmer-managed irrigation systems in Nepal'. *Asia-Pacific Journal of Rural Development* 10 (2), 67–92.

Kiser, L. L., and Ostrom, E. (1982). 'The three worlds of action: a metatheoretical synthesis of institutional approaches'. In Ostrom, E. (ed.), *Strategies of Political Inquiry.* (pp. 179–222). Beverly Hills, CA: Sage.

Kreps, D. M., Milgrom, P., Roberts, J., and Wilson, R. (1982). 'Rational cooperation in the finitely repeated prisoners' dilemma'. *Journal of Economic Theory,* 27, 245–252.

Lam, W. F. (1998). *Governing Irrigation Systems in Nepal: Institutions, Infrastructure, and Collective Action.* Oakland, CA: ICS Press.

Lansing, J. S. (1991). *Priests and Programmers: Technologies of Power in the Engineered Landscape of Bali*. Princeton, NJ: Princeton University Press.

Levine, G. (1980). 'The relationship of design, operation, and management'. In Coward, E. W. (ed.), *Irrigation and Agricultural Development in Asia*. (pp. 51–64) Ithaca, NY: Cornell University Press.

Lobe, K., and Berkes, F. (2004). 'The Padu system of community-based fisheries management: Change and local institutional innovation in south India'. *Marine Policy*, 28, 271–281.

Marshall, G. R. (2004). 'Farmers cooperating in the commons? A study of collective action in salinity management'. *Ecological Economics*, 51, 271–286.

McCay, B. J., and Acheson, J. M. (1987). *The Question of the Commons: The Culture and Ecology of Communal Resources*. Tucson: University of Arizona Press.

Mehra, S. (1981). *Instability in Indian Agriculture in the Context of the New Technology. Research Report no. 25*. Washington, DC: International Food Policy Research Institute.

Netting, R. McC. (1993). *Smallholders, Householders: Farm Families and the Ecology of Intensive, Sustainable Agriculture*. Stanford, CA: Stanford University Press.

NRC (National Research Council). (2002). *Drama of the Commons. Committee on the Human Dimensions of Global Change*, eds. E. Ostrom, T. Dietz, N. Dolšak, P. C. Stern, S. Stonich, and E. Weber. Washington, D.C.: National Academy Press.

Ostrom, E. (1990). *Governing the Commons: The Evolution of Institutions for Collective Action*. New York: Cambridge University Press.

Ostrom, E. (1998). 'A behavioral approach to the rational choice theory of collective action'. *American Political Science Review*, 92 (1), 1–22.

Ostrom, E. (2005). *Understanding Institutional Diversity*. Princeton, NJ: Princeton University Press.

Ostrom, E., Agrawal, A., Blomquist, W., Schlager, E., Tang, S. Y., et al. (1989). *CPR Coding Manual*. Bloomington: Indiana University, Workshop in Political Theory and Policy Analysis.

Ostrom, E., Gardner, R., and Walker, J. (1994). *Rules, Games, and Common-Pool Resources*. Ann Arbor: University of Michigan Press.

Ostrom, V., Feeny, D., and Picht, H. (eds.) (1993). *Rethinking Institutional Analysis and Development: Issues, Alternatives, and Choices*. (2nd ed). Oakland, CA: ICS Press.

Palanisami, K. (1982). *Managing Tank Irrigation Systems: Basic Issues and Implications for Improvement*. Presented at the workshop on Tank Irrigation: Problems and Prospects. Bogor, Indonesia: CIFOR.

Panayotou, T., and Ashton, P. S. (1992). *Not By Timber Alone: Economics and Ecology for Sustaining Tropical Forests*. Washington, DC: Island Press.

Pinkerton, E. (ed.) (1989). *Co-operative Management of Local Fisheries: New Directions for Improved Management and Community Development*. Vancouver: University of British Columbia Press.

Poudel, R., Pandit, K. N., Adhikari, K., Shakya, S. M. Yadav, D. N. and Joshi, N. R. (1994) *Inventory and Need Assessment of Irrigation Systems in North-Eastern Tanahu (Volume 1)*, Rambpur, Chitwan, Nepal: Irrigation Management Systems Study Group, Institute of Agriculture and Animal Sciences.

Repetto, R. (1986). *Skimming the Water: Rent-Seeking and the Performance of Public Irrigation Systems*. Research report no. 4. Washington, DC: World Resources Institute.

Schlager, E. (1990). *Model Specification and Policy Analysis: The Governance of Coastal Fisheries*. Ph.D. diss., Indiana University.

Schlager, E. (1994). 'Fishers' institutional responses to common-pool resource dilemmas'. In Ostrom, E., Gardner, R., and Walker, J. (eds.), *Rules, Games, and Common-Pool Resources*. (pp. 247–266) Ann Arbor: University of Michigan Press.

Schlager, E., Blomquist, W., and Tang, S. Y. (1994). 'Mobile flows, storage, and self-organized institutions for governing common-pool resources.' *Land Economics*, 70 (3), 294–317.

Schlager, E., and Ostrom, E. (1992). 'Property-rights regimes and natural resources: A conceptual analysis'. *Land Economics*, 68 (3), 249–262.

Seixas, C., and Berkes, F. (2003). 'Dynamics of social-ecological changes in a lagoon fishery in southern Brazil'. In Berkes, F., Colding, J., and Folke, C. (eds.), *Navigating Social-Ecological Systems*. (pp. 271–298). Cambridge: Cambridge University Press.

Sengupta, N. (1991). *Managing Common Property: Irrigation in India and the Philippines*. New Delhi: Sage.

Shepherd, G. (1992). *Managing Africa's Tropical Dry Forests: A Review of Indigenous Methods*. London: Overseas Development Institute.

Shivakoti, G., and Ostrom, E. (eds.) (2002). *Improving Irrigation Governance and Management in Nepal*. Oakland, CA: ICS Press.

Shukla, A., Gajhurel, K. P., Shivakoti, G., Poudel, R., Pandit, K. N., Adhitkari, K. R., Thapa, T. B., Shakya, S. M., Yadav, D. N., Joshi, N. R. and Shrestha, A. P. (1993) *Irrigation Resource Inventory of East Chitwan Rampur*, Chitwan, Nepal: Irrigation Management Systems Study Group, Institute of Agriculture and Animal Sciences.

Singleton, S. (1998). *Constructing Cooperation: The Evolution of Institutions of Co-management in Pacific Northwest Salmon Fisheries*. Ann Arbor: University of Michigan Press.

Singleton, S., and Taylor, M. (1992). 'Common property economics: A general theory and land use applications'. *Journal of Theoretical Politics*, 4 (3), 309–324.

Tang, S. Y. (1992). *Institutions and Collective Action: Self-Governance in Irrigation*. San Francisco, CA: ICS Press.

Tang, S. Y. (1994). 'Institutions and performance in irrigation systems'. In Ostrom, E., Gardner, R., and Walker, J. (eds.), *Rules, Games, and Common-Pool Resources*. (pp. 225–245). Ann Arbor: University of Michigan Press.

Taylor, M. (1982). *Community, Anarchy, and Liberty*. New York: Cambridge University Press.

Theesfeld, I. (2004). 'Constraints on collective action in a transitional economy: The case of Bulgaria's irrigation sector'. *World Development*, 32 (2), 251–271.

Thomson, J. T. (1977). 'Ecological deterioration: Local-level rule making and enforcement problems in Niger'. In Glantz, M. H. (ed.), *Desertification: Environmental Degradation in and around Arid Lands*. (pp. 57–79). Boulder, CO: Westview Press.

Thomson, J. T., Feeny, D., and Oakerson, R. J. (1992). 'Institutional dynamics: The evolution and dissolution of common-property resource management'. In Bromley, D. W., et al. (eds.), *Making the Commons Work: Theory, Practice, and Policy*. (pp. 129–160). Oakland, CA: ICS Press.

von Wright, G. H. (1966). 'The logic of action: A sketch'. In Rescher, N. (ed.), *The Logic of Decision and Action*. (pp. 121–136). Pittsburgh, PA: University of Pittsburgh Press.

Wade, R. (1994). *Village Republics: Economic Conditions for Collective Action in South India*. San Francisco, CA: ICS Press.

Weissing, F. J., and Ostrom, E. (1991a). 'Irrigation institutions and the games irrigators play: Rule enforcement without guards'. In Selten, R. (ed.), *Game Equilibrium Models II: Methods, Morals, and Markets*. (pp. 188–262). Berlin: Springer-Verlag.

Weissing, F. J., and Ostrom, E. (1991b). 'Crime and punishment'. *Journal of Theoretical Politics*, 3 (3), 343–349.

Williamson, O. E. (1975). *Markets and Hierarchies: Analysis and Antitrust Implications*. New York: Free Press.

Williamson, S., Brunckhorst, D., and Kelly, G. (2003). *Reinventing the Common: Cross-Boundary Farming for a Sustainable Future*. Sydney, NSW: Federation Press.

Wilson, J. A. (2002). 'Scientific uncertainty, complex systems, and the design of common-pool institutions'. In Ostrom, E., Dietz, T., Dolšak, N., Stern, P. C., Stonich, S., and Weber, E. (eds.) (Committee on the Human Dimensions of Global Change), *The Drama of the Commons, National Research Council.* (pp. 327–359). Washington, DC: National Academy Press.

Wilson, J. A., Acheson, J. M., Metcalfe, M., and Kleban, P. (1994). 'Chaos, Complexity, and Community Management of Fisheries'. *Marine Policy*, 18, 291–305.

Yandle, T. (2001). *Market-Based Natural Resource Management: An Institutional Analysis of Individual Tradable Quotas in New Zealand's Commercial Fisheries.* Ph.D. diss., Indiana University.

Yandle, T., and Dewees, C. (2003). 'Privatizing the commons . . . twelve years later: fishers' experiences with New Zealand's market-based fisheries management'. In Dolšak, N., and Ostrom, E. (eds.), *The Commons in the New Millennium: Challenges and Adaptations.* (pp. 101–27). Cambridge, MA: MIT Press.

3

The Challenge of Maintaining the Salience of Common Property Rights with Increasing Cultural and Socio-economic Heterogeneity

Katrina Myrvang Brown

Introduction

In the UK, and elsewhere in Western Europe, there are many examples of historically enduring common property regimes (e.g. Stevenson, 1991; Brouwer, 1995; Short, 2000; Carlsson, 2001; De Moor, 2002). From a survey of English-language literature it is estimated that approximately nine per cent of the land area of Western Europe is historically enduring common land (Brown, 2005). However, contemporary demographic shifts coupled with demands for greater multifunctionality of agricultural land have put pressure on the formal and informal institutional arrangements used to govern such commons. In particular, the in-migration of people from other – often urban – areas (Jedrej and Nutall, 1996; Stockdale et al, 2000), the decline in agricultural returns (Kinloch and Dalton, 1990; Sutherland and Bevan, 2001; Cook and Copus, 2002), and the growing need to provide public goods, such as scenery, recreational opportunities and biodiversity (Wilson, 2001; Pretty, 2002), unsettle previously established ways of using, thinking about, and exerting control over the land. Economically, rightsholders depend much less – or at least less directly – upon the land for their livelihood, and find a greater variety of values attached to the land than in the past; a trend exacerbated by the growing socio-economic and cultural heterogeneity of rightsholders caused by counter-urbanization. Maintaining the salience (or importance) of the common land rights to rightsholders is made more challenging because many of these values relate to public goods, which by definition are difficult to capture value from in pecuniary terms. Such commons trends concur with Kant (2000) who observes that dependence upon the resource goes down and user-heterogeneity goes up with economic growth.

Both *salience* and *heterogeneity of user groups* have been established as key variables in the common property literature. For example, several theorists have identified *salience*, or similarly *dependence*, as of substantial importance in providing impetus to the formation and operation of effective institutions for resource management (Agrawal and Yadama, 1997; Gibson and Becker, 2000; Ostrom, 2001; Vatn, 2001; Gibson, 2001). Ostrom (2001) asserts that a resource is highly salient when 'appropriators are dependent on the resource for a major portion of their livelihood or other important activity' (p. 22), which matters because 'if appropriators do not obtain a major part of their income from a resource ... the high costs of organizing and maintaining a self-governing system may not be worth their effort' (ibid. p. 25). Gibson (2001) goes so far to imply that *dependence*, along with scarcity, is a prerequisite of self-organization of resource management institutions. *Heterogeneity of user groups* has also been frequently flagged up in the literature as important to the collective organization of resource management institutions (Baland and Platteau, 1999; Kant, 2000; Varughese and Ostrom, 2001; Bardhan and Dayton-Johnson, 2002; Poteete and Ostrom, 2004), although less agreement exists over precisely how it affects such collective action.

There is evidence that decreasing dependence on common land for livelihoods in Western Europe is influencing the robustness of their governing institutions (e.g. Kissling-Naf et al, 2002; Brown, 2005). However, there are difficulties in conceptualizing resource salience, and its link to institutional *health*, in any straightforward way – as in the common property literature mentioned above – because salience is a function, not only of *external* factors such as market and policy signals, but also of what the group of rightsholders themselves perceive as valuable, or as a potentially valuable opportunity (Brown, 2006a). A greater heterogeneity of rightsholders is likely to influence the degree and nature of the salience of the resource to those rightsholders, as well as the more frequently examined costs of negotiating and sustaining agreements amongst the group. However, there has been little attempt to unpack this relationship between salience and heterogeneity. In cases such as Western European commons, where maintaining salience is increasingly problematic, it is imperative to examine the dynamics of introducing new users or rightsholders with potentially different ideas, values, and norms, and how this affects the way values are attached to, and in turn captured from, the land. The case of historical grazing commons in Scotland will be employed to explore the central issue of how to maintain or restore the salience of common property rights in the face of the economic and demographic pressures of contemporary rural change.

Pressures of Rural Change for Enduring First-World Commons

Background of common grazings in Scotland

Crofting common grazings constitute the most prevalent examples of historically enduring land-based common property regimes in Scotland, with over 800 administrative units covering nearly 5,000 km², which is seven per cent of its total land area (Crofters Commission, 1999). They are found only in the former Crofting Counties of Scotland (Figure 3.1), coinciding largely with the Highlands and Islands. Common grazings form part of the crofting system – which has always been a part-time agricultural endeavour supplemented by other activities such as fishing or weaving – in which use and management rights are linked to the tenure of small individual plots of land known as *crofts* or *inbye*.

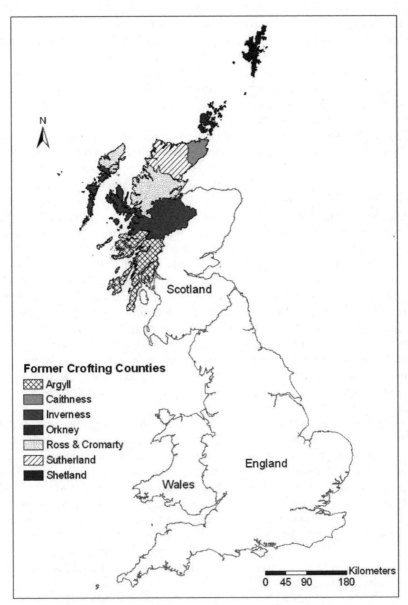

Figure 3.1 The former Crofting Counties of Scotland

Source: Based on Boundary Data from ED-Line Consortium and the Post Office, OS © Crown Copyright

Past centuries saw the dissolution of the vast majority of common property regimes in Western Europe and their replacement with forms of private property, contemporaneous with industrialization, population growth, urbanization, expansion of the market economy, and often supported by specific legislation (Demsetz, 1967; North and Thomas, 1973; Dahlman, 1980; Devine, 1994). Common grazings survived in Scotland, partially due to their inferior agricultural quality and remote location, but largely due to the passing of the Crofters Holdings (Scotland) Act 1886 and the Crofters Common Grazings Regulation Act in 1891, which preserved the basic pattern of land tenure. This legislation was passed as a response to the growing civil unrest caused by years of eviction, resettlement in poorer quality areas, emigration and famine; symptoms of landlords drive for agricultural *improvement* through increasing the land's productivity and profitability. The legislation conferred on crofters a set of rights unavailable to any other kind of tenant farmer in the UK, crucially including security of tenure and fair rent (Hunter, 1976; Devine 1988). Rights to the common grazings were specified for grazing livestock, cutting peat and collecting seaweed from the common grazings, but allowed landlords to retain title to the land, and the sporting and mineral rights.

Subsequent legislation has extended and amended crofters common grazings rights. The Crofters (Scotland) Act 1955 allows rightsholders, with permission from the Crofters Commission (a quasi-governmental body devoted solely to the development and regulation of crofting), to take an apportionment of part of the common grazings in order to obtain the exclusive use of that area. The Crofting Reform (Scotland) Act 1976 entitles rightsholders to 50 per cent of any development value coming from the common grazings, for example, from the resumption of land by the landlord for a housesite or windfarm. The Crofter Forestry (Scotland) Act 1991 enables the Grazings Committee to use any part of the common grazings to plant trees, provided that they obtain the written consent of the landlord and the approval of the Commission. The crofting community right-to-buy mechanism in the Land Reform (Scotland) Act 2003 allows the enforced purchase of inbye and common grazings, including mineral, sporting and development rights, provided certain conditions are met.

The formal institutional arrangements for governing common grazings exist on a number of levels. At the constitutional level there are several Acts of Parliament that define the legal rights and responsibilities, and provide for the Crofters Commission. At the operational level, there is a voluntary, elected Grazings Clerk who is responsible for administrative duties, and a voluntary, elected Grazings Committee, which has statutory powers and duties with respect to the management, maintenance and improvement of the resource (MacCuish and Flyn, 1990). Most grazings have a set of regulations dealing with aspects of stock management and resource maintenance, such as individual stock quotas, which, when endorsed by the Crofters Commission, become legally binding.

Consequently, crofting is a complex and somewhat paternalistic system, in which the arrangements of common property rights still reflect to a large extent the (previously valid) assumption that livestock production is central to gaining a livelihood from the land. This assumption has been undermined, however, by the current set of opportunities and constraints for common grazings as delineated by the contours of rural change.

Opportunities and constraints of rural change for common grazings

The pressures of rural change are manifest in the Highlands and Islands of Scotland in such a way that it is difficult to realize livelihood value from exercising common grazings rights, particularly from traditional agriculturally based activities. Cook and Copus (2002) describe how agricultural product prices in the Highlands and Islands, primarily relating to store sheep and cattle, fell sharply in the mid- to late 1990s due to the strength of UK currency, world price commodity slump, and the removal of protection from global competition. Problems in the livestock sector reached a peak in 2001 with an episode of FMD (Foot and Mouth Disease). Although improved prices have been experienced in the wake of FMD, ultimately the sheep sector is still recovering from a historically low base of net farm income in 2001/02 (SEERAD, 2004), compounded by a declining level of subsidy over the same period (Cook and Copus, 2002).

Concurrently, there is evidence that other sources of income are becoming of greater importance to croft households. Over the past three decades researchers have noted the growing financial significance of non-agricultural, off-croft work (e.g. Mewett, 1977; Sutherland and Bevan, 2001). According to the latest economic report on Scottish agriculture, non-farming incomes have increased by an average of 11 per cent from the previous year, with off-farm employment and pensions/investments largely accounting for the increase (SEERAD, 2004). Decreasing agricultural incomes are compounded by the economically marginal nature of most of the Highlands and Islands area, and the difficulty of capturing the economic value of the common grazings in other ways due to the prevalence of public good characteristics. Current market opportunities for the region relate primarily to tourism and renewable energy. However, the current bundle of agriculturally based common grazings rights, and the low availability of capital in low-input crofting systems, do not aid the capture of this. Policy opportunities for agricultural businesses relate primarily to environmental management activities (Futureskills Scotland, 2004). The opportunities exist in the domain of provision of goods such as scenery, amenity, habitats and biodiversity (SEERAD, 2003), although until now such funding has been extremely limited and highly competitive.

Furthermore, rural communities all over Scotland appear to be increasingly heterogeneous. A study of counter-urbanization in Scotland by Stockdale et al. (2000) found that within the sample of rural areas including a key crofting area, 28 per cent were long-term residents, 35 per cent had moved locally (less than 15km) and 37 per cent were incomers (had moved more than 15km). Moreover, the findings showed that long-term residents and incomers tended to differ in terms of age, income, level and location of employment, expenditure patterns, educational status, aspirations and cultural background.

Migrants were predominantly part of a service sector class who were 'commonly perceived to be responsible for changing rural communities' (p. 254). Of course, not all in-migrants to crofting areas acquire common grazings rights, but many do due to croft tenancies providing one of the main housing opportunities. According to the literature, such heterogeneity can make collective resource management more difficult based on the presumption that groups from diverse sociocultural backgrounds will encounter problems of distrust and lack of mutual understanding (Varughese and Ostrom, 2001).

Overall, the formal institutional framework of common grazings has changed very little whilst the informal institutions have changed a great deal, particularly regarding the expectations and benefits of holding such common property rights, in comparison with the past. Although over the years rights-holders have acquired limited extra rights relating to apportionment, development and forestry, exercising them relies heavily upon the agreement of the landlord and/or the Crofters Commission. In short, the current set of rights is partial and contingent, and to acquire the full rights through the recently added crofting community right-to-buy mechanism requires the *community* to pass a set of criteria defined by the Scottish Parliament.

Implications for Common Property Institutions

General implications of rural change for land use and governance

A postal survey of Grazings Clerks with a response rate of 49 per cent allowed an overview of the current state of common grazings use and governance using quantitative and qualitative data. The survey confirmed that there was great pressure to reduce or abandon use of common grazings primarily due to the comparative financial advantage of off-croft employment in relation to live-stock farming and the consequent time constraints that preclude a full contribution to cooperative, extensive livestock production.

Respondents reported that grazings shares were formerly very much in demand, and that it was rare to have unused shares or non-using rightsholders. Currently, however, an average of 76 per cent of shares are actually used, and that the average proportion of rightsholders that use the commons is 50 per cent. This comprises only 78 per cent of the number of rightsholders using the resource ten years ago. Nor is it just grazing use that is in decline; peat-cutting, once a feature of virtually all common grazings, now only takes place in 40 per cent of cases.

The extent and rate of decline vary greatly between individual cases (Table 3.1). Nine per cent of common grazings are in a situation of de facto privatiza-tion with only one active rightsholder; 12 per cent of common grazings are tending towards de facto privatization, with only two active rightsholders; and seven per cent of common grazings have effectively been abandoned completely. Only 11 per cent of cases have five or more active rightsholders.

There is also evidence for a decline in cooperative ways of working on common grazings (see Tables 3.2 and 3.3.). Daily or weekly cooperation was widespread 20–30 years ago, particularly for stock gathering and management, but now only occurs on 18 per cent of common grazings.

Table 3.1 *Variation of grazier numbers between common grazings*

No. of Graziers Using Common Grazings	0	1	2	3	4	5 OR MORE
Percentage of Common Grazings Cases	7%	9%	12%	35%	26%	11%

Source: Brown (2006a)

Table 3.2 *Regularity of co-operation on common grazings*

Regularity of Co-operation	Mean Percentage of Cases
Every day	3%
Every few weeks	15%
Every few months	37%
Once or twice a year	27%
Never	18%

Source: Brown (2006a)

Table 3.3 shows that only 68 per cent of common grazings have any communal stock gathering. These cooperative activities are now typically carried out by three to five rightsholders when once they were social occasions involving everyone.

Table 3.3 *Cooperative activities on common grazings*

Collective Activity	Stock Gathering	Stock Management (e.g. sheep dipping)	Resource Maintenance (e.g. fencing repairs)	Resource Improvement (e.g. reseeding)	Stock Club
% of Commons on which Activity Occurs	68%	49%	63%	24%	7%

Source: Brown (2006a)

In a stock club a livestock herd is administrated and managed wholly as one unit in order to produce an annual dividend for rightsholders.

The practical importance of many rules and regulations has reduced, as demonstrated in 54 per cent of cases where grazings regulations (e.g. the stock quotas) are not enforced. The role now demanded of Grazings Clerks and Committees tends to be less about regulating appropriation of resource 'units' and more about entrepreneurship and identifying and capturing a range of

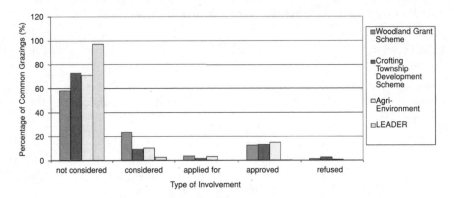

Figure 3.2 Common grazings-related engagement with development schemes

Source: Brown (2006a)

alternative benefit streams, usually from projects requiring competitive bidding. However, over 55 per cent of common grazings have not considered entry into one of the main schemes available, and less than 20 per cent have had a proposal approved (Figure 3.2).

Despite the general decline in commons salience, use and regulation, a minority of cases (eight per cent) evaded the general trend with high rates of use and users, high rates of cooperation and the successful initiation and completion of commons-related schemes and projects. This counter-trend is a crucial finding as it highlights the variety of institutional responses to the pressures of rural change. It shows that decline is not inevitable as clearly some institutions have the impetus to use and organize – e.g. the rightsholders are finding a way that the salience can be maintained or regenerated – whilst some do not. The question thus raised concerns why this should be, given that the opportunities for pecuniary gain are similar for all common grazings.

Part of the answer is that salience can only exist to the extent that it is perceived by group members, regardless of any exogenous measure of actual or potential benefits for livelihoods or other measure of well-being. This is acknowledged in the literature that deals with salience in that the *expected* benefits and costs of organizing for collective resource management are those held to comprise the calculus of individual group members (e.g. Ostrom, 2001). However, the literature rarely problematizes the corollary of this acknowledgement, which is that the expectations or perceptions underpinning *salience* are contingent on the social and cultural setting in which group members are situated. Consequently, the implications of salience as something that is perceived are poorly appreciated, particularly with respect to its relationship with other identified key factors such as heterogeneity. If it is perceived salience that matters, then it also matters how group members negotiate and contest what constitutes legitimate aspects of land use as part of the processes of enacting their common property rights.

The mechanisms of property enactment

To understand the processes at work here it is helpful to draw on the field of critical legal scholarship and particularly the work of Blomley and Rose, in which 'property is not a static, pregiven entity, but depends on a continual active *doing* ... property is an enactment' (Blomley, 2004, p. xvi). Property rights are conceptualized not as a relationship between people and particular resources, but as part of a situated, social process involving relationships between people with respect to resources (Fortmann, 1996; Li, 1996; Blomley, 1998). In this process the power to both communicate with others and persuade them that a property right exists is vital (Rose, 1994), and, accordingly, sustaining property rights and relations relies upon their continual enactment and re-enactment through representational, practical or material means (Blomley, 2004).

Enactments occur on multiple levels of governance and include: formal legal channels, such as court hearings; technologies, such as mapping; construction of material fixtures, such as fences; internalized everyday practices, such as tending a hedge; and, subtle discourses, such as those constructing a '*right*' to a parking space on the street outside one's house (Blomley, 2002). Discursive enactments take place through processes of negotiation and contestation over definitions of key categories. Struggles over resources are simultaneously struggles over meaning (Berry, 1989) and having the 'power to define, to attribute meaning, and to assign labels' (Peters, 1987, p. 193). Successful enactments signal dominion to others whilst objectifying and naturalizing the *doing* of property and the social relations of power that produce and maintain it (Rose, 1994; Peters, 1994; Blomley, 2004).

A key implication of the social nature of property relations is that they can, and do, change as society changes. What is valued about land, what constitutes a legitimate claim to a right and who is considered a legitimate claimant can vary both spatially and temporally (Peters, 1994), with economic, social and environmental consequences. Even if there is little change at a formal institutional level, as in the case of crofting common grazings, there can be a great deal of change at the informal level with implications for who gets access to and control over resources *on the ground*. Since patterns of access and control do not necessarily reflect the *official*, state authorized, configurations of rights (Meinzen-Dick and Pradhan, 2001), the analyst must examine the social spaces in which de jure and de facto rights and formal and informal institutions interact, where various resource claims are constantly being constructed, negotiated and contested in the struggle for legitimacy (Mehta et al, 2001).

Heterogeneity and common property enactment

Property relations can change when the reproduction of salience amongst the group changes. The issue for common grazings is how increasing heterogeneity through the introduction of new rightsholders with potentially different ideas, values and norms affect the way that values are attached to, and captured from, commons resources. This heterogeneity impacts how salience is perceived and socially reproduced, and in turn the impetus to manage collectively is sustained.

In-depth investigation of eight common grazings case studies showed that enactment processes had undoubtedly become more contested in line with the growing demands for multifunctionality and the increased heterogeneity of rightsholders, which together have disturbed previously stable assumptions of what and whom crofting was for. Of particular note, however, is that the actual heterogeneity of the group in terms of diverse backgrounds, interests, endowments mattered less than perceived heterogeneity (see Brown, 2006b, for full explanation). Rightsholders did not necessarily differentiate between each other along strictly defined social, economic or cultural differences – as many commons-related studies of heterogeneity do – but constructed differences amongst themselves relating to their land use practices, their land use objectives and their identity or role as a user or beneficiary. The two may be related but they cannot be conflated.

Table 3.4 *Axes that delineate legitimate uses, objectives and users*

1. **Deontology – Labour and Practice of Land Use**
a. Application of labour
b. Ethics of (hard) work
c. Types of land use
d. Link to past practices
2. **Teleology – Motives, Functions and Objectives of Land Use**
a. Agriculture as livelihood, lifestyle or pastime
b. Betterment and socio-economic heterogeneity
c. Progress and development
d. Constructions of the 'common good'
3. **Identity and Subject Formation**
a. Gender
b. Age
c. Localness
d. Agricultural involvement

As part of a struggle over the conceptual and material territory of crofting, rightsholders were contesting the moral right to the legal right, with one informant clearly demonstrating that they cannot be assumed to overlap: 'just because they have a right to a croft, doesn't mean they have the right to interfere in crofting' (grazier). For example, some in-migrants were labelled *incomers* but some were not, with implications for how they can act with respect to the resource. Constructions of difference in the degree and nature of moral right were used to legitimate or undermine particular resource claims as they were negotiated and contested amongst the group. Table 3.4 shows the three principal axes of practices, objectives and identities along which group members were differentiated, with examples under each one as found in common grazings cases. Although differentiation occurred across similar axes in the common grazings cases (as denoted in the table), the processes of negotiating legitimacy unfolded differently, with different results, in each case because the precise meanings attached to each axis, and the way they are invoked in relation to each other, depended on the precise context.

Returning to the imperative for resource salience, the key question is whether what is legitimate – and therefore (re)produced as salient – to the group is also salient in terms of financially viability. In economically marginal crofting areas, there remains the need for group members to be able to *afford* to enact property in line with their morally underpinned notions of land use. For generating or maintaining the impetus to organize collective resource management, the practices and objectives of land use carrying the greatest legitimacy within the group, must overlap sufficiently with the opportunities for contributing to livelihoods. What is *sufficient*, therefore, depends very much on the alternative income sources such as part-time employment and pensions that group members have access to. However, even rightsholders possessing an independent, secure income can often see the importance of allowing others income-generating opportunities in order to sustain a viable economic and social infrastructure in fragile areas. Yet the degree to which they do so comes back to the legitimacy of the people, practices and objectives with respect to the moral assumptions they hold about land use.

Illustrative Scenarios of Response to Pressures of Rural Change

The following four common grazings scenarios will be used to demonstrate the range of institutional responses to rural change that alters the way heterogeneity is constructed and the way salience is reproduced, enabling common property to be enacted in particular ways and not others. The scenarios represent simplified 'types', when in practice there is a spectrum of grey area between them.

Abandonment

Where there are no graziers using the common grazings and no established Grazings Committee, the land can be considered abandoned, which occurred in seven per cent of cases. Either there was insufficient salience perceived in the resource by rightsholders, or the salience of the resource was reproduced in such a way that dominant ideas of legitimate use did not concur sufficiently with the income-generation necessary for contributing to livelihoods. This can be exacerbated when certain biophysical and policy circumstances create thresholds by demanding a minimum number of participants for common grazings activities. For example, sheep cannot be gathered on some common grazings without a minimum of five people, so when resource salience is such that less than five active graziers remain, the other four have to quit using the land even if it is still salient to them. Similarly, if a rural development scheme requires that a majority of rightsholders participate, the opportunity cannot be taken up even if 49 per cent of rightsholders find it salient.

De facto privatization

A situation of only one remaining active grazier using the common grazings occurs in nine per cent of cases. One particular case featured a rightsholder who was exercising his own and everyone else's sheep quota (without their permission). Many of the other rightsholders were not able to keep stock due to the time constraints of other employment, but were keen to use their rights to plant trees as part of a communal forestry project in order to generate some funds for the township. However, the grazier justified his effective blocking of this plan through constructions of the *localness* of the rightsholders and their desire to maintain *traditional* practices for the *common good*. In the grazier's view, the best use of common grazings land was *traditional* use, by which he meant grazing use. Furthermore, he asserted that the main way the common grazings could serve the objective of the 'common good' was to provide a significant livelihood contribution in order to maintain population in the area, but which can only be done through *traditional* practices for one rightsholder using economies of scale (e.g. using all the shares). He also described the township as predominantly composed of *locals*, who are not able to *use* the land themselves (e.g. for grazing), but implied that they would thus share this interpretation of *best use* as a function of being *local*. In actual fact, the majority of rightsholders had recently migrated to the area, but neither they, nor their objectives – and in turn their resource claims – were given any visibility in the discourses of the dominating grazier. They were unable to resist the grazier's constructions, particularly given the legitimacy that *tradition* and the *common good* carried, and their desire to be accepted as *locals* as much as possible.

Residual traditional cooperation

In 73 per cent of cases there is some functioning of commons institutions through residual agricultural cooperation, usually on a much reduced scale compared to the past; often just above the threshold of minimum numbers of participating graziers willing and available to carry out related tasks. The justifications for maintaining *traditional* use are often very similar to those described in the section above, but in contrast, the graziers place very little store in making a profit as they have an independent income, usually from a pension that still allows them time to cooperate. On the surface these commons can appear to work well, with informants reporting that small numbers make consensus easier to reach. Nevertheless, such arrangements are very vulnerable to future reductions in available labour, as participants tend to be old and, therefore, will imminently be unable to play an active role in commons management. Moreover, the sustained legitimacy of sheep grazing as *tradition* often prevents the infiltration of new ideas – and thus younger rightsholders who might find the resource salient in other ways – into these commons management institutions. Wherever one originates, they are only considered *local* if they support established practices. This compounds the lack of adaptability to future changes.

Diversification

In 11 per cent of cases, common grazings rights are used in a variety of ways, with all rightsholders involved or benefiting in some way through the provision of income-generating opportunities and social, cultural and environmental public goods. Types of diversification found include new sport and recreational uses (e.g. football, athletics and pony trekking), tourism (e.g. nature trails, accommodation), power generation, conservation management and forestry. A particularly vibrant example has 50 per cent of rightsholders still exercising their grazing rights for sheep, cattle and horses, as well as forestry; recreation by both locals and tourists; paid conservation management; peat cutting; and sites for community facilities such as the fank, dipper and community storage shed. Many community projects take place here, mostly catalysed by the community enterprise company, such as a feed cooperative, machinery ring, garden centre and tree nursery, art studio, videoing service, shop and museum. There are also plans to refurbish some disused shielings as backpacker accommodation. Directly, the grazing of animals provides primarily non-pecuniary benefits, but indirectly, along with other activities, generates benefits for rightsholders such as employment in projects or tourist businesses, economies of scale in buying agricultural inputs, and shared equipment and facilities. Atypically, the Grazings Committee holds sufficient legitimacy to be viewed as a tier of local government, and all the money generated by communal projects go into the Committee fund, where the profits pump-prime further projects. Over half of the rightsholders (and the Committee) are in-migrants who happen to be sympathetic to past uses – and therefore do not disenfranchize those for whom past uses have great symbolic importance – but can see through 'tradition' as a changing construction that needs to adapt to current rural development opportunities. Dominant discourses serve to expand the definition of crofting, drawing heavily on the moral axes of the common good, livelihoods, progress and development. They also employ broad interpretations of land use type (including forestry conservation and amenity) and application of labour (where many kinds of contributions are valued and labelled as *active*). They construct the crofting *way of life* fluidly, where new elements are not seen as compromising *old* elements but as helping to sustain them in some form. This disturbs the assumption commonly found elsewhere that the label of *local* and *agricultural practices* must go together.

Conclusion

Two key pressures on land-based, historically enduring common property regimes in Western Europe are the declining direct dependence upon the resource by rightsholders for their livelihoods and the increasing cultural and socio-economic heterogeneity of rightsholders. These reflect broader trends of primary-industry decline and counter-urbanization found in many developed countries. Since dependence or at least high salience of the resource to its users/rightsholders is flagged up in the common property literature as crucial to sustaining effective resource management institutions, the question is raised of how this salience might be maintained or regenerated.

In the example of common grazings in the Highlands and Islands of Scotland, the extent of dependence upon the resource has declined due to lower returns from agriculture and the reliance on external employment or pensions as income sources. Furthermore, maintaining high salience had been problematic because of the difficulty in capturing pecuniary value from the goods that are currently demanded. These demanded goods are often a) public goods; b) require high capital outlay to be realized; and c) cannot be accessed through the traditional bundle of rights. Nevertheless, the land is still very much valued in most cases – and therefore in a sense has high salience – but in an increasing variety of ways by an increasing variety of people.

Although the absence of common grazings rights may not cause imminent livelihood collapse for most rightsholders, it matters that the resource is managed for a number of reasons. Principally, use and governance of common grazings contributes to the quality of life of both locals and visitors, and allows the provision of environmental, social and cultural public goods, as well as the possibility of generating pecuniary value. Absence of use and governance could indirectly cause negative economic impact, especially on income from tourism.

The common property literature, although clear about the importance of salience and heterogeneity as variables in the initiation and evolution of collective institutions, has very little to say about the institutional response in circumstances where salience or dependence is not high, or about the relationship between salience and heterogeneity. Ostrom (2001) notes that *expected*, rather than *actual*, benefits are those that matter to rightsholders when deciding whether it is worth investing in commons management. However, the literature rarely problematizes the corollary of this acknowledgement, which is that the expectations or perceptions underpinning *salience* – and indeed heterogeneity – are contingent on the ways they are negotiated amongst group members in specific social and cultural settings. Thus, despite being related, perceived salience and actual opportunities to benefit, as well as perceived heterogeneity and actual socio-economic differences, if confused will only obscure understanding in analysis.

Common grazings examples demonstrate that, in terms of providing the impetus for collective management, the opportunities to benefit from resource rights are only important to the extent that they are perceived as such by rightsholders. Resource salience is a function of market and policy drivers mediated and negotiated through the groups' cultural values and moral norms. It is an issue of negotiating legitimacy of particular land use options as well as their costs and benefits, which is often poorly appreciated in the literature. Common grazings rightsholders negotiate – and sometimes contest – what is legitimate regarding the objectives for land use, the practices of land use and whom ought to use and benefit from the land. Thus, salience cannot be assumed away as high, uniform or static, nor as an *external* variable in order to concentrate on more 'internal' institutional variables, as it is partially determined by *internal* factors. Instead it must be understood as part of an iterative process in which it is produced and reproduced through the continual enactments of common property.

Heterogeneity affects the reproduction of salience by a collective of right-sholders in different ways. On one hand, differences in socio-economic and cultural background increase the likelihood that ideas, values and norms will diverge. Therefore, one might expect greater contestation amongst the group regarding what is salient about the resource. On the other hand, such differences increase the chances that at least some values will be aligned with those underpinning the policy instruments and market opportunities.

The most crucial finding of the study was that perceived heterogeneity is as important as heterogeneity in some kind of *actual* sense. The way differences were constructed amongst common grazings rightsholders was not necessarily aligned with straightforward measures of socio-economic or cultural back-ground. Instead, differentiation came from the drawing of moral boundaries between people, practices and objectives: how land should be used; what purpose it should serve; and who should use and benefit from the land. The main reason the 'diversification' case resisted decline was the innovative ways that rightsholders considered the resource salient, negotiated through moral values that allowed the conceptual expansion of crofting.

Poteete and Ostrom (2004) point out that institutions can be adapted to cope with heterogeneity. This study suggests that institutions might also be adapted to cope with declining or changing salience. For common grazings to cope with declining salience and increasing heterogeneity, policy needs to facil-itate the provision and discernment of opportunities by:

a. extending the bundle of common property rights that crofters hold (e.g. through the Land Reform (Scotland) Act 2003);
b. encouraging the capture of value from public goods provision (e.g. through grant schemes for conservation or tourism initiatives on common grazings);
c. providing favourable loans for projects with high start-up costs (e.g. wind power).

Policy also needs to recognize that even when the above measures have expanded the opportunities for benefit provision, perceived salience may or may not have changed in tandem. Alignment between 'perceived' and 'real' benefits (or salience) will depend on how the legitimacy of various aspects of land use is negotiated amongst the group.

References

Agrawal, A. and Yadama, G. N., (1997). 'How do local institutions mediate market and population pressures on resources? Forest Panchayats in Kumaon, India'. *Development and Change*, 28, 435–465.

Baland, J. M. and Platteau, J. P., (1999). 'The ambiguous impact of inequality on local resource management'. *World Development,* 27 (5), 773–788.

Bardhan, P. and Dayton-Johnson, J., (2002). 'Unequal irrigators: Heterogeneity and commons management in large scale multivariate research'. In Ostrom E. et al. (eds). *The Drama of the Commons.* (pp. 87–112). Washington, DC: National Academy Press.

Berry, S., (1989). 'Social institutions and access to resources'. *Africa,* 59 (1), 41–55.

Blomley, N.K., (2002). 'Mud for the land'. *Public Culture,* 14 (3), 557–582.

Blomley, N.K., (2004). *Unsettling the City: Urban Land and the Politics of Property.* London: Routledge.

Blomley, N.K., (1998). 'Landscapes of property'. *Law and Society Review,* 32 (3), 567–612.

Brouwer, R., (1995). 'Common goods and private profits: Traditional and modern communal land management in Portugal'. *Human Organization,* 54 (3), 283–294.

Brown, K.M., (2005). *Contemporary Rural Change and the Enactment of Common Property Rights: The Case of Crofting Common Grazings.* Unpublished doctoral thesis, University of Aberdeen.

Brown, K.M. (2006a). 'New challenges for old commons: The role of historical common land in contemporary rural spaces'. *Scottish Geographical Journal,* 122(2), 109–129.

Brown, K.M. (2006b). 'The role of moral values in contemporary common property enactment'. *Norsk Geographisk Tidsskrift-Norwegian Journal of Geography,* 60(1), 89–99.

Carlsson, L., (2001). 'Keeping away from the Leviathan: The case of the Swedish Forest Commons'. *Management of Social Transformations (MOST) Discussion Paper* No. 51.

Cook, P. and Copus, A., (2002). *Agricultural Forecasts for the Highlands and Islands Enterprise Area.* Report for Highlands and Islands Enterprise, Aberdeen: Scottish Agricultural College.

Crofters Commission, (1999). *Annual Report.* Crofters' Commission: Inverness.

Dahlman, C. J., (1980). *The Open Field System and Beyond.* Cambridge: Cambridge University Press.

De Moor, M. (2002). 'Common land and common rights in Flanders'. In De Moor et al. (eds). *The Management of Common Land in North West Europe, c.1500–1850.* (pp. 113–141). Utrecht: Brepols.

Demsetz, H., (1967). 'Toward a theory of property rights'. *American Economic Review,* 57 (2), 347–359.

Devine, T. M., (1988). *The Great Highland Famine: Hunger, Emigration and the Scottish Highlands in the Nineteenth Century.* Edinburgh: John Donald.

Devine, T. M., (1994). *Clanship to Crofters' War: The Social Transformation of the Scottish Highlands.* Manchester: Manchester University Press.

Fortmann, L. (1996). 'Bonanza! The unasked questions: domestic land tenure through international lenses'. *Society and Natural Resources,* 9, 537–547.

Futureskills Scotland, (2004). *Industry Profile: Land Based Industries in the Highlands and Islands.* Inverness: Highlands and Islands Enterprise.

Gibson, C. C. and Becker, C. D., (2000). 'A lack of institutional demand: Why a strong local community in Western Ecuador fails to protect its forest'. In Gibson, C. C., McKean, M. A., and Ostrom, E. (eds). *People and Forests: Communities, Institutions, and Governance.* (pp. 135–161). London: MIT Press.

Gibson, C. C., (2001). 'Forest resources: Institutions for local governance in Guatemala'. In Burger, J., Ostrom, E., Norgaard, R. B., Policansky, D., Goldstein, B. D. (eds). *Protecting the Commons: A Framework for Resource Management in the Americas.* (pp. 71–89). Washington, DC: Island Press.

Hunter, J., (1976). *The Making of the Crofting Community.* Edinburgh: John Donald.

Jedrej, C. and Nutall, M., (1996). *White Settlers: The Impact of Rural Repopulation in*

Scotland. Luxembourg: Harwood Academic.

Kant, S., (2000). 'Extending the boundaries of forest economics'. *Forest Policy and Economics*, 5 (1), 39–56.

Kinloch, M. and Dalton, G., (1990). *A Survey of Crofting Incomes – 1989*. Report for the Scottish Crofters Union. Edinburgh: Scottish Agricultural College.

Kissling-Naf, I., Volken, T. and Bisang, K., (2002). 'Common property and natural resources in the Alps: The decay of management structures?' *Forest Policy and Economics*, 4 (2), 135–147.

Li, T. M., (1996). 'Images of community: Discourse and strategy in property relations'. *Development and Change*, 27 (3), 501–527.

MacCuish, D. J. and Flyn D., (1990). *Crofting Law*. Edinburgh: Butterworths/Law Society of Scotland.

Mehta, L., Leach, M. and Scoones, I., (2001). 'Editorial: environmental governance in an uncertain world'. *IDS Bulletin*, 32 (4), 1–9.

Meinzen-Dick, R.S. and Pradhan, R., (2001). 'Implications of legal pluralism for natural resource management'. *IDS Bulletin*, 32 (4), 10–17.

Mewett, P. G., (1977). 'Occupational pluralism in crofting: The influence of non-croft work on patterns of crofting agriculture in the Isle of Lewis since about 1850.' *Scottish Journal of Sociology*, 2, 31–49.

North, D. C. and Thomas, T. H., (1973). *The Rise of the Western World: A New Economic History*. Cambridge: Cambridge University Press.

Ostrom, E., (2001). 'Reformulating the commons'. In Burger, J., Ostrom, E., Norgaard, R.B., Policansky, D. and Goldstein, B.D. (eds). *Protecting the Commons: A Framework for Resource Management in the Americas*. (pp. 17–41). Washington, DC: Island Press.

Peters, P. E., (1987). 'Embedded systems and rooted models: the grazing lands of Botswana and the commons debate'. In McCay, B. J. and Acheson, J. M. (eds.) *The Question of the Commons: The Culture and Ecology of Communal Resources*. (pp. 171–194). Tucson: University of Arizona Press.

Peters, P .E., (1994). *Dividing the Commons: Politics, Policy, and Culture*. London: University Press of Virginia.

Poteete, A. R. and Ostrom, E., (2004). 'Heterogeneity, group size and collective action: The role of institutions in forest management'. *Development and Change*, 35 (3), 435–461.

Pretty, J. N., (2002). *Agri-Culture: Reconnecting People, Land and Nature*. London: Earthscan.

Rose, C. M., (1994). *Property and Persuasion: Essays on the History, Theory and Rhetoric of Ownership*. Boulder, CO: Westview.

SEERAD, (2003). *Custodians of Change*. Edinburgh: Scottish Executive Environment and Rural Affairs Department.

SEERAD, (2004). *Economic Report on Scottish Agriculture*. Edinburgh: Scottish Executive Environment and Rural Affairs Department.

Short, C., (2000). 'Common land and ELMS: A need for policy innovation in England and Wales'. *Land Use Policy*, 17, 121–133.

Stevenson, G. G., (1991). *Common Property Economics: A General Theory and Land Use Applications*. Cambridge: Cambridge University Press.

Stockdale, A., Findlay, A. and Short, D., (2000). 'The repopulation of rural Scotland: Opportunity and threat'. *Journal of Rural Studies*, 16 (2), 243–257.

Sutherland, R. and Bevan, K., (2001). *Crofting in the 21st Century: Report on Survey of Croft Incomes and Responses to Policy Changes*. Aberdeen: Scottish Agricultural College.

Varughese, G. and Ostrom, E., (2001). 'The contested role of heterogenity in collective action: Some evidence from community forestry in Nepal'. *World Development*, 29 (5), 747–765.

Vatn, A., (2001). 'Environmental resources, property regimes, and efficiency'. *Environment and Planning C: Government and Policy,* 19, 665–680.

Wilson, G. A., (2001). 'From productivism to post-productivism ... and back again? Exploring the (un)changed natural and mental landscapes of European agriculture'. *Transactions of the Institute of British Geographers,* 26, 77–102.

Part III

Institutional Misfit

4

Traditional and Customary Land Tenure and Appurtenant Rights: Reflections on Critical Factors of an Ecologically Sustainable Australian Outback

Alex Amankwah

Introduction

Property is one of the most complex of human institutions. The complication is the result of humanity's efforts to subordinate nature's creations to human desires and emotions. Humans see themselves as apart from nature, rather than as a part of nature. And, instead of working in cooperation with nature, humankind in attempting to dominate nature actually ends up being the loser, always working against their own interests.

Emerson described this succinctly when he wrote:

> *Nature never wears a mean appearance... The flowers, the animals, the mountains, the mountains reflected the wisdom (of nature)...*
>
> *The charming landscape which I saw this morning is undoubtedly made up of some twenty or thirty farms. Miller owns this field, Locke that, and Manning the woodland beyond. But none of them own the landscape. There is property in the horizon which no man has...* (Emerson, 2003)

A leading modern authority on property law would seem to have no quarrel with Emerson's observation (Gray, 1991).

Christian theology in its positioning of humankind at the centre of the universe creates the misleading impression that humankind are the sole beneficiaries of nature's benevolence (Genesis 1: 26: 'God was said to have created man in his own image and gave him 'dominion over the fish of the sea and over the birds of the air, and over cattle, and over all the earth, and over every creeping thing that creeps upon the earth.'). Hence the claimed rights of use and abuse of what constitutes one's own property, something carved out of or appropriated from nature's bounty. As to how humankind actually exercises dominion over things in nature so as to generate property in them, human imagination does not lack capacity to fabricate and create fictions to justify all types of appropriations (Cohen, 1954; Macpherson, 1978; Posner, 1998).

If humanity is constituted by variegated forms of races and peoples, is it not obvious that property would mean different things to different people? In the current global social, political and economic environment, however, there is a dominant culture (the dominant paradigm) whose property connotations a thing must embrace and approximate in order to deserve the appellation property.

Property Regime: What Paradigm?

Academics begin every analysis and discussion of property by emphasizing that property in its multifarious manifestations is nothing more than an aggregation of rights that a person may assert in relation to worldly things, which the ordering of society takes into account with a view to enforcing them (Penner, 1996). Land (realty) exemplifies the most concrete representation of property and includes the hard surface of a piece of the earth, and water, the space above it and the soil and sub-soil below (Megarry and Wade, 2000). Property in land on occasions amounts to nothing more than a right of way over another person's land, or something amounting to 'a beneficial attribute' of property, e.g. the right of enjoyment of a garden abutting a house in common with other land owners whose houses are in close proximity to that garden (Ellenburough Park, 1956; Bradbrook and Neave, 2000).

Some forms of property, though concrete and tangible, are not considered as valuable as land because of the ease of their movability and their susceptibility to pass from one person to another as personalty or chattels or goods (Tyler and Palmer, 1973). Property can further be subdivided into tangible (corporeal) and intangible (incorporeal) property. There is also a species of property in which rights can be vindicated only by the initiation of action based on a piece of document – *choses in action* – which includes all kinds of negotiable instruments (Cornick, 1989). Finally, the law rewards investments of an intellectual kind, and so endows such products as arise through exertion of the intellect with proprietary indicia, that is intellectual property (Sherman and Bentley, 1999). Property in human parts is beyond the scope of this chapter (Cal. 1990; Summer, 1994; Churchill, 1994).

The gamut of property rights and interests outlined above, though originating in the Western hemisphere, are recognized globally because they are considered as coming within the ambit of 'properly designed property rights' (Bromley, 1991). Every other type of interest or right in property is a fortiori 'improperly designed', according to that perception of property.

Nature of the Dominant (Real) Property Regime

The dominant property regime is grounded in the ideologies of individualism and laissez faire. Individual ownership of land is idolized as the lifeblood of the economic system in which market forces determine economic growth and outcomes. Land affords ready access to finance by way of outright alienation or through other dealings short of alienation, for example mortgage security or leasing.

Alienation of land under the common law is an indispensable incident of ownership, an idea that flies in the face of the feudal doctrine that the Crown, or the State in lieu of the Crown, is indeed the real owner of all lands, and that what individual citizens actually 'own' is a slice of time, an estate which is measured with reference to duration – freehold estate, life interest, leasehold, etc. (Gray, 1991).

Unhampered transferability of an interest in land is a function of the system of land registration a legal system maintains. In the case of Australia, it is the Torrens System that ensures indefeasibility of title, which consequently facilitates marketability (Whalen, 1982). Today, the worth of land lies in its marketability as a commodity and individualism underscores the right of use and abuse of land.

The Traditional (Customary) Property (Real) Paradigm

In *Re Southern Rhodesia* ([1919], AC 211), the Privy Council said:

> *The estimation of the rights of Aboriginal tribes is always inherently difficult. Some tribes are so low in the scale of social organization that their usages and conceptions of rights and duties are not to be reconciled with the institutions or the legal ideas of civilized society. Such a gulf cannot be bridged. It would be idle to impute to such people some shadow of the rights known to our law and then to transmute it into the substance of transferable rights of property as we know them... On the other hand, there are Indigenous peoples whose legal conceptions, though differently developed, are hardly less precise than our own. When once they have been studied and understood they are no less enforceable than rights arising under English law...* ([1919] AC 211 at 233–234).

It is therefore neither fruitful nor honourable to deny the existence of customary law as a functioning system of law, let alone deny the enforceability of rights arising under such a system (Amankwah, 1994).

After two centuries of such denial by the judiciary in Australia (*Coe v Attorney General* (1979) 53 ALJR 403 at 408 per Gibbs J; *Milirrpum v Nabalco Pty. Co.* (1971) 17 FLR 141.), the High Court finally pronounced in favour of the existence of traditional or customary or native title interests *in land* (*Mabo v Queensland* (No. 2) (1991) 175 CLR 1). The Court said relevantly:

> *Native title to particular land (whether classified by the common law as proprietary, usufructuary or otherwise), its incidents and the persons entitled thereto are ascertained according to the laws and customs of the Indigenous people who, by those laws and customs, have a connection with the land. It is immaterial that the laws and customs have undergone some change since the Crown acquired sovereignty provided the general nature of the connection between the Indigenous people and the land remains. Membership of the Indigenous people depends on biological descent from the Indigenous people and on mutual recognition of a particular person's membership by that person and by the elders or other persons enjoying traditional authority among those people.*
> (Ibid at 69–70 per Brennan J; emphasis added)

Rather than leave the matter to the courts to develop a native title jurisprudence on a case by case basis, the government seized on the decision in *Wik Peoples v Queensland* ((1996) 187 CLR 1; 141 ALR 129), to the effect that pastoral leases did not necessarily extinguish native title rights, to amend the Native Title Act (1992). The Act (Native Title Act No 97 1998 Cth) virtually annihilated the gains of the Mabo case.

However, there can be no gainsaying the fact that among the world's traditional and Indigenous people, ownership of proprietary rights is characterized by communalism rather than individualism. Such rights are pressed into the service of the cultural and spiritual ethos of the people rather than their economic well-being and aspirations. With regard to land in particular, communal ownership operates to constitute land into an ancestral trust to be enjoyed by the present generation and passed on to generations yet unborn (*Amadu Tijani v Secretary Southern Nigeria* (1921) AC 399 (PC)). Amankwah states the rationale of the principle among the communities of West Africa thus:

> *The complexity and bewildering spectre of confusion of the land use control apparatus at customary law must indeed confound the foreign observer. But all this seemingly incomprehensible and exotic system was designed by our ancestors to make it difficult, if not well-nigh impossible for the living to deplete land resource to the prejudice of those who have a beneficial future interest in the res. The mystic attributes of land, the trusteeship concept, the stamping of corporate identity of property which was once individual property etc., all ensure that limitations are placed on land use thus promoting land preservation.* (Amankwah, 1990)

More than a decade after *Mabo* the view still persists in Australia that native title is an anachronistic leftover of a forgotten age. Chris Pearson asserts:

> *It's a leftover from the Arcadian fantasy era in which our very own noble savages were expected to wander off happily ever after to*

their dreaming sites and practice self-determination, in mystic communion with the land. When land rights seemed a panacea to cure all ills, land grants were expected to provide homelands and sacred sites for traditional nomads, along with capital bases through pastoral leases and mining leases and administrative bases for huge, Aboriginal-controlled regional councils. Far too little thought was given to the various immediate, interim and long-term uses to which the land might be put.

For example, there was no model envisaged capable of providing building blocks in settlements that individuals could buy, develop and leave to their children. This meant that everything from quasi-surburban quarter-acre allotments to million-acre spreads were held by the same cumbersome means, with all control vested in land councils... These days the councils linger on as the last surviving Marxist enclaves in our part of the world. (Pearson, 2004)

In the same paper, it was reported that the Prime Minister was now willing to consider a Norfolk Island land tenure system in which the legal system based on Australia's sanctions private ownership of land by families, that is group ownership, however, with the protection from outside takeovers (Shanahan and Karvelas, 2004). This comes over a decade after the *Mabo* decision and the roll-back effect of the Native Title Amendment Act.

Although Australia prides itself on multiculturalism, the legal system considers legal pluralism, which makes it possible for the incorporation of culturally diverse legal ideas into a dominant legal regime, an anathema (See *Coe v Attorney General* (1979) 53 ALJR 403; Also, Amankwah H A, 'Post-Mabo: The Prospects of the Recognition of Customary Law', note 19 supra.). Times were when, in England, judges confronted by the imperatives of justice fashioned new legal doctrines to accommodate new rights that were evolving outside the established common law regime. Do we have judges today of the calibre and mental acumen of Lords Eldon, Ellesmere and Nottingham (considered the father of equity), individuals who charted the undefined horizons of the common law? (Holdsworth, 1903–1904)·

It must be said in passing that traditional law also makes a distinction between land and chattels, which are not subject to such rigorous doctrinal restraints on alienation as operate on land. Chattels are freely disposable by their owners, although in the case of vital life-sustaining implements such as guns, hunting knives, bows and arrows, complex rules of succession govern their devolution upon the death of their owners (Amankwah, 1970). However, under traditional law, there is no norm for the categorization of property as either tangible or intangible. The reason for this is not difficult to see: all aspects of traditional existence are permeated by cultural indicia, which though cognizable cannot be felt or touched.

Traditional Knowledge

Traditional knowledge in non-western cultures

A crucial component of the traditional proprietary paradigm is traditional knowledge, also referred to as local knowledge in minuscule group settings. Experience gained from the colonial existence of non-western cultures suggests that whenever western values and institutions come into conflict with those of non-western culture the later must yield to the primacy of their western counterparts. Non-western cultural values and institutions – political, social and legal – deserved recognition and protection only to the extent that they approximate their western counterparts. Pluralism or coexistence of multiple cultural values and institutions was at best tolerated (Getz, 1983).

The position is not any different in respect of traditional knowledge. The discourse of intellectual property excludes any consideration of traditional knowledge as a species of interest or right informed by proprietary indicia. If land, the most concrete representation of property, was not so long ago considered as encompassed by Indigenous ideas of property (*Milirrpum v Nabalco Pty Ltd* (1971) 17 FLR 141; contra *Mabo v Queensland* (1992) 175 CLR), is it any wonder that Indigenous products of the intellect are excluded from the categories of legally recognizable and protectable rights and interests?

The globalization process has even exacerbated the problem in its drive toward the evolution of a universal commercial monoculture in which goods and services are beyond the regulatory powers of individual territorial sovereigns (Martin, 1999).

However, it is simplistic to generalize about the conception of traditional/Indigenous knowledge, for to do so will be an experiment in trivialization. Most of such knowledge is context specific, designed for the solution of localized problems. It is therefore important that its indicia be determined. It must be critically evaluated and validated. Such validation will enhance its protection and prevent indiscriminate dissemination and exploitation.

Indigenous people assert ownership rights to their peculiar knowledge and practices relating to the bush, which enabled them, and their forebears before them, to nurture and sustain the regenerative qualities of the country in fishing, hunting and gathering and controlled burning of the bush. Additionally, Indigenous people possess knowledge of the medicinal and curative properties of plants and vegetation, which have been scientifically validated and are in great demand by pharmaceutical companies in western countries (Davies, 1999).

This knowledge has been transmitted in a continuum through oral tradition from generation to generation and cannot be said to belong to particular individuals as its creators. Indigenous people are under enormous pressure to concretize such knowledge, reducing it into writing, which makes it more amenable to piracy. The term biopiracy was not coined by Indigenous people. Biopiracy is the unauthorized appropriation of plant-related substances for development into commercial commodities, such as pharmaceuticals, cosmetics and pesticides. This is the crux of the concern of traditional peoples today regarding intellectual property; the non-recognition of traditional knowledge and its protection from commercial exploitation.

Just as the proverbial Tropical African tree, the baobab tree, which is so large that it is said it cannot be encompassed by one person, traditional knowledge can not be encompassed by one definition. It is embodied in the norms, customs and traditional practices of a people and passed down by oral tradition from generation to generation. It is sacred and cannot be revealed to outsiders. It is inextricably bound with the land and its tenure. Entitlement to its use and enjoyment is communal and resides in the group. It embraces knowledge of places and of their ecology, knowledge of vegetation and plants and their properties as food to sustain life or as medicine to assist in curing maladies and diseases, knowledge of minerals and their uses etc. And just as there is no such thing as knowledge but systems of knowledge (Cooper and Packards, 1997), so also there are many systems of Traditional Knowledge (Brokensha et al, 1980). And there could be knowledge according to sex, age, status or other social stratification (Fairhead, 1992).

Intellectual property in this context will be confined to patent law and away from copyright law because of the nexus between the World Intellectual Property Organization's (WIPO's) Trade Related aspects of Intellectual Property Rights regime and traditional knowledge (Blakeney, 1997).

Ownership of traditional knowledge

The emergence of traditional/Indigenous knowledge as an intellectual expression has serious implications for development and scientific exploitation of natural resources outside the predominantly western industrialized nations. Western and industrialized nations have tended to idolize intellectual prowess as the product of formal education buttressed in schools, colleges and universities. This posture has nurtured the inauguration of a monocultural intellectualization, which would not countenance the existence of other systems of knowledge in a world made up of multiple cultures. Non-western forms of knowledge are denigrated as unscientific and dismissed as based on superstition. The realization now, albeit grudgingly conceded, that knowledge can be formal or informal, means there has to be a re-evaluation of those interests, rights and claims built on the presumption of a universal monolithic intellectual culture. The North/South cleavage palpably demonstrates the correctness of the dichotomy of formal and informal knowledge systems (Getz, 1983, note 32 supra, Chapter 6).

By relying on the knowledge of local people about resources and their properties, those interested in the acquisition of such knowledge save themselves the expense and trouble of engaging in long and drawn out experiments. However, even when such secret knowledge has been revealed by local people to bioprospectors, there is still the task of validating it scientifically.

The question of ownership of traditional knowledge does not lend itself to an easy solution. It could begin initially as the thought of one individual which was then subsequently embraced by direct descendants and later practised by the community as a whole (*Bulun Bulun v R and T Textile Pty Ltd* (1998) 157 ALR 193 at 210 per Von Dousa J).

Mobility, the extended family system and inter-tribal marriage could lead to the transportation of the knowledge, so that over time it spreads over regions and even countries and is transformed or refined into other knowledge products. As Sillitoe observes, local knowledge 'is never still' (Sillitoe, 1998). Sikana echoes the same idea when he says local knowledge 'is dynamic and strategic' (Sikana, 1994).

Native title claims in Australia demonstrate how difficult identifying the beneficiaries of a native title interest can be. Shiva states the matter eloquently:

> *Within Indigenous communities, despite some innovations being first introduced by individuals, innovation is seen as a social and collective phenomenon and results of innovation are freely avail-able to anyone who wants to use them. Consequently, not only the biodiversity but its utilization has also been in the commons, being freely exchanged both within and between communities. Common resource knowledge based innovations have been passed on over centuries to new generations and adopted for newer uses, and these innovations have over time been absorbed into the common pool of knowledge about that resource. This common pool of knowledge has contributed immeasurably to the vast agricultural and medici-nal plant diversity that exists today.* (Shiva, 2001)

It is perhaps therefore not feasible to always determine with finality who are entitled to payment of compensation for a particular knowledge, whether a group or tribe, because they are considered currently to be the rightful owners of some knowledge. Doing so could well work injustice on unidentified but potential beneficiaries (Smith, 2003; see also Chapter 5 of this book).

Sustainable Development and Harmonization of the Conflicting Property Paradigms: The Relevance of Environmental Law

After centuries of ruthless exploitation of the world's natural resources, often accomplished through subjugation of local populations, the real owners and custodians of such resources by metropolitan powers, the realization has dawned on humankind that such natural resources, despite nature's bound-less bounty, are not inexhaustible. Unless humankind's patterns of exploitation and use of natural resources are drastically adjusted, there will be nothing left to bequeath posterity and future generations. The conception of the ideology of sustainable development and its institutional gestation resulted in the United Nations Conference on Environment and Development (UNCED), also called the 'Earth Summit', in 1992 at Rio de Janeiro, and is very critical to humankind's survival. Among the outcomes of the UNCED, three instruments are significant and pertinent to the theme of this gathering viz:

1　The Rio Declaration on Environment and Development (UN Doc. A/CONF. 151/26/Rev.1).
2　Agenda 21; (Adopted in the United Nations Conference on Environment and Development, Rio de Janeiro, June 14 1992).
3　The Convention on Biological Diversity (CBD), (UN Doc. A/RES/51/182 entered into force December 29 1993; further discussed in Chapter 5).

(1) The Rio Declaration on Environment and Development is significant for its recognition of the potential of Indigenous and other traditional or local peoples for the management and development of the ecosystem through the deployment of their traditional knowledge systems. Principle 22 states:

> *Indigenous people and their communities, and other local communities, have a vital role in environmental management and development because of their knowledge and traditional practices. States should recognize and duly support their identity, culture and interests and enable their effective participation in the achievement of sustainable development.*

(2) Agenda 21 is a comprehensive plan of action implementable on global, national and local proportions. Though more hortatory than a legally binding document, it wields a moral force and provides a yardstick by which the performance of states could be measured. Its significance lies in the recognition it accords the 'holistic tradition of scientific knowledge of their lands, natural resources and environment' of Indigenous, traditional and other local peoples (Ribis and Mascarenhas, 1994).

(3) The CBD, the world's first legal instrument on biodiversity and its conservation, is the most significant in its impact on the world's traditional peoples not only for its objective of the conservation of biological diversity and the sustainable use of its components but also for its objective of equitable sharing of benefits from the exploitation and use of genetic resources. To that effect Article 8(j) enjoins Each Contracting Party:

> *Subject to its national legislation, respect, preserve and maintain knowledge, innovations and practices of Indigenous and local communities embodying traditional lifestyles relevant for the conservation and sustainable use of biological diversity and promote their wider application with the approval and involvement of the holders of such knowledge, innovations and practices and encourage the equitable sharing of the benefits arising from the utilization of such knowledge, innovations and practices.*

Article 10 buttresses Article 8(j) by obligating Each Contracting Party to:

> *c. Protect and encourage customary use of biological resources in accordance with traditional cultural practices that are compatible with conservation and sustainable use requirements...*

d. Support local populations to develop and implement remedial action in degraded areas where biological diversity has been reduced.

As is always the case with governance whether national or global, good intentions are not enough. Since the CBD is short on details of mechanisms for the implementation of Articles 8(j) and 10(c) and (d), the issue of the 'equitable sharing of the benefits arising from the utilization of (traditional) knowledge, innovations and practices' is still mired in endless debate. This is because in recognizing traditional knowledge and requiring that users of such knowledge pay for the product, the rich and developed countries see an end coming to their monopoly and stranglehold on the economic gains arising from intellectual property rights. Such a proposition sounds odious and preposterous to corporate interests. Traditional knowledge must remain entrenched in the public domain and exploitable without compensation being paid to their so-called owners.

However, there is an obvious correlation between securing legal protection of Indigenous knowledge and the dictates of biodiversity – e.g. the variety of all life forms – the different plants, animals and microorganisms, the genes they contain, and the ecosystem of which they form a part (Art. 2 Convention on Biological Diversity, UN Doc A/RES/51/182, June (1995); 31 ILM 818) and the integrity of the environment. It is the fact that in recognizing and protecting one, interests in the other are enhanced automatically. Needless to say that in ratifying the Convention on Biological Diversity in 1993, Australia is under an international obligation to take legal measures to protect the rights of Indigenous people relevant to biodiversity related knowledge and practices. Further discussion on this subject can be found in Margulies, 1993; Hubbard, 1994; Bodansky, 1995; Horton, 1995; Huft, 1995; Kushan, 1995; Roht-Arriaza, 1996; Jacoby and Weiss, 1997 and Cottier, 1998.

Advent of Trade Related Aspects of Intellectual Property Rights (TRIPs)

Developing countries, home for the majority of the world's traditional and Indigenous peoples, find it difficult to understand the trappings of intellectual property law, which is essentially a European legal contraption (Forsythe, 2003). Some such laws were designed solely to protect patents already granted by the parliament of a colonial power (Ahmadu, 1998). Be that as it may, the introduction in 1994 of the Trade Related Aspects of Intellectual Property Rights (TRIPS) into the Uruguay Round of the GATT negotiations by the United States of America can be regarded as the turning point in the world's intellectual property regime. This contrasts sharply with the most significant of the objectives of the Uruguay Declaration of 1986; namely, 'to ... bring about further liberalization and expansion of world trade to the benefit of all countries, especially less developed contracting parties, including the improvement of access to markets by the reduction and elimination of tariffs, quantitative restrictions and other non-tariff measures and obstacles' (Para B (iv); see (1986) 25 ILM 1623). It was a move strategically designed to foist on the rest of the world a US-type intellectual property regime. The idea was conceived and hatched by the Intellectual Property Committee (IPC) of the United States, made up of 13 US-based multinational corporations (MNC), and assisted by industry associations of Europe and Japan. The membership of the US IPC consisted of corporations such as Bristol Myers, Dupont, General Electric, General Motors, Hewlett Packard, IBM, Johnson and Johnson, Merck, Monsanto, Pfizer, Rockwell and Warner (Croome, 1995; Buderi, 2000). The TRIPS regime is an outgrowth of the World Trade Organization's (WTO's) objective of forging a global or multilateral trade system by '[P]romoting sustainable growth and development while contributing to a more stable and secure climate in international relations.' (Para 2, Singapore Ministerial Declaration, 1996)

Here was the genesis of the agenda linking global trade and the environment, an issue which would exacerbate the North/South cleavage with disastrous consequences for future WTO deliberations. At the Seattle Ministerial Conference in 1999, matters came to a climax with developing state members' refusal to accept or condone any such linkage. Developing countries regard the linkage as a diversion from legitimate trade and economic issues. The conference ended in a fiasco (Subedi, 2003).

TRIPS was therefore not a case of a negotiated agreement by the GATT member nations. However, with the establishment in 1994 of the World Trade Organization (WTO), as the administrative body of GATT, the success of the scheme was assured. It was obligatory for member states to take steps to legislate the law by January 1, 2000. For developing nations this entails amendments to existing legislation on intellectual property. The least developed nations were given until 2005 to sign up. In the case of Australia, for example, this was accomplished by the Patents Amendment (Innovation Patents) Act 2000, No 140 (Cth). In adopting an amending legislation, the concerns of Australia's Indigenous population regarding the sustenance of their traditional existence and livelihood would assume critical dimensions in the general debate on Indigenous people's assertion of and entitlement to proprietary rights and interests in land and knowledge of the land (GAAT, 1994).

Problems emanating from the TRIPS Agreement

The first thing to note about this agreement is that it was not negotiated in the manner multilateral treaties are customarily negotiated and concluded among nations. As noted earlier, it was more an imposition than a negotiated outcome. Second, by affirming in the Preamble the exclusivity of patent rights as conferring private and individual rights, communal interests and interests of groups such as those held by Indigenous people based on group entitlement are denied legal recognition (GATT, 1994, Article 28). Thirdly, the agreement flies in the face of the sovereignty of nations over their natural resources enshrined in several United Nations documents and reiterated in the Convention on Biological Diversity as it treats national natural resources as up for grabs under the TRIPS regime of the agreement (Van Caenegem, 2002). The question is: which of the two takes precedence over the other? Without a doubt, nations would place the integrity of their sovereignty over and above every other consideration (see the seminal discussions on reconciling the two documents: McManis, 1998; Cullet, 1999; Kruger, 2001; Verna, 2001; Young, 2001; Mishra, 2002; and Helfer, 2004). The exceptions of human, animal or plant life in Article 27(2) from patentability on grounds of public order or morality is stultified by the provisions of Article 27(3). This is a very controversial provision, the interpretation of which has attracted much commentary (for examples, see Braga and Carlos, 2000; Braga, 2000; Mathur, 2001; The Economist, 2001; Cunningham, 2002; Chaytor, 2002; Elwyn-Jonas, 2002; Viswanathan, 2002; Stegemann, 2003; and Pretorius, 2002).

The United States is unlikely to accept any *sui generis* system that does not meet the rigorous standard of Article 8, that is, 'appropriate measures' that are 'consistent with the ... Agreement'. These are the same expressions employed in section 301 of the United States Trade and Competitiveness Act 1988 under which the US often retaliates against nations whose intellectual property laws are not consistent with standards ordained by the United States Government.

Domestic implementation of the TRIPS Agreement

The implementation of the TRIPS agreement, as indicated earlier, was accomplished through amending existing patent legislation in many countries (for example, the Indian Patent (Amendment) Act 1999 amending the Patent Act 1970 to remove the exceptions from patentability of food, medicine and drugs in the old legislation, see Shiva, 2001). In Australia the Patents (Amendment) Act 2000 No 140 (Cth) was passed amending the Patents Act 1990 (Cth) 'by repealing the petty patent scheme (old s62) and providing for innovation patents...'. A new Section 7 defines 'innovative step'. It states:

> (4) For the purposes of this Act, an invention is to be taken to involve an innovative step when compared **with the prior art base** unless the invention would, to a person skilled in the relevant art, in the light of the common general knowledge as it existed in the patent area before the priority date of the relevant claim, **only vary from the kinds of informative set out in subsection (5) in ways that make no substantial contribution to the working of the invention.** [emphasis original]

It is ironic that when existing knowledge is 'shuffled around' it is considered a new knowledge and therefore patentable. However, in the case of traditional knowledge which is not always reduced into recorded instruments or documents, it is regarded as part of the public domain and therefore exploitable by those with the means and ability to do so.

A new subsection added to Section 18 defines patentable inventions. Applied to existing traditional knowledge that is of unquestioned antiquity, it becomes a new idea because although it is practised openly ('not secretly used in the patent area') it has become a novelty through its encounter with another culture's so called 'innovative step'.

Again, Section 18 is amended to include two new subsections – which together provide for the exceptions to patentability. They read:

> *(3) For the purposes of an innovation patent, plants and animals, and the biological processes for the generation of **plants and animals, and not patentable inventions.***
> *(4) Subsection (3) does not apply if the invention is a **microbiological process or a product** of such a process.* [emphasis original]

Section 18(4) reverses everything that Section 18(3) is designed to accomplish. It is, however, consistent with the intention behind Article 27.3(b) of the Agreement on Trade Related Aspects of Intellectual Property Rights and the US Supreme Court decision in *Diamond v Chakrabarty* (447 US 303, 1980). All the amendments were carried through without any hint of consultation with Australia's Indigenous people who order their lives around traditional knowledge.

TRIPS and plants and seed

For developing nations and Indigenous peoples the most troubling aspect of the TRIPS regime is its effect on peoples' daily livelihood and traditional existence – food, plants (medicine), and seed (farming). Indeed traditional existence is encompassed by the entire philosophy of biodiversity. This has been overwhelmed by external economic and monopolistic forces over which they have no control.

Newly invented plants are patentable in the developed nations. In the US since 1930 this has been the case (Plant Patent Act, 1930). In 1970 the Plant Variety Protection Act was passed, which allowed farmers to sell seeds among themselves. That privilege was taken away by the Plant Variety (Amendment) Act 1994, which established virtual monopoly over seed in favour of the US seed industry (*Asgrow Inc v Winterboer* (1987), Monsanto's Round Up Ready Gene Agreement. See also *JEM Ag Supply Inc v Pioneer Hi-Bred Int'l Inc.* 534 US 124 (2001)). In Australia the new Plant Breeders Act 2000 accomplishes similar objectives.

Since the US Supreme Court handed down its decision in *Diamond v Chakrabarty* (see note 46 supra) to the effect that an invention of a new bacterium genetically engineered to degrade crude oil was patentable because the microorganism 'is not...a hitherto unknown natural phenomenon but a nonnaturally occurring manufacture or composition of matter – a product of human ingenuity...a discovery that is not nature's handiwork...' (Ibid). The stage was set for human claims to nature's products. The Court even went further: 'anything under the sun made by man' was patentable (Ibid at 309)! The mere shuffling of genes and changing of already existing bacteria constitutes invention? The discovery of a hitherto unknown phenomenon of nature is not patentable 'if there is to be invention for such a discovery it must come from the application of the law of nature to a new and useful end'(*Funk Bros Seed Co v Kalo Co.* 333 US 127, 130 (1948)).

The controversial 'appropriation' of the neem plant (Azadirachta indica) of India by W. R. Grace and the patenting of chemical compounds obtained from the seed for the processing and manufacture of pesticides was challenged in the European Patent Office by over 200 organizations, which instituted action in respect of two of the patents. The claims were vindicated in spite of the arguments on behalf of the patentee that 'The neem tree itself has not been patented, nor have its parts such as leaves, twigs, roots, stems etc' (Shiva, 2001, note 44 supra at p. 60). However, in the USA itself the US Patent and Trade Mark Office continues to protect the operations of W. R. Grace.

Again the patenting of Indian aromatic *basmati* rice lines and grains by RiceTec Inc of Texas in 1997 is an example of how the traditional knowledge of a whole subcontinent can easily be appropriated. Basmati rice is as Indigenous to India as the neem tree. By patenting basmati the patentee is assured 'novelty' rights and privileges appurtenant to it. It is exported under the brand names *Kasmati, Texmati* and *Jasmati*. However, it is in the area of medicinal plants that the issue becomes quite acute. The examples are numerous. A few cases will be referenced here:

- The Fox Chase Centre of Philadelphia applied for a patent on *Phyllanthus niruri* for the treatment of hepatitis to the European Patent Office citing an Indian text, *India Materia Medica*, which reports that the chemical substance derives from the Indian tree, *Bhudharti*, or *Jar amla* or *Bhuin amla* and is used to treat jaundice. Since both diseases relate to liver malfunctioning, the success of the application can only be described as an example of biopiracy (Shiva, pp54–55).
- Again Cromak Research Inc, a New Jersey based medicinal company, obtained a patent on *Karela* or *jamun*, an Indian plant used in the treatment of diabetes in Indian traditional medicine (Ibid at p.55).
- Brazil's effort to manufacture and promote its AIDS cocktail, which would reduce the cost of AIDS treatment and make AIDS drugs cheaper under its *Patent Law* 1997, has been resisted by US drug companies assisted by the US Government (Onaga, 2001).
- In Australia Davis records the Western Australia case of the Smokebush plant (*Conospermun*), which the US National Cancer Institute collected and screened under licence from the WA Government in the 1980s. The plant has medicinal properties, which, it is believed, could assist in curing AIDS (Davis, 1998).

The current posture of the WIPO on traditional knowledge is clearly the reverse of other agencies of the UN, which actively promote self-reliance and self-sufficiency in developing nations by providing financial support for institutional programmes that foster integration of traditional and non-traditional institutions and practices. For example the World Bank (International Bank for Reconstruction and Development) has demonstrated how cooperation –

e.g. engaging traditional medicinal practitioners in bioprospecting rather than antagonism towards them – can be beneficial to all concerned (World Bank, 2003).

Whose interest is really served by bioprospecting?

Staggering corporate profits resulting from the diversion of biological resources from developing to developed nations belie the altruistic posturing of the companies involved, which claim they are assisting with poverty allevia-tion in developing nations (Sillitoe and Wilson, 2003). Only state intervention, whether legal or political, can halt the depletion and waste of a nation's natural resources. However, such state legislative action as has been taken is directed at revenue collection not at forest protection.

State laws are typically designed to protect state interests in biodiversity, thus exposing Indigenous interests to exploitation (see for example Biodiscovery Act 2003 (Queensland): while bioprospecting is seemingly based on consent, biopiracy is not!). Indigenous people are therefore left to their own devices and usually find solace in the only legal option available to them, i.e. entering into contracts with bioprospecting companies. The unequal bargain-ing powers of the parties in such situations clearly leads to unfair deals. Thus, while the state appears interested in *cashing in* on the loot of *nature's pharmacy* by commercial conglomerates, the depletion of our forests continues unabated. As Onaga observes:

> *The whole business structure is aimed at making human beings richer, not making forests conserved. However, the growing under-standing that destroying rain forests means depleting Mother Nature's medicine cabinet has raised the expectation among conser-vationists that some of these profits could, and should, be used to finance measures to preserve biodiversity, particularly in species-rich developing countries.* (Onaga 2001, note 77 supra).

Traditional knowledge of herbs and medicinal plants

Alternative medicine, a burgeoning health care area, is medicine based on non-western medicinal precepts. In Africa, Asia and North America, long before the introduction of European type medicine, plants and herbs provided the only sources of medicine. In West Africa *Dalziets treatise* (Burkill, 1964) is a classic text on such matters supplemented by research outcomes of the Centre for Scientific Research into Plant Medicine (CSRPM) in Ghana and its coun-terpart in Nigeria, Nigeria Institute of Pharmaceutical Research and Development (NIPRD). In Australia there are numerous texts on Indigenous pharmacology (Levitt, 1981).

In Asia, China and India are leaders in the field (Shiva, 2001; Liu, 2003). In Central and Southern Africa the situation is the same (Esegu, 2002). In the South Pacific region, Vanuatu, Fiji and Papua New Guinea, are leaders in the production of kava reputed for its medicinal quality in the alleviation of stress-related ailments.

What Prospects for the Future?

Uneven apportionment of rights and obligations in any legal setting bespeaks discrimination and unequal treatment. Democracy thrives only in environments suffused with equalitarian ideals. The current TRIPS regime is an affront to the dignity and self-sufficiency of Indigenous populations all over the world as it is weighted against their interests while upholding the primacy of the interests of western and industrialized countries. Injustice breeds alienation, which in turn fosters temptation to resort to extralegal means for redress. The closure of the Bouganville copper mine by forces opposed to the operations of the Australian mining giant BHP Billiton in Papua New Guinea is a pointer to this modality of self-help (Silitoe and Willson, 2003). Only fairness can ensure social tranquillity and the reign of law.

Review process

Article 27.3 of the TRIPS agreement provides for the review of its provisions four years after coming into force of the WTO Agreement in 1999. Not much has happened on that front since the fiasco of the Seattle and Cancun Conferences. Shiva has argued that a review should have preceded the coming into force of the Agreement (Shiva, 2001, note 44 at 117). This writer argues that the shortcomings of any instrument become evident only after it has gone into force. Without experiencing problems with implementation, review and reform is otiose and meaningless. First, it is not just Article 27 that must be reviewed, the entire Agreement must be reworked because it is important to resolve the discrepancy between the Convention on Biological Diversity and the TRIPS Agreement and to enshrine the primacy of the former. Second, it is important to provide for the recognition and protection of traditional knowledge. Third, traditional knowledge should be patentable in its own right, and the problem of biopiracy ought to be addressed as well.

Challenging patent applications

Some have hailed the Indian success at getting the European Patent Office to revoke European Patent No 0436257 on neem tree oil granted to W. R. Grace as a victory for developing countries and shows that developing countries have clout and the wherewithal to have their rights vindicated (Kadidal, 1997). However, the expenditure involved in such litigation is prohibitive and beyond the financial resources of most Indigenous peoples and developing countries.

Adoption of *sui generis* system

Countries which rushed into meeting the deadline for the implementation of the TRIPS Agreement believing that a safety net has been provided in Article 27.3 for the protection of their peculiar national intellectual property interests now realize that the Article 27.3 protection is illusory. The conjunction of 'non-biological' and 'microbiological' in Article 27.3(b) is to say the least a red herring, for while they undoubtedly refer to biotechnology involving genetic engineering, that is the mixing of animal and plant genes, the consequential production of permutations of animals and plants are essentially reproduction through *biological* processes. Views on the moral and ethical implications of human involvement in nature's reproduction processes are discussed in detail in publications such as International Plant Genetic Resources Institute report (IPGRI, 1997). Further, TRIPS Article 27.5.3(b) aims at the protection of plant varieties by patents or a *sui generis* system, without reference to the time-honoured practices of ordinary farmers and peasants across the globe. This is the part of the Agreement that threatens most the survival of peasant farmers worldwide. The plant varieties are of course those connected with the system of plant breeders rights recognized under the International Union for the Protection of New Varieties of Plants (UPOV) 1961–1991.

Article 8(1) enjoins member states when formulating or promulgating their national laws to implement the TRIPS Agreement to: adopt measures necessary to protect public health and nutrition, and to promote the public interest in sectors of vital importance to their socio-economic and technological development, provided that such measures are consistent with the provisions of this Agreement.

Other measures necessary to 'prevent the abuse of intellectual property rights by right holders or the resort to practices which unreasonably restrain trade or adversely affect the international transfer of technology' run the risk of being considered inconsistent with the provisions of the Agreement (Article 8(2)).

These provisions, when juxtaposed with Article 8(j) of the Convention on Biological Diversity (CBD), evince an indisputable contradiction. Article 8(j) of CBD places on each contracting party the obligation, as far as possible and appropriate, to:

> [R]espect, preserve and maintain knowledge, innovation and practices of Indigenous and local communities embodying traditional lifestyles relevant for the conservation of sustainable use of biological diversity and promote their wider application with the approval and involvement of the holders of such knowledge, innovations and practices and encourage the equitable sharing of benefits arising from the utilization of such knowledge, innovations and practices.

It seems apparent, therefore, that whereas the CBD seeks to promote in-situ conservation of resources, the TRIPS Agreement ordains their exploitation, removal and depletion.

An example of a *sui generis* regime is The Model Law for the Protection of Traditional Knowledge and Expression of Culture (The Model Law), 2002 crafted by the South Pacific Commission and Pacific Island Forum in collaboration with UNESCO and endorsed by the Forum Regional Ministers in the same year. The Model Law seeks to protect traditional knowledge and expressions of culture as traditional cultural rights and not as things in the public domain and therefore amenable to private appropriation by outsiders (s 7.). Culture in the South Pacific embraces all traditional practices, usages and knowledge of the peoples of Melanesia, Polynesia and Micronesia. The rights are perpetual (s 9.), inalienable (s 10.), but, subject to the consent of the owners, who may be constituted as a Cultural Authority are exploitable in a manner that ensures appropriate profit sharing (Part 4.). These rights are not categorized as tangible or intangible and do not negate or supplant the extant intellectual property regime, hence their *sui generis* character.

Adoption of a compulsory registration system and disclosures

Some advocate a system of compulsory registration of traditional knowledge, which provides for the granting of licence to those who require access to it (see Cottier, 1998, note 51 supra). Some people advocate just the opposite; that is giving developing nations access to information obtained by developed nations in respect of traditional knowledge (Ibid). Neither system, however, addresses the perennial issue of ownership of traditional knowledge. Similar to the idea of registration is the call for the establishment of a system of disclosure of the source (e.g. country of origin) of traditional knowledge employed in a biotechnology process (Ibid). This is akin to the requirement of acknowledgment and attribution of authorship implicit in the moral rights regime of the Australian copyright law (Copyright Amendment (Moral Rights) Act 2000 (Cth)). It is a mere palliative measure that protects the integrity of the work of an author and does not address economic issues, which is of concern to the customary owners of traditional knowledge.

Capacity building

The deficit in Indigenous peoples' ability to negotiate and enter into contracts with well-heeled corporate entities, some believe, can be cured through a process of training euphemistically labelled 'capacity building'. By this it is thought that Indigenous peoples' representatives could be tutored in particular western and corporate-based techniques of management and technical legal know-how to position them to deal with business people and other corporate structures and institutions on equal footing. It were as if overnight people could be imbued with corporate wisdom and transformed into shrewd business executives appreciative of and competent in the processes of negotiation and contract formation, the logic of the capital market system, resource and environmental protection laws and myriad internationally ordained ethical and legal prescriptions regarding the exploitation of natural resources. Contracts that the Canadian-based advocacy group Rural Advancement Foundation

International (RAFI) has argued could usher in economic opportunities – training, employment, infrastructure – but they do not address the perennial and critical Indigenous concerns – that is control and ownership of the outcomes of bioprospecting (see, for example, Merck/National Biodiversity Institute (INBio) Costa Rica Agreement, 1996 or Oddie, 1998).

Change in corporate culture

It has been appropriately observed:

> *When the company officials step out of their offices and into the village or into the forest clearing to meet with landowners they step into a customary law setting. When liaison officers make their regular trips to villages to hear the 'talk', they hear verbiage which comes from a customary law context and insofar as the talk raises disputations matters they are so in reference to the villagers' aspirations for justice to be done according to custom. Land is the physical basis of the sovereignty of the community and customary law is the cultural and legal basis of the sovereignty of the community. In order to deal with these matters effectively community liaison officers must have a knowledge of, and sympathy for, customary law issues.* (Rivers and Amankwah, 2003)

That observation in relation to mining operations in Papua New Guinea holds good for all investments in development projects. The locus and situs of such initiatives are quite different from the environment in which corporate decisions are made. Often development agencies enter such alien terrain with their own corporate ideas – operation of market forces, the logic of capital, representative bodies to negotiate with, principles of accountability, majoritarian decision-making processes, management by hierarchies etc. – which are all foreign to Indigenous institutions and traditional practices. They then expect local people to understand such matters and play the game according to the rules. If local people exhibit an attitude of non-cooperation or antagonism as a consequence of their ignorance of such matters, developers are irked and become impatient and adopt a strategy of compliance through imposition. Without an appreciation of the cultural climate of these places, developers would be 'playing with fire' as Sillitoe and Wilson have demonstrated in respect of mining in Papua New Guinea (Sillitoe and Wilson, 2003).

The authors provided an example of how fatal a lack of understanding of the implications of compensation payment in Melanesia in respect of mining on land could be. A 'one for all time' lump sum payment to landowners in Melanesia is a fond hope in a culture in which relationships are viewed as continuing. They assert:

> *Compensation is one of the key aspects of the company and community relationship. The egalitarian ethos that informs land rights should influence the process by which a mine recompenses local*

> *people for damages and disruption of lifestyle. People equate mining company compensation payments with traditional indemnity payments such as those given in repatriation for kin killed in tribal fights. Both involve negotiated recompense for loss. **The corporate view of transactions is single cash payments made to settle claims for loss or damage. In contrast, the traditional view embraces long-term reciprocity, consolidation and reconciliation involving a web of associated persons.*** (Ibid at 265; emphasis added)

Obviously a change in the paradigm of corporate culture will go a long way to improving the climate of economic development in a non-western cultural terrain.

Two high-ranking officers of the Monsanto Corporation, a United States multinational corporation (MNC), recently issued a report in which they called for a change in United States corporate policy on patents which is antithetical to the realization of food security in developing nations (Taylor and Cayforth, 2003). A change in policy, they argued, could simultaneously augment food sufficiency in developing nations and the broader global interests of the United States. The authors of the report argue:

> [T]*he richest and most powerful country in the world...has a duty to avoid actions and policies with unnecessary and avoidable adverse impacts on progress elsewhere. This includes patent policies that adversely affect food security in developing countries.* (Ibid)

Agroforestry strategy

Several years' scientific studies have concluded that sustainable agricultural development globally is achievable only through agroforestry. Implicit in agroforestry is the integration of multipurpose trees into farming systems. Agroforestry, the studies indicate, has long been understood and embraced by subsistence farmers in poor developing nations (Schulze and Mooney, 1993; Leakey and Newton, 1996; Leakey et al, 1996; Arnold and Deweer, 1997; Guarino, 1997; Buck et al, 1999; Collins and Qualset, 1999; Huxley, 1999; Simmonds and Smartt, 1999; Kindt, 2002; Laird, 2002; Schroth et al, 2004; van Hoordwijk et al, 2004; and Palm et al, 2005). Clearly not only is commercial agriculture based on indiscriminate tree clearing (as is the practice in some Australian States) incompatible with the tenets of agroforestry, it is also antithetical to the principle of sustainable development.

Conclusions

A change is also required in peoples' perceptions of rights and interests under traditional laws and customs. In the real world today, land is an economic asset. Land per se is valueless unless it can be put to some economic use. The concept of property under the general law encompasses all things, tangible and intangible. In respect of traditional and customary rights, however, interests and rights are consigned to a legal terrain of relicts and souvenirs of antiquity devoid of economic viability. They remained embedded in the past while new property rights are constantly being forged and evolved for all other species of interests. A knowledgeable Peruvian leader was quoted to say recently:

> *The land is the only thing you cannot forge. Once you have that, you can build mortgages and secondary mortgages, and then securities based on mortgages, and then you can create chattel mortgage systems and relate them like ships relate to the coast... And then you forget the land. But the land is the crucial information system.* (Botsman, 2003)

Land under traditional tenure remains inalienable today. The anomaly this situation represents today in terms of economic viability is emphasized by Richie AhMat, the Cape York Land Council Chief Executive:

> *Indigenous land for good reason is inalienable. It must remain so. However, inalienability represents a huge difficulty for our economic development. It is a difficulty we must overcome.* (Ibid)

That goes for traditional knowledge and all its attributes also. And to attempt to balance the imperatives of economic development and those of cultural survival of developing nations and Indigenous populations outside the matrix of sustainable development is quixotic and an exercise in futility.

References

Ahmadu, M. (1998) 'Vanuatu's Accession to the WTO and the WIPO: A Reflection on Patent and Pharmaceutical Technology', *Journ. South Pacific Law*, 2, 30.

Amankwah, H. A. (1970) 'Ghanaian Law: Its Evolution and Interaction with English Law', 4 *Cornell Int'l Law Journal*, 37.

Amankwah, H. A. (1990) *The Legal Regime of Land Use in West Africa*. Hobart: Pacific Law Press.

Amankwah, H. A. (1994) 'Post Mabo: The Prospect of the Recognition of Customary Law in Australia', *UQLJ*, 18, 15.

Arnold, J. E. and Deweer, P. A. (1997) *Farms, Trees and Farmers: Responses to Agricultural Intensification*. London: Earthscan Pubs.

Bannerman R. H. et al (1993) *Traditional Medicine and Health Care Coverage*. Geneva: WHO.

Blakeney, M. (1997) 'Bioprospecting and the Protection of Traditional Medicinal Knowledge of Indigenous Peoples: An Australian Perspective', *EIPR,* 19, 298

Blakeney, M. (1998) 'Biodiversity Rights and Traditional Resource Rights of Indigenous Peoples', *Bio-Science Law Rev*, 2, 52

Blakeney, M. (1999) *Intellectual Property Aspects of Ethnobiology*, Sweet and Maxwell: London, at p1

Bodansky, D. M. (1995) 'International Law and the Protection of Biological Diversity', *Vand J Transnat'l L.* 28, 623.

Botsman, P. (2003, December 11) 'Aboriginal Prosperity Through Property', *The*

Australian, p. 11.

Bradbrook, A. and Neave, M. (2000) *Easements and Restrictive Covenants in Australia*, 2nd ed. Sydney: Butterworths.

Braga, P. (2000) 'Intellectual Property Rights: Imperatives for a Knowledge Industry', *World Patent Information*, 22, 167.

Braga, P. and Carlos, A. (2000) 'International Transactions in Intellectual Property and Developing Countries', *Intern'l Journ. Of Tech. Manag.*, 19, 35.

Brokensha, D. et al. (1980) *Indigenous Knowledge Systems and Development*. Maryland: University of America Press

Bromley, D. W. (1991) *Environment and Economy: Property Rights and Public Policy*. Oxford: Basil Blackwell Inc.

Buck, L. E. et al. (1999) *Agroforestry in Sustainable Agricultural Systems*. New York: CRC Press and Lewis Publishers.

Buderi, R. (2000) *Engines of Tomorrow: How the World's Best Companies are Using Their Research Labs to Win the Future*. New York: Simon and Schuster.

Burkill, H. M. (1964) *The Useful Plants of Tropical Africa*, Rev. ed., London: Oxford University Press

Cal. (1990) *Moore v Regents of the University of California*, 793 P 2d 479

Chambers, R. (2001) *An Introduction to Property Law in Australia*. (pp. 37) Sydney: LBC Information Services.

Chaytor, B. (2002) 'The Convention on Biological Diversity: Exploring the Creation of a Mediation Mechanism', *Intern'l Journ. of World I. P.*, 5, 157.

Churchill J. (1994) 'Patenting Humanity: The Development of Property Rights in Human Body', *Intellectual Property Journal*, 8, 249.

Cohen, F. (1954) 'Dialogue on Private Property', *Rutgers Law Rev*, 357.

Collins, W. W. and Qualset, C. O. (eds), (1999) *Biodiversity and Agroecosystems*. New York: CRC Press.

Cooper, F. Packards R, (1997) *International Development and the Social Sciences: Essays in the History of Politics of Knowledge*, University of California Press: Berkley, at pp 1–41.

Cornick, B. (ed), (1989) *Richard's Law of Negotiable Instruments*. London: Butterworths.

Cottier, T. (1998) 'The Protection of Genetic Resources and Traditional Knowledge', *Journ. of Inter'l Econ. Law*, 10, 555.

Croome, J. (1995) *Reshaping the World Trade System: A History of the Uruguay Round*, WTO, Geneva

Cullet, V. (1999) 'Revision of the TRIPS Agreement Concerning the Protection of Plant Varieties', *Journ World I. P.*, 2(4), 617.

Cunningham, R. (2002) 'Rights for All', *Managing Intellectual Property*, Issue No 120. pp. 34–37.

Davies, M. (1999) 'Indigenous Rights in Traditional Knowledge and Biodiversity: Approaches to Protection', *Australian Int'l Law Rev*, 4, 1.

Davis, M. (1998) 'Biological Diversity and Indigenous Knowledge Research Paper', No 17, June 29, Canberra Parliamentary Library

The Economist (2001) 'The Right to Good Ideas', *The Economist*, Vol. 359 Issue No 8227, pp. 25–29 (2001)

Ellen, R. et al. (eds) (2000) *Indigenous Environmental Knowledge and Its Transformation*. London: Zed Books.

Ellenburough Park (1956) Ch 131; (1955) 3 All ER 667 (CA) at 176, 698 per Lord Evershed

Elwyn-Jonas, S. (2002) 'Report of the Commission on Intellectual Property Rights', *Bio-Science Law Rev*, 5(3), 101.

Emerson, R. W. (2003) 'Nature', In Robinson D M (ed) *The Spiritual Emerson: Essential Writings,* Boston: Beacon Press, p 25

Esegu, J. F. (2002) *Research in Medicinal Plants in Uganda Kampala*, Forest Resources Research Unit

Fairhead, J. (1992) *Indigenous Technical Knowledge and Natural Resources Management in Sub-Saharan Africa*, New York, Social Science Council.

Forsythe, M. (2003) 'Intellectual Property Laws in the South Pacific: Friend or Foe', *Journ. South Pacific Law*. 6, 8

Fourmile, M. H. (1996) 'Protecting Indigenous Property Rights in Bio-diversity', *Current Affairs Bulletin*, 36, Feb/Mar.

GATT (1994) 'The Results of the Uruguay Round of Multilateral Trade Negotiations' 365 reproduced in ILM (1994), 33, 1179.

Getz, (1983) *Local Knowledge: Further Essays in Interpretive Anthropology*. New York: Basic Books Publishers.

Gray, K. (1991) 'Property in Thin Air', *Cambridge Law Journal*, 5, 252.

Gray, K. (1993) *Elements of Land Law*, 2nd ed. London: Butterworths:, at p 28

Guarino, L. (1997) *Traditional African Vegetables*. Rome: International Plant Genetic Resources Institute.

Helfer, L. (2004) 'Regime Shifting: The TRIPs Agreement and New Dynamics of Intellectual Property Lawmaking', *Yale J. Int'l Law*, 29, 1.

Holdsworth, W. S. (1903–1904) *A History of English Law*, London;

Horton, C. M. (1995) 'Protecting Biodiversity and Cultural Diversity under Intellectual Property Law: Toward a New International System', 10 *J. Envtl L. and Litig*. 10, 1.

Hubbard, A. (1994) 'The Convention on Biological Diversity's Fifth Anniversary: A General Overview of the Convention – Where has it Been and Where is it Going?', *Tul Envtl L. J*. 10, 415.

Huft, M. H. (1995) 'Indigenous Peoples and Drug Discovery Research: A Question of Intellectual Property Rights', *Nebraska UL Rev*, 89, 1678.

Huxley, P. (1999) *Tropical Agroforestry*. London: Blackwell Science.

IPGRI (International Plant Genetic Resources Institute) (1997) *Ethics and Equity in Conservation and Use of Genetic Resources for Sustainable Food Security*, Proceedings of a Workshop to Develop Guidelines for the CGIR', 21–15 April 1997 IPGRI: Rome

Jacoby, C. D.; Weiss, C. (1997) 'Recognizing Property Rights in Traditional Biocultural Contribution', *Stan. Envt'l. L. J.*, 16, 74.

Kadida, S. (1997) 'Subject-Matter Imperialism? Biodiversity, Foreign Prior Art and the Neem Patent Controversy', *IDEA* , 37, 371.

Kindt, R. (2002) *Methodology for Tree Species Diversificaiton Planning for African Ecosystems*, PhD Thesis, University of Ghent

Kruger, M. (2001) 'Harmonizing TRIPS and the CBD: A Proposal from India', *Minnesota Journ Global Trade. 10,* 169.

Kushan, J. P. (1995) 'Biodiversity: Opportunities and Obligations', *Vand J. Transnat'l L,* 28, 755.

Laird, S. A. (2002) *Biodiversity and Traditional Knowledge: Equitable Partnerships in Practice*. London: Earthscan.

Leakey, R. R. and Newton, A. C. (1996) *Tropical Trees: The Potential for Domestication and the Rebuilding of Forest Resources*. London: HMSO.

Leakey, R. R. et al. (eds), (1996) *Domestication and Commercialization of Non-Timber Forest Products for Agroforestry, Non-Wood Forest Products,* No. 9, FAO: Rome

Levitt, D. (1981) *Plants and People: Aboriginal Uses of Plants on Groote Eylandt*, Aust Inst. Ab. Studies: Canberra

Lewinger, J. et al (1992) *Diversity, Farmer Knowledge and Sustainability*. Ithaca: Cornell University Press.

Liu, Y. (2003) 'IPR Protection for New Traditional Knowledge: A Case Study of Traditional Chinese Medicine', *EIPR,* 25, 194.

Macpherson, C. B. (1978) *Property: Mainstream and Critical Positions*, University of

Toronto Press: Toronto.

Margulies, R. L. (1993) 'Protecting Biodiversity: Recognizing International Property Rights in Plant Genetic Resources', *Mich. J. Int'l L.*, 14, 322.

Martin, H. P. (1999) *The Globalization Trap*. London and New York: Zed Books

Mathur, S. K. (2001) 'Domestic Challenges and the TRIPS Agreement: The way Forward for India', *Journ of World I. P.*, 4(3), 337.

McManis, C. R. (1998) 'The Interface Between Intellectual Property and Environmental Protection: Biodiversity and Biotechnology', *Washington U L Quarterly,* 76(1), 255.

Megarry, R. E. and Wade, H. W. (2000) *The Law of Real Property*, 6th ed, Sweet and Maxwell: London, at p 928

Mishra, J. P. (2002) 'Biodiversity and Intellectual Property Rights: Implications for Indian Agriculture', *Journ World I. P,* 3(2), 211.

Moran, K. et al (2001) 'Biodiversity Prospecting: Lessons and Prospects', 30 *Annual Rev. Anthropol.* 505.

Munzer, S. R. (1993) 'Kant and Property Rights in Body Parts', 6 *Canadian J. L. and Jurisp.* 319

Oddie, C. (1998) 'Bio-prospecting', 9 *Australian Intellectual Property Journal*, 18–19.

Oguamanan C, 2003, 'The CBD and Intellectual Property Rights: The Challenge of Indigenous Knowledge', *Southern Cross ULR,* 7, 89.

Onaga, L. (2001) 'Cashing in on Nature's Pharmacy', 2(4) *European Molecular Biology Organization (EMBO) Reports* 263.

Palm, C. A. et al. (2005) *Slash and Burn: The Search for Alternatives.* New York: Columbia University Press.

Pearson, C. (2004, December 11–12) 'Case to put the Land Right', *The Weekend Australian*, p. 18.

Penner, J. E. (1996) 'The "Bundle of Rights" Picture of Property', *UCLA Law Rev*, 43, 711.

Pollock, F. and Maitland, F. W. (1968) *The History of English Law*, 2nd ed, SF Milsom. Cambridge: Cambridge University Press.

Posner, R. A. (1998) *Economic Analysis of Law*, 5th ed, Oxford University Press: New York

Pretorius, W. (2002) 'TRIPS and Developing Countries: How Level is the Playing Field', in P. Drahos (ed), *A Philosophy of Intellectual Property*, Hanover, NH: Dartmouth Publishing Group

Ribis, N. and Mascarenhas, A. (1994) 'Indigenous Peoples after UNCED', 18 *Cultural Survival Quarterly*, available at www.culturalsurvival.org (September 3, 2004)

Rivers, J. and Amankwah, H. A. (2003) 'Sovereignty and Legal Pluralism in Developing Nations: A Reappraisal of the PNG Case', *James Cook ULR* , 10, 85 at 108.

Roht-Arriaza, N. (1996) 'Of Seeds and Shamans: The Appropriation of the Scientific and Technical Knowledge of Indigenous and Local Communities', *Mich J Int'l L*, 17, 919.

Schroth, G. et al. (2004) *Agroforestry and Biodiversity Conservation in Tropical Landscapes.* Washington: Island Press.

Schulze, E. D. and Mooney, H. A. (eds), (1993) *Biodiversity and Ecosystem Function.* Berlin: Springer Verlag.

Shanahan, D. and Karvelas, P. (2004, December 11–12) 'PM Considers New Land Rights, *The Weekend Australian*, p. 4.

Sharp, L. R. (1937) 'The Social Anthropology of a Totemic Society in Northern Australia', Unpublished PhD Dissertation, Harvard University

Sherman, B. and Bentley, L. (1999) *The Making of Modern Intellectual Property.* Cambridge: Cambridge University Press.

Shiva, V. (2001) *Protect or Plunder: Understanding Intellectual Property Rights*, London and New York: Zed Books.

Sikana, P. (1994) 'Indigenous Soil Characterization in Northern Zambia', in Scoones, I. and Thompson, J. (eds), *Beyond Farmer First: Rural Peoples Knowledge, Agricultural Research and Rural Practice*. (pp. 80–82) London: Intermediate Technology Publications.

Sillitoe, P. (1998) 'The Development of Indigenous Knowledge: A New Applied Anthropology', *Current Anthropology*, 39, 223–252.

Sillitoe, P., and Wilson, R. A. (2003) 'Playing on the Pacific Ring of Fire: Negotiation and Knowledge in Mining in Papua New Guinea', in J. Pottier et al (eds) *Negotiating Local Knowledge: Power and Identity in Development*, London: Pluto Press

Simmonds, N. W. and Smartt, J. (1999) *Principles of Crop Improvement*, Oxford: Blackwell Science.

Singapore Ministerial Declaration (1996) *Singapore Ministerial Declaration*, World Trade Organization, Geneva

Smith, B. R. (2003) 'All Been Washed Away Now: Tradition, Change and Indigenous Knowledge in Queensland Aboriginal Land Claim', In Pottier, J. et al (eds), *Negotiating Local Knowledge: Power and Identity in Development*. (pp. 127–131) London: Pluto Press.

Stegemann, K. (2003) The TRIPS Agreement as an Alliance for Knowledge Production. *Journ. of World I. P.*, 6(4), 529.

Stewart, G. (undated) *People, Plants and Wangarr Wirws: Notes on Traditional Healing*, Kowanyama Aboriginal Land and Natural Resource Management Office.

Subedi, S. (2003) 'The Road from Doha: The Issues For The Development Round of The WTO And The Future of International Trade', *ICLQ*, 52, 425.

Summer (1994) 'An Uneasy Case Against Property Rights in Body Parts', Society of Philosophy and Policy, cited in Penner, *The 'Bundle of Rights' Picture of Property*

Taylor, M. and Cayforth, J. (2003) 'US Should be More Flexible on Patent Law', In Dickson D (ed) *Science and Development Network*, www.scidev.net/News/Index.cfm?fuseaction=readNews&itemid=1049&language=1

Tyler, E. L. and Palmer, N. E. (eds), (1973) *Crossley Vaines' Personal Property*, 5th ed,: London: Sweet and Maxwell.

Underkuffler, L. S. (1990) 'On Property: An Essay', 100 *Yale L. J.* 127

Underkuffler, L. S. (1991) 'The Perfidy of Property', *Texas L. R.* 293.

Van Caenegem, W. (2002) 'The Public Domain: Scientia Nullius?' *EIPR* , 24, 324.

van Hoordwijk, M. et al. (eds), (2004) *Below-ground Interactions in Tropical Agrosystems: Concepts and Models with Multiple Plant Components*. Cambridge: CABI.

Verna, S. K. (2001) 'Access to Plant Genetic Resources and Intellectual Property: The Case of India', Spring/Summer *CASP* Newsletter, Seattle, WA

Viswanathan, A. (2002) 'From Marrakesh to Doha: WTO's Passage to India for Pharmaceutical Patents', *World I. P. Report*, 17, 22.

Whalen, J. (1982) *The Torrens System in Australia*, Law Book Company: Sydney

Woodman, R. A. (1970) 'The Torrens System in New South Wales: One Hundred Years of Indefeasibility of Title', 44 *Australian Law Journal* 96.

World Bank, (2003) 'Traditional Medicine Practice in Contemporary Uganda', *I K Notes* No 54, March 2003

Young, S. (2001) 'The Patentability of Maori Traditional Medicine and the Morality Exclusion in the *Patents Act* (NZ) 1953', 32(1) *V U Wellington LR* 1.

Ziff, B. H. (2000) *Principles of Property Law*. Toronto: University of Toronto Press.

5

Substantive and Procedural Dimensions of Old and New Forms of Property: IPRs, the CBD and the Protection of Traditional Ecological Knowledge

Michael Jeffery

Introduction

The law of property under English Common Law has occupied a significant position within the legal system. Its antecedents can be traced back many centuries and much of what today is afforded protection under the constitution or similar constating instruments such as Bills of Rights can find their origins in the context of private property rights. It is not all that long ago that women were considered chattels at law and their basic human and civil rights were subjugated to that of their husband, the basis of which in English law was founded on a concept of 'property'. Similarly, the right to hold elected or appointed public office was often based on the prerequisite of owning property, as was the right to vote and/or take part in matters of governance.

Property law in modern times involves a number of general categories comprising laws over real or fixed property (freehold/leasehold), chattels, *choses in action*, intellectual property rights (IPRs) with an emphasis on private property rights, as well as equally significant categories of public and communal property rights.

The specific rationale and principles underlying each of these categories have withstood concerted assaults from time to time by legislatures, the courts and the weight of public opinion in the name of reform, a process that is ongoing and necessary as inequities and injustices are identified and cry out for redress. Some of these issues are further discussed in Craig, Chapter 7 and Venn, Chapter 8.

It is beyond the purview of this chapter to trace and record this evolution in depth and no attempt will be made to do so. Rather the chapter will focus on recent developments in the area of IPRs and their appropriateness and ability to provide adequate protection of Indigenous knowledge and practices. The contextual platform on which I will raise and discuss these issues is the urgent need for the global community to accelerate its efforts to protect and conserve biological diversity, particularly biological diversity associated with genetic resources.

The chapter will argue for the urgent need to move toward the creation of new forms of property right protection that link conventional property rights, environmental principles and human rights if we are to achieve an equitable and sustainable use of essential resources in the future.

In presenting my thesis for a new and more enlightened approach to what has occurred to date, a strong case will be made for the need to focus upon and incorporate some of the public interest dimensions such as the right to information, the right to adequate legal and technical resources, and the right to participate in environmental decision-making, upon which the new forms of property might be constructed. The Aarhus Convention will be briefly discussed as an example of one such development.

Rationale Behind a Global Response

One does not have to go back very far in recent history to find the beginning of what today is categorized under the broad heading of environmental law. The term *environment* was found in no constitution prior to the middle of the twentieth century, and the concept of environmental law had yet to be invented. Prior to the 1950s the environmental regulatory response of the nation state was confined primarily to ensuring a supply of potable water and adequate and safe sewage treatment facilities. What legislation existed was closely identified with health legislation and little attention was paid to the protection and conservation of essential resources such as air, water and species. In the early 1960s the introduction in many jurisdictions of *command and control* environmental protection regimes proliferated as governments at the national, state and municipal levels sought to control what were finally recognized as serious pollution issues. Thus most jurisdictions introduced environmental protection legislation under the generic categories of clean air acts, clean water acts, contaminated land legislation etc... There was little thought given, however, to the impending depletion and scarcity of these essential resources but rather a recognition that increases in population coupled with rapid industrial expansion following the Second World War necessitated a much more comprehensive regulatory response.

The development of the environmental impact assessment legislations started in the early 1970s. This development was partly precipitated by a number of environmental incidents that occurred over a short period of time. The incidents have highlighted both the inadequate compliance and enforcement efforts as well as the lack of capacity and resources governments had available to deal with the clean-ups. Environmental impact assessment legislation was therefore designed as a planning tool to weed out projects that were likely to cause significant adverse environmental impacts before they were implemented and thus negate the need for costly mitigation and/or cleanup after the fact.

It is important to note that the various approaches associated with environmental protection regulatory regimes are not mutually exclusive and thus, in almost every jurisdiction, we find that both command and control as well as environmental impact assessment are used together to achieve a better environmental outcome.

From a property rights perspective the development of environmental law, as a specific subset of administrative law (administrative law, as one of the key formal institutions, is discussed in Smajgl and Larson, Chapter 1), has significantly curtailed the freedom of the individual to do what he or she wishes in the context of their own property. The common law of nuisance has to a large extent been subsumed under the mantle of environmental protection legislation and most jurisdictions have taken both procedural and administrative steps to enhance the power of the state to control and curtail polluting activities. The introduction in the late 1970s of the *public welfare* offence leading to the imposition of strict liability for such offences, a category of offence that covers most environmental regulatory offences, resulted in fundamental changes to the existing environmental regulatory regimes. Public welfare offences effectively shift the burden of proof from the prosecution to the defendant (first referred to in a decision of the Supreme Court of Canada *R v Sault Ste. Marie* (1978) 85 D.L.R.3d 161). Furthermore, the law assigns the responsibility for industry breach of environmental legislation to directors and officers (the imposition of Director's and Officer's liability received a significant boost as the result of the decision of an Ontario, Canada Court in *R v Bata Industries Ltd* [No 2] (1992) 70 CCC (3rd) 394).

The latter half of the last century also witnessed a concerted effort on the part of specific countries and the wider international community to place some defined limits on the wanton destruction of habitat and the introduction of measures to protect endangered species. In addition to a number of jurisdictions enacting endangered species legislation, the Convention on International Trade in Endangered Species of Flora and Fauna (CITES), was adopted (27 U.S.T. 1987, T.I.A.S No. 8249, reprinted in 12 I.L.M. 1085 (1973).

The involvement of the international community in the context of environmental protection and evidenced by the proliferation of a multitude of multilateral environmental agreements (MEAs) and a number of important treaties and conventions, heralded a new phase of international cooperation and recognition that many of the serious environmental problems facing the planet required a coordinated global response.

The difficulties encountered in the negotiation and drafting stages of many of these treaties, most of which significantly interfere with the unfettered sovereignty of nation states, were reflected in the time it took to arrive at a final text and the compromises that were necessary in order to ensure that a significant number of states were prepared to adopt and ratify the treaty. In addition, it was recognized that the piecemeal ad hoc approach to concerns such as biodiversity conservation should be replaced by framework treaties, building upon existing conventions and under which specific issues could be addressed in separately negotiated protocols.

Examples that readily come to mind are the treaties involving the Law of the Sea (UNCLOS – UN Doc A CONF.62 122, reprinted at 21 I.L.M. 1261 (1982)), Climate Change (UNFCCC – May 29, 1992, 31 I.L.M. 849 (1992) (entered into force March 21, 1994)) and its subsidiary instrument – the Kyoto Protocol (Kyoto Protocol to the United Nations Framework Convention on Climate Change, December 10, 1997, 37 I.L.M. 22 (1998), and the Convention on Biological Diversity (CBD- 21 I.L.M. 1261) including the recently adopted Biosafety Protocol (Cartagena Protocol on Biosafety).

The international community's approach to some basic concepts resulted in some major changes to what had hitherto been the norm. For example, prior to the adoption of the CBD in 1992, genetic resources had been characterized as a *common resource* of humankind and therefore freely available to all states. In recognition, however, that genetic resources and other components of biological diversity are found in areas under national jurisdiction in most instances, the CBD entrenched the concept of a state's right to exploit its own resources as set out in Principle 21 of the Stockholm Declaration. Thus, both the Preamble and Article 15 of the CBD clearly acknowledge the sovereign right of states over their own biological resources including controlling access to them. Instead of biological resources being considered common resources of humankind, the CBD introduced the concept that biological resources were to be considered a *common concern* of humankind, implying a need for collective international responsibility for their protection and conservation. Further discussion on rights, obligations and restrictions (RORs), the way they are currently shaped and proposals for future developments are presented in Lyons et al, Chapter 11.

The protection and conservation of biological diversity is an extremely broad and diverse topic. In the time and space permitted, I propose therefore to discuss certain property issues of concern in the context of the CBD and focus upon IPRs and their particular application to the preservation of the knowledge, innovations and practices of Indigenous and local communities embodying traditional lifestyles.

Intellectual Property Rights under the CBD

The CBD is predicated upon the recognition of states' sovereign rights over their natural (genetic) resources which, in turn, affirms that the authority over access to these genetic resources lies with national government and is subject to national legislation (CBD, Article 15(1)). There is no obligation on states to provide access but rather each Contracting Party shall endeavour to create conditions to facilitate access to genetic resources for environmentally sound uses by other Contracting Parties and not to impose restrictions that run counter to the objectives of the Convention (CBD, Article 15(2)). A key element in the context of providing access is that it shall be subject to prior informed consent (PIC) of the Contracting Party providing such resources, unless otherwise determined by that Party. Access, where granted, shall be on *mutually agreed terms* (emphasis added) (CBD, Article 15(4)).

The CBD requires that Contracting Parties shall implement these provisions by taking legislative, administrative or policy measures, as appropriate and in accordance with Articles 16 and 19, and, where necessary, through the financial mechanism established by Articles 20 and 21 with the aim of sharing in a fair and equitable way the results of research and development and the benefits arising from the commercial and other utilization of genetic resources with the Contracting Party providing such resource. Such sharing shall be upon mutually agreed terms (CBD, Article 15(7)).

It should be noted that there is no specific reference in Article 15(7) to intellectual property rights, however, the obligations imposed on the parties to facilitate the fair and equitable sharing of benefits in accordance with Article 16 requires the Contracting Parties to take measures in a manner that is 'on terms which recognize and are consistent with the adequate and effective protection of intellectual property rights'.

Article 16 of the CBD specifically relates to access to and transfer of technology which is considered to be essential if the objectives of the CBD are to be achieved.

Article 16(1) includes in its definition of technology, biotechnology and specifically 'technologies that are relevant to the conservation and sustainable use of biological diversity or make use of genetic resources and do not cause significant damage to the environment'. By defining technology in this way it ensures that traditional and Indigenous applied knowledge also falls within the category of technology.

Under Article 16(2) access to and transfer of technology shall be provided and/or facilitated under fair and most favourable terms, including on concessional and preferential terms where mutually agreed. The terms *fair and most favourable* and *concessional and preferential* are not defined within the convention, however, the language is consistent with the United Nations Framework Convention on Climate Change (UNFCCC), the Protocol on Substances that Deplete the Ozone Layer (Montreal Protocol) and Agenda 21.

Of particular note is the fact that Article 16(2) explicitly recognizes and protects existing intellectual property rights. It provides that in the case of technology subject to patents and other intellectual property rights, such access and transfer shall be provided on terms that recognize and are consistent with the adequate and effective protection of intellectual property rights. As might be expected, the protection of existing IPRs proved to be one of the make-or-break issues during the negotiations leading up to the adoption of the CBD and it is doubtful that the negotiations would have been successfully concluded without this explicit recognition of existing intellectual property rights.

Once again, there is no specific obligation on Contracting Parties for the transfer of the technology that makes use of the resources to the Contracting Party that is providing the genetic resources, and, like under Article 15, the CBD merely provides for the establishment of legislative, administrative or policy measures that would facilitate the access and transfer of the technology, with the manner in which this obligation is to be met left to the parties to decide (CBD Article 16(3)).

An important caveat is inserted, however, under Article 16(3) in that any transfer of technology that does take place is to be in accordance with international law. This would therefore include any international law that applies to intellectual property rights such as the TRIPS Agreement, World Intellectual Property Organization (WIPO) administered multilateral treaties, and bilateral agreements and other regional treaties such as the European Community Directive on the Legal Protection of Biotechnological Inventions.

The principal IPRs that are relevant to the protection and conservation of biological diversity are patents, trade secrets and plant breeders' rights (PBRs) (Glowka et al, 1994). Each of these will be discussed briefly in the context of both the CBD and their interface with the protection of traditional knowledge and practices.

In order to overcome the concern that recognition and protection of existing intellectual property rights might in fact not support the objectives of the CBD, Article 16(5) was inserted. It provides that the 'Contracting Parties, recognizing that patents and other intellectual property rights may have an influence on the implementation of this Convention (and by implication on its goals and objectives) shall cooperate in this regard subject to national legislation and international law in order to ensure that such rights are supportive of and do not run counter to its objectives.'

Incompatibility of Traditional Forms of IPRs in Protecting Traditional Knowledge and Practices

The CBD under Article 8(j) specifically requires each Contracting Party to obtain the consent of the holders of Indigenous knowledge, innovations and practices and to encourage the equitable sharing of benefits arising from the use of such knowledge (CBD, Article 8(j)). Implementation of Article 15 in accordance with the objectives of the CBD cannot be achieved without considering the requirements of this provision.

Unlike Article 15 that refers only to genetic resources, Article 8(j) has a much wider scope as to the resources it includes. The qualification that the article's implementation is subject to national legislation was introduced in order to maintain a relationship that had been established between some states and Indigenous groups prior to the Convention being complete (supra note 7 at 15). Article 10(c) is considered to be a natural consequence of Article 8(j) as it requires that Parties 'protect and encourage customary use of biological resources in accordance with traditional cultural practices that are compatible with conservation or sustainable use requirements'. There is, as a result, a necessity that in considering the development of policy and legislation with regard to access to genetic resources, state governments must consider the customary use of these resources (Ibid, p. 16).

As Graham Dutfield (Dutfield, 2000) notes, it is significant that the use of the word *holder* suggests that there is some type of ownership or legal entitlement at the least, and so have some rights over their 'knowledge, innovations and practices' (CBD, Article 8(j)) regardless of whether or not they can attract intellectual property right protection. This Article of the CBD is an acknowledgement by the international community that they understand the importance and value of traditional 'knowledge, innovation and practices' to modern society (Glowka et al, 1994, supra note 7 at 15).

In order to appreciate the difficulties one confronts in the context of attempting to harmonize the various legal mechanisms that have been put in place, a brief comment on the Agreement on Trade Related Aspects of Intellectual Property Rights (the TRIPS Agreement) must be inserted at this juncture (see also discussion on TRIPS agreement presented in Amankwah, Chapter 4). The TRIPS Agreement sets the minimum level of intellectual property rights that must be provided by all state parties to the General Agreement on Tariffs and Trade (GATT, 1947) and subsumed by all member states of the World Trade Organization (WTO). Unlike states having the flexibility to decide whether or not they wish to ratify a specific international treaty or convention or subsequent protocol adopted under a particular treaty or convention, all members of the WTO are obliged to adhere to and be bound by all agreements administered by the WTO by virtue of their membership of the WTO.

With respect to the TRIPS Agreement, members may implement more extensive protection provided that such protection does not contravene the provisions of the TRIPS Agreement. Intellectual property under the TRIPS Agreement is not defined in its own right but rather refers to seven categories of IPRs: namely: copyright and related rights, trademarks, geographical indications, industrial designs, patents, layout designs of integrated circuits and protection of undisclosed information (including trade secrets or test data). Of these categories, patents are potentially the most useful in terms of genetic resources, but trade secrets may also be relevant, as well as geographical indications and possibly trademarks (Downes, 1999).

Through Article 27, the TRIPS Agreement places an obligation on member states to enact legislation that will make patents available for both products and processes in all fields of technology provided that they are 'new, involve an inventive step and are capable of industrial application'. The rationale behind this article is to ensure that no material is excluded from patentability laws, including drugs and medicines, farm chemicals and products produced outside of the country. It should be noted however that there are some allowable exclusions within the context of Article 27, namely an exception excluding what is referred to as '*ordre public* or morality' (Article 27(2)).

Although this term is not defined, the Article states that it includes the protection of 'human, animal or plant life or health or to avoid serious prejudice to the environment'. This raises some interesting propositions for, in some societies or cultures, the patenting of life-forms and their components in general would be considered inherently immoral. In addition, many traditional societies have put forward the view that monopoly protection of products derived from traditional ecological knowledge and community-based resources is exploitative and morally wrong.

Further possible exclusions relate to diagnostic, therapeutic and surgical methods as well as plants and animals (other than micro organisms) and biological processes (other than microbiological processes). On this point the TRIPS Agreement states that members have the obligation to provide protection of plant varieties either through patents, or an 'effective' *sui generis* system, or a combination of the two (TRIPS Agreement Article, 27(3)b).

Also relevant to IPR protection and biodiversity is the International Convention for the Protection of New Varieties of Plants (the UPOV Convention, 1991), which provides a framework for intellectual property rights (IPR) protection of plant varieties, referred to as plant breeders' rights or plant variety rights.

Unfortunately traditional ecological knowledge, by its very nature, is not capable of being protected under conventional IPR regimes. IPRs (in particular patents) grant monopoly rights as incentive for technological innovation, or 'development'. For this reason, they protect only private rights and do not take into account IPRs in the public domain. This limited recognition and protection of intellectual property is problematic as it fails to acknowledge systems of knowledge that have evolved over time, as scientific knowledge does, but whose evolution has not taken place in a laboratory (Biswajit et al, 2001).

This poses a problem for Indigenous communities whose local knowledge is used by bioprospecting companies to locate and understand the properties of biological organisms to be used in creating a patentable product. In most cases traditional knowledge, passed down through generations, has lost its novelty and has become part of the public domain and therefore incapable of patent protection under existing patent regimes.

It has been suggested that the 'trade secret' could prove useful in the protection of traditional ecological knowledge. This is based on the fact that not all knowledge within traditional communities is shared, and that some individuals may have access to information due to their status in the group, which may be converted into a trade secret to be owned by that individual or the group as a whole. This practice is underway in Ecuador where a database of traditional ecological knowledge trade secrets is being developed for intended use by the private sector. It is, however, debatable whether the TRIPS agreement goes far enough in providing for protection of Indigenous knowledge under trade secrets.

Public Interest Dimensions Associated with the Protection of Indigenous IPRs

As noted at the outset of this chapter, the ability of the law to be used for the purpose of providing 'effective' protection to Indigenous communities for the use by others of their traditional ecological knowledge depends to a large extent upon both the moral and political will of the Contracting Parties and in particular the nation states responsible for carrying out the objectives and goals of the CBD in the context of national implementation. Because of significant legal impediments, some of which are outlined above, it will be necessary to assess and incorporate some fundamental public interest principles into any legislative reforms that are urgently required.

In the context of access and benefit sharing under the provisions of the CBD there is specific provision made for the obtaining of the prior informed consent of the Contracting Party providing access to the genetic resource (Article 15(5)).

The issue of prior informed consent and the degree of information that needs to be provided prior to such consent being obtained must be discussed in the context of the ownership question, as it will in all cases involve a determination as to whose consent is required. The term prior informed consent is notably absent from the definitions section of the CBD (Article 2); however, it is a concept that has been used in the Convention on the Control of Transboundary Movements of Hazardous Wastes (the Basel Convention), which entered into force on 5 May 1989. It has also been used in the FAO's International Code of Conduct on the Distribution and Use of Pesticides (FAO RES 10/85/1985 as amended by RES 6/89/1989).

There appears to be general agreement that the essential elements of any PIC must contain at least the following:

> *the party providing the genetic resources before granting consent is entitled to require any potential user of genetic resource to obtain prior authorization or consent; and the potential user must furnish information setting out how and by whom the genetic resources will be subsequently used, providing a basis upon which the provider might properly decide upon whether to withhold or grant access and upon what terms; and in addition to provide a basis upon which to effectively evaluate and facilitate benefit sharing.*
> (Mugabe et al, 1996)

Such access must be on mutually agreed terms (CBD, Article 15(4)) and must be shared in a fair and equitable way (CBD, Article 15(7)).

The fundamental concepts of access and benefit sharing that lie at the very heart of the CBD are further complicated when one considers the ownership question. Who within the provider country is legally entitled to provide the consent required to facilitate access to the genetic resources and is entitled to receive compensation arising from their use? This issue is often more complex when the genetic resources are held collectively by Indigenous communities as their concept of ownership is radically different from that of non-Indigenous societies.

One must bear in mind at all times each Contracting Party to a treaty under international law is a nation state, not individuals, territories, dependencies, communities or societies that do not have nation state status. Consequently while the sovereignty of a state over its genetic resources is recognized by the CBD, the assigning of property rights over these resources rests with the tenure and ownership systems of each Contracting Party and will impact upon the participation of a state in regulating access. It has been noted that tenure and ownership systems are neither uniform across all countries, nor are they clearly defined in any given country. A particular country's ownership arrangements will depend on both its legislative heritage and cultural traditions and may range from traditional common tenure to state-enforced private rights to land and natural resources, including genetic resources (see discussion in Columbia University

School of International and Public Affairs study report, 1999). As a broadest example, the Common Law often regards natural resources as private property affording the state little participation in regulating access, while Roman Law grants property to the state, holding natural resources as national patrimony.

Organisation for Economic Co-operation and Development (OECD) countries generally do not regulate access to genetic resources subject, in some cases, to conservation and endangered species legislation. Consequently, prior informed consent from the state would not be required, only the specific landowner's consent or permission to access the resource on private land. In contrast, some Latin American countries comprising the Andean Pact, such as Peru, designate genetic resources and their derivatives as the property or patrimony of the state and thus prior informed consent is governed by a state-owned property regime.

In many developing countries, traditional and Indigenous communities have continued to apply their own tenure system for biological resources that, for the most part, find their basis in collective ownership and may have religious or mystical importance for the community. In such cases, determining who should regulate access is a complex issue. Further, traditional community tenure may or may not be recognized by a particular nation's property rights. This, in turn, relates to numerous other issues and concerns about the interface between Indigenous rights and laws and the dominant legal system. Many legal systems fail to recognize Indigenous rights to own and control their genetic resources and there are many impediments to Indigenous participation in the dominant decision-making process. The community form of tenure may not have a legal institutional form capable of representing and protecting Indigenous concerns and serious difficulties often arise when outsiders seek a *majority* or representative view in determining access issues.

It should therefore be noted that although the CBD requires PIC only of the *state* providing access to the genetic resources, it does not prevent a country's national law from applying the concept to all individuals and/or communities whose consent or permission may be required, including Indigenous communities (Fourmile, 1998).

Need for Adequate Technical and Legal Resources

In light of the fact that, in most cases, the state will under its national legislation or practice endeavour to obtain the PIC from those in actual control of the genetic resources as well as the traditional ecological knowledge associated therewith, it is of critical importance, in this writer's view, to provide the necessary technical and legal resources to properly assess and evaluate whether or not consent should be given and under what conditions. Likewise, given the complexity of the field of biotechnology, it would be difficult if not impossible to arrive at a fair and equitable sharing of benefits in the absence of both the information and the technical expertise to evaluate that information and incorporate it into a legally binding access and benefit sharing agreement.

The need to establish an appropriate funding model capable of providing adequate resources to underwrite an effective PIC process, particularly in the case of poorly resourced Indigenous communities, is absolutely essential if the objectives of the CBD are to be achieved.

This debate is not only confined to the protection and conservation of biological resources but has been of persistent concern to environmentalists and conservationists over the past three decades. Most developed countries provide a process designed to encourage citizen participation in environmental decision-making.

Meaningful citizen participation encourages government accountability, ensures continuation of a participatory democracy and can, in an environmental context, stimulate inventive and socially acceptable answers to environmental problems (Anand and Scott, 1982).

It is also increasingly evident that the general public remains mistrustful and sceptical of government's ability to adequately and apolitically represent the public interest. The same would invariably be the position of Indigenous and local communities if they were not directly involved in the prior informed consent process. However, to require their participation in the absence of providing the necessary financial resources for legal and technical advice is tantamount to what this writer has in the past referred to as 'participatory tokenism' (Jeffery, 2002).

One must realize that the other party to the access and benefit sharing agreement is often a multi-billion dollar pharmaceutical company attempting to obtain the traditional knowledge necessary to formulate its next multi-billion dollar pharmaceutical product. To suggest that this party will not have access to adequate legal and technical advice in negotiating an access and benefit sharing agreement would be an understatement of the first magnitude.

Other Public Interest Initiatives in the International Law Arena

The recent development in the international law arena of linking environmental and human rights is worthy of consideration in the context of the preceding discussion.

The Convention on Access to Information, Public Participation in Decision-making and Access to Justice in Environmental Matters (the Aarhus Convention) was adopted at the fourth ministerial conference – 'Environment for Europe' in Aarhus, Denmark on June 25, 1998. Approximately 40 countries from Europe, Central Asia and the European Union have since signed it and it entered into force October 30, 2001. It contains a number of important fundamental principles.

The Aarhus Convention grants the public rights and imposes on Contracting Parties and public authorities obligations regarding access to information and public participation. It reinforces these rights with access to justice provisions and covers obligations that Contracting Parties have to the public rather than obligations of Parties to each other. More importantly it links environmental protection to human rights norms and raises environmental rights to the level of other human rights.

It is suggested that basic rights such as *the right to know, the right to partic-ipate, the right to have one's cultural heritage adequately protected* and *the right to have a clean and safe environment*, when characterized as human rights, will result in greater respect and enhanced protection in the context of both international and domestic legal systems.

Concluding Comments

International law since the 1970s has experienced a remarkable growth and unity of purpose. The international community comprised of both developed and developing states have both appreciated the need to act in a concerted, collective manner and have been prepared to take the first tentative steps to putting in place global strategies to redress a number of pressing global environmental concerns.

Climate change and in particular greenhouse gas emissions and the protection and conservation of biological diversity have undoubtedly been catapulted to the forefront of media attention, however, the development of a number of important principles that now have routine application should not go unnoticed. In many cases these principles are non-binding and referred to in the context of international environmental law as 'soft-law'. In some cases these principles have developed to the stage of being considered customary international law and therefore binding or 'hard-law'.

Principles such as the precautionary principle, the principle of inter- and intra-generational equity, the polluter-pays principle and the principle of common but differentiated responsibility, to name but a few, have significantly enhanced our ability to achieve sustainable development and to approach environmental issues in a much more fair and equitable manner.

The CBD and its explicit recognition of both existing intellectual property rights and the important role played by Indigenous and local communities in the quest to protect and conserve biological diversity, is an important first step in providing a workable framework treaty that attempts to bridge the North-South divide.

Acknowledgement

The author gratefully acknowledges the assistance of Meredith Rose, student-at-law, Osgoode Hall, York University, Toronto Canada.

References

Anand, R. and Scott, I.G., (1982). Financing Public Participation in Environmental Decision-making. *CAN. BAR. REV.*, 60 (81), 151–152.
Biswajit, D,; Sachin, C. and R.V., (2001). *Anuradha, Regime of Intellectual Property Protection for Biodiversity: A Developing Country Perspective*. India: RIS and IUCN.
Columbia University School of International and Public Affairs, (1999). Access to

Genetic Resources: An Evaluation of the Development and Implementation of Recent Regulation and Access Agreements. *Environmental Policy Studies Working Paper 4*. Columbia: Biodiversity Action Network.

Downes, D., (1999). *Integrating Implementation of the Convention on Biological Diversity and the Rules of the World Trade Organization*. Gland and Cambridge: IUCN.

Dutfield, G., (2000). *Intellectual Property Rights, Trade and Biodiversity: Seeds and Plant Varieties*. UK: Earthscan Publications/IUCN.

Fourmile, H., (1998). Using PIC procedures under the Convention on Biological Diversity to protect Indigenous Traditional Ecological Knowledge and Natural Resources Rights. *Indigenous Law Bulletin*, 16, 27.

GATT, General Agreement on Tariffs and Trade, 30 October, (1947). 61 Stat. A3, 55 U.N.T.S. 187.

Glowka, L. et al, (1994). *A Guide to the Convention on Biological Diversity*. Gland and Cambridge: IUCN.

Jeffery, M., (2002). Intervenor Funding as the Key to Effective Citizen Participation in Environmental Decision-making. *Arizona Journal of International and Comparative Law*, 19 (2).

Mugabe et al, (1996). Managing Access to Genetic Resources: Towards Strategies for Benefit Sharing. In Mugabe, J. et al, (eds). *Biopolicy International Series No. 17*. (pp. 5). Kenya: ACTS/Initiatives Publishers/WRI.

UPOV Convention, (1991). *International Convention for the Protection of New Varieties of Plants*. Reprinted at www.upov.org. As adopted in Paris, 1961 and revised in 1972, 1978 and 1991.

6

Myth, Embeddedness and Tradition: Property Rights Perceptions from the Pacific

Spike Boydell

Introduction

Myth, embeddedness and tradition

This essay is introduced by delving into the myth, embeddedness and tradition that surrounds people's perceptions of property rights. In all societies the property rights of individuals are subject to both political and legal regulation, whether this is by custom, modern legal instruments, or both. In the Pacific there is often a confusion and conflict between constitutional and customary law. Embeddedness, or preconception from prior upbringing, clouds and confuses attitudes to property and land ownership.

Is there such a person as a customary landowner in the Pacific Islands or is society actually adopting inappropriate *borrowed* western language? To answer this question, it is necessary to explore the concept of communalism, which is accepted practice in many Pacific island countries, and investigate how it is, like most things in the Pacific, grounded in relationships.

The South Pacific in context

Before discussing property rights issues in the region, it will help to contextualize the Pacific Island nations and their sustainable development challenges. The Pacific Island Countries and Territories (PICs) comprise 12 nations to 22 nations depending on the definition of various regional organizations.[1] The Pacific islands region is unique because of the combination of geographical, biological, sociological and economic characteristics (Miles, 1999). The region occupies a vast 30 million km² of the Pacific Ocean. The 22 countries and territories comprise some 550,000km² of land with 7.5 million inhabitants. Notably, if the largest landmass, Papua New Guinea, is excluded from the summation, the remaining 21 nations comprise 87,587km², with a total population of

2.7 million. The region comprises three sub regional groupings: Micronesia, Polynesia and Melanesia, with a diversity of people and cultures – over 2,000 different languages are spoken across the region.

The common characteristics of the region include remoteness and geographic isolation; environmental fragility; rapid population growth; limited land resources; poorly functioning and immature land markets; land access issues, with 83–100 per cent remaining vested in the Indigenous owners; informal housing; dependency on marine resources; (relative) poverty; limited diversification; limited capacity; and vulnerability to critical environmental, ecological, and economic risks (Boydell, 2004).

Through colonization, a broad range of external tenure influences have been brought into the region. In many Pacific Island countries, these influences result in a plural system whereby western notions of freehold and leasehold operate alongside customary regimes. The influences can be summarized thus:

- United Kingdom: Fiji, Solomons, Gilbert Ellice (Tuvalu) and partly New Hebrides;
- France: New Caledonia, French Polynesia, Wallis and Futuna and partly New Hebrides;
- Germany: (until 1914) for north-eastern New Guinea, Western Samoa, Nauru, Caroline and Marshall Islands;
- Netherlands: until 1962 for West New Guinea (now called Irian Jaya);
- Indonesia: (since 1963) for Irian Jaya;
- Australia: Papua (since 1906), north-east New Guinea (since 1914) and Nauru (1914 to 1968);
- New Zealand: Cook Islands and Niue (since 1901) and Tokelau Islands (since 1925) and Western Samoa (1914 to 1962);
- Spain: Guam, Mariana and Caroline Islands (till 1899);
- Japan: Mariana, Marshall and Caroline Islands (from 1914 to 1945);
- US: Mariana and Caroline Islands (from 1945) and Hawaii;
- Chile: Easter Island.

This chapter will focus on the investigation of the compatibility of the United Kingdom system as introduced over the traditional system in Fiji.

As Farran and Paterson highlight, one of the difficulties with the approach that looks at property as rights in the South Pacific is that 'in English common law, the notion of property as rights is seen as the relationship between the individual – or legal person – and the thing' (Farran and Paterson, 2004). A similar challenge is present in considering ownership from a western and an Indigenous perspective – the former being an individualistic paradigm, the latter often being grounded in communalism, prioritizing the relationship between native peoples and the land.

A survey of the relationships between various native peoples and their land reveals that, typically, the relationship has two dimensions – spiritual (or metaphysical) and material (relating to the political economy of land)(Small, 1997). Philosophically and spiritually, there is a deep-rooted belief in the stewardship of land. The current generation has a responsibility in respect of the land that relates to the spirits of their ancestors along with the expectations of their descendants, in addition to the needs of the current generation. Descendants, as future members of the tribe, are regarded as having the same rights of access to land as those tribe members currently alive. For the same reasons, children cannot be charged for access to the land of their parents. Land is free for the use of current tribe members on the basis that it will be passed on, without degradation, for the use of future members. The communalism of the tribe, the timeless stewardship afforded the land and the idea of land as a common legacy, are concepts often difficult for westerners to appreciate (Boydell and Small, 2003). They differ from the standardized model of private exclusive ownership that has now been disseminated in most developed societies (Hann, 1998).

Table 6.1 *Property rights summarized*

Right	Explanation
Direct use	Rights to plant, harvest, build, access and similar, maybe shared rights
Indirect economic gain	Such as rights to tribute or rental income
Control	Conditions of direct/indirect use, held by persons other than the user
Transfer	Effective power to transmit rights – by will, sale, mortgage, gift or other conveyance
Residual rights	Remaining rights at the end of a term (such as lease, death, eviction), includes reversionary rights
Rights of identification (symbolic rights)	Associated with psychological or social aspects with no direct economic or material function
Duration	Length of time property right is held, indicating profits and/or savings
Flexibility	Right should cater for modifications and alterations
Exclusivity	Inverse of the number of people with shared or similar rights, more relevant to water property
Quality of title	Level of security that is available as tenure shifts from the optimum of notional freehold
Divisibility	Property right can be shared over territories, according to season, etc.
Access	Entry/admission onto the land
Withdrawal (extraction)	Extraction of resources by owner despite leasing property
Management	Be able to make decisions on how and by whom a thing shall be used
Exclusion	Disallowing others from entry and use of resources
Alienation	Transfer of an interest (right) in property to another, in perpetuity
Usufruct rights	Collection of fruits or produce
Chiefly rights	Inherited by a headman in communal ownership (tribe, clan, village)

Source: Adapted from Crocombe, 1975; Bromley, 1991; Payne, 1997; Rigsby, 1998; Sheehan and Small, 2002; World Bank, 2003; Farran and Paterson, 2004

There are many different interpretations, or lists, of property rights. Table 6.1 provides a list combined from several different sources. On closer inspection it will be noted that some of these *rights* (e.g. duration and flexibility) are actually attributes of more fundamental rights, rather than separate individual rights. Chapter 1 of this book provides definitions and further discussion on property rights in general.

Property Rights and Spiritual Materialism

It is only by reflecting on particular cases that the essential and universal aspects of property may be abstracted. In this way the meta-consideration of cultural responses to the problem of property may yield an understanding of property that can then be redeployed to refine existing property institutions. Implicit within this methodological approach is the recognition that the western institution of property is as much in need of refinement as any customary approach (Boydell and Small, 2003).

Eroni's story

The first investigation is grounded on the example of Eroni, an educated, respected and humble man. While Eroni lives in Suva, Fiji, and works at the university, he is head of the Tokatoka (tribe) back in the village near Savusavu where his family comes from. In a cruel example of the spiritual materialism that surrounds Pacific property rights, Eroni almost died last year. There is a view coined by, among others, Ravuvu (Ravuvu, 1983) that land holds a special place in the Pacific. The reality is that land holds a special place in all societies on economic, social and environmental grounds, but that the difference in the Pacific is that much of the land was never alienated through colonialism and remains in the communal ownership of the Indigenous islanders.

Living alongside Indigenous and settler communities in the Pacific expands a researcher's appreciation of the spiritual connection of humankind with not just their land but particularly their property rights. This chapter uses the phrase *their land* with both caution and circumspection, having previously presented a convincing argument that those Indigenous Fijians who believe themselves to be land owners have no legal ownership in a western legal context, but instead collectively own a bundle of property rights (Boydell and Shah, 2003). Interestingly, that view has evolved in the light of a subsequent appeal judgment of the Supreme Court, which recognized lessons from the *Mabo* case and now gives legal identity (locus standi) to members of a Mataqali (*Native Land Trust Board v Narawa* May 21, 2004).

So, back to Eroni's story, in a land where *Christianity* (Methodism in this instance) and *vakadranikau* (black magic) are as strong as ever and work alongside one another in the plural spirituality of many educated as well as less fortunate Fijians (as is well documented in, among others, Katz, 1993). Katz simplifies the definitions of *western* and *Indigenous* in a pragmatic manner, alluding to two different but overlapping and interrelated ways of being, which are themselves dynamic and evolving. He suggests the application of the term *western* to people and institutions affected by forces such as modernism, capitalism and urbanism. In contrast, *Indigenous* applies to people and institutions more affected by traditionalism, cooperative economics and rural or *bush* life. Katz does indeed qualify this in identifying Indigenous people as being descended from the first or original inhabitants of a place, acknowledging that while they are *more* traditional, they are often influenced by the western values of the larger nation within which they reside.

Eroni is head of a Tokatoka, a chiefly communal grouping which is smaller than a Mataqali. He took over this responsibility on the death of his father in 2003. Operating in the plural societies of urban Suva and the bush village near Savusavu, with responsibilities and obligations in both, exemplifies the stress that can be placed on an individual in a communal society. With responsibility and obligation comes the need to make decisions for and on behalf of members of the Tokatoka. When Eroni became sick with a necrotic tropical ulceration of the leg (and near lethal blood pressure) he initially sought solace and relief in bush medicine. Time passed. By the time medical evacuation to Australia was facilitated, he had taken to his bed with Fijian Methodist Bible in hand in the hope that it would protect him from the black magic being cast in his direction by his villagers, in anger for a property rights decision he had made on behalf of his kinsfolk in the Tokatoka. For Eroni, property rights almost became last rites.

Happily, Eroni responded to appropriate health care in a Sydney hospital, and lives to tell the tale. His life and his leg were saved and the physical wound is healing. The deeper wound that underlies his mind–body challenge may take longer to heal. He recently returned to the village to address the underlying issues in the oxymoron that is the spiritual materialism (Roy, 2004) of property rights. How did Eroni make amends for a property rights dispute that allowed his kin to almost spiritually kill him? With materialism, of course; by paying for expensive visa fees for members of the Tokatoka to apply to serve as (comparatively) well-paid security officers in Iraq.

Eroni's story has introduced the concept of property rights. It is important to reflect on these rights and review the confusion that seems to surround them – confusion that can lead to all manner of land tenure conflicts. The next section reviews what is meant by property rights and they are then contextualized by putting a Pacific 'spin' on them by using another investigation, this time of Jale and the differing rights that he has from both a customary and western perspective.

Property rights as a human and spiritual concept

Our understanding of property rights can be enhanced by using anthropological explanations to look at institutions. There is no property in nature – the concept of property and property rights is a human construct. Taken in isolation, such as in the world of Robinson Crusoe, property rights play no role (Demsetz, 1967). It is only when another person, group of people, clan or larger society are involved that a sense of territoriality becomes important.

Humans need to define what is ours, and like many animal species, humans will defend their space – with their lives if necessary. Our perception of value is affected by others needs – a monetary value is placed on property rights within the economic structure of society. Material value is very tangible and it can be measured in economic terms. Spiritual value is intangible. Just because spiritual value cannot be quantified in conventional economic terms, its importance in Indigenous societies cannot be overemphasized.

Society accepts that land holds a special place in the Pacific for many reasons. As mentioned above, one of the most important reasons is that it was never alienated as a result of colonization in the way that the Aborigines had their land taken in Australia and likewise the Maori had much of their land taken as a result of white European settlement. Alienation means the transfer of ownership (property rights) in property to another, e.g. sale of a freehold, grant of a lease or the taking of customary land.

We need to define what we mean by property and investigate what we value. Taking the Demsetz example, when Robinson Crusoe was shipwrecked his first concern was not what property rights he had, rather his very survival, the need to find food and fresh water, the need for some form of shelter. With time he would have accepted his environment and with his basic needs satisfied he may have started to take his environment for granted, until he felt threatened that someone may try and take his *world* away from him. At that point, his value systems would have started to change as he became territorial and felt that his informal property rights might be affected.

There is a similar transition evolving in Pacific small island developing states today. Many Pacific Islanders have in recent generations, since settlement and a move to colonial rule after the law of the *club* (tribal warfare), become more settled in their environments. Perhaps they too have taken some things for granted. However, the move to a global market, access to natural resources and the capitalist paradigm have placed more emphasis on economic value in relation to property rights, as opposed to cultural, spiritual or subsistence value.

Land tenure as an evolving paradigm

When we think of land, we find levels of understanding and levels of confusion. This is compounded by the difference between the western *real estate* definition of property and the Indigenous explanation.

The real estate definition of property is that which is capable of being owned: classified as personalty and realty. Examples of personal property would include furnishings, artwork, jewellery, machinery and household goods. In other words personal items; as opposed to real estate.

> *They say that land, like financial and human capital, is a factor of production, which helps drive economic and social development, generates national income, wealth, jobs and government revenue, combats poverty, improves the standard of living of all and ultimately entrenches social and political stability in any country. Land*

> *tenure, like culture and tradition, stands to evolve organically over time within a society. As in all things, changes and solutions have to be made and formulated. Solutions must be formulated from within and must reflect national, family and individual needs and aspirations and the changing global, regional, national economic, social and political dynamics that determine our destiny.*
> (Siwatibau, 2002)

The definitions themselves can become confused. The US Dictionary of Real Estate Appraisal (3e) suggests that 'real property comprises all interests and rights related to the ownership of physical real estate' (Appraisal Institute, 1993). This indicates the inclusion of different interests and different parties. Conversely, the UK Glossary of Property Terms defines real property (realty) as 'freehold land, but not leaseholds; the latter are defined as personalty or personal property' (Jones Lang Wootton, 1989).

If contemporary western society cannot agree on what we mean by real estate and real property, the whole picture becomes even more clouded when we try to explain it from an Indigenous perspective. The Indigenous explanation is grounded in social relationships and how people (individually or communally within a group) own, value and dispose of things.

Property Rights in Communal Context

Property rights in the communal context: Jale's story

Jale is an Indigenous Pacific islander. To provide context, it will be assumed that he is from Fiji. He lives on customary land *belonging* to his clan (Mataqali), but just outside of the main village. He worked for many years in the capital, but is now leading a simpler rural life. However, he has learned many ideas in the city and while being very respectful of tradition is not content to stick with a customary subsistence village lifestyle.

Jale was *given* land by his village/clan to construct a home. He has always contributed to the communal well-being of his kinsfolk and is a respected member of the clan. He has identified an opportunity to establish a small piggery adjacent to his home, a modest commercial venture that will allow him to generate an income and continue contributing to the village, now that he is no longer in paid employment.

As a member of the community, he is living on communal land. He needs some financial support to establish his piggery, so he approaches the manager of the local bank. The bank manager is interested in his initiative and keen to support Jale's venture. He agrees to lend Jale some money, provided Jale can offer him some collateral, some security for the bank if Jale fails to meet his mortgage/loan repayments. The bank asks Jale for title to his land to be pledged as a guarantee of the repayment of the loan, to be forfeited in case of default. The bank asks for this because Jale has no other security.

Problem 1: Jale does not *own* the land in the western (or bank security) context. As stated, it is held communally by his clan. However, his clan does have the ability to alienate parcels of land outside of the village, provided that the land is not needed for subsistence purposes by the villagers, now or in the anticipated future.

Problem 2: Jale is a member of the village, so if he needs the land for subsistence there is a Catch-22 situation. Jale, as a member of the village, is seen as needing the land, which by inference may prevent the land from being released for his subsistence piggery.

Not daunted by this, Jale prepares a tabua (traditional gift) for his chief and asks that the elders agree to allow the Native Land Trust Board to create a lease for him. If he has a lease, he has formal property rights that can be used as security – a long lease is considered adequate security by a bank, as long as the lease term is longer than the length of the loan.

The chief is not happy with Jale's proposal, even though it has the potential for Jale to provide some financial support to his fellow villagers. Why would the chief not be happy?

The chief knows Jale, has faith in his business acumen, and is happy for Jale (as a member of the village) to work the land. But what will happen if Jale defaults on his loan (fails to make his mortgage repayments)? If Jale uses a long lease as security against his bank loan, this means that the bank has enforceable property rights to foreclose and sell Jale's interest (Jale's property rights) in the land. A forced sale may result in an outsider buying the lease, with resultant temporary loss of community ... a sense that the land could be lost from the village for future generations. The reality is that the communal 'ownership' rights of the village to the land would only be *lost* for the duration of the lease term, rather than in perpetuity.

It could also be that the chief may feel insecure and intimidated by the modest wealth that Jale may generate, making Jale more respected by the community, and, critically perhaps, more respected than the chief in the eyes of some. Apparently, with no alternative security to raise venture capital, Jale is being unrealistic in expecting the village to formalize his property rights to the land he already occupies (for which he would pay rent, whereas he currently occupies the land for no *direct* cost) so that he can feel more (individualistically) secure in building a piggery.

In this example, the chief declines Jale's request to obtain a lease from the communal landholding. As a result, the bank manager is unable to satisfy his lending criteria and has to refuse Jale's loan application. This leaves Jale without finance to establish his piggery, and without any title (property rights) to land to invest in. Is this progress? Who has benefited in the short term? Not Jale, not the bank and probably not the community as they will not receive any rent or any formal financial contributions from Jale.

And the long-term view? The village land remains intact, but the land is less productive than it could be.

Property rights of different parties in communal context

Reinforcing the oxymoronic nature of spiritual materialism in dealing with land issues, power relationships come to the fore when interpreting property

Table 6.2 *Summarizing the property rights of different parties*

	Jale's Customary Rights	Jale's Lease Rights	Village's Communal Rights	Bank Rights with Lease as Loan Security
Direct use	Yes, at grace of village	Yes	No	No
Indirect Economic Gain	Only if land is leased out and he is a beneficiary	Yes, he could sub-lease	Yes, as co-beneficiaries of any lease arrangement – and direct from Jale	Yes, interest payments on debt
Control	No	Yes	Yes, unless leased	Only in the event of repossession
Transferability	To descendants, but only with the grace of the village	Yes, dependent on lease covenants to assign or sub-let	Right to grant lease, or to give access by grace and favour	The bank can sell or transfer the debt, but can only transfer the physical assets in the event of foreclosure
Residual Rights	Assuming Jale has heirs, at the grace of the village	Yes, dependent on wording of lease	The land (and improvements) should revert to the village as communal landowner on lease expiry	Nil
Rights of Identification (Symbolic Rights)	Communal	Communal	These need not be lost by the grant of a lease	Nil
Duration	Guardianship for life	Rights for duration of lease	In perpetuity	Rights limited to mortgage and/or lease term
Flexibility	No	Yes, subject to lease covenants	Yes	No
Exclusivity	No	Yes	No	No
Quality of Title	Poor	Good	Unclear	Good
Divisibility	No	Potential, subject to lease terms	Potential	No
Access	Yes, by the grace of the village	Yes	Communal	No
Withdrawal (extraction)	No	Yes, subject to lease terms	Communal	No
Usufruct	Possibly	No	Possibly	No
Chiefly Rights	No	No	For chief	No
Management	No	Yes	Communal	No
Alienation	No	No	No	No

rights. These relationships can be explained by investigating the above property rights and the parties involved in Jale's piggery scenario (Table 6.2).

As Table 6.2 highlights, there are different property rights relating to different institutions. Jale's property rights will vary depending on if he has a lease (and thus a title and defined property rights) or if his situation remains communal and informal. The main powers of the bank only come into play in the eventuality of Jale defaulting on his loan and the bank exercising its powers of foreclosure and selling on the lease.

In this example, the concept of development in its widest sense is limited both by a lack of flexibility by the chief and a lack of flexibility by formal credit systems. As is demonstrated in Table 6.3, if Jale decides to pursue his piggery venture without access to domestic savings, his de facto communal tenure will force him to seek credit from informal lenders, inevitably at a higher interest rate (to reflect the lack of security) than structured credit through a formal lender.

Table 6.3 *Credit and tenure options according to levels of security*

CREDIT	TENURE De facto – No Title, Communal Land rental	Regularized – No Title Use Rights Contract Licence	Freehold Leasehold Tenant – Statutory Tenant – Contract
Formal Credit System			X
Credit Unions Savings Banks Public Grants Guaranteed Loan		X	X
Domestic Savings Informal Credit Loan *Sharks*	X	X	X

Source: Payne (1997)

Criteria for Assessing Tenure and Property Rights

Clear criteria are needed for assessing tenure and property rights. These criteria are based around clarity, efficiency, equity and *de jure* and *de facto*. Each of these criteria will be explored in turn. This section also presents discussion on potential consensus and on institutional arrangements in contemporary Pacific society.

Clarity of tenure status

Clarity can be formalized through the registration of all property rights, measured by the difference between *de jure* and *de facto* status. *De jure* means according to law whereas *de facto* means in fact – a phrase describing an accepted situation, which is accepted for all practical purposes, but that may not be *legal* or may be extra-legal (*vakavanua* in the Fiji context). This is a very unclear explanation because of the status of customary law versus constitutional law in the Pacific Island countries. Indeed, this pluralism highlights two related, but quite different, realities. It implies that *de jure* includes our *formal institutions* whereas *de facto* includes our *informal institutions*. However, Pacific societies exist in a legal environment where the concepts of *de jure* and *de facto* overlap significantly in many aspects of everyday life, more strongly than in many other societies. At the end of the day, perhaps we are just confusing ourselves by trying to fit the Pacific systems into a western model that has evolved over 2,000 years ... and we are still using the Latin words to explain the concepts.

How compatible are the concepts of *de jure* and *de facto* to contemporary institutions in the Pacific? Should we be finding a Pacific solution? These questions are raised because, as demonstrated by Jale's scenario, we are tying to make a customary ownership situation *fit* a western lending requirement. Unfortunately, as the banks hold the *power* because they are holding the money, there is pressure on Jale, and the rest of society, to conform to their reality, rather than the bank adapting its systems to allow lending flexibility within the customary framework it is trying to operate in. The tail (the bank) is clearly wagging the dog (the communal landowners).

Fundamental to an efficient tenure and property rights system is simplicity. The existing structures are not straightforward, so how can we simplify the system and who are we trying to simplify it for? Presumably, the simplification will benefit all parties who want access to land and capital. To simplify, we may need to find (or develop) a new Pacific model (or hybrid), rather than relying on an imported colonial system, which was designed to keep people in their place.

As pointed out in Chapters 2 and 3 of this book, flexibility is one of the key characteristics of successful institutions. Certainly the banks are not demonstrating flexibility. The banks are showing an embeddedness of lending policy which was designed for an Anglo-Australian institutional framework rather than a Pacific Islands institutional framework grounded in post-colonial evolved traditional and customary systems.

Transferability of both property rights and of the investment return (or surplus of productivity, e.g. rent) is seen as important from a western perspective, but if Pacific Islanders adopt their traditional spiritual approach, they are guardians for their ancestors' spirits as well as those of their descendants. Why would you want to transfer that sociological and spiritual responsibility under a façade of spiritual materialism?

Further to institutional compatibility, a good tenure system requires land management compatibility. This implies the potential for improvement of the land resource over time, be it the land's propensity to either generate income or to be more efficient in its productive output of food or other natural resources, or the ability to generate additional income from land/property, subject to planning regulations and other statutory restrictions.

In his Discourse on the Origin of Inequality (1754) Rousseau reminded us that 'you are lost if you forget that the fruits of the earth belong to all and the earth to no one' (de Botton, 2004). This challenges the oversimplified but popularized clarion call to regularize land title to enable the land/property to be used as collateral (de Soto, 2000), as the apparent solution to Jale's stalemate with the bank in particular and the concept of development in general. When Rousseau meets de Soto, we have to make a compromise within our spiritual materialism to acknowledge that earth is vested in the Almighty rather than in an individual (Boydell and Shah, 2003). The bank does not require Jale to *own* the earth in order to provide collateral security; what the bank requires is for Jale to have clearly defined and enforceable property rights.

The tenet of equity demands accessibility to property rights by all socio-economic groups, with sufficient security to encourage investment by residents. Equity also requires transferability (and a share in investment return) and balanced property rights between all parties – owner, head leaseholder, sub-tenants. Did Eroni experience equity if his rank in society requires that he has to make decisions that may be construed as unpopular by his kin, and then suffer the consequences of misplaced spiritual materialism? Like Eroni, Jale is an Indigenous Fijian and thus seen by most as favoured in society as a member of the supposed landowner class. The ownership myth has previously been challenged (Boydell and Shah, 2003), and any doubts Jale may have had over his ownership have been confirmed by the bank, which uses his lack of enforceable property rights as grounds not to lend him the venture capital funds to realize his piggery dream.

Seeking consensus

As we have seen from the Eroni and Jale stories, spiritual materialism is, perhaps, less of an oxymoron in the Pacific than in western cultures. I try to demonstrate this point by conducting each year tutorial discussions with students who study land management. A new cohort of islander students is asked about their values. The answers from these would indicate that valuers/land managers are not measured in monetary dollar or materialistic terms. Their relationship to the land is strong, both in terms of family and of spirit, the seen and the unseen. When the same question is repeated with grad-uating students at the end of their course, to find out what they aspire to do with their skills, the majority of students prioritize economic goals both at home and overseas above returning to their roots to benefit the community with their new found knowledge. However, the communal expectation to send remittances back to their kinsfolk remains a priority and a major obligation.

As Eroni's example also demonstrates, material dissatisfaction can result in spiritual negativity. The critically important but unspoken quandary of spiri-tual materialism, which affects land and daily life in the Pacific, merits further investigation.

Institutional arrangements

One of the biggest challenges for sustainability is how to provide an institutional framework that allows for sustainable management of landscape, water, air, biodiversity and industries and communities (CSIRO, 2003).

As discussed in Smajgl and Larson, Chapter 1, the rules influencing human behaviour can be broken down into two categories, formal – which tend to be enforceable and informal – which are in many cases unenforceable (Table 6.4).

Table 6.4 *The rules influencing human behaviour*

Formal Institutional Arrangements	Informal Institutional Arrangements
Constitutions	Relationships
Statutes	Social expectations
Regulations	Family
Plans	Firm
Policies	Community
Title	Traditional Laws and Customs

As Eroni's and Jale's scenarios demonstrate, the difficulty in contemporary Pacific society is with the overlap that exists between formal and informal institutional arrangements, and their interface with society's needs and aspirations. The overlap and interface were considered at length during the FAO/USP/RICS Foundation South Pacific Land Tenure Conflict Symposium in 2002 and are further discussed in Boydel et al (2002).

Finding a Way Forward

This essay did not promise solutions to the major development dilemma surrounding property rights in the Pacific. Instead it provides an insight into the myth, embeddedness and tradition that surrounds and confounds property rights in one particular Pacific Island country, grounded in two sample investigations. As has been stated before, the solutions must evolve as land tenure does, locally and appropriately to the culture, tradition and reality of those they affect. This essay is intentionally personal, grounded on the informed interpretation of actual experiences.

To be effective, local property institutions need to respect local culture and tradition, as well as incorporate elements that recognize the needs and dignity of persons beyond the confines of the tribal *owners*. It is only in this way that the broader level of cooperation that is nascent within western commerce and culture may be made available to customary people (Boydell and Small, 2003). This essay highlights the need for a systematic reappraisal of the very fundamentals of the institution of property and property rights in a manner that will facilitate appropriate regional solutions.

What is important is that such interpretations may assist others from beyond the shores of Pacific Islands to better understand the realities surrounding property rights from an Indigenous perspective. Through understanding comes clarity, and the potential for the better appreciation of property rights by grounding theory on local experience.

Note

1   The University of the South Pacific (USP) incorporates 12 Pacific Island Nations, the Pacific Island Forum Secretariat (PIFS) incorporates 16 members including Australia and New Zealand, whereas the South Pacific Geoscience Commission (SOPAC) has a membership of 19 Pacific Island Countries/ Territories. The South Pacific Games (SPG 2003) in Fiji included 22, encompassing the full width of the Pacific Ocean, with an administrative responsibility for one-seventh of the earth's surface (i.e. double that of the USA and almost triple the area of Australia).

References

Appraisal Institute. (1993). *The Dictionary of Real Estate Appraisal*. Edited by S. Shea-Joyce. 3 ed. Chicago: Appraisal Institute (U.S.).

Boydell, S. (2004). Alleviation of Poverty: the role of surveyors, land economists and related professions in the Pacific Islands. Paper read at *Commonwealth Association of Surveying and Land Economy (CASLE) Technical Conference for Built Environment Professions*: 'Alleviation of Poverty: The Role of Surveyors, Land Economists and Related Professions', at Danbury Park Conference Centre, Anglia Polytechnic University, Chelmsford, UK (21–24 April 2004).

Boydell, S., and Shah, K. (2003). An Inquiry into the Nature of Land Ownership in Fiji. Paper read at *International Association for the Study of Common Property (IASCP)*. Brisbane, Australia.

Boydell, S., and Small, G. (2003). The Emerging Need for Regional Property Solutions – A Pacific Perspective. Paper read at *Pacific Rim Real Estate Society (PRRES) Ninth Annual Conference*, 19–22 January, 2003. Brisbane, Australia.

Boydell, S., Small, G., Holzknecht, H., and Naidu, V. (2002). *Declaration and Resolutions of the FAO/USP/RICS Foundation South Pacific Land Tenure Conflict Symposium*. Suva: Fiji, 10–12 April 2002, Web based PDF available from www.usp.ac.fj/landmgmt/PDF/SPLTCDECLARATIONRESOLUTIONS.PDF

Bromley, D. (1991) *Environment and Economy: Property Rights and Public Policy*. Cambridge, MA: Basil Blackwell, Inc.

Crocombe, R. (1975). An Approach to the Analysis of Land Tenure Systems. In *Land Tenure in Oceania*, edited by H. P. Lundsgaarde. Honolulu: University of Hawaii Press.

CSIRO. (2003). *Reshaping Australians for Australia, Feature Article*. Commonwealth Scientific and Industrial Research Organization [cited 2003]. Available from www.csiro.au.

de Botton, A. (2004). *Status Anxiety*. London: Hamish Hamilton.

de Soto, H. (2000). *The Mystery of Capital: Why Capitalism Triumphs in the West and Fails Everywhere Else*. New York: Basic Books.

Demsetz, H. (1967). Toward a theory of property rights. *American Economic Review* (57), 347–359.

Farran, S., and Paterson, D.E. (2004). *South Pacific Property Law*. Sydney: Cavendish Publishing Limited.

Hann, C.M. (1998). Introduction: the embeddedness of property. In *Property Relations – Renewing the anthropological tradition*. edited by C. M. Hann. Cambridge. UK: Cambridge University Press.

Jones Lang Wootton. (1989). *The Estates Gazette Limited, and South Bank Polytechnic: The Glossary of Property Terms*. London: Estates Gazette.

Katz, R. (1993). *The Straight Path: A Story of Healing and Transformation in Fiji*. Reading, Massachusetts: Addison-Wesley.

Miles, G. (1999). *Pacific Islands Environment Outlook, Global Environmental Outlook (GEO) of UNEP*. Apia, Samoa: Copublication of SPREP, UNEP and EU.

Native Land Trust Board v Narawa [2004] FJSC7; CBV0007.02S. (May 21, 2004). In the Supreme Court, Fiji Islands, at Suva.

Payne, G. (1997). *Urban Land Tenure and Property Rights in Devloping Countries: A Review*. London: Intermediate Technology Publications/Overseas Development Administration (ODA).

Ravuvu, A. (1983). *Vaka i Taukei: The Fijian Way of Life*. Suva: Institute of Pacific Studies, University of the South Pacific.

Rigsby, B. (1998). 'A Survey of Property Theory and Tenure Types'. *Marine Tenure in Australia: Oceania Monograph* 48. N. Peterson and B. Rigsby. Sydney: University of Sydney pp22–46.

Roy, R. (2004). Spiritual Materialism. *Yoga and Health* (December 2004):12, 18.

Sheehan, J. and Small, G. (2002) 'Towards a definition of property rights', working paper, UTS Property Research Unit.

Siwatibau, S. (2002). *Welcome Address for the FAO/USP/RICS Foundation South Pacific Land Tenure Conflict Symposium*. Suva: Fiji, 10–12 April 2002, Web based PDF available from www.usp.ac.fj/landmgmt/WEBPAPERS/WELCOMEADDRESS.PDF

Smajgl, A., Vella, K., and Greiner, R. (2003). *Frameworks and models for analysis and design of institutional arrangements in Outback regions*. Digital Library of the Commons – International Association for the Study of Common Property [cited 2004]. Available from http://dlc.dlib.indiana.edu.

Small, G. (1997). A Comparative Analysis of Contemporary Native and Ancient Western Cultural Attitudes to Land. Paper read at *Pacific Rim Real Estate Society (PRRES) Annual Conference*, at Massey University, Palmerston North, New Zealand.

World Bank (2003) *Land Policies for Growth and Poverty Reduction*, ed. K. Deininger, Oxford University Press/World Bank, Washington, DC.

7

Indigenous Property Right to Water: Environmental Flows, Cultural Values and Tradeable Property Rights

Donna Craig

Background

Indigenous peoples have integral and unique relationships with the earth, including land, seas, resources and wildlife. They do not fragment or compartmentalize their rights and obligations relating to their ecological, spiritual, cultural, economic and social dimensions (Posey, 1999).

The spiritual and cultural connection that Aboriginal people have with the lands and waters has been part of their existence for thousands of years. This needs to be understood and recognized when decisions are made that affect those lands and waters. Aboriginal people have their own traditions, customs and laws relating to water and access to water that are not being recognized in modern Australian water management. This lack of legal recognition flows from a deeper lack of recognition and understanding of Indigenous spiritual values and cultures (Lingari Foundation, 2002).

To date where the rights of Indigenous people have received any acknowledgement at all, they have been included as merely another *stakeholder*. Aboriginal and Torres Strait Islander peoples have not received recognition of their distinctive rights, or of their distinctive relationship to the water resources of their country (Lingari Foundation, 2002).

This distinctive relationship is evident in the concern of many Aboriginal people about the fate of the water systems in Australia. Proposals to draw more water for irrigating agriculture or for growing cotton are of great concern to the Aboriginal communities. Aboriginal communities in the Kimberley region have expressed their concern about the effects of taking too much underground water. They fear that the underground rivers or streams will be irrevocably deprived of water, and that their water sources will as a consequence dry up or become salty (Yu, 2000). They tell stories about what has occurred in the past:

At one time they trialed cotton. Nobody knew about the cotton. We were just wondering what was wrong, what was happening here. Couldn't work out why everything was dying on us. And then somebody said, 'Oh. They're growing cotton over there. Trial One.' That's when we found out what was happening to the animals that were dying. (Yu, 2000, p.11)

These are the sorts of problems that can occur when the traditional laws and customs relating to water are not followed:

The importance of water in the area of the Daly River is highlighted by the Tjinimin myth that upon the death of the father-figure, humans were granted perennial water, life-giving waters, for it was in them that, somehow, he also placed the spirits of all children who have been born since. (Jackson, 2004, p.24)

The landscape/waterscape is a complex cultural network of significant places along the watercourses within the river system to which individuals and groups have spiritual connections and cultural responsibilities. The different groups are culturally connected through their participation in and responsibilities to water-related law and ceremonies (Jackson, 2004).

Water sources are generally considered spiritual places, and the laws and traditions that are linked with water sources reflect this. There are traditions among many Aboriginal communities of having to seek permission from those whose country you are in, by those who are not from the country to access water, as well as the custom of *baptizing* newcomers to land with water so that the country knows them. This practice is recounted in Jackson (2004) in relation to a Rainbow Dreaming Place on the Daly River:

… Rainbow there, Rainbow smell the sweat. That's where you get the rain. When stranger come … wash 'em on your head. Wash your sweat on his head so he don't get sick. Talk to that Rainbow when you take people who aren't from that country. If you don't do that you get a flood. A stranger might make that big rain. Spirits can hear the talk and smell the sweat. (Jackson, 2004, p.28)

Aboriginal accounts of traditional land and water management practices also imply that they do know how to care for water resources in a sustainable manner:

Every jila *[living waterhole] has its own songs, stories and skin group. A watersnake lives in the* jila, *he was human before he turned into the snake and went into water. Without the snake underneath the water will go away. Our old people know how to sing and talk to the snake. If you want rain or food you can sing to the snake and he'll bring it. If the* jila *is dry we know the proper way to dig them out and when we take the sand and clay out we*

> *know the right story to sing as we dig and how to do it properly.*
> (Yu, 2000, p.13)

Among many Aboriginal people there are mythological accounts of the consequences of poor water management, which highlight their awareness of the need to properly care for and manage water resources. The dreamtime stories and strong clan traditions handed down through the generations serve as parables about the consequences of unwise water use. Mark Casey, President of the Nauiyu Council, recounts one such story:

> *In the dreamtime, all the animals came together to have a corroboree. They asked sand frog to come along, but he said no. When all the other animals had left, sand frog said, 'I will do something to these animals.' So he went away and drank up all the water from the rivers, the creeks and the billabongs. The animals were having their corroboree and they got thirsty. They went looking for the water but could not find any. Bush bee flew around and found a billabong that had just been emptied. He saw, sitting on a big rock, sand frog. He flew back down and told all the other animals where sand frog was, so they all went over to see sand frog. They said 'Give us back our water: we are thirsty.' He said no and ignored them. So they got their weapons and threw them at him, hitting him to try to get him to release the water – but he would not. Brolga grabbed a spear and flew up high. He threw the spear, hitting sand frog in the guts. All the water came out, filling up the rivers, creeks and billabongs again. All the animals were happy. They drank and they continued their corroboree. Today, you will never see a sand frog in the dry season. He is buried deep in the sand, too ashamed to come out.* (Jackson, 2004, p.29)

However, it is important to note that Aboriginal laws and customs relating to water are *sui generis* to each clan or group. There may be many commonalities and overlaps, but each clan or group maintain their own laws and customs in relation to their land and waters, at particular sites or places that are of cultural and spiritual significance. Therefore, the contours of traditional laws and customs relating to any one place and people may be considered as personal and distinctive as a fingerprint. But the broad characteristics of the law relating to water sites described here are common throughout Australia. And since each individual community maintains its own customs and traditions – 'current scientific knowledge cannot be called upon to support one over another given the large uncertainties about various ecological interactions and the value-laden character of most contemporary water problems' (Jackson, 2004, p. 23).

The important connection between Indigenous traditional owners and their resources is becoming widely recognized and acknowledged and mechanisms are being put in place to protect that knowledge and enhance the rights of traditional owners. There are many sources of international and domestic law that support the right of Aboriginal peoples to have their customary relationships to water recognized and respected. These include International Human Rights law, particularly the emerging discourse of a human right to water; the Right to Self-Determination of peoples; Protection of Cultural Heritage and broader frameworks bound up with Adaptive Ecosystem Management and Ecologically Sustainable Development. The next section briefly discusses the implications of some of those laws.

Legislative Context and Developments

International human rights and human right to water

Within international human rights discourse there is a growing concern with the rights of Indigenous peoples to access and use traditional water resources as well as their traditional lands.

Paragraph 5 of Recommendation 23 of the Convention on the Elimination of All forms of Racial Discrimination (CERD), states that:

> *The Committee especially calls upon State parties to recognize and protect the rights of Indigenous peoples to own, develop, control and use their communal lands, territories and resources and, where they have been deprived of their lands and territories traditionally owned or otherwise inhabited or used without their free and informed consent, to take steps to return these lands and territories.*

The reference to *resources* in this context would include both land and water resources. In addition, Articles 25 and 26 of the Draft United Nations Declaration On the Rights Of Indigenous Peoples contain direct reference to water as a human right:

> *Article 25: Indigenous Peoples have the right to maintain and strengthen their distinctive spiritual and material relationship with the lands, territories, waters and coastal seas and other resources which they have traditionally owned or otherwise occupied or used, and to uphold their responsibilities to future generations in this regard.*

> *Article 26: Indigenous peoples have the right to own, develop, control and use the lands and territories, including the total environment of the lands, air, waters, coastal seas, sea-ice, flora and fauna and other resources which they have traditionally owned or otherwise occupied or used.*

Within the broader context of human rights, the right to water is emerging as a crucial element that inheres with other rights (Scanlon et al, 2003), such as the right to life (International Covenant on Civil and Political Rights, 1966) or the right to an adequate standard of living (Universal Declaration of Human Rights Article 25). Without access to a supply of clean water these rights could essentially be considered a misnomer. An effective right to water necessarily involves fulfilling both the procedural and substantive aspects of this right. The substantive aspect of this right includes ensuring that there is both an adequate quantity and quality of water. In regards to procedural rights it could include having: a right to information; a right to participate in decision-making; and a right to recourse for environmental harm suffered. When these procedural and substantive aspects are addressed through capacity building programmes, Aboriginal people could then have an effective right of equal access to water, which has often been lacking in the past.

Self-determination

The recognition of the rights of Aboriginal and Torres Strait Islander peoples to water should be consistent with, and carry forward, a broader platform for the just recognition of the rights of Australia's Indigenous peoples. An Aboriginal right to water is not simply one right being sought; it would be part of a broader framework. Aboriginal people seek to have more control of their destinies, to empower their communities, and to seek recognition of this empowerment in the broader context of national and international law and policy. An Aboriginal right to water is part of a broader discourse of a right to self-determination, which is recognized in Article 1 of the International Covenant on Cultural, Economic and Social Rights (ICESCR), which states:

> *1(1) All peoples have the right of self determination. By virtue of that right they freely determine their political status and freely pursue their economic, social and cultural development.*

> *1(2) All peoples may, for their own ends, freely dispose of their natural wealth and resources without prejudice to any obligations arising out of international economic cooperation, based upon the principle of mutual benefit and international law. In no case may a people be deprived of its own means of subsistence.*

Self-determination is also a feature of several of the international instruments that deal specifically with Indigenous rights. Among these are ILO Convention 169, particularly Articles 7, 13(1), 13(2) and 14 (3), and the Draft Declaration on the Rights of Indigenous Peoples under Articles 24, 25, 26 and 29. Participation and consultation regarding decisions that affect Indigenous peoples, and the resources they depend on, are highlighted in both of these agreements. However, there are also conflicting international instruments, in particular, the General Assembly resolution 1803 (XVII) 1962, which declares that a state has permanent sovereignty over its natural resources. However, Erica-Irene Daes, former Chairperson of the UN Working Group on Indigenous Populations, believes that the basic principle of permanent sovereignty over natural resources applies well to Indigenous peoples, one of the reasons being that the natural resources originally belonged to the Indigenous peoples concerned and were not freely and fairly given up (Daes, 2002a).

Indigenous peoples Kyoto water declaration

The relationship that Aboriginal people maintain with water is recognized in the Indigenous Declaration on Water, which was a result of the Third World Water Forum, held in Kyoto, March 2003. This Declaration recognizes the special relationship that Indigenous peoples have with water; the environmental threats to water, such as pollution and depletion; and recognizes the right of Indigenous peoples to make decisions at all levels regarding water. Importantly it recognizes that consultations include the conduct of the consultations under the communities' own systems and mechanisms and the provision of the means for Indigenous peoples to fully participate in such consultations (Indigenous Peoples Kyoto Water Declaration, 2003).

Heritage protection

Water sites are generally considered places of special cultural significance by Aboriginal people. There are several international conventions that have as their objective the conservation of cultural heritage. The most widely recognized is the Convention Concerning the Protection of the World Cultural and Natural Heritage (1972), which provides for the identification and protection of cultural and natural heritage that is of 'outstanding universal value'. The convention works through the United Nations Educational, Scientific and Cultural Organization (UNESCO), which compiles a list of areas of significant natural and/or cultural heritage. Examples of protected World Heritage sites areas that are culturally significant to Aboriginal people in Australia include Uluru and Kakadu.

Although the Convention can provide a mechanism for the protection of areas of water that are of significant cultural value, it is a slow and cumbersome process to get areas recognized and is still dependent on state action for protection of those areas (Craig and Shearing, 2004). In the Living Water Report, Yu (2000) indicates that for the traditional owners in the territory of the study all water sites are culturally significant, although they might not all be recognized in legislation as significant areas. Under the traditional law it is the cultural responsibility of the traditional owners to maintain the water sources.

One of the more recent international conventions, the Convention for the Safeguarding of the Intangible Cultural Heritage (2003), has been established to safeguard intangible cultural heritage (ICH), ensure respect for intangible heritage of communities, groups and individuals, raise awareness at the local, national and international levels of the importance of ICH and provide for international cooperation and assistance. This Convention protects the knowledge, practices, expressions and skills of Indigenous peoples, which includes ICH that may be related to water.

Ecologically sustainable development and the Millennium Development Goals

Sustainable development seeks to create a balance between social, environmental and economic concerns and to ensure that meeting the needs of the current generation does not negatively affect future generations. The Brundtland Report (WCED, 1987) has popularized the concept of sustainable development. Taken out of the context of the Report, such popularity is under-standable. It implies that economic growth can be sustained at present and increasing future levels, so long as we develop *better* ways of managing the environment. Thus the word *sustainability* is an ambiguous western cultural construct, which while originating in the sustenance of the yields of biological and physical resources for present patterns of economic growth, its fluidity as a concept has enabled its interpretation to be extended to the socio-economic realm. Hence, with such an extension the goal is no longer limited to sustain-ing the level of physical stock or physical production from an ecosystem over time, but some sustained increase in the level of societal and individual welfare. This broader context was generated by the WCED because of their concern to alleviate poverty, which is accelerating in developing countries, and requires a wider range of other economic, social and cultural changes to be incorporated into its precepts.

The WCED report (1987) has created a new awareness of the concerns of Aboriginal people, and created new avenues for them to assert their rights. The Rio Declaration (1992), Agenda 21 (1992), the World Summit on Sustainable Development: Plan of Implementation (2002), the UN Millennium Development Goals and the Millennium Project Report (2005) have been supporting comprehensive and specific poverty reduction strategies as one of the key pillars of achieving sustainable development. Several international environmental conventions are indicative of this movement.

Conservation conventions

The Convention on Wetlands of International Importance Especially as Waterfowl Habitat (1971) (Ramsar Convention) was one of the earlier interna-tional environmental conventions. The focus is on preserving wetlands that constitute a resource of great economic, cultural, scientific and recreational value, the loss of which would be irreparable. As well as being important habi-tats for flora and fauna they are critical in regulating water flows and water levels. As the cultural significance of wetlands is recognized in the preamble of the Convention, this could be argued by Indigenous people to promote the protection of wetlands that are culturally significant to them.

In more recent times, international environmental law has introduced a new path for the preservation and protection of Indigenous cultural values. This path is highlighted in the Convention on Biological Diversity Article 8(j) and is already discussed in Amankwah (Chapter 4) and Jeffery (Chapter 5).

Indigenous perspective

Indigenous communities throughout the world have learnt to prosper in all different types of environments by adapting to the conditions, and by learning how to manage the resources they found there. As the first inhabitants of the areas, Indigenous peoples can be seen to have special knowledge and insight into management of their surrounding environments, including management of waters, both onshore and offshore. This knowledge can be used to enhance management of waters in Australia. Indigenous communities should be seen as partners in the management of water resources that are vital to sustaining life.

The Karajarri (one of the Aboriginal tribes of Western Australia) characterize their environmental responsibilities as *palanapayana tukjana ngurra* – everybody looking after country properly (Yu, 2000). This essentially encompasses undertaking holistically the cultural, spiritual and environmental caring for the welfare of the country. The conception of having responsibilities towards the environment is found in most Aboriginal communities and, having this long experience with caring for their environment, their knowledge should be sought out for the benefit of better environmental management.

Aboriginal people have been excluded from planning and land use decisions, particularly relating to water. There is often little account taken of Aboriginal perspectives, and where Aboriginal people are consulted there is often no follow up. This historical legacy of negligible Aboriginal involvement in research and planning is likely to play a significant part in Aboriginal people's assessment of their capacity to influence contemporary decisions and negotiate as equals.

Participatory rights are essential for Aboriginal people when it comes to decision-making surrounding water issues, in light of their special connection and knowledge. Aboriginal people should be consulted in the management of natural resources, and that consultation should be meaningful, and should be followed up. Aboriginal people should be kept fully informed about developments that affect those resources. It is necessary for legal regimes and market mechanisms to institutionalize and incorporate public rights and the rights of Indigenous people. Participatory rights such as these are the foundation of the Convention on Access to Information, Public Participation in Decision-Making and Access to Justice in Environmental Matters (Aarhus Convention). This mainly European convention is further discussed in Jeffrey, Chapter 5.

Native Title and Recognition of Customary Law in Australia

The definition of native title is set out in section 223 of the Native Title Act (NTA) (Cth):

> (1) *The expression* native title *or* native title rights and interests *means the communal, group or individual rights and interests of Aboriginal peoples and Torres Strait Islanders in relation to land or waters, where:*
> a) *the rights and interests are possessed under the traditional laws acknowledged, and the traditional customs observed, by the Aboriginal peoples or Torres Strait Islanders; and*
> b) *the Aboriginal peoples or Torres Strait Islanders, by those laws and customs, have a connection with the land or waters; and*

> c) the rights and interests are recognized by the common law
>   of Australia.

Under the Native Title Act 1993 (Cth) a non-exclusive possessory right in
section 211 is recognized for native title rights to land and waters, which means
that there is no control over access to water resources or who has use of such
resources. In addition, if native title is recognized in *waters* and a determination is made for the exercise of those rights, section 212(1)(b) of the NTA
confirms the 'existing right of the Crown in that capacity to use, control and
regulate the flow of water'. Further, section 212(2) confirms the right of the
commonwealth, state or territory to allow public access and enjoyment of the
specified watercourses within its provisions.

Section 24HA of the Native Title Act also allows for the management and
regulation of water and airspace, so that future legislative acts by a state or the
Northern Territory government may repeal, or amend, the management and
regulation of: surface and subterranean waters (24HA(1)(a)); and living
aquatic resources. Under this section water is also said to include the granting
of access and taking of water.

In *Millirrpum v. Nabalco Pty Ltd*, Justice Blackburn said:

> *There is an unquestioned scheme of things in which the spirit ances-
> tors, the people of the clan, particular land, and everything that
> exists on and in it, are organic parts of one indissolvable whole*
> (1971, 17 FLR 14 at 167).

Therefore, the forms of intellectual and real property in the dominant legal
system, where rights and interests are compartmentalized and clearly defined
for a specific individual's exclusive possession and alienability, is distinct
from Aboriginal conceptions of rights and interests in *country*. Indigenous
relationships with land and waters are essentially a spiritual connection and
form a significant part of Indigenous cultural identity. This cultural identity
is a manifestation of spiritual connections, which unites families and communities and maintains the continuity of traditional societies through
ceremonies and initiation, teachings by community elders and religious rituals where ancestral beings of the dreamtime are worshipped and revered.
However, these rights and interests of Indigenous nations and communities
need to be considered when new forms of property and water trading
systems emerge. Failure to do this will further entrench historic and contemporary injustices and disadvantage (Native Title issues are also discussed in
Amankwah, Chapter 4).

In determining what native title rights and interests to water resources do
exist, in relation to those asserted by a claimant, the court attempts to understand the holistic view of country that is presented in evidence by Indigenous
peoples about relationships with land and waters. The intertwined and often
inseparable social, economic, spiritual, cultural and environmental sense of
being has been interpreted as a *bundle of rights*. Although such an approach
has been criticized on the basis that it doesn't adequately explain the right to

property, it is an approach favoured by the court in its attempted interpretation of Indigenous relationships with land and waters.

Those rights and interests that have a normative content and survive a *cultural translation* may be recognized in common law of Australia.

This process is said to be undertaken because:

> *Native title has its origin in the traditional laws acknowledged and the customs observed by the Indigenous people who possess the native title. Native title is neither an institution of the common law nor a form of common law tenure but it is recognized by the common law. There is, therefore, an intersection of traditional laws and customs with the common law.* (Mabo v Queensland *(No. 2)* *[1992] HCA 23* per Brennan J at 64).

The location of the intersection of these native title rights and interests and the conception of sovereignty is to be located by reference to the Native Title Act 1993 (Cth).

However, a further qualification to the recognition of native title rights is that those rights must be able to be described within common law tenets and they must not be inconsistent with the legal rights already created in others by the Crown in the same area.

In the case of *Yanner v Eaton*, the importance of the recognition of the spiritual as well as the secular aspects of native title was emphasized by the majority: 'And an important aspect of the socially constituted fact of native title rights and interests that is recognized by the common law is the spiritual, cultural and social connection with the land' (1999, 201 CLR 351 at 38).

In the case *Yarmirr v The Northern Territory Government* (Mary Yarmirr and Ors v The Northern Territory of Australia and Ors [1998] 771 FCA (6 July 1998) at 126 and 127), 'the Croker Island case', Justice Olney elaborated upon the claimed right to safeguard cultural knowledge – the right to receive, possess and safeguard the cultural and religious knowledge associated with the estate and the right and duty to pass it on to the younger generation. There was no discussion, however, about how effect might be given to a right of access to *protect* places or safeguard knowledge.

However, the majority of the High Court in *Western Australia v Ward* doubted that 'a right to maintain, protect and prevent the misuse of cultural knowledge is a right in relation to land of the kind that can be the subject of a determination of native title' (HCA 28 at 57–61). It refused to provide *sui generis* protection for *cultural knowledge* because the limits and boundaries of such subject matter have been ill-defined. In addition, Callinan, in his judgment in Ward, said:

> *the requirement 'in relation to land' although having a wide ambit in the NTA must be construed in context. It is in relation to land or waters and not knowledge about or reverence for it, no matter how culturally significant that knowledge or reverence might be.* (Ibid at 644)

Managing and Commodifying Water:
Environmental Flows and Cultural Values

With the deterioration of many natural watercourses, from human interference in the natural flows of water, has come the realization that these watercourses need a certain amount of water flow to maintain their health. This has become embodied in the concept of environmental flows. Environmental flows have been defined as:

> *the water regime provided within a river, wetland or coastal zone to maintain ecosystem and their benefits where there are competing waters uses and where flows are regulated.* (Dyson et al, 2003, p.3)

The needs of the ecosystem must be preserved to protect environmental flows. Allocation of water to the environment, sufficient to maintain its health, should take priority over any other consumptive uses of water.

Environmental flow setting can be best done within the context of wider assessment frameworks for river basin planning:

> *These frameworks are part of Integrated Water Resources Management and assess both the wider situation and river health objectives. They build on stakeholder participation to solve existing problems and include scenario-based evaluation of alternative flow regimes.* (Dyson et al, 2003, p. vi)

This concept of environmental flows is being increasingly implemented in various jurisdictions throughout the world. Examples in Australia include the Murray-Darling River area (which covers New South Wales, South Australia, Victoria and Queensland), and the Daly River in the Northern Territories, where allocation of water for environmental purposes is being given primary consideration in water allocation decisions. For instance, Queensland Water Act 2000 (section 47) requires the best scientific information available to be used in the assessment of the duration, frequency and timing of water flows necessary to support the natural environment. And in NSW, experts with appropriate qualifications are appointed to Water Advisory Councils, to investigate matters affecting the management of water sources throughout the state (Water Management Act 2000 (NSW) section 387).

Providing for an adequate environmental flow has in the past been seen as generally sufficient to meet the cultural needs of Aboriginal communities. 'In the Kimberley, environmental water requirements have served as a surrogate for protecting the cultural values' (Yu, 2000, p. 23). Indeed a healthy river or water system is essential to maintain the cultural values of Aboriginal communities. 'One of the principal findings of the project is that, from an Indigenous perspective, their health, and that of their communities, is linked to the health of their land and waters. Making sure that the environment is healthy and sustains the community is an inherent right. Land and waters must be healthy so that Indigenous peoples remain healthy. Land and waters are a living body, and water quality directly affects the Indigenous peoples' inherent rights' (Yu, 2000, p.72).

However, this requirement for an environmental flow should be kept distinct from the cultural values of the water. Although both the concepts of environmental and cultural flows may overlap in their content or definition, protecting cultural values will require consideration of different values, such as the care of particularly significant sites. Rather than being synonymous with environmental flows, water flows that are needed to protect cultural values should be seen as overlapping. With this recognition has come the notion of a *cultural flow* requirement. This has been discussed in various reports and the idea encompasses 'the provision of a water allocation to each Indigenous Nation for cultural purposes, will ensure that cultural obligations to the health of the Rivers can be better met, as well as cultural responsibilities to the country of neighbouring Indigenous Nations' (Yu, 2000, p.14).

In allocating water for environmental flows, different factors are taken into account. Although the division of water resources must be made through consultation with the community and taking into account many different factors, such as economic, aesthetic and recreational factors, the process to determine how much water the environment needs will be one that is heavily influenced by scientific factors. Protection of particular sites of significance to Aboriginal people will not necessarily factor into the calculation of environmental flows. For example:

> in Central Arnhem Land, amongst Aboriginal clans generally there is a wide spread belief that a clan has a sacred spring or waterhole that is the most important spiritual site for that clan. People believe that at conception the spirit enters women from the sacred clan billabong. After death, if the proper ceremonies take place, that spirit returns to the billabong. (Jackson, 2004, p.64)

Ensuring that particularly significant springs or waterholes are protected and receive adequate water to keep them active may not necessarily be a factor in allocating water to environmental flows. In determining the amounts necessary for environmental flow, the scale is likely to be much larger, taking into account whole catchments or water basins, and in the process, smaller, but nonetheless significant, waterholes may be overlooked.

A Malak Malak story about the Dreamtime origins of the Daly River told recently reveals the way in which flowing water is considered to provide the basis for life and dispense collective good and well-being (Jackson, 2004). While altering the course of flowing water may have little significance in environmental terms, it can have a tremendous impact culturally if that flow alters the dispensation of collective good and well-being:

> Cultural flows should be an essential component of river management. A cultural flow *can be set and monitored as sufficient flow in a suitable pattern to ensure the maintenance of Aboriginal cultural practices and connections with the rivers. In circumstances*

> *where rights to water are being turned into a commodity and schemes for tradable water rights being expanded, it becomes increasingly important to ensure that Aboriginal cultural flows are secured in legislation as a non-tradable interest. Aboriginal people do not have the means to purchase those water flows on the open market. Indeed, the entire purpose of those markets is to direct the resource in a utilitarian manner rather than in a way that accommodates Aboriginal perspectives on that resource.* (Behrendt and Thompson, 2003)

Aboriginal communities should have full decision-making power over any *cultural flow* allocated to them. It remains with the community to decide how best to manage those rights, what is the best use. Restrictions on the use of the resource that impact upon that decision-making power should not be permitted.

Determining how much water should be allocated to cultural flows is a difficult problem. Because cultural values are difficult or impossible to capture in traditional utilitarian calculus or market transactions should not mean they should be ignored, or receive less attention. Ultimately these decisions must be made with the full participation of all stakeholders, and it is imperative that Aboriginal communities are part of the process.

Tradeable Water Rights in Australia

Indigenous concepts of *property* appear to generate insecurity in the dominant society because of their potential breadth and lack of *certainty* (usually because they are defined through applicable customary law). However, there is much more fluidity, flexibility and change in the concept of property, evolving in the Australian legal system, than is commonly understood:

> *Property does not refer to a thing; it is a description of a legal relationship with a thing. It refers to a degree of power that is recognized in law as power permissibly exercised over a thing. The concept of* property *may be elusive. Usually it is treated as a* bundle of rights. *But even this may have limits as an analytical tool or accurate description, and ... 'the ultimate fact about property is that it does not exist it is an illusion'... Much of our false thinking about property stems from the residual perception that* property *is itself a thing or resource rather than a legally endorsed concentration of power over things and resources.* (Yanner v Eaton (1999) 105 LGERA 71)

The movement towards tradeable water rights in Australia could be seen as an opportunity for Aboriginal peoples to gain greater recognition of their rights, as this new form of property develops. It is instructive to look at how the movement to tradeable property rights has impacted on Indigenous people in other jurisdictions. One particularly well-known example is the Treaty of Waitangi

Fisheries Settlement (23 September 1992) with the Maori people of New Zealand. This settlement is further discussed in the next section.

The concerns expressed by the Indigenous nations of the lower Murray Darling River Basin (MLDRIN) over the privatization of water rights may be indicative of more widely held fears. These concerns were stated in the NSW Parliament during discussion over the proposed amendments to the Water Management Act (NSW) 2000 (Cohen, 2004). The concerns expressed were the:

- lack of negotiation and informed consent with the nations;
- repercussions of future Act established through the granting of perpetual water licences on native title claims in NSW and claims to water;
- omission in the legislation of the inherent rights of the Nations to water;
- granting of licences to Aboriginal interested parties after the granting of perpetual licences is offensive;
- lack of time for response from the nations; and
- questionable adherence and commitments to the MoU signed between MLDRIN and DIPNR (NSW Dept. of Environment and Natural resources).

Also expressed to Parliament during the reading of the bill was that the NSW Aboriginal Land Council and NSW Native Title Services had created seven steps towards water equity for the Aboriginal people of NSW, that could assist in securing more favourable outcomes for Aboriginal people in relation to water rights (Cohen, 2004):

- a commitment from the government to enter into Indigenous Land Use Agreements (ILUAs) before perpetual water licences are granted;
- protection for environmental flows;
- a commitment from the government not to extend the term of a Water Sharing Plan unless Aboriginal rights and interests have been adequately addressed, with an audit of the Water Sharing Plans to assess the adequacy of each plan;
- standards and targets should be implemented that reflect the obligations to Aboriginal interests under various pieces of legislation;
- a broad basis for Aboriginal cultural and economic access licences and a commitment that these will not just be tokenistic;
- an Aboriginal Water Trust to commence operation as a matter of urgency and to be permanent; and
- increased allocations to this Aboriginal Water Trust with a fixed and stable source of funds, for example, through the allocation of stamp duty received from the sale of water licences, and Commonwealth contributions.

The rights and concerns of Indigenous nations and communities need to be considered when new forms of property and water trading evolve. Failure to do this will further entrench historical and contemporary injustice and disadvantage regardless of the exact legal position of Indigenous nations. However, the legal issues may be crucial as market mechanisms rely heavily on *certainty* in property rights. Potentially unextinguished native title and failure to observe standards relating to human rights, environmental law and heritage law raise serious concerns about the infatuation with market *solutions* and fundamental ethical and political concerns for all sectors of society.

New Zealand Fisheries and Maori Rights: A Comparative Experience with Market Mechanisms

The 1840 Treaty of Waitangi, the Maori treaty with the British, recognized Maori rights over their resources, including their fisheries. Article 2 of the Treaty guarantees to the Maori 'the full, exclusive and undisturbed possession of their ... fisheries ... for so long as it is their wish and desire to retain the same in their possession' according to the English version. However, the rights said to be guaranteed in the Treaty have not in the past carried much weight. Early claims by the Maori were rejected by the courts. For example *Wi Parata v Bishop of Wellington* held that any claim Maori may have to rights that were in any way associated with the Treaty were moral alone, binding only upon the honour of the Crown (Robinson, 1993). And in *Waipapakura v Hempton*, the court interpreted section 77(2) of the Fisheries Act 1908, which stated that nothing in that Act affected any Maori fishing rights, as meaning any rights conferred by statute. Despite these early legal set backs, Maori have continued to claim their right to the fisheries under the Treaty, and have had more success in recent claims.

In *Te Weehi v Regional Fisheries Officer* ([1986] 1 NZLR 680) was the turning point for the recognition of Maori fishing rights. The court found that Te Weehi, who had been charged with violating a regulation of the Fisheries Act 1983, had been exercising a customary fishing right under s88(2) of the Fisheries Act, which was essentially the same as section 77(2) of the 1908 Act, which stated that nothing in the Act affected any Maori fishing right. The court found that 'any Maori fishing rights' included rights that Maori had retained to their fisheries in accordance with the doctrine of Aboriginal title (McHugh, 1991). Following the success of this claim, there was a barrage of claims by Maori.

Also around the time of the Te Weehi case the government was considering a change to fisheries management. During the 1960s the government provided numerous subsidies and loans to the fisheries industry, and removed some of the rigid licensing scheme, which led to a rapid expansion in commercial fisheries. However, few Maori were able to benefit, having little collateral for loans, and therefore were further squeezed out of the industry. Also in the early 1980s fishing licences were not granted to those who did not earn at least 80 per cent of their income from fishing, which prevented even more Maori from participating (Guth, 2001–2002).

The rapid growth of the fisheries resulted in growing conservation concerns. In order to address these conservation concerns and to bring the fishing industry to a sustainable level the government enacted the Fisheries

Amendment Act 1986 that privatized the fisheries by creating a Quota Management System (QMS), and allocated individual transferable fishing quotas. These rights were allocated to existing fishers largely in accordance with their catch history (Waetford, 1993), which of course severely limited Maori participation in the new fishing scheme. Maori were not consulted in this fisheries revolution. The Maori also perceived what they considered to be their treaty rights being quantified, labelled, divided and parcelled out to the highest bidder, who, for the most part, were not Maori. Following the introduction of the Fisheries Amendment Act there was a number of legal claims and complaints to the Waitangi Tribunal directed at halting the privatization of fisheries.

In *Ngai Tahu Maori Trust Board v Attorney General* (1987, 1 NZLR 641), the High Court granted an interim declaration against the ministry allocating any more fishing quotas. The Court relied on the traditional rights of the Maori, as protected by s88 (2) of the Fisheries Act. The Court further found that 'before 1840 Maori ... fisheries had a commercial element and were not purely recreational or ceremonial or merely for the sustenance of the local dwellers' (Ibid p.6) Therefore, not allowing Maori to fish commercially without obtaining a quota was an infringement of Maori rights.

As well as granting the injunction, the High Court ruling established a joint working group of Crown and Maori to determine how best to settle the claim. The Maori negotiators were told to settle for no less than 50 per cent of the fisheries because although the Treaty already guaranteed them 100 per cent, in the spirit of fairness they were willing to share. However, no agreement was reached in the first round of negotiations, and an interim agreement granted ten per cent of the total allowable catch to the Maori, as well as compensation of NZ$10 million. To manage the quota for the Maori, the settlement also created the Maori Fisheries Commission.

When New Zealand's largest fishing company, Sealord Products, was put up for sale, the government and the Maori saw an opportunity. The government would arrange for the Maori to purchase a half share of Sealord, which would substantially increase their share in the fisheries. A Memorandum of Understanding was struck and sent around to seek Maori approval. This Memorandum was then incorporated into the final Deed of Settlement. Although there was hardly majority support for the agreement, the Crown concluded there was a mandate from the Maori to formalize the Memorandum.

The settlement, in exchange for discharging and extinguishing all commercial fishing rights of the Maori, as well as non-commercial rights and interests in fisheries, gave the Maori a half share of Sealord Products, as well as 20 per cent of any quota added for new fish species. The extinguishment of Maori fishing rights was of great concern for many Maori, who did not wish to give up their rights in exchange for a share in the commercial fisheries. Therefore opposition to the Deed was almost immediate. Less than a week after the Deed was signed several Maori groups sought an injunction to prevent the settlement, which ultimately failed. However, the Court found that the Deed did not bind non-signatories, and that the Deed was a contract of a political kind.

Although the Deed may not have been binding, it was quickly enacted by the government into legislation with the passage of the Treaty of Waitangi (Fisheries Claims) Settlement Act.

Although the Fisheries settlement occurred in 1992, it has taken over ten years to reach an agreement on the distribution of the proceeds to all the Maori, and the settlement of the distribution remains controversial (Guth, 2001–2002).

Whether the fisheries settlement is ultimately beneficial for the Maori or not, the Treaty of Waitangi recognized that the Maori had an unextinguished claim to the fisheries, which has been possible without the recognition by the courts. With the recognition of this right, the court was willing to grant an injunction to stop the privatization of the fisheries, which forced the government to negotiate. The government was eager to reach an agreement in order to allow New Zealand to get back into the fisheries market. In his speech introducing the Settlement Bill, then Minister of Fisheries Doug Kidd stated:

> *If the Government wanted to move further to develop our vital fishing industry it had to get the matter out of the courts, and to do that it had to resolve the Maori fishing claims. The way will now be clear to introduce sustainable management across all our fisheries, which will assure the future of those fisheries and result in export earning that will, over time, far outweigh the cost of these claims.* (Kidd, 1992)

With the recognition by the High Court in Australia that Aboriginal rights in land and water exist, where they have not been extinguished (*Mabo v Queensland* (NO.2) (1992) 175 CLR 1), Aboriginal people can try and protect this interest in water if the government seeks to privatize the resource.

Future Directions: A *Sui Generis* Regime for Water Trading?

The term *sui generis* denotes uniqueness or *one of a kind*. This description is used when the existing legislation cannot handle the required changes needed to achieve an efficient management of a resource. Within environmental law, this description has been attached to many legal situations with some degree of success.

Sui generis systems can be effective if they are conceived to be relevant in time, specific to the subject matter to be protected and adaptable to the socio-economic environment in which they are to be implemented. A *sui generis* system needs to give legal recognition to the river ecosystem, which is distinct from those rights conferred under water allocations or extraction licences, designed under the static and unnatural characteristics of the established property rights regime. This potential right should be based on the specific needs of ecosystems, that is, one that recognizes its dynamic behaviour. The right will not represent an amount of water, but a continuous movement of water. The result is the recognition of a right that is associated with the health of a river provided by its own river flow.

A hybrid approach combining the use of regulatory approaches to meeting the minimum levels of water needed for ecosystem health and addressing basic human and Indigenous rights could be suggested. Water trading may operate for flows above the levels required for these purposes with an allocation of a share of the new property rights to Indigenous peoples. The environmental flows will dictate the two areas for operation of the regime.

This unique regime will set the rules over two key areas. The first of these two areas will be a free stock exchange market based on the upper level of flows (determined as environmental flows) and the maximum possible level of transactions according to the free forces of the market. A percentage of the water from this area will be assigned to cover the needs of Indigenous peoples, farmers and landowners. The remaining percentage will be for the purposes of market exchange activity.

The free market should not govern the second area, essential for ecosystem health and Indigenous rights. This area is the water that represents the level between the environmental flows and the seasonal drought of the river. Therefore, the regime would be divided in two parts: one on the free market, and the other on conservation. The borderline between them will be the environmental flows of the river. The proposed regime recognizes a free market within the safe boundaries for the ecosystem. The regime would be a hybrid because of the mixture of two different policies to control and manage natural resources.

Conclusion

The necessary steps to be taken towards the recognition that Indigenous rights to the access and use of water are human rights begin with the recognition that:

> *Indigenous peoples have the right to determine and develop priorities and strategies for the development or use of their lands, territories and other resources, including the right to require that States obtain their free and informed consent prior to the approval of any project affecting their lands, territories and other resources, particularly in connection with the development, utilization or exploitation of mineral, water or other resources. Pursuant to agreement with the Indigenous peoples concerned, just and fair compensation shall be provided for any such activities and measures taken to mitigate adverse environmental, economic, social, cultural or spiritual impact.* (Daes, 2002b, item 5(b))

This necessarily involves a much greater level of participation and empowerment of Indigenous peoples, cross-cultural research, education and policy and institutional change in the area of water planning, allocation and management. Indigenous practices and values do not separate land and water and this is very consistent with modern approaches to ecosystem management. Similarly the need for ecological heath of rivers overlaps with the need for *cultural flows*.

These aspects of Indigenous rights to water, for basic needs and cultural purposes, can only be reflected in Australian water resource issues by allowing Indigenous voices and values to be expressed directly by them and for new approaches to be developed that respect customary law and related institutions of Indigenous governance. This chapter has argued for a *rights-based approach*, supported by international human rights and environmental law, to ensure wider recognition of Indigenous rights to water.

The current emphasis in national water policy, laws and administration on *efficiency* undervalues often excludes the Indigenous *property* such as native title. This has been reinforced by the models and approaches to market mechanisms, such as water trading. This chapter has been arguing that Indigenous rights and disadvantage need to be specifically addressed in the development of market mechanisms to avoid further entrenching injustice and disadvantage. Australian governments and *experts* are rushing towards the adoption of these approaches with an inadequate appreciation of the implications for equity, social justice and Indigenous rights. In the end, many questions remain unanswered:

- How will the new property rights affect existing property rights and interests in water?
- Who will be able to afford the new commodified rights to water?
- From what perspectives and values will *efficiency* in water allocation and transactions be judged?
- What values and uses of water should be *entitlements* and not left to the market?

Indigenous relationships to land and water are inextricable. However, they are being bargained away by other more powerful sectors in our society.

Acknowledgements

Research assistance was provided for this chapter by Nik Hughes, Volunteer, Centre for Environmental Law, Macquarie University and Meredith Rose, Intensive Program in Aboriginal Resources and Governments, Osgoode Hall Law School, York University, Canada. The views expressed are my own.

References

Behrendt, J. and Thompson, P. (2003). *The Recognition and Protection of Aboriginal Interests in NSW Rivers*. OCP 1008, Healthy Rivers Commission of NSW.
Cohen, I. (2004). *Water Management Amendment Bill*. Second Reading Speech. June 23, 2004. NSW Legislative Council Hansard. www.parliament.nsw.gov.au.
Craig, D. and Shearing, S. (2004). *Best Practice Models and Approaches for Indigenous Engagement in the Murray Darling Basin*. Research Report Prepared for Murray Darling Basin Commission for the Development of the Indigenous Action Network. Macquarie Centre for Environmental Law.

Daes E.-I., A. (2002a). *Prevention of Discrimination And Protection Of Indigenous Peoples*. United Nations Economic and Social Council. Sub-Commission On The Promotion and Protection Of Human Rights: Fifty-forth session, E/CN.4/Sub.

Daes E.-I., A. (2002b). Special Rapporteur, Article 30: Commission On Human Rights Sub-Commission on the Promotion and Protection of Human Rights Fifty-fifth session. Item 5(b) of the provisional agenda: *Prevention Of Discrimination Prevention And Protection Of Indigenous Peoples' Permanent Sovereignty Over Natural Resources*. Preliminary report. Submitted in accordance with Sub-Commission resolution.

Dyson, M., Bergkamp, G. and Scanlon, J. (2003). *Flow: The Essentials of Environmental Flows*. Gland and Cambridge: IUCN, The World Conservation Union.

Guth, H. K. (2001–2002). Dividing the Catch: Natural Resource Reparations to Indigenous Peoples – Examining the Maori Fisheries Settlement. *U. Haw. L. Rev.*, 24 (179), 191.

Indigenous Peoples Kyoto Water Declaration (2003): www.indigenouswater.org/IndigenousDeclarationonWater.html

Jackson, S. (2004). *Preliminary Report on Aboriginal Perspectives on Land-Use and Water Management in the Daly River Region, Northern Territory*. A report by CSIRO for the Northern Land Council.

Kidd, D. (1992). *Speech Introducing the Treaty of Waitangi* (Fisheries Claims). Settlement Bill (Dec. 3, 1992), in Guth, ibid at 204, fn 165.

Lingari Foundation, (2002). *Indigenous Rights to Water Report: Lingiari Report to ATSIC*. Canberra, ATSIC.

McHugh, P. (1991). Maori Magna Carta: New Zealand Law and the Treaty of Waitangi. Oxford University Press. In Nettheim, G., Meyers, G. D. and Craig, D. *Indigenous Peoples and Governance Structures*. Canberra: Aboriginal Studies Press.

Posey, D.A. (1999). *Introduction: Culture and Nature – The Inextricable Link*. In UNEP. Cultural and Spiritual Values of Biodiversity. London.

Robinson, M. (1993). The Sealord Fishing Settlement: An International Perspective. *Auck U. L. Rev.*, 7 (402), 559.

Scanlon, J., Cassar, A. and Nemes, N. (2003). Water As A Human Right. Paper prepared for *Water as the Web of life, 7th International Conference on Environmental Law*. Sao Paulo, Brazil: Law for a Green Planet and IUCN Environmental Law Programme.

Waetford, A. M. (1993). Treaty of Waitangi (Fisheries Claims) Settlement Act 1992. *Auck U. L. Rev.*, 7 (402), 402.

World Commission on Environment and Development, WCED, (1987). *Our Common Future*. Oxford: Oxford University Press.

Yu, S. (2000). *Ngapa Kunangku: Living Water, Report on the Aboriginal Cultural Values of Groundwater in the La Grange Sub-Basin*, 2nd edition. Prepared by the Centre for Anthropological Research University of Western Australia, for the Water and Rivers Commission of Western Australia.

8

Commercial Forestry: An Economic Development Opportunity Consistent with the Property Rights of Wik People to Natural Resources

Tyron J. Venn

Introduction

Relative to other Australians, Wik, Wik-Way and Kugu people (referred to hereafter for anthropological convenience as Wik people) living in Aurukun Shire on the west coast of Cape York Peninsula (CYP) are socio-economically disadvantaged. They are largely outside the market economy and are financially dependent on government welfare, including the work-for-welfare Community Development Employment Program (CDEP). Nevertheless, elders aspire for their people to be economically independent and self-reliant (Venn, 2004a). While opinion varies about how to promote economic development in remote Indigenous communities, there is an emerging consensus among economists (e.g. Duncan, 2003; Altman, 2004) and Indigenous leaders (e.g. Pearson, 2000; Ah Mat, 2003) that economic development is urgent and necessary to improve the welfare of inhabitants and for the survival of Australian Indigenous cultures.

Wik people are poor in terms of financial and (western) human capital. However, the High Court judgement in *Wik Peoples v State of Queensland and Others* 1996, the granting in 2000 and 2004 of native title over a portion of the Wik land claim, and legislated future changes of land tenure under the Queensland Aboriginal Land Act 1991, indicate that Wik people may become relatively rich in natural capital. In the late 1990s, Balkanu Cape York Development Corporation (Balkanu) representatives of Wik people identified commercial utilization of the Darwin stringybark (*Eucalyptus tetrodonta*) native forest timber resource on customary land as one potential engine with which to drive the elders' vision of economic independence. In 2000, the author was invited by Balkanu and the Australian Centre for International Agricultural Research (ACIAR) to investigate the potential for a forestry industry to generate employment and income for Wik people as a PhD project. That research indicated the potential commercial viability of a Wik timber industry (Venn, 2004a).

Wik forestry opportunities will be shaped by the incidence of property rights to timber, which are dependent upon the legal interpretation of numerous pieces of Queensland and Federal Government legislation, past and pending native title court rulings, and continuing negotiations between representatives of Wik people and the Queensland Government. There is no practical or legal precedent for commercial timber harvesting on Indigenous land tenure in Queensland and it became apparent that considerable uncertainty surrounded Wik rights to timber, because the combined effect of various court cases and pieces of Federal and Queensland Government legislation had never been contemplated. Furthermore, recent High Court judgements (e.g. *Commonwealth v Yarmirr* 2001 and *Western Australia v Ward* 2002) have compounded the obstacles to development faced by native title holders by reflecting a *frozen in time* approach to Indigenous laws and customs.

Economists of the private property rights tradition (e.g. Coase, 1960) are of the view that alienable and secure individualized land tenure is desirable, even essential, for wealth creation, economic efficiency and ecological sustainability. The 'Tragedy of the Commons' model popularized by Hardin (1968) failed to distinguish between open-access resources, for which his model is valid, and communally managed resources, including the grazing commons in his illustrative example. Economists who have followed Hardin have also typically assumed that communally managed resources can be modelled as open access. Therefore, it is not surprising that some economists and Indigenous leaders have argued that the collective and inalienable nature of Australian native title property rights to land present an obstacle to the development of Indigenous communities (Williams, 1993; Warby, 1997; Karvelas, 2004, 2005; Hughes and Warin, 2005). However, there are theoretical and empirical alternatives to the Hardin model. For example, Ostrom (1990) reported many examples of self-governed commons where institutional arrangements have been defined, modified, monitored and sustained by the users, and management outcomes have been sound. Dahlman (1980) discussed the specific case of grazing commons and concluded that they were not subject to open access.

This chapter examines the property rights of Wik people to native forest timber and assesses whether a forestry-based economic development strategy is consistent with inalienable and communal native title to land. The following section describes the study area, timber resources and the forestry objectives of Wik people. Next, rights to natural resources conferred by native title are discussed and Wik rights to timber are outlined. A discussion of the compatibility of Wik native title rights with forestry-based economic development follows.

Study Area, Timber Resources and Wik Forestry Objectives

Wik people have an historical and spiritual connection with land along the west coast of CYP between Napranum and Pormpuraaw and east to the Great

Dividing Range (Dale, 1993). Encroaching settlers demanded greater control of the *wild tribes* on CYP, which led to the establishment in 1904 of Aurukun Mission to 'settle' Wik people (Anderson, 1981). Wik people were encouraged and sometimes forced to settle in the village (Balkanu, 1999) and by the 1970s the last of the Wik had left the *bush* on a permanent basis (von Sturmer, personal communication, cited in Dale, 1993). Today, Aurukun town is home for about 900 Wik people, accounting for 88 per cent of the town's population (ABS, 2002). The town's Indigenous population is not a cohesive group of people, but a complex of 23 allied and competing clans with variable status, power and authority (Dale, 1993). Inter-clan and inter-racial cultural differences have periodically led to social disorder (Anderson, 1981; Leveridge and Lea, 1993; Voss, 2000).

Balkanu defined an 841,500ha study area for this research (approximately 30 per cent of the Wik native title claim) including Aurukun Shire and part of Mining Lease 7024 in Cook Shire adjacent to the north-west boundary of Aurukun Shire. This area is highlighted in Figure 8.1 and is hereafter referred to interchangeably as the *Aurukun area* or *study area*. In 2004, the study area consisted of land with four distinct combinations of land tenure and title, namely (author's estimates, based on data supplied by the Queensland Department of Natural Resources and Mines, 2000):

1   Aurukun Shire lease land within the Wik Part A native title determination area (503,000ha);
2   Aurukun Shire lease land in the Wik Part B native title determination area with no other titles or interests (69,900ha);
3   Aurukun Shire lease land in the Wik Part B native title determination area, which was formerly covered by Mining Lease 7032 (165,200ha); and
4   Unallocated State-owned land in Cook Shire covered by Mining Lease 7024 (103,400ha).

The study area is topographically level to gently undulating and dominated by two major vegetation groupings, namely Darwin stringybark forests and wetlands, with the former covering approximately 70 per cent of the Aurukun area. The high level of interest of Wik people and Balkanu in native forest timber harvesting is partly due to the fact that 230,000ha of commercially valuable Darwin stringybark forests in the Aurukun area grow on deep red kandosols that contain valuable bauxite deposits situated on mining leases (Venn, 2004a). No mining operations have commenced in the Aurukun area.

Following consistent failure of the holders of Mining Lease 7032 to meet obligations stipulated within the lease agreement, laws cancelling that lease were passed through the Queensland Parliament in May 2004. The Beattie Queensland Labor Government has been publicizing its intention to call for expressions of international interest in the forfeited bauxite resource and, while the Government is committed to a consultation process with customary Wik landholders about a new mining agreement, it has stipulated that Wik people will not have the right to veto the project (Hodge, 2003). Bauxite mining by Comalco Pty. Ltd. in Darwin stringybark forest on Mining Lease

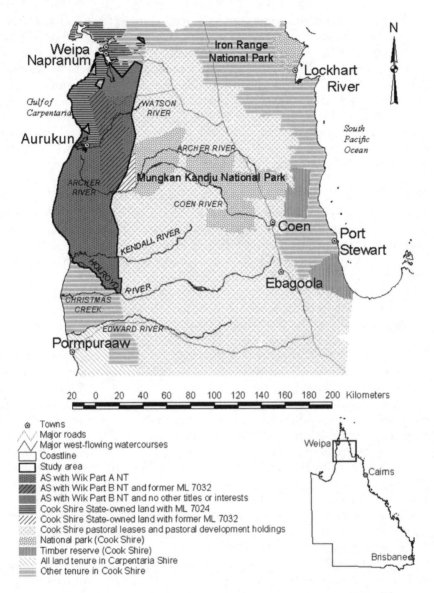

Figure 8.1 The study area and surrounding land tenure on central CYP

Notes: AS is Aurukun Shire Special Lease land; NT is native title; and ML is mining lease.

7024 near Weipa is proceeding at a rate of up to 1000ha per annum (Annandale, 2004). Currently, Comalco prepares land for open-cut bauxite mining by clearing vegetation with bulldozers and chains, windrowing woody debris and then burning, which represents an enormous waste of a valuable timber resource.

Darwin stringybark forests contain several commercially valuable timber species, particularly *Eucalyptus tetrodonta* (Darwin stringybark), *Corymbia nesophila* (Melville Island bloodwood) and *Erythrophleum chlorostachys* (Cooktown ironwood). A timber inventory undertaken in the study area found that, while the total standing volume of millable and harvestable timber is large at approximately 2,300,000m³ to 3,700,000m³ (depending on merchantability specifications), this is distributed over 400,000ha of forest where standing volumes are typically less than 7m³/ha to 10m³/ha (Venn, 2004a). Scarce growth data for timber species in these forests suggest the trees are slow growing and have led Department of Primary Industries (DPI) Forestry personnel to recommend a 100-year rotation for selective logging operations (Crevatin, 2000). Much of the timber resource on Wik land is remote from roads and over half of the standing volume in the study area is located south of the Watson River. Processing of timber harvested south of the Watson River in Aurukun town would require hauling over relatively long road distances to utilize existing river fords, transporting logs by river barge or bridge construction over *wild* rivers that flood annually.

Freshwater and estuarine wetlands surround and extend south of Aurukun town along the coast to the Edward River. These have been identified by conservation groups, including the Wildlife Preservation Society of Queensland, as areas that may prove to be equivalent in biological diversity to Kakadu National Park (Smyth, 1993). Throughout CYP, including the study area, most soil types are deficient in macro- and micro-nutrients, are weakly structured and are erosion prone following clearing of native vegetation, which limits the land's suitability for intensive agriculture (CYRAG, 1997). Carrying capacities for open-range grazing of cattle on native grasses and other native vegetation in the study area average between 21ha and 56ha per beast (CYRAG, 1997).

According to Sutton (1988, cited in Martin, 1993), for Wik people *there is no wilderness*. Darwin stringybark forests have been managed with regular burning to provide many valuable economic and cultural goods and services that are important to sustain their people and culture, including native (and in recent history, exotic) plant and animal foods; customary tools, arts and crafts; classrooms for passing on Indigenous knowledge to the children; settings for important Dreamtime stories; habitat for clan totem beings; and venues for ceremonies. Western natural resource extraction practices that can be modified to be culturally appropriate, such as selective logging, are considered by Wik people to be consistent with their way of life, land management objectives, and conservation ethic.

Wik people have multiple objectives for a timber industry operating on customary land (Venn, 2004a, 2004b). Employment generation, not profit maximization, is the highest priority forestry objective, particularly generation of on-country (outside of town) employment to encourage population decentralization, reduce social problems in Aurukun town and facilitate better connection of young people with country. As the Wik envisage ecotourism becoming a major economic activity in the future, another non-pecuniary objective is to limit logging in forests outside of mining leases, especially within the catchments of wetlands.

Wik Rights to Timber in the Aurukun Area

There is continuing debate about whether *terra nullius* – the fiction that the land was unoccupied at the time of European settlement – was ever part of law relied on to justify settlement of Australia (Connor, 2004; Pearson, 2004). Nevertheless, settlement of Australia proceeded as if the land was *terra nullius* and, post-1788, Wik people had no enforceable property rights to any land or natural resources until limited rights were conferred with the establishment of the Aurukun Mission. It was not until the High Court's judgement in *Mabo v State of Queensland* 1992 that Indigenous people were legally recognized as the first inhabitants of Australia and native title was introduced to Australian law. The Federal Native Title Act 1993 addressed many of the fundamental unde-cided issues of the Mabo case and established a process by which Indigenous Australians could obtain native title. A key element of the Act is that while native title holders and claimants may surrender their native title to govern-ment under an agreement with the Federal or a state or territory government, native title cannot be transferred to someone outside the clan, group or community. In Section 223(1) of the Native Title Act 1993, native title or native title rights and interests are defined as:

> The communal, group or individual rights and interests of the Aboriginal peoples or Torres Strait Islanders in relation to land or waters, where:
> a.   the rights and interests are possessed under the traditional laws acknowledged, and the traditional customs observed, by the Aboriginal peoples or Torres Strait Islanders; and
> b.   the Aboriginal peoples or Torres Strait Islanders, by those laws and customs, have a connection with the land and waters; and
> c.   the rights and interests are recognized by the common law of Australia.

In another landmark High Court ruling that became known as the Wik case,[1] the Court ruled that the granting of pastoral leases over the traditional land of Wik people (living in Aurukun town) did not necessarily extinguish all native title rights. The majority of judges found that native title rights can co-exist with the rights of a lessee under pastoral leasing legislation, so long as those rights are not inconsistent with the rights of the pastoralist. This was a politi-cally explosive outcome and the Howard Federal Coalition Government attempted to reduce uncertainty surrounding the judgement with the Native Title Amendment Act 1998, which many commentators perceived as reducing native title rights in favour of miners and pastoralists.

Together the Mabo and Wik Cases and the Native Title Act 1993 and Native Title Amendment Act 1998 established a framework for the application for native title, determining the exclusive existence or co-existence of native title on particular land tenures, protecting native title and specifying proce-dures for negotiating future land uses that may affect native title. However, no Act or court ruling has specified exactly what rights are conferred by native title. Instead, it has been left for the detail of native title rights to be determined on a case-by-case basis, depending on the local law and custom of each Indigenous community claiming native title. For example, one group's entitlement may be to traverse the land for periodic gathering or harvest of bush foods, while another group's rights may be exclusive and constant occupation and use of the land (Brennan, 1998).

The Mabo decision does make it clear, however, that Aboriginal tradition is not a *fixation of the past*. The six justices in the majority concluded that provided any changes do not diminish or extinguish the relationship between a particular tribe or other group and particular land, subsequent developments or variations do not extinguish the title in relation to that land. For example, the use of present day tools in harvesting plants and animals, including firearms, boats and nets made of present-day materials, still comprise the exercise of a customary right, albeit in a modern way (Sweeney, 1993). The High Court ruling in *Yanner v Eaton* 1999 confirmed that legitimate native title holders have the right to hunt game for customary use with present-day tools in the areas in which native title is held by that group or individual. But there remains much uncertainty about whether native title in Australia includes rights to non-traditional uses of natural resources or uses of resources that had not traditionally been exploited.

Meyers (2000) observed that the Federal Trial Court and Full Federal Court judgements in *Western Australia v Ward* (Mirruwung Gajerrong) case found that where native title in Australia includes the right of occupation, this creates an interest in land or possessory native title (the High Court's judgement in *Western Australia v Ward* 2002 did not reject this argument (Strelein, 2002).

> The prescript announced in Mabo (No 2) that native title is given
> its meaning by the traditions and customs observed by the
> claimants, means that in a case of exclusive possession, those
> customary and traditional uses of the land define the area under
> claim, not the extent of the rights associated with exclusive occu-
> pancy of the land. (Meyers, 2000, p. 6)

According to Meyers (2000) and Cape York Peninsula Indigenous leader and lawyer, Noel Pearson (2003), possessory native title should confer a generally unencumbered right to manage and determine uses of the land as native title holders see fit to support their economic and cultural development, as well as diminished sovereign rights to manage the land, in the same manner as holders of native title in the United States and non-Aboriginal freehold title in Australia. However, High Court judgements involving possessory native title in *Commonwealth v Yarmirr* 2001 and Mirruwung Gajerrong have reflected a *frozen in time* approach to Indigenous laws and customs, compounding the obstacles to development faced by native title holders. For example, the justices in Mirruwung Gajerrong concluded that the Indigenous claimants did not hold a native title right to ownership or the right to use (e.g. extract and process) minerals and petroleum, because they had not demonstrated laws and customs related to the use of minerals. Pearson (2002) described the justices' anthropological rather than common law conception of native title as a *great travesty [of justice] for Australia.* The issue of whether holders of native title may exercise native title rights to commercially utilize natural resources has not yet been answered conclusively in Australia and will certainly continue to be fought over in Australia's courts.

The characteristics of property rights that Wik people hold over timber resources differ between the land tenure-title combinations in the Aurukun area. Further complicating the issue is that land tenure-title combinations and Wik property rights will change with anticipated future native title rulings, the issuing of a new mining lease over former Mining Lease 7032 and the transfer of Aurukun Shire lease land to Aboriginal freehold tenure under the Queensland *Aboriginal Lands Act 1991.*

Property rights of Wik people to timber resources on native title land in Aurukun Shire

For the purposes of native title determination, the 27,000km² Wik native title claim area was split into two parts: Part A, approximately 6,000km² confined to areas that have only ever been unallocated state land or land under forms of title granted for the benefit of Aboriginal people; and Part B, the remaining 21,000km² that incorporates seven pastoral leases and four mining titles. In October of 2000 and 2004, the Federal Court granted Wik people native title over all of Part A and 12,500km² of Part B, respectively (Pryor, 2000; Gerard, 2004). Negotiation is continuing over the remaining Part B Wik claim area. Both the Part A and B native title determination areas include land outside the study area. Figure 8.1 illustrates native title land within the Aurukun area only.

Justice Drummond conferred upon Wik people the right to possess, occupy, use and enjoy the Part A determination area, including rights to (Federal Court of Australia, 2000, Order 3):

> (e) *make use of the determination area by:*
>   (i) *engaging in a way of life consistent with the traditional connection of the native title holders to the determination area ...*
> (f) *take, use and enjoy the natural resources from the determination area for the purposes of:*
>   (i) *manufacturing artefacts, objects and other products;*
>   (ii) *disposing of those natural resources and manufactured items, by trade, exchange or gift save that the right of disposal of natural resources taken from the waterways (as that term is defined in the* Fisheries Act 1994 (Qld) *as at the date of this determination) of the determination area is only a right to do so for non-commercial purposes.*

The definition of *natural resources* in Order 3 of the ruling included forest products as defined in the Forestry Act 1959 (Qld). Order 3 also conferred the right upon native title holders to 'determine as between native title holders what are the particular native title rights and interests that are held by particular native title holders in relation to particular parts of the determination area'. Order 8 stated that 'subject to Orders 4 and 5, [the native title rights and interests of Wik people confer] possession, occupation, use and enjoyment of the determination area on the native title holders to the exclusion of all others, except those having rights and interests identified in Order 6'. No rights and interests identified in Order 6 appear to degrade the Wik peoples' exclusive right to timber in Part A of the determination.

The Part B judgement handed down in 2004 consisted of two schedules: an exclusive areas determination; and a non-exclusive areas determination. All Part B determination areas within the Aurukun area are exclusive areas.[2] The rights of Wik people to timber on the exclusive areas of Part B are identical to Part A with the exceptions that points (i) and (ii) from Order 3(f) of the Part A determination (reported above) are not included, and there are different parties identified as holding valid rights and interests in the native title area. There are presently no 'other rights and interests' identified in Order 6 of the Part B exclusive determination areas schedule that could degrade the Wik peoples' exclusive right to timber in the Aurukun area. However, presumably some rights to timber will be affected by the granting of a new mining lease over former Mining Lease 7032.

The Federal Court has granted Wik people possessory native title over the Part A and Part B exclusive determination areas. Section 45 of the Forestry Act 1959 (Qld) includes a provision that forest products are the absolute property of the Crown *unless and until the contrary is proved*. These native title judgements have proved the contrary. Selective logging of timber appears to be consistent with the traditional connection of Wik people to their land and the Part A determination explicitly conferred the rights to manufacture artefacts, objects and other products out of *natural resources* taken from the land, and to dispose of these manufactured items through trade, exchange or gift.[3] Wik people also appear to have been conferred a right to conduct commercial forestry on native title land within the study area without a permit from or payment of royalties to DPI Forestry. Forestry activities would be subject to legislation that applies to forestry operations on freehold land elsewhere in Queensland. Operations will also be subject to the Queensland Code of Practice for native forest timber production on private lands when it is complete.

Property rights of Wik people to timber resources conferred by the Local Government (Aboriginal Lands) Act 1978 (Qld)

The Local Government (Aboriginal Lands) Act 1978 (Qld) established Aurukun Shire as a 50–year lease to Aurukun Shire Council. Until the granting of native title in 2000, this Act defined the legal rights of Wik people to timber throughout Aurukun Shire. The rights of Aurukun Shire Council and Wik people to natural resources in Aurukun Shire are specified in sections 29 to 31 of the Act. Section 31 specifies that all forest products within the meaning of the Forestry Act 1959 (Qld) are reserved for the Crown, as if the Shire was a Crown holding within the meaning of that Act. The Forestry Act 1959 gives the chief executive of DPI Forestry the power to authorize persons to enter and extract forest products from the forests of Aurukun Shire. Therefore, under the Local Government (Aboriginal Lands) Act 1978 (Qld), Wik people do not have the right to exclude others from timber within Aurukun Shire. Aurukun Shire Council may authorize the harvesting of timber for use on the lease without payment of a royalty to DPI Forestry. However, a permit must be sought from DPI Forestry to undertake commercial timber harvesting, logging must comply with all environmental and other legislation that affects such activities on state-owned land elsewhere in the state, and royalties for harvested timber are legally payable to the Queensland Government. Prior to the cancellation of Mining Lease 7032, Wik rights to timber on the lease were also subject to the condition that they did not interfere with the rights and obligations of the lessee.

The Wik Part A and Part B native title determinations identified Aurukun Shire Council, with its rights defined by the Local Government (Aboriginal Lands) Act 1978 (Qld), as one of the *other interests* in relation to the determination areas. The rights to timber conferred to Aurukun Shire Council under this Act prevail over native title rights to the extent of any inconsistency. council activities are largely organized by a non-Indigenous chief executive officer and non-Indigenous administration and technical teams working under democratically elected Indigenous councillors and an Indigenous mayor. Therefore, it is unlikely that the Aurukun Shire Council will invoke its power under the Local Government (Aboriginal Lands) Act 1978 (Qld) to deliberately override native title rights.

Property rights of Wik people to timber resources on mining leases in the Aurukun area

The establishment of Mining Leases 7024 and 7032 in the study area were facilitated by the special mineral development Acts, the Commonwealth Aluminium Corporation Pty Limited Agreement Act 1957 (Qld) and the Aurukun Associates Agreement Act 1975 (Qld), respectively. These were entered into as agreements between the mining company and the Queensland Government and gave lessees rights to utilize timber on the leases for construction, erection and maintenance of plant buildings, roads and other works necessary to directly or indirectly carry out their operations, without payment of a royalty to DPI Forestry.

Under the Queensland Forestry Act 1959 and Mineral Resources Act 1989, control of access to commercially utilize timber resources on mining leases on state-owned land in Queensland is vested with the Crown. DPI Forestry can authorize commercial forestry operations on these leases provided those activities do not interfere with the rights and obligations of the lessees. All legislation applicable to forestry operations on state-owned land in Queensland are, by strict definition of the law, also applicable to forestry operations on mining leases within the Aurukun area.[4]

Wik people hold no legal rights to timber resources on Mining Lease 7024 in Cook Shire. Wik people can apply to DPI Forestry for a permit to commercially harvest timber from forests on the lease, but are obliged to pay royalties for harvested timber to DPI Forestry. It is unclear what, if any, restrictions Comalco Pty. Ltd. (the holder of Mining Lease 7024) may place on forestry activities within their lease area. Wik rights to commercially utilize timber on land that was formerly Mining Lease 7032 are presently those conferred by the Part B exclusive areas determination, but these rights are likely to be affected when a new mining lease is granted to the bauxite resource.

Property rights of Wik people to timber resources on Aboriginal freehold

As prescribed by the Aboriginal Land Act 1991, Aboriginal freehold over Aurukun Shire lease land (including former Mining Lease 7032) is likely to arise within the study area in the near future. Aboriginal freehold title reserves to the State the rights to all minerals and petroleum on or below the land surface. Section 43 of the Aboriginal Land Act 1991 provides for the reservation of forest products (and quarry materials) to the Crown, if the Crown desires. Assuming the Queensland Government transfers the rights to timber with Aboriginal freehold land title, the characteristics of property rights of Wik people to utilize timber resources will be the same as freehold land title holders in Queensland. A Wik forestry industry would not be required to obtain a harvest permit from DPI Forestry or pay royalties for harvested timber, but would still be subject to legislation relating to vegetation management on freehold land. However, existing interests in the land continue in force, e.g. the granting of Aboriginal freehold over Aurukun Shire lease land with an existing mining lease, would not diminish the mining leaseholder's right to demand that forestry activities must not interfere with their rights and obligations. Presumably, to the extent of any inconsistency between native title rights and Aboriginal freehold rights, the more comprehensive rights for Wik people will prevail.

Legislative and other constraints potentially affecting the rights of Wik people to commercially utilize timber in the Aurukun area

Legislation enacted by Australian Federal and Queensland Parliaments,[5] regional planning policy (e.g. CYRAG, 1997; Commonwealth of Australia, 1998; Department of the Premier and Cabinet, 2000), and industry regulations and codes of practice (e.g. EPA, 2002) can affect the rights of entrepreneurs and landholders with any tenure to manage and utilize timber resources on CYP. These constraints are discussed in Venn (2004a). In summary, with the exception of the Federal Government World Heritage Properties Conservation Act 1983, legislation, policy and codes of practice can affect how and where forestry operations are conducted in the Aurukun area, but cannot completely prohibit selective logging in native forest.

Compatibility of Forestry-Based Economic Development for Wik People with Inalienable and Communal Native Title to Land

Economists have argued that the inalienable and communal nature of native title is an obstacle to economic development in remote Australian Indigenous communities. For example, Williams (1993) asserted that collective property rights reduce incentives to improve land (management that increases the stream of benefits produced by the land) and manage land in an ecologically sustainable manner. Warby (1997) argued that inalienability prevents land from being put to its economically efficient use by people who most value the land. Furthermore, he contended that, in comparison with individualized land tenure, the communal nature of native title property rights increases transaction costs, thereby reducing the number of wealth generating exchanges that will take place. Duncan (2003) observed that inalienability limits the capacity of native title holders to raise capital by mortgaging land. Indeed, Nagy (1996) reported that traditional owners of several Aboriginal-owned pastoral leases in the Northern Territory, which have been converted to inalienable Aboriginal freehold land under the Northern Territory Land Rights Act 1976, were unable to raise finance to maintain and develop their pastoral enterprises.

The socio-economic environment of the Aurukun area and the high importance Wik people place on non-pecuniary objectives is unfamiliar to Australian finance lenders – a Wik forestry industry will be judged as a high-risk venture irrespective of whether Wik rights to land are alienable and held individually. The argument that the inalienability of native title land tenure will prevent the land from being put to its most economically efficient use has limited relevance to the Aurukun area. Remoteness, poor soils and low cattle carrying capacity suggest that the opportunity cost of agricultural production foregone is likely to be small.

The criticism that inalienability precludes Indigenous landholders from raising finance to drive economic development through mortgaging land is simplistic both in its narrow conception of rights potentially conferred by native title and because in determining credit worthiness, financial lenders not only consider an applicant's collateral, but also their ability to repay the loan. Altman and Cochrane (2003) and Duncan (2003) have highlighted the potential for long-term leases conferring rights to particular natural resources on native title land (as distinct from interests in the land) to be accepted by banks as security for loans. With possessory native title that includes rights to commercially utilize timber, Wik people could potentially raise finance using long-term leases to timber resources as collateral, as distinct from the land.

The high importance of connection with country for the spiritual well-being of Wik people raises ethical and practicality issues surrounding the alienability of Wik native title land. Suppose Wik people were granted alienable native title and defaulted on repayments of a mortgage over their traditional land. Presumably the lender would wish to sell the property to recover the debt, but what would happen to Wik people? Eviction would be politically intolerable. This suggests that even if Wik native title land became alienable, the government would be required as the guarantor on a private loan or source of *seed* funding to facilitate economic development.

The argument that without individual land rights there are reduced incentives to manage natural resources to improve the land (increase the flow of future benefits) has less relevance for an extensively managed native forest system than, for example, an intensively managed annual cropping system. Discounted revenues arising from native forest management practices, such as timber stand improvement (removing unmerchantable trees to promote regeneration), are negligible at any realiztic discount rate.

Collectively, Wik people have aspirations for a timber industry that will have limited detrimental effects on other potential economic development opportunities, e.g. ecotourism in wetlands and forests outside of mining leases. Presently, various pieces of legislation and operational prescriptions restrict how and where timber harvesting can be undertaken on native title land, but do not prohibit logging (with the potential exception of the World Heritage Properties Conservation Act 1983). A profit maximizing individual native title landholder in the upper catchment of wetlands has no economic incentive to refrain from harvesting timber and will not account for the cost of likely increases in sediment loads in watercourses and subsequent damage to the ecology and ecotourism potential of wetlands on other individual native title landholdings downstream. In contrast, collective resource management on communal native title land may lead to a more socio-economically efficient outcome for Wik people, as all members of the native title claimant group can share in the benefits and costs of logging and conservation in particular areas.

The relatively low harvestable volume of timber per hectare in forests of the study area indicates it is unlikely that individualized native title holdings would include sufficient timber volume to supply a moderate-sized milling operation over a time period that would justify investment in necessary plant and equipment. On the other hand, establishing a forestry industry with access to a large pooled resource, as under the communal native title Wik people presently hold, would provide a large resource, permit logging to be concentrated initially in the most accessible (least cost) areas and facilitate a high degree of operational flexibility (e.g. provide areas for wet weather harvesting and the ability to meet orders for less common timbers, including Cooktown ironwood).

In the culturally diverse and historically troubled social environment of Aurukun town, government financial assistance, whether as *seed* funding or as guarantor on a private loan, is probably best directed towards collective economic development projects in which all clans in the Aurukun area have a stake. This will reduce the prospect that a project will be seen as favouring particular clans over others. Communal native title appears to be more conducive than individualized native title for the provision of economic development assistance in the study area.

Social and Cultural Obstacles to Economic Development in Remote Indigenous Communities

The current property rights regime appears to be satisfactory for establishment of a Wik timber industry on CYP and research by Venn (2004a) has highlighted the potential of such an industry to generate employment and income for Wik people. However, a plethora of resource development projects have been implemented in the Aurukun area from the earliest days of Mission activity, all of which failed when the community-based brokers who initiated them became dispirited or departed (Dale, 1993; Venn, 2004b). Dale (1993) highlighted several reasons for project failure, but principally the limited support and interest of Wik people in the projects, and a lack of participatory and technical planning.

CYP Indigenous leaders have argued that reconciliation of social and cultural considerations with private enterprise is the main obstacle to economic development (Pearson, 2000; Ah Mat, 2003), an issue that has hardly been addressed by research. Cultural differences and low western education and skill levels have left Wik people outside the real economy labour force. A passive welfare economy has been created by government where personal sustenance is received without the recipient being required to work or provide anything in return. This regime has corrupted Wik social relationships, values, expectations and aspirations.

Custom requires Wik people to fulfil cultural obligations such as social engagements (e.g. participation in mortuary rituals) and customary management responsibilities within clan estates (e.g. hunting and fire management). It is sometimes impractical for these activities to be postponed until the end of the working week. For a timber industry to have a chance of success in Aurukun, employment opportunities need to be designed that recognize the inappropriateness of a 40-hour working week and the relatively low labour productivity of people with no market economy work experience and limited western education and skills training. Another feature of Wik and other Australian Indigenous cultures is the obligation to distribute gains among extended families. This makes it difficult for the Wik to accumulate capital or obtain and service a bank loan.

Social and cultural factors are substantial obstacles for a commercially viable, employment-generating Wik forestry industry. Enterprise development in Aurukun will require a transition period between the welfare and the market economies. During this phase, culturally appropriate employment generation and development of human capital and entrepreneurial expertise will take precedence over profit maximization. Quiggin (2004) asserted that arguments similar to those used to justify tariff protection for particular industries are relevant for infant Indigenous industries. Subsidizing the high effective labour costs in the study area, perhaps through the CDEP, is one policy option that could be explored.

Concluding Comments

There has been much political rhetoric in Australia about sustainable economic development in remote Indigenous communities, yet governments have appeared reluctant to grant Indigenous people property rights to natural resources – the single economic factor remote Indigenous communities have in their favour. To avoid impeding development opportunities for Indigenous communities, native title must confer comprehensive and exclusive rights to at least some economically important natural resources. As possessory native title holders, Wik people appear to have an unencumbered right to manage and determine uses of their native title land, including rights to commercially utilize timber without a permit from and payment of royalties to the Queensland Government. However, this right will be affected by the Queensland Government's intention to grant a new mining lease over part of the Wik native title area. Outside native title determination areas Wik people are legally obliged to obtain harvest permits and pay royalties to commercially harvest timber. Forestry operations within and outside the native title areas must comply with all legislation applicable to activities on freehold and state-owned land respectively.

Several issues, including reconciliation of social and cultural obligations with engagement in the market economy, cultural diversity within the Indigenous population of Aurukun town and low western skill levels, make economic development for Wik people a challenging undertaking. By comparison, the inalienable and communal aspects of native title appear to be second-order development obstacles. If Wik native title land became alienable and individualized, it is unlikely enterprise development in the Aurukun area would become less challenging. The fact that forestry enterprises have harvested and continue to harvest timber from native forests on state-owned and freehold land in Queensland without alienable and individualized rights to land also indicates that the inalienable and communal nature of native title is unlikely to be a major impediment for native forest-based economic development in the Aurukun area. Native forest logging provides an economic development opportunity for Wik people that is compatible with their property rights to natural resources.

Acknowledgements

The author is grateful to the Australian Research Council, Rural Industries Research and Development Corporation, the Cape York Partnerships unit in the Queensland Department of Premier and Cabinet, and the Australian Centre for International Agricultural Research for funding this research. Critical in-kind support was also provided by Balkanu Cape York Development Corporation, Aurukun Shire Council and DPI Forestry. The following Wik elders are thanked for generously giving their time to discuss their forestry objectives and opportunities: Joe Ngallametta; Rotana Ngallametta; Pamela Ngallametta; Joshua Woolla; Ron Yunkaporta; Hersey Yunkaporta; Maurice

Holroyd; Anthony Kerenden; Gladys Tybingoompa; and Denny Bowenda. The editing assistance of anonymous government experts in land tenure, property rights issues and conservation significant flora and fauna is also appreciated.

Notes

1   There were actually two native title cases before the High Court in the Wik case, *Wik Peoples v State of Queensland and Others* 1996 and *Thayorre Peoples v State of Queensland and Others* 1996. The Court decided to hear both cases together because the claims overlapped.
2   The Part B non-exclusive determination area consists mostly of pastoral leases on which Wik people have been conferred less comprehensive rights. For example, Wik people cannot engage in a way of life consistent with the traditional connection of native title holders, live on or erect residences on non-exclusive native title areas. Also, Wik people have no right to control access to or use of Part B non-exclusive determination areas.
3   The right to produce and sell goods manufactured from the natural resources within the Part B exclusive determination area, which includes former Mining Lease 7032, is unclear
4   The intention of granting special bauxite mining leases is for all land under the lease to be cleared of vegetation and mined. Therefore, there may be grounds for regulations or restrictions imposed by particular environmental legislation on forestry operations to be relaxed on the mining leases within the study area. The Queensland Department of State Development and Innovation has indicated that it will support this argument for proposed forestry operations on bauxite mining leases on CYP (Taylor, 2003). Nevertheless, it is likely that the longer the period of time between harvesting and subsequent clearing for mining, the fewer the number of regulations and restrictions that will be waived (Taylor, 2003).
5   Important Federal and State legislation that can affect forestry operations in Queensland, include the Export Control Act 1982 (Fed), the World Heritage Properties Conservation Act 1983 (Fed) and the Environmental Protection and Biodiversity Conservation Act 1999 (Fed), the Forestry Act 1959 (Qld), Timber Utilization and Marketing Act 1987 (Qld), Nature Conservation Act 1992 (Qld), Land Act 1994 (Qld), Environmental Protection Act 1994 (Qld), Integrated Planning Act 1997 (Qld) and Vegetation Management Act 1999 (Qld).

References

ABS (Australian Bureau of Statistics) (2002). 2001 Census Basic Community Profiles and Snapshots. Online: www.abs.gov.au/Ausstats/abs@census.nsf/Census_BCP_ASGC_ViewTemplate?ReadFormandExpand=1, accessed 25 August 2003.

Ah Mat, R. (2003). The Moral Case for Indigenous Capitalism. *Paper presented at the Native Title on the Ground Conference,* Alice Springs. Online www.capeyorkpartnerships.com/richardahmat/index.htm, accessed 2 September 2003.

Altman, J. (2004). *Economic Development and Indigenous Australia: Contestations Over Property, Institutions and Ideology?* Centre for Aboriginal Economic Policy Research, The Australian National University, Canberra. Online: www.anu.edu.au/caepr/.

Altman, J.C. and Cochrane, M. (2003). *Innovative Institutional Design for Sustainable*

Wildlife Management in the Indigenous-owned Savanna. Centre for Aboriginal Economic Policy and Research paper number 247/2003, Australian National University, Canberra. Online: www.anu.edu.au/caepr/.

Anderson, C. (1981). Queensland. In N. Peterson (ed.), *Aboriginal Land Rights: A Handbook, Australian Institute of Aboriginal Studies.* (pp53–114). Canberra.

Annandale, M. (2004). *Principal State Development Officer (Indigenous Economic Support)*, Queensland Department of State Development and Innovation. Personal communication.

Balkanu Cape York Development Corporation (1999). *The People.* Online: http://balkanu.com.au/people.htm, accessed 16 May 2000.

Brennan, F. (1998). *The Wik Debate: Its Impact on Aborigines, Pastoralists and Miners.* Sydney: UNSW Press.

Coase, R. H. (1960). The problem of social cost. *The Journal of Law and Economics, 3* (October), 1–44.

Commonwealth of Australia (1998). *Cape York Natural Heritage Trust Plan 1997 to 2001.* Canberra: Department of the Environment.

Connor, M. (2004, July 9). Dispel myth of terra nullius and historians are on shaky ground. *The Australian*, p. 13.

Crevatin, M. (2000). District Manager, DPI Forestry, Atherton, personal communication.

CYRAG (Cape York Regional Advisory Group) (1997). *Cape York Peninsula Land Use Strategy – Our Land Our Future: A Strategy for Sustainable Land Use and Economic and Social Development.* Cairns: Cape York Peninsula Land Use Strategy, Department of Local Government and Planning; Canberra: Department of the Environment, Sport and Territories.

Dahlman, C. (1980). *The Open Field System and Beyond.* Cambridge: Cambridge University Press.

Dale, A. P. (1993). *An assessment of planning for government-funded land use development projects in Australian Aboriginal communities*, unpublished PhD thesis. Brisbane: Faculty of Environmental Sciences, Griffith University.

Department of the Premier and Cabinet (2000). *Cape York Partnerships: Some Practical Ideas.* Brisbane: Queensland Government.

Duncan, R. (2003). Agricultural and resource economics and economic development in Aboriginal communities. *Australian Journal of Agricultural and Resource Economics*, 47(3): 307–24.

EPA (Environmental Protection Agency) (2002). *Code of Practice for Native Forest Timber Production.* Brisbane: Environmental Protection Agency.

Federal Court of Australia (2000). *Wik Peoples v State of Queensland.* Online: www.austlii.edu.au/au/cases/cth/federal_ct/2000/1443.html, accessed 8 May 2003.

Gerard, I. (2004). Wik people win back their land. *The Australian*, 14 October, p. 2.

Hardin, G. (1968). The tragedy of the commons. *Science*, 162(3859), 1243–1248.

Hodge, A. (2003, October 25–26). Abandoned town still waiting for rush. *The Weekend Australian*, p. 4.

Hughes, H. and Warin, J. (2005). A New Deal for Aborigines and Torres Strait Islanders in Remote Communities. Issue Analysis no. 54. Sydney: The Centre for Independent Studies.

Karvelas, P. (2004, December 10). Land rights may be privatized. *The Australian*, p. 4.

Karvelas, P. (2005, February 18). Plan to privatize land for blacks. *The Australian*, pp1–2.

Leveridge, V. and Lea, D. (1993). *Takeback: Planning for Change in Aurukun.* Casuarina, Darwin: Australian National University North Australia Research Unit.

Martin, D. F. (1993). *Autonomy and Relatedness: An Ethnography of Wik People of Aurukun, Western Cape York Peninsula*, unpublished PhD thesis. Canberra:

Australian National University.

Meyers, G.D. (2000). The content of native title: questions for the Miriuwung Gajerrung appeal. *Land, Rights, Laws: Issues of Native Title*, 2(7). Canberra: Native Title Research Unit, Australian Institute of Aboriginal and Torres Strait Islander Studies.

Nagy, J. (1996). Raising finance on native title and other Aboriginal land. *Land, Rights, Laws: Issues of Native Title*, (11), Canberra, Australian Institute of Aboriginal and Torres Strait Islander Studies.

Ostrom, E. (1990). *Governing the Commons: the Evolution of Institutions for Collective Action*. New York: Cambridge University Press.

Pearson, C. (2004, July 10–11). Naive lie of an empty land. *The Weekend Australian*, p. 18.

Pearson, N. (2000). *Our Right to Take Responsibility*, Noel Pearson and Associates Pty Ltd, Cairns.

Pearson, N. (2002, August 28). Native title days in the sun are over. *The Age*. Online: www.capeyorkpartnerships.com/noelpearson/index.htm, accessed 28 April 2003.

Pearson, N. (2003). *The High Court's Abandonment of 'the Time-Honoured Methodology of the Common Law' in its Interpretation of Native Title in Mirriuwung Gajerrong and Yorta Yorta*. Sir Ninian Stephen Annual Lecture, 17 March, Law School, University of New Castle. Online: www.capeyorkpartnerships.com/noelpearson/index.htm, accessed 28 April 2003.

Pryor, C. (2000, October 4). New struggle looms after Wik people win six-year land battle. *The Australian*, p. 5.

Quiggin, J. C. (2004). Professor and Federation Fellow, School of Economics, The University of Queensland, Brisbane, personal communication.

Smyth, D. (1993). *A Voice in all Places: Aboriginal and Torres Strait Islander Interests in Australias Coastal Zone*. Consultancy report commissioned by Coastal Zone Inquiry. Canberra: Resource Assessment Commission.

Strelein, L. (2002) *Western Australia v Ward* on behalf of Mirivwung Gajerrong, 8 August 2002, [2002] HCA 28. Paper presented at the Native Title Conference 2002, Geraldton Western Australia, 3–5 September 2002.

Sweeney, D. (1993). Fishing, hunting and gathering rights of Aboriginal peoples in Australia. *University of New South Wales Law Journal*, 16(1), 97–160.

Taylor, M. (2003). *Manager, Resource Assessment and Planning*. Forest Policy Group, Department of State Development, Brisbane, personal communication.

Venn, T .J. (2004a). *Socio-economic Evaluation of Forestry Development Opportunities for Wik People on Cape York Peninsula*, unpublished PhD thesis, School of Economics. Brisbane: The Univertsity of Queensland.

Venn, T. J. (2004b). Visions and realities for a Wik forestry industry on Cape York Peninsula, Australia. *Small-Scale Forest Economics Management and Policy*, 3(3), 431–51.

Voss, N. (2000, June 18). Mission impossible: tribal wars still take grim toll in far north. *The Sunday Mail*, pp38–39.

Warby, M. (1997). *Past Wrongs, Future Rights*. Melbourne: Tasman Institute.

Williams, P. L. (1993). Mabo and inalienable rights to property. *Australian Economic Review*, (103), 41–44.

9

Coping with a Tragedy
of the Australian Aboriginal Common

Rolf Gerritsen and Anna Straton

Introduction

The conditions of Aboriginal people on remote settlements in northern and central Australia are very much worse than for non-Aboriginal people in the same regions, let alone in the rest of Australia. The lifetime outcomes of Indigenous Australians in those settlements, as revealed by headline indicators of health, income, education and home ownership, for example, are far worse than for Australians generally. Life expectancy for Indigenous males is 20.9 years less than for non-Indigenous males, and 24.7 years less than their non-Indigenous counterparts for Indigenous females; median gross weekly individual income is $372 less for Indigenous people than for non-Indigenous people; and home ownership is 15.2 per cent for Indigenous people versus 52.1 per cent for non-Indigenous people (SCRGSP, 2005). These discrepancies are especially pronounced for Aboriginal people living on remote communities in outback Australia (Productivity Commission, 2003; SCRGSP, 2005).

The reasons usually advanced to explain this ubiquitous phenomenon include inadequate levels of government expenditure in Aboriginal communities (Taylor and Stanley, 2005), lack of access to conventional labour markets, and failure of service delivery programs because their design is inappropriate to Aboriginal social norms and values. In the latter instance, for example, health programs can fail because Aboriginal people have different understandings of what are considered acceptable health levels (Senior, 2001). This is but one example of the mutual cultural incomprehension between Aboriginal and non-Aboriginal Australians that underpins all of these explanations:

> *Those Aborigines I know seem to me to be still fundamentally in struggle with us. Their struggle is for a different set of things, differently arranged, from those which most European interests want them to receive. Neither side has clearly grasped what the other seeks.* (Stanner, 1979, pp42–43)

Since Stanner wrote that over 25 years ago, the problem of official incomprehension of the substance and importance of Aboriginal culture has persisted:

> *One of the messages that came through clearly during consultations on the draft framework back in 2002 and 2003 was that there was no single indicator of culture which could adequately reflect the place of culture in the lives of Indigenous people. Indeed culture was so important that it was pervasive in every aspect of their lives.* (SCRGSP, 2005, p. 2.11)

This chapter seeks to further diagnose the nature of this cultural incomprehension through the notions of rules and rule (in)compatibility. This diagnosis provides a basis for innovative opportunities and solutions to issues of program delivery to Aboriginal settlements.

The core problem examined here is that official policies targeted at helping Aboriginal people reflect a misunderstanding of Aboriginal culture and rules by assuming that Aboriginal people living on remote settlements are in fact communities, sharing common norms, values and purposes. This assumption leads to the belief that Aboriginal people on these settlements form a well-structured and cohesive group (Davies, 2003) that can and needs to be *mobilized*, in the sense of the conventional community development approach (Ife, 1995). That is not the case. Rather, the larger Aboriginal settlements in central and northern Australia today almost universally comprise people from different clan and language groups,[1] and this creates a complex set of social relationships and competition that directs the distribution of welfare programme benefits throughout these communities. Misunderstanding of these relationships and inter-group competition, rather than simply the individual Aboriginal irresponsibility that seems to underpin the Commonwealth's mutual obligation contractual approach to Aboriginal welfare, is advanced here as being partly responsible for the failure of government programmes.

This chapter focuses on the ineffectiveness of targeted welfare and service delivery programs, positing one of the major causes of this as having to do with the incompatibility between official government rules for welfare distribution and Aboriginal cultural rules and practices of social interaction. The heterogeneity of Aboriginal groups within remote settlements is highlighted, and aspects of Aboriginal culture and history that currently impede the success of targeted, specific purpose, programs as designed by government bodies are discussed. A solution to address the rule incompatibility is then proposed and conclusions are drawn about the potential impacts of this solution in terms of establishing a set of cooperative social commons on Aboriginal settlements.[2]

Issue: Ineffective Distribution of Benefits to Aboriginal People on Remote Settlements

There are two main ways in which the Australian government distributes welfare to Aboriginal people in remote areas.[3] The first is through income transfers to individuals or families – welfare payments mostly controlled by the Commonwealth's Centrelink agency (even if delivered by a local agent, such as the Community Government). Income transfers include *kidsmoney* (family benefits/payments), *UB* or *sit-down* money (unemployment payments) and *pension money* (all other pension payments). Such income transfers are appropriate for distributing welfare to individuals and to a degree within family groups, although within Aboriginal society they can be problematic because they may be subject to cultural rules of distribution that negate their purpose to reduce particular individuals' income disadvantage (Daly, 1999; Sanders, 2001).

However, our attention here is on governmental programme payments to Aboriginal communities or organizations, rather than to individuals. These are the second means of monetary distribution, through Specific Purpose Payments programs such as those for health, education and training, which are almost entirely delivered by state and territory government officials.

The standard method for the delivery of such programmes is that the funding agency will have an agent within the Aboriginal settlement. This is most often the settlement's official local government but can be the administrators of the Community Development Employment Program (CDEP), health clinic, school, or the governing body of an Aboriginal organization within the community (such as the general store or the housing association). The agent will usually appoint a person with responsibility for the programme. The person may be from within the community, a part-time employee of the Community Council, or be employed on the CDEP. In the latter two cases that person would have their wage *topped-up* in return for working part time on delivering the designated programme. Sometimes one individual might have the responsibility for delivering two or more programmes.

For various reasons this system is not effective, and is partially responsible for poor development outcomes for Aboriginal people on remote settlements. One set of reasons for this is to do with the design and application of administrative rules. At its simplest this is because programmes are designed for mainstream Australia and are not easily transferable to the Aboriginal settlements of northern and central Australia. These settlements comprise less than one per cent of Australia's population (though scattered over half the country's landmass), so there is little incentive for policy makers to design programmes specifically for these Aboriginal communities. In some cases, such as the technology for renal failure, the technology for the program can be ill-fitted for the Aboriginal community situation (Willis, 1995); although in this case improvements are occurring. The Northern Territory Government's rules for educational expenditure – based upon a fee-for-service model – systematically disadvantage Aboriginal communities by creating a feedback loop of reduced funding because of low school retention and attendance rates, which in turn cannot be remedied because of the low funding (Taylor and Stanley, 2005, p67ff.).

There are also reasons for failure that are internal to Aboriginal settlements. It is upon this factor that we now concentrate.

Aboriginal Society and the Administrative Domain

The governmental programmes, especially the specific purpose programmes, delivered to Aboriginal communities are based on two sets of assumptions, the first about the nature of the problems they are intended to remedy and the second about Aboriginal people and communities. These assumptions mainly come from two directions: the inertial historical legacy of orthodox community development theory, and a misunderstanding of Aboriginal culture and its adaptation to modern *whitefella* business, presuming the romanticized characterization of Aboriginal people as *noble savages* and so inherently egalitarian. This perspective is evident in statements such as:

> *Aboriginal political life is characterized by the uniform distribution of rights, privileges and duties throughout a social order based on kinship and suffused by egalitarian ideology.* (Hiatt, 1986, p. 177)

Aboriginal society is only superficially egalitarian. Its egalitarian image is probably as much a reflection of Aboriginal people traditionally owning few goods that *whitefella* outsiders could see as having value. It may also be either as much a reflection of the analyst romanticizing Aboriginal society or as a pedagogic contrast to the failings of western society (for example, Bell, 1983[4]). Yet Aboriginal society has always been hierarchical and to a degree competitive. The bases of power and accumulation in Aboriginal society lay in the inter-linkage between the ownership/control of women (Berndt and Berndt, 1965, pp159–60) and ceremonial business. Multiple wives produced more followers and the food supplies necessary to devote to ceremony. Ceremonial *spiritual* power conferred the status that allowed men to accumulate more wives (Hiatt, 1968, p. 175). In Aboriginal society the great majority of older men had only one wife; young men rarely had any. A few older men had several wives. Meggitt (1962, p. 78, table 9) provides an analysis of the Walpiri; 115 of the men had only one wife, 60 had two or more. Eight men in his sample had four or more wives. If wives are an indicator of the distribution of goods of value, then Walpiri society was profoundly unequal, as were many if not most traditional Aboriginal societies (Hiatt, 1965; see also Maddock, 1982, p. 67ff.). Hart and Pilling (1960) reported an even greater range in the number of wives among the Tiwi.

Aboriginal societies were hierarchical in a particular way. Leaders, the hierarchs, had reciprocal obligations. As Myers (1980, p. 320) notes of the Pintubi, 'the capability of seniors to "look after" dependants in a material sense was the moral basis of their authority'.

The modern political dynamic of the Aboriginal settlements of northern and central Australia has been comparatively neglected by anthropologists and other students of Aboriginal society (Rowse, 1992). Essentially studies originating from such disciplinary approaches either ignore government and its impacts and concentrate upon the purely Aboriginal domain or assume that Aboriginal people are the passive recipients of governmental activities on their settlements. A few descriptions exist that indicate that some Aboriginal people have a more active, even controlling, role over this process (for example, Gerritsen, 1982a, 1982b).

As noted above, the political dynamic of these settlements is essentially one of active competition to control the distribution of governmental programmes or *whitefella* business (cf Anderson, 1989; Smith, 1989; Rowse, 1992 pp50–58). Control over the local implementation of these programmes confers upon the relevant brokers (or *dominant men*) the control over the largess consequent upon these programmes – such as access to vehicles, cash and employment – which can then be distributed to their affines, thereby cementing the dominant men's control over the settlement. In each settlement the losers greatly outnumber the winners from this competition. Important features of modern Aboriginal society, such as the outstation movement, are partly explained by a reaction to this dynamic (Gerritsen,1982b; Christie and Greatorex, 2004).

In essence the Aboriginal brokers of these settlements have taken programmes designed with the Weberian rationality of impersonal distribution and based upon assumptions of equal access and applied them to suit their society – one where competition and control are important – thus negating the bureaucrats' intent. Also of influence is the fact that the person selected for the programme delivery will most likely be identified with one of the *parties* in the political contestation (described below) within the community. That means that members of the other *party* will greet his/her efforts with apathy if not hostility. Or they may not even feature in the distribution of the goods and benefits (for example, access to vehicles and employment, respectively) that the programme is intended to deliver. In addition, any person employed is likely to be in a kinship-based avoidance relationship with significant segments of the population (for example, with their classificatory mothers-in-law), which obviously inhibits effective service delivery. None of these examples are statements about a negative intention of Aboriginal people; rather they describe outcomes that have emerged from the interaction (and mismatch) of government-designed rules and cultural rules.

Consequently, governmental programmes are proving to be generally ineffective in delivering and widely distributing the beneficial outcomes they intend, partly as a result of the bureaucratic failure to anticipate the unequal distribution of the benefits of those programmes through misunderstanding of the complex social relations guiding behaviour, especially resource distribution, on these settlements. This leads to perverse effects upon programme delivery priorities. For example, governmental expenditure can be distorted towards the symptoms of dysfunction, such as medical services that focus upon dealing with chronic illness and violent assaults, rather than preventative health programmes and means to lessen the social tensions that create the chronic illness and alcohol-fuelled violent assaults.

One outcome of the failure of government programmes appears to be that arguments are currently being put forward by the federal government for the concepts of community mobilization and the application of *mutual obligation* arrangements. The federal government is currently establishing Shared Responsibility Agreements (SRAs) with Aboriginal communities. These SRAs are built on the assumption that Aboriginal communities exist and can express and negotiate about a *community* point of view. Such debates may still be missing a crucial point to do with the differences between how Aboriginal people distribute resources and how Australian bureaucracies deliver resources; how incorrect assumptions about Aboriginal processes inhibit effective outcomes for Aboriginal welfare. Mutual obligation, like orthodox community development,[5] assumes that there is an Aboriginal community commons whose purpose is community mobilization and impersonal and egalitarian distribution of benefits.

Problem Specification: The Incompatibility of Assumed and Actual Rules

Any activity that humans engage in whereby they are interacting with each other and with the world around them is structured by a set of rules. For example, interactions with colleagues at work are guided by informal rules of etiquette and interpersonal relationships, and by formal rules described by reporting relationships and contractual obligations.[6] While individuals can choose whether to follow these types of rules, they cannot change them without input and action from others.[7] Formal and informal rules arise from processes, institutions and people interacting with each other. These rules exist at the level of the system of interacting humans rather than at the level of individuals.

Cultural norms are an institution, being a set of rules, as are bodies such as local, state and federal governments, and written guidelines such as natural resource management plans and legislative acts. Interactions between people, behaving in accordance with various cultural and social institutions, and institutions of governance, such as the distribution of specifically targeted programs to Aboriginal people on settlements, can be conceptualized as taking place between sets of rules.

Previous sections discussed how the community network on any given remote Aboriginal settlement is fragmented and the sets of rules for social interaction are diverse and result in complex cultural institutions. This reflects a phenomenon that can explain most cases where welfare efforts are ineffective, or, even worse, result in perverse and negative outcomes:

> *If the individuals who are crafting and modifying rules do not understand how particular combinations of rules affect actions and outcomes in a particular ecological and cultural environment, rule changes may produce unexpected, and at times, disastrous outcomes.* (Ostrom, 2005, p. 1)

Aboriginal world views and behaviours (rules) are generally different to those of non-Aboriginal people in a number of domains, and are also different between Aboriginal groups. And these differences have important implications for public policy. For example, Folds (2001, pp42ff) describes the Pintupi attitude to government as one in which the government is characterized as *holding* (e.g. being responsible for) the Pintupi people. This is the consequence of the government encouraging the Pintupi out of the western desert during the 1960s. Governments did this for humanitarian reasons (according to the mainstream Australian view), but the Pintupi interpreted this as the government offering to take full responsibility for them. *Holding* the Pintupi produced the situation that the current *mutual obligation* debate defines as dependence, but the Pintupi see as the government only carrying out its proper obligations:

> *Pintupi have kept their part of the bargain, living in settlements under various arbitrary administrations and participating, in a somewhat desultory fashion, in the plethora of programs devised for them. They naturally consider it treacherous of government to try and foist the responsibility for their physical well-being back onto them, especially now that the traditional life they were enticed away from is utterly irretrievable.* (Folds, 2001, p.43)

Issues often arise when sets of rules interact. For example, there have been many attempts to *assimilate* Aboriginal people into the capitalist economy and western society since the mid-twentieth century (some of which had very questionable bases in principles of human rights). Many such attempts have taken place in the settlement of Maningrida in the Northern Territory of Australia since its establishment in 1957 as a government settlement (Hughes, 1996). The Welfare Branch and then the Department for Aboriginal Affairs ran a range of development projects, including a large forestry project. This project shared several features with many others in Maningrida:

> *They were established with government funds; came under close scrutiny and tight regulation; Yolngu participation in deciding to set them up was minimal; and those which were released from direct government control were transferred to Aboriginal corporations with white managers, rather than to individual entrepreneurs or kinship groups.* (Hughes, 1996)

While these projects were originally designed to train Aboriginal people to be self-supporting, they often failed to achieve this goal. The sets of rules, both written and unwritten, by which the forestry project operated were incompatible with those of the Aboriginal people involved. There are several examples of this. First, incompatibility between traditional and introduced technologies of forestry fire management hampered Aboriginal people's attempts to hunt. Second, there were incidents such as the building of a forestry road over a clan estate that passed through and disturbed an important dreaming site. The inability of the (then) modern approach to forestry to accommodate respect for the cultural needs of Aboriginal people led to further alienation. Hughes writes:

> *After a decade of life in town, Yolngu began to reject the hierarchical control, dependency and impersonal relationships of planned*

development. A trickle of families began leaving Maningrida to resume life on their clan estates about 1969. This became a flood... By 1980, 32 permanent homeland communities with populations from five to 100 were officially recognized, as well as a number of seasonal camps. These small self-managing communities use traditional and modern technologies to attain a standard of living higher than that available in Maningrida. (Hughes, 1996)

The problems and perverse outcomes of the attempted development project arose when a rule or rules from one institution did not embed well or *fit* within the rule set of another. The examples above – of the different approaches to fire management for commercial forestry purposes versus those for subsistence purposes, and the reaction of those running the forestry project to cultural needs – are but two in a smorgasbord of cases of incompatibility of sets of rules between Aboriginal and non-Aboriginal institutions.

The incompatibility of sets of rules can happen in several ways. First, as per the previous example, the informal rules of one group may not fit within formal existing institutions. For example, Aboriginal people's perspective of their country is that it is owned communally, and that some features in the landscape are not negotiable, transferable or substitutable. This does not fit well within western private property rights regimes based on divisible and transferable rights held by single entities, and this incompatibility is at the root of discussions about the ability of Aboriginal traditional owners to use their land to create jobs, welfare and financial security. Particular perspectives regarding land and ownership and social institutions, such as those required for certain types of conflict resolution and business practice, are needed to support engagement with the western capitalist system. Modified institutions enabling Aboriginal people to engage with the western system will be required to reconcile the traditional Indigenous and western paradigms of property rights to land and other natural resources.

Second, the rules of a formal institution might not embed well within the cultural rules of a group of people. This is how we conceptualize the issue at hand: the Australian government's rules for the distribution of welfare do not fit with the rules of social interaction in Aboriginal communities, including the networks through which resources are distributed. Welfare projects based on the assumption of a distribution network like that in Figure 9.1(a) will struggle when the actual set of connections is like that in Figure 9.1(b).

There are also variations on these two processes. Hughes (1996) wrote of a situation where:

In their homelands people follow a lifestyle in which some elements of Western culture are incorporated into a traditional structure... This is the reverse of the situation in Maningrida, where elements of traditional culture were incorporated into a Western structure of knowledge and power.

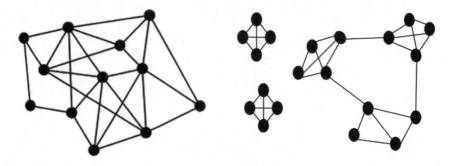

(a) Example of a network structure of resource distribution relationships commonly assumed by welfare institutions when there is little understanding of social relations. The dots represent people and the lines represent distributive relationships. The spread of distributive connections is relatively even throughout the whole network of people.

(b) Likely network structure of resource distribution relationships on Aboriginal settlement. The different clusters represent people of different subgroups within the whole community. The network is fragmented and distribution relationships are between specific people in each group. Resources must pass through certain people to get to others, and some groups are not connected at all.

Figure 9.1 Assumed and actual network structures of resource distribution on Aboriginal settlements

This is an example of how aspects of one set of rules – elements of western culture – can embed well within another in certain contexts, including the traditional structure of Aboriginal families on their homelands. The very same elements do not fit together, however, in other contexts: for example, when elements of traditional culture out of its homeland context did not fit into the western institutions and ways of coordinating activity.

While the phenomenon of the incompatibility between sets of rules would seem to have been captured before through notions such as the clash of cultures, and throughout the continuing debates about assimilation, self-determination and now mutual obligation, there has been little discussion of the actual sets of rules that are embodied in the organizations involved in Aboriginal rights and welfare, the mechanisms that they use and the rules that they follow and assume of each other. Discussion focuses instead on symptoms and does not seem to approach these root causes.

Failures of welfare distribution policies in remote Indigenous communities are essentially failures of cultural comprehension, coupled with and underpinned by the historical legacy of Aboriginal treatment, negligible Aboriginal involvement in research and planning, the lack of Aboriginal experience in negotiating and contributing to programme processes, plus entrenched power imbalances, including those within Aboriginal settlements. The examination of the institutions – formal, tangible organizations, legislation and regulations, and the unwritten social and cultural norms – will enable a more thorough understanding of exactly where and why conflicts and perverse outcomes occur, and, more positively, how programmes and policies can be developed based on seeking out and creating compatibilities between sets of rules.

We now turn to a way forward for the distribution of welfare to Aboriginal people on remote settlements. The following discussion is based on understanding the sets of rules governing the dynamics and processes on remote settlements and designing policies and projects based on compatible institutions. It is intended that the improved conditions arising from programmes based on compatible institutions will enable the building of trust between Aboriginal and government groups, and so the shifting of perspectives. This, in turn, may further enable all participants to restructure their sets of rules to better serve their shared purposes (Ostrom, 2005).

Attempts in this vein have been made before with the establishment of incorporated councils representing the interests of Aboriginal people in particular areas (Aboriginal Councils and Associations Act, 1976). Dodson (1996, p. 9) wrote, 'These initiatives, amongst others, were attempts to fundamentally restructure the relationship between Aboriginal and Torres Strait Islander peoples and governments.' The matching of sets of rules is possible. It does require, however, a more thorough understanding of the root causes and mechanisms guiding the behaviour of all parties.

Solution: Building Self-Defined Networks and Institutional Trust

The problem specification outlined above enables a recasting of the issue at hand. The question now becomes one of finding sets of rules that match and that can deliver on the objectives of the programme funding body and Aboriginal people. As there are different rules across different groups within a settlement, Australian governments may need to explore options that maximize rule compatibility in each circumstance. This will need considerable resources, as the aim is initially not to create *an Aboriginal common*, but to identify multiple commons in each Aboriginal community.

Here social capital theory (Woolcock, 2001; Productivity Commission, 2003) also provides a clue as to the way forward. This is through its emphasis upon *trust*. Trust exists when all parties accept that the rules are legitimate and fairly applied. Where trust exists, cooperative commons can form (Falk and Kilpatrick, 2000). Trust can be built up by successful cooperation within primary social interaction groups expanding to build trust in the larger institutional rule sets of society. Broader social cooperation, or a commons, can then exist.

Aboriginal people need to define their own intra-community *trust* networks as relevant to a targeted programme. For example, their relevant network for delivering on women's health may be individual families or households. Or the relevant network for delivering skills and education training for young men may be the leaders of the major parties, clans or language groups on the settlement and it may be appropriate for the training to be delivered separately to each party.

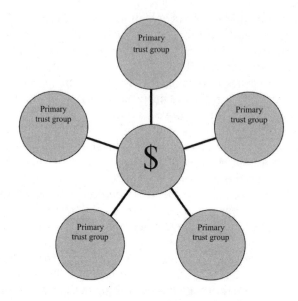

Figure 9.2 Primary trust groups connected to a funding body
through separately negotiated agreements

The first task in each case is to identify the primary trust groups (Woolcock, 2001; Productivity Commission, 2003) that will be directly connected to the funding body through the person or people who carry out the programme (see Figure 9.2).

Each primary trust group will have a separately negotiated agreement with the funding body that reflects the realities of delivering and distributing the programme outcomes within the particular set of rules of that primary trust group. Ideally, these agreements will reflect the needs and aspirations of each primary trust group, and will be able to respond to changes in these needs. Implementation may initially involve significant transaction costs and the extent to which arrangements can be contractual may be limited. However, this approach of multiple bilateral mutual obligation agreements, rather than blanket applications to whole communities, will distribute benefits more effectively, build Aboriginal trust in government institutions, and build more effective institutions that can learn, and are sensitive to the particular ways in which Aboriginal Australians see and interact with the world.

Conclusions

Australia's policy makers have not adequately understood the cultural norms, aspirations and life choices of Aboriginal people. This has resulted in an inadequate understanding of the impact of government-imposed rules and rule changes on remote Aboriginal settlements, most obviously, the impact of policies that placed Aboriginal people of different clan and language groups together on these settlements. The major Aboriginal settlements that exist today seldom reflect the original Aboriginal communities of Australia. The social relationships that exist in these mixed communities are far more complex than recognized by decision makers. As noted above, the Aboriginal people on these so-called communities cannot be considered homogenous groups of people; they do not necessarily share common norms, values, purposes and ways of doing things. Thus, the community network on any given settlement is fragmented in ways not yet understood by Australia's policy makers. The sets of rules for social interaction are diverse and result in complex cultural institutions.

Debate to date about the distribution of welfare to Aboriginal people on remote settlements, and of Aboriginal welfare generally, has focused more on the symptoms of the problems rather than their root causes. Misinterpretation, historical legacies, confusion over objectives and disagreements on the appropriate analysis have all played a role in inhibiting informed discussions about these root causes. The causes essentially relate to tension between the ways in which Aboriginal people see the world and interact with others in it, and the ways in which non-Aboriginal people see the world and characterize Aboriginal people, for example, as *noble savages* or, more recently, as needing to be *encouraged* out of passive welfare dependence.

A system that allows different methodologies to be applied within each settlement and between settlements would encourage a better fit between programmes and Aboriginal communities. Success would eventually establish intra-settlement trust and perhaps allow multiple family or clan commons over time to develop into single settlement commons that at present do not exist.

Conversely, maintaining current approaches would continue inefficiency within public outlays. Taylor and Stanley (2005) described how governmental expenditure on the Wadeye settlement in the Northern Territory is skewed towards law and order and medical services that focus upon dealing with chronic illness and violent assaults rather than preventative health programmes. These are the symptoms of failure, and this failure is being *rewarded* by disproportionate outlays. A better system, such as the one we advocate, would instead reward success because delivery of programmes is predicated on having working primary trust groups and agreements.

Currently the national Indigenous policy agenda is for Shared Responsibility Agreements between governments (at the moment principally the federal government) and Aboriginal communities. The community receives funding for a particular desired project in return for agreeing to enforce some particular behaviour (such as ensuring that the settlement children attend school, etc). These Agreements, like most innovations, may bear short-term fruit but are destined not to provide a long-term *solution* (sic) to the nexus between adequate provision and efficient utilization in service delivery. That is because the agreement process is still predicated upon the premise of a united community. Eventually the process will founder on the politics of each Aboriginal settlement. We would argue that recognizing the fundamental reality that these settlements are occupied by numbers of *families* that are potentially prepared to cooperate, the more decentralized approach advocated here would provide a better long-term framework. It would provide more congruence between governmental rules, institutional rules and Aboriginal social rules.

Acknowledgements

We would like to thank Alan Andersen, Tyron Venn, Jim Binney, Harvey Creswell, Michael Christie and two other referees for their comments and critiques.

Notes

1   The Aboriginal communities considered in this chapter are the major settlements, usually having over 200 residents at the seasonal peak and containing stores, schools, health clinics and other rudimentary appurtenances of the wider Australian society. Outstations – usually of between 15 and 150 people – are formed by a different dynamic (see Gerritsen, 1982b) and may be less socially and economically internally competitive arenas because they are less socially heterogeneous. They can even be interpreted as a consequence of persons deliberately removing themselves from the contested arenas of large settlements (Gray, 1977). Some observers claim that, unlike on the larger settlements, outstations are places where Aboriginal social capital exists and works beneficially (cf Christie and Greatorex, 2004).

2   We are aware that the term *common* suggests Garrett Hardin's seminal 1968 article (Hardin, 1968). In this chapter we use the common as a metaphor for social cooperation in the tradition of game theory (i.e. the prisoner's dilemma) and collective action theory, in which the failure to cooperate or the existence of distributional coalitions leads to sub-optimal social outcomes. For a discussion see Ostrom (1990, ch.1).

3   This account ignores the flows of income derived from mining royalties and land rents and other similar payments (e.g. see Pritchard and Gibson, 1996, p. 28–32). It could be argued that these payments eventually create further inequalities, but this has not been examined here.

4   The realities, for example, in the case of the position of women in Aboriginal society, can be less romantic (Bolger, 1991).

5   It is only fair to note that contemporary work on community development practice has incorporated the conundrum of whether community representatives actually do 'represent' the community (e.g. Jewkes and Murcott, 1998).

6   Ostrom (2005, pp210ff) distinguishes between rules, norms and shared strategies. For current purposes, the description of rules here is adequate, however, any further conceptualization of a potential research agenda based on the ideas presented in this chapter will consider Ostrom's framework.

7   What individuals can change is their strategy with regards to rules and the way they will negotiate the situations in which they find themselves.

References

Anderson, C. (1989). Centralization and group inequalities in North Queensland. In Altman, J. (ed.) *Emergent Inequalities in Aboriginal Australia*. Sydney: Oceania Monograph No. 38. University of Sydney.

Bell, D. (1983). *Daughters of the Dreaming*. Melbourne: McPhee Gribble.

Berndt, R. and Berndt, C. (1965). *The World of the First Australians*. Sydney: Ure Smith (2nd ed.).

Bolger, A. (1991). *Aboriginal Women and Violence*. ANU: North Australia Research Unit.

Christie, M and Greatorex, J. (2004). Yolgnu life in the Northern Territory of Australia: the significance of community and social capital. *Asia Pacific Journal of Public Administration*, 26 (1), 55–69.

Daly, A. (1999). Prospects for Indigenous Australians in the welfare system. *Agenda*, 6 (1), 5–16.

Davies, J. (2003). Contemporary geographies of indigenous rights and interests in rural Australia. *Australian Geographer,* 34, 19–45.

Dodson, M. (1996). *Assimilation versus self-determination: no contest*. Discussion Paper No. 1. Canberra: North Australia Research Unit.

Falk, I. and Kilpatrick, S. (2000). What is social capital? A study of rural communities. *Sociologia Ruralis*, 40 (1), 87–110.

Folds, R. (2001). *Crossed Purposes. The Pintupi and Australian Indigenous Policy.* Sydney: University of NSW Press.

Gerritsen, R. (1982a). Blackfellas and Whitefellas. In Loveday, P. (ed.), *Service Delivery to Remote Communities*. Darwin: ANU, North Australian Research Unit.

Gerritsen, R. (1982b). Outstations, differing interpretations and policy implications. In Loveday, P. (ed.), *Service Delivery to Outstations*. Darwin: ANU, North Australian Research Unit.

Gray, W. (1977). Decentralization trends in Arnhem Land. In Berndt, R. (ed.) *Aborigines and Change: Australia in the 70s*. Canberrra: Australian Institute of Aboriginal Studies.

Hardin, G. (1968). The tragedy of the commons. *Science*, 162, 1243–1248.

Hart, C and Pilling, A. (1960). *The Tiwi of North Australia*. New York: Holt.

Hiatt, L. (1965). *Kinship and Conflict*. Canberra: Australian National University.

Hiatt, L. (1968). Gidjingali marriage arrangements. In Lee, R. and DeVore, I. (eds) *Man the Hunter*. Chicago: Aldine Publishing Co.

Hiatt, L. (1986). Aboriginal political life. In Edwards, W. H. (ed.), *Traditional Aboriginal Society*. South Melbourne: MacMillan.

Hughes, I. (1996). Yolngu rom: indigenous knowledge in north Australia. In Blunt, P. and Michael Warren, D. (eds), *Indigenous Organizations and Development*. London: Intermediate Technology Publications.

Ife, J. (1995). *Community Development. Creating community alternatives – vision, analysis and practice*. Frenchs Forest NSW: Longman.

Jewkes, R. and Murcott, A. (1998). Community representatives representing the community? *Social Science of Medicine*, 46(7), 843–858.

Maddock, K. (1982). *The Australian Aborigines: A Portrait of their Society*. (2nd ed.) Ringwood, Vic: Penguin Books.

Meggitt, M. (1962). *Desert People. A study of the Walbiri people of Central Australia.* Sydney: Angus and Robertson.

Myers, F. (1980). A broken code: Pintupi political theory and temporary social life. *Mankind*, 12(4), 311–326.

Ostrom, E. (1990). *Governing the Commons: The evolution of institutions for collective action*. New York: Cambridge University Press.

Ostrom, E. (2005). *Understanding Institutional Diversity*. Princeton: Princeton University Press.

Pritchard, B. and Gibson C. (1996). The Black Economy: regional development strategies in the Northern Territory. Darwin: ANU, North Australia Research Unit Report Series No. 1.

Productivity Commission (2003). *Social Capital: Reviewing the concept and its policy implications*. Melbourne: Productivity Commission Research Paper.

Rowse, T. (1992). *Remote Possibilities. The Aboriginal domain and the administrative imagination*. Darwin: ANU, North Australia Research Unit.

Sanders, W. (2001). Indigenous Australians and the rules of social security: Universalism, appropriateness and justice. Discussion Paper No. 212, Canberra: ANU, Centre for Aboriginal Economic Policy Research.

SCRGSP (Steering Committee for the Review of Government Service Provision) (2005). *Overcoming Indigenous Disadvantage: Key indicators 2005*. Canberra: Productivity Commission.

Senior, K. (2001). Health beliefs and behaviour: the opportunities and practicalities of 'looking after yourself'. In Ngukurr, South East Arnhem Collaborative Research Project Working Paper No. 5, Wollongong: ISCCI, University of Wollongong.

Smith, B. (1989). The concept 'community' in Aboriginal policy and service delivery. *NADU Occasional Paper No. 1*. Darwin: North Australia Development Unit, Department of Social Security.

Stanner, W.H. (1979). *The Aborigines. White Man got no Dreaming, Essays, 1938–73*. Canberra: ANU Press.

Taylor, J. and Stanley, O. (2005). *The Opportunity Costs of the Status Quo in the Thamarrurr Region*. ANU, Centre for Aboriginal Economic Policy Research.

Willis, J. (1995). Fatal attraction: do high technology treatments for end stage renal disease benefit Aboriginal people in central Australia? *Australian and New Zealand Journal of Public Health*, 19(6), 603–609.

Woolcock, M. (2001). The place of social capital in understanding social and economic outcomes, ISUMA: *Canadian Journal of Policy Research*, 2(1), 11–17.

Part IV
_____

Experiences in Dealing with Institutional Dynamics

10

Designing Robust Common Property Regimes for Collaboration towards Rural Sustainability

David J. Brunckhorst and Graham R. Marshall

Introduction

Sustainability of many human communities in agricultural and pastoral regions is diminishing. In many parts of the world, a significant contributor is natural resource degradation within these regions. The Australian *National Action Plan for Salinity and Water Quality* (Commonwealth of Australia, 2000) estimated that land and water degradation costs Australia at least $3.5 billion annually. The real cost to society is probably much greater through the interdependency of social-ecological systems. The effects on rural communities, their social systems and economies, are increasingly visible.

Institutions – socially-accepted rules for interaction of humans with one another and nature (see Ostrom, 1990; Bromley, 1992a) – affect the resilience of ecological systems. Ecological and social resilience in Australian rural communities appears elusive within contemporary policy frameworks (Reeve 1992, 1997; Dovers, 2000). Despite increasing efforts to reduce social and environmental costs by encouraging structural adjustment in agriculture, there remain substantial obstacles to adjustment. These obstacles include existing institutions, social values and cultural norms relating to land use (Reeve, 1998). Conventional attempts to address these issues are hampered too frequently by an entrenched narrow focus on individual property rights (particularly in respect of land tenure), as well as by institutional arrangements implemented at inappropriate scales for sustainable landscape futures (Lee, 1993; Reeve, 1997, 1998; Brunckhorst, 2000, 2001). Intertwined with the cultural dimensions of property rights and its influence on natural resources management is a complex social ecology. This social ecology is a web of both formal and informal social behaviours and structures that influence landowners' attitudes about issues related to property rights and the environment. It also affects their willingness to support or oppose initiatives for improved sustainability.

It is important to clarify our understanding of the above-mentioned terms such as *institutions property* and *property rights* in the context of designing more sustainable resource governance arrangements (see Smajgl and Larson, Chapter 1). The socially accepted rules defined above as institutions comprise not only formal rules (e.g. laws, regulations, contracts, memoranda of understanding, etc) but also informal rules (e.g. customs, norms, conventions, etiquette, etc.). Rules are institutions where they are actually followed by most individuals to which they apply (i.e. they are *working rules*) (Ostrom, 1990).

The concept of *property* encapsulates a claim to a benefit (or income) stream, and a *property right* is a claim to a benefit stream that can be enforced against claims by others by virtue of the strength of prevailing institutions (Commons, 1968; North, 1990; Ostrom, 1990). In other words they are endorsed, respected and upheld by humanly devised constraints, enforcement and other interactions that effectively maintain their legitimacy. Property rights are thus the individual components of the sets of relationships comprising institutions (Schmid, 1972). Conversely, property rights *regimes* can be regarded as institutional mechanisms people use to control their use of the environment and their behaviour with each other (Hanna et al, 1996). Bromley (1992b) considered a property rights regime for a particular natural resource as the totality of social and institutional arrangements by which individuals are aware of what parts of the resource are their and others' property, and what duties are imposed on them by virtue of others' property rights.

The strength of the institutions underpinning property rights in a particular domain, and thus the enforceability of these rights in that domain, depends considerably on the legitimacy afforded the institutions by those expected variously to comply with, monitor and enforce them. In some cases, the legitimacy afforded customary institutions (e.g. verbal agreement sealed by shaking hands in the presence of witnesses) for defining a new property right (e.g. for one landholder to borrow another's tools) may provide all the institutional strength desired. Other cases may warrant some supplementation of this customary legitimacy with the added legitimacy that may be gained by introducing higher authority. For example, a decision by a catchment management committee on how to allocate incentive funds for on-ground works between groups of landholders may be regarded as more legitimate if the committee comprises representatives nominated from local landholders within those communities reflecting a particular domain. Moreover, the socially accepted authority of the committee may provide all the legitimacy that is needed for many of the decisions arising within this domain, with decisions referred to yet higher levels of authority (perhaps ultimately to government and/or the legal system) only when its legitimacy in respect of such decisions becomes unduly stretched. Similarly within particular land-use domains, Indigenous cultural rights maintained and upheld over thousands of years have legitimacy, unwritten in law, that is increasingly accepted by land title holders.

Five types of property rights can be distinguished in respect of natural resources, namely rights of: access, withdrawal, management, exclusion and alienation (Schlager and Ostrom, 1992). In turn, rightsholders differ in how many of the different types of property rights they hold in respect of a particular resource. Only where rightsholders hold all five types of property rights in respect of a resource can they be regarded properly as *owners* of that resource (Schlager and Ostrom, 1992).

The situation of *non-property* or *open access* exists either where a property claim has not been made or where the claim is unprotected by an accepted legitimate authority. This situation often characterizes ecosystems, which, because they overlap different land tenure systems, no single property holder is motivated to sustain in their entirety. Both state and individual land-tenure systems are increasingly implicated in observed failures to sustain such ecosystems (Reeve, 1997, 1998). These failures stem in significant part from the high transaction (including political) costs of enforcing the rights and responsibilities established by these property systems, as well as from entrenched institutional arrangements for resource governance that deal poorly with ecosystem functions crossing interdependent scales (i.e. managing externalities; see Reeve, 1992, 1998; Lee, 1993; Brunckhorst et al, 1997; Marshall, 2002, 2004b,c, 2005).

Given the tendency of property systems and associated ideologies inherited from the past to remain *locked in* despite escalating change pressures from negative environmental externalities, there is increasing value in institutional experimentation designed to explore innovative paths forward. In this chapter, we are concerned particularly with the innovative use of various business structure entities that can provide supporting strength (*robustness*, sensu Anderies et al, 2004) to collaborative arrangements of groups of landholders of multiple resources that occur across the landscape and land titles. We draw on lessons from practical on-ground experiments, which in turn were informed by multi-disciplinary research into long-enduring institutional arrangements for collaborative resource use and management often referred to as *common property regime*. Margaret McKean (2000b, p.30) describes a common property regime as 'a property-rights arrangement in which a group of resource users share rights and duties toward a resource'. The focus of common property research has been on understanding what gives common property regimes both the strength and flexibility required to manage natural resources sustainably in the face of uncertainty and flux. The institutional experimentation reported here drew deeply from the insights gained from research on common property regimes and collective action by Ostrom and others (see for example: Ostrom, 1990, 1992; Bromley, 1992a; McKean, 1992, 1997, 2000a, b; Berkes and Folke, 1998; Ostrom et al, 2002; Marshall, 2005). Some of the features of successful common property regimes identified in this research for institutional adaptability in managing natural resources are summarized in the next section. Identification of such characteristics helps build our capacities for responding to accelerating change pressures on interdependent social-ecological systems (see for example, *Science*, vol 302, 2003).

A recent advance in this discussion has arisen from Anderies et al, (2004), who asked 'what makes a social-ecological system robust?' Anderies and co-authors differentiated resilience, which arises from spontaneous self-organizing processes within a system (such as an ecosystem or a social network), from robustness that arises in addition from conscious efforts to increase a system's capacity to adapt to internal and external stresses. The more we understand how to facilitate robustness in linked social-ecological systems, the better equipped we become to design institutional arrangements capable of enhancing the resilience of those ecosystems we depend on (Anderies et al, 2004). The on-ground experiments discussed in this chapter seek particularly to understand how groups of farmers can move towards sustainable natural resource management and enterprise development by crafting institutional arrangements enabling them to manage their combined resources cooperatively. Such arrangements can contribute both resilience and robustness. In building robustness, we are particularly interested here in how to take advantage of opportunities the existing suite of business structures (supported by a state's legal system) might contribute to robustness of common property regimes.

The *outback* of Australia represents a large part of the continent, and is characterized in large part by rangelands – arid and semi-arid landscapes with occasional monsoon-like rains and low productivity soils used primarily for grazing. These social-ecological systems can be differentiated as particular biocultural or landscape regions, such as the northern savanna. Despite the sometimes large distances between neighbours, these are interdependent systems with external influences, including those of distant governments. In understanding, facilitating, or possibly redesigning institutional arrangements for collective action and resource governance in the outback, knowledge by local people of the design characteristics of robust community-scale institutions will be important. Appropriate business structures might offer a supportive framework for collective decisions that facilitate adaptive management enhancing sustainability and endurance.

After summarizing the characteristics of enduring common property regimes, we draw on three projects we have been closely involved with to describe how legal entities or corporate structures might be employed to enhance robustness of the institutional arrangements. All are Australian grazing systems, one in the mallee rangelands and Riverland in South Australia, and two on the relatively richer soils of the New England Tablelands of New South Wales. Each example involves the development of a form of common property regime for collective decision-making, action and governance of landholder groups and/or communities. Facilitating and supporting (but not stifling) this institutional development through legal entities or corporate structures can contribute robustness. Balancing individual versus collective rationale, and risk management of internal and external stresses enhances robust capabilities. Some corporate structures or combinations of entities might, in different ways, be useful in the development and evolution of robust institutional arrangements for collective use and governance of various resources across multiple scales of ownership.

Characteristics of Robust Commons

Numerous instances of long-enduring common property regimes, referred to here as *commons*, have now been identified and studied. The fact that social-ecological systems of this kind are found so widely and often have a track record stretching over a long period, suggests they can be highly adaptive and robust. Their operational characteristics (Netting, 1976; Ostrom, 1990, 1992; Berkes and Folke, 1998; McKean, 2000a, b; Ostrom et al, 2002), if able to be generalized and translated to contemporary circumstances, would help us respond to and manage change pressures, functions, and dynamics in ways that add resilience and robustness to existing social-ecological systems.

In building on the design principles of Elinor Ostrom's (1990) synthesis, and the work of others, McKean (1992, 1997, 2000a, b, 2002) identified several internal and external features of common property regimes that help explain robust instances of such institutional arrangements. Features regarding relationships among regime co-owners or collaborators are termed internal features, and include the following (after Ostrom, 1990; McKean 2000a, b, 2002):

1   There are clearly defined boundaries to the resource system, and to the group of individuals with rights of access to resource units.
2   The collective owners of land, water or other resource rights are a self-conscious and self-governing group. Dynamics are best managed if the group is relatively small (or, if large, consists of small sub-groups) and has a history of shared values and social capital (built on trust and social norms including reciprocity).
3   Within-group homogeneity of identities and interests assists cohesion. Heterogeneity of skills that contribute to group interdependence and capacity is also valuable. Members, including the young educated, with external networks to decision-makers or others in positions of power, can be useful.
4   The rules of engagement and operation are of local origin and design, easily understood, easy to enforce and ecologically conservative (to assist matching to ecological context and resource capacity).
5   Distribution of benefits from the commons is equitably proportional to the effort (time, labour, infrastructure, money) invested in the commons by members.
6   The group has an internal mechanism for resolving conflict.
7   The rules provide for monitoring of adherence behaviour and application of appropriate graduated sanctions.
8   Those guarding or monitoring the commons, and its officials, are accountable to the co-owners. In a globalizing world, pressures on a group of co-owners will come from an increasing number of different directions. A group's characteristics in terms of relationships between its members and the outside world are termed external features.

In addition to those eight internal features, McKean (2000a, b, 2002) identified three external features of successful common property regimes:

9   It is better for the group of co-owners to have independent jurisdiction or autonomy. Groups will be more robust when their members possess long-term tenure to resource rights and are free to design their own institutional

arrangements unchallenged by external authorities. Governments that defend and support the group's independence can play an important role.

10 Both ecological and political scale and context are important to the success of common property regimes in managing natural resources sustainably. Common property regimes operate better in managing resource allocation, monitoring and use when their boundaries match the scale and context of local ecological resources.

11 Across spatially extensive ecological resource systems and/or large groups of users, it is important to nest layers of governance for decision-making and responsibility.

Experimental common property regime models designed in accordance with these features can be expected to strengthen the robustness of the rural social-ecological systems into which they are introduced, and increase sustainability of resource use within such systems. The contribution towards robustness of a particular tactic in common property regime design is explored in the following brief summaries of projects with which we have been involved. This tactic involves a group of co-owners organizing themselves through state-supported legal structures capable of accommodating and consolidating the 11 features listed above – feature nine most obviously. These legally recognized business entities will henceforth be referred to simply as *structure/s*.

Contemporary Commons in Australia: Reinventing Commons through Cross-Property Collaborative Structures

Farmers in nations like Australia, Canada and the USA are constrained (spatially, socially, economically and ecologically) in their capacity for sustainable resource use. Institutional impediments include an individualistic property rights system (Marshall et al, 2005) and a political-economic system that demands ongoing productivity increases to make up for declining terms of trade despite frequent accompanying declines in the productive capacity of the natural resource base. These demands typically come without commensurate pressures on farmers to account for the external costs, environmental or social, that satisfying them often generates.

A contemporary approach to institutional design for rural common property regimes acceptable to rural landholders and their families involves the parcelling up of individual titles of nearby farms to gain both ecological and socio-economic benefits. This would help overcome some mismatches between the scale of ownership for rural land, the scale of ecological functional capacity, and the scale at which costs are incurred from its utilization. Three institutional experiments that pursue such an approach are discussed below. Each of these experiments follows a model wherein individual land titles were retained while bundling up a much larger collective resource pool having greater capacity to deliver economies of scale and manage the resources within their functional capacity. The experiments were designed to answer key questions including the following: How do we design and implement cross-tenure resource use and management in a modern nation state? What business structures or entities are available to support design and operation of a common property regime? Can a common property regime supported by a formal business structure remain adaptive while protecting both the individual and collective interests of participating landholders?

Bookmark biosphere: Common property and cross-tenure resource management

The UNESCO Biosphere Reserve programme provides an international umbrella for developing and testing community-based adaptive-management or *learning-by-doing* models. This approach has begun to develop at the Fitzgerald River Biosphere in south Western Australia (Watson, 1993), and at the Bookmark Biosphere in the South Australian portion of the Riverland region through which the lower reaches of the Murray River flow (Brunckhorst et al, 1997; Brunckhorst, 2000, 2001).

Riverland communities of South Australia, Victoria and New South Wales living along the Murray River are faced with a number of human-created environmental challenges. Soil loss, landscape degradation and species loss, combined with the infusion of saline ground waters, decreasing water quality, and disappearing wetlands, collectively threaten the sustainability of all these communities.

The semi-arid Mallee ecosystems of lower Murray region are uniquely Australian, consisting of a few eucalyptus species adapted to the harsh dry conditions. Productivity of the Mallee ecosystem is low. Soils are fragile and poor, with deficiencies in structure and nitrogen content. Characteristically, vegetation is multi-stemmed and squamose, and possesses peculiarly shaped leaves enabling the canopy to intercept about 15 per cent of available rainfall with a further 30 per cent running down the multiple trunks. The region receives an average of 240 millimetres of annual rainfall with annual evaporation rates potentially greater than 2,300 millimetres.

Droughts are frequent and are punctuated by erratic floods. The hydrology of the floodplain and wetlands of the Murray River has been altered by a variety of engineering projects designed to support agriculture and irrigation development. Problems of groundwater salinization have been compounded by other factors, including loss of deep-rooted vegetation through land clearing for timber and pastoral use throughout the past century. Many of the land degradation problems within the biosphere reserve are replicated throughout the drainage systems of the Murray River and its tributary, the Darling, which together drain one-seventh of the continent.

Bookmark Biosphere covers a region of more than 9,200 square kilometres and encompasses the interconnected Murray river, its anabranch creeks and floodplain, and mallee-eucalypt dominated uplands. This is the environment that the local communities identify with – the *Riverland*. Several small townships occur in the region. Large-scale landscape recovery and species restorations are necessary and integral to the pursuit of ecologically sustainable development initiatives.

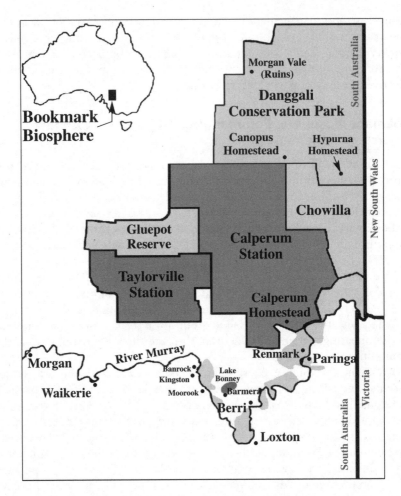

Figure 10.1 Bookmark biosphere in South Australia: Generalized map showing
major land parcels including the common property, *Calperum*

Source: Map courtesy Australian Landscape Trust and Bookmark Biosphere Trust

The Bookmark Biosphere common property regime is made up of 40
different parcels of land of varying tenure, including: conservation reserves;
game and forestry reserves; national trust land; large (private) pastoral leases;
and, individual private title (Figure 10.1). It was initiated in 1992, through the
purchase of the 2,000 square kilometre *Calperum* pastoral lease, with funds
provided jointly by a Chicago benefactor and the Australian Government. The
community was given title to, and responsibility for, the land and water
resources through a *Deed in Trust*. This stimulated an evolving collaboration
across many other landholders in the ensuing years. *Calperum* became a
community focal point to trial innovative sustainable land uses and large-scale
restoration. In joining this collective together, governments have vested the

community with ownership rights and responsibility for selecting goals for management of this entire regional landscape for their future.

The flood plains of Bookmark Biosphere Reserve are recognized as internationally significant wetlands for waterfowl and migratory species (e.g. RAMSAR). *Calperum*, which incorporates many of these wetlands of international significance, is also the focal point for the community to experiment with novel ecologically restorative industries. This is not only on the land it encompasses, but also across adjacent privately owned lands and government conservation lands (Brunckhorst et al, 1997a).

The Riverland communities, through nominated representatives, manage the land within the Biosphere Reserve and accomplish required tasks through a citizens' committee known as the Bookmark Biosphere Trust, which is constituted under South Australian legislation. The Trust is the formal management body responsible for Bookmark Biosphere Reserve and for making collective decisions, organizing, monitoring and controlling cross-land tenure activities. State and federal agencies and private sector professionals assist the Trust in understanding and implementing management options.

Creation of the Bookmark Biosphere involved a bold commitment to support *bottom-up* capacities to accomplish conservation goals, political harmony, and innovative working relationships for leveraging available resources, commitment and talent. It provides for a combination of capacity building from the *bottom (community)-up, top (government)-down* and *sideways (private sector)-in* (Brunckhorst, 2000). In addition to the community co-owned *Calperum* land, it involves a common property regime institutional arrangement encompassing multiple land tenures and parcels by means of a combination of structures.

The Bookmark region and its Trust are supported through several interesting capacity-building partners and structures. The first of these is a non-profit philanthropic foundation, the Australian Landscape Trust (ALT), a progeny of the Ian Potter Foundation. The ALT provides more than funds for innovative land management and recovery enterprises. It also contributes capacity building and analysis to support the community decision-making. Enterprises developed, such as a horticultural business producing drought and salt resilient cultivars, were established using limited liability company and non-profit foundation structures, but with some characteristics of cooperatives. The ALT and Bookmark Biosphere Trust, in turn, provide governance for a nested system of informal Landcare groups that have been delegated responsibilities for smaller areas (within or across properties) of the Bookmark Biosphere region.

Tilbuster Commons

The Tilbuster Commons is a common property regime established collaboratively by local landholders and facilitated as a deliberate experimental model by researchers and Land and Water Australia for a period of three years (see Coop and Brunckhorst, 1999, 2001; Brunckhorst and Coop, 2003; Williamson et al, 2003). It is located in the Tilbuster Valley, on the New England Tablelands in northern New South Wales. The land covers approximately

1,300 hectares and is an amalgamation of the privately owned parcels of land of four grazing families, with individual properties varying in size.

The social and ecological issues facing the landholders in the Tilbuster Valley are similar to those that face many rural communities. Among these pressures are an ageing rural population, small size of landholdings, and ecological and economic decline. Consistent also with many rural communities, the members of the valley tend to provide both a supportive environment and assistance to each another. Another factor in the selection of the Tilbuster resident landholders was their concern for the long-term future of the valley and their willingness to recognize many of the issues associated with collaborative management.

Four grazing families contributed land, livestock, infrastructure and labour to form the common property arrangement. The entire group as a single enterprise, collectively known as the Tilbuster Commons, manages these combined resources. The members and their families are establishing a grazing arrangement with the aim of testing whether the common property regime model is capable of delivering improved economic returns while ensuring the sustainability of the productive resource. The model relies on achieving a scale of operation at which integrated management of resources for maintenance of ecological integrity, as well as grazing purposes, becomes possible (Figure 10.2). Figure 10.2 provides diagrammatic illustration of how the Tilbuster Commons refocuses strategic decision-making from spatial units based on individual land titles, to considering the resource base as a collective. This enables more efficient and appropriate use of the ecological resources, time and labour, while providing additional scales of economy and risk management.

After two years of discussion facilitated by researchers and a local leader, the landholders formed an informal (unconstituted) arrangement in 1999, known as the Tilbuster Common Resource Cooperative (Coop and

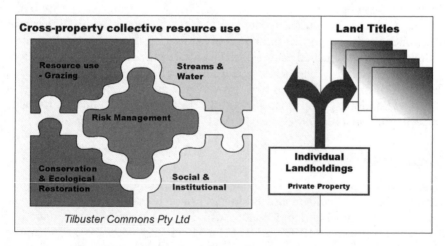

Figure 10.2 Diagrammatic illustration of refocusing of the strategic decision-making at the Tilbuster commons

Brunckhorst, 1999). While this had no legal standing, it provided an important social vehicle for the group to begin building the necessary social capital required for the transformation towards whole system planning, resource allocation and collective decision-making (Brunckhorst, 2001, 2002; Brunckhorst and Coop, 2003).

The initial decision to participate was not based on a set of hard and fast rules that were already in existence. Rather, it was based on shared values and aspirations, together with attempts to apply in practice some of the guiding features of successful common property regime institutions that were listed earlier. This *philosophy* of explicit shared direction became, and continues to be, an important set of criteria against which to test decisions. This probably marks the beginning of the informal institutionalization of the Tilbuster Commons. Since its inception, trust, credibility and acceptance of each other's strengths and weaknesses have grown. Over time, each participating member has been able to see the advantages of collaborating. A collective confidence was gained in the group's capability to negotiate equitable outcomes with multiple benefits (see Singleton, 1998; Wondolleck and Yaffee, 2000, on building trust, collaboration and cooperative informal institutions).

The group then started to consider the kinds of structures and corporate arrangements they needed. The group felt strongly that a simple structure providing flexibility would serve them best. The range of decisions included livestock management, planned grazing, pasture management, the strategic allocation of conservation and environmental rehabilitation areas, and operational issues. Operational rules began to evolve that reflected the design features of long-enduring common property regimes discussed earlier. Issues at the forefront of discussions included allocation of land to the common (excepting small areas nominated for private use, primarily around member's homes), selection of key infrastructure items, development of a *formula* representing the interests of each member, and allocation of land/resources to maintaining ecosystem functions recognized as underpinning the productive sustainability of the common. Expected labour inputs simply became a matter of a landholder family looking after the herd of cattle when they were on their land, according to the collectively decided grazing plan. Labour inputs therefore automatically equated to the proportion of the land area contributed by a landholding family and their expected share of the net profits. The rules and processes that govern the management of the Tilbuster Commons continued to evolve through this collaborative process, guided by testing decisions against agreed values and goals (Brunckhorst and Coop, 2003; Williamson et al, 2003).

The group considered various structures suitable to undertake the management and enterprise development of the commons, including partnership, trust, cooperative and company arrangements. They decided that a limited liability company (Pty Ltd) structure seemed to provide the best arrangement (Williamson et al, 2003). In a common property regime with this structure, there is a useful tension between individual landholders' interests and the collective interests of the group of landholders represented in the company. With both hats on, individuals must consider the options that best benefit both themselves and the collective interests of the Tilbuster Commons Company. In other words, there is a healthy *conflict of interest* for collective action across individual land tenure boundaries (Brunckhorst and Coop, 2003).

The landholders, as directors of the company, each have a share calculated using the *formula* agreed by all. The formula represents the proportion of original contributions of land, stock, equipment, expected labour input, etc. contributed by individual landowners. It also forms the basis for sharing profits in the form of allocated dividend shares. As company directors they make collective decisions for running the enterprises of the company, and to manage the portion of the whole resource base represented by their land and the creek that runs through it (Figure 10.2). Initially an informal tenancy at will was created with the landholders as lessors and the company as lessee. This allowed the company to start rotational grazing across all properties. The arrangement was trialled as a renewable fixed-term lease for the three years of the experiment, but was later renewed. A fixed-term lease provides a mechanism with some stability and protection for both individuals (i.e. retaining land title) and the company (Williamson et al, 2003).

Individual and collective social benefits of this common property regime include freeing up of time and labour and the pooling of a variety of expertise. This in turn helps build robustness for common property regime institutions and resilience of the ecosystems supporting its resource base. Some simple but highly regarded benefits enjoyed by the Tilbuster Commoners include more efficient accounting and management practices, and reduced labour inputs, for example, by eliminating the need to crop for winter feed. This permits families to *get away* to have a real holiday, and to leave gates open when the livestock are on someone else's landholding.

At broader ecological scales across the landscape, the common property regime provided opportunities for long-term conservation and maintenance of rare, basalt associated ecosystems and the restoration of woodland and stream environments (e.g. creek bed and riparian vegetation). The Tilbuster common property regime therefore incorporated several different levels of rights and rules – for example, limiting certain uses and fencing the creek across properties and facilitating stream bed and riparian restoration. Such landscape-scale resource use and restoration, based on assessment of the natural resources base across an ecological landscape and a regime of informally upheld rights, can build resilience and sustainability at the same time as providing good economic returns. As Ostrom (1990) has pointed out, the higher level authority of the group to devise future operational level rights is what makes collective-choice rights so powerful.

Under conventional individual ownership regimes, a typical landholding may comprise some high-quality soil that is suitable for farming, grazing land that is generally not suitable for farming, and some poorer areas barely suited to grazing. The type and mix of these areas will vary depending on the topography and soils of the region. Faced with various family and economic pressures and with only these resources at the landholder's disposal, there is often no option but to overuse, or inappropriately use, each type of resource. The productive riparian land is inevitably cropped, possibly for both summer and winter feed for livestock. The mid-quality land will be grazed throughout the year, and the poorer areas will slowly decline due to the impacts of livestock *wintering over*. Input costs tend to increase to counter negative trends of water quality, parasite load and reduced natural productivity of both cropped and grazed areas.

A valuable aspect of the Tilbuster common property regime is the ability to allocate the available resources more efficiently, but within their functional capacity. It could be considered a modern version of the *scattering* that occurred on the old agrarian commons of Europe (Dahlman, 1980), but updated with new pasture management knowledge and aid from modern tools such as GIS (geographic information systems). By recognizing the distinction between resource allocation and land tenure, the Tilbuster Commons land-holders consolidated their herds to graze them across all of their properties (Figure 10.2). This allows the utilization of grazing techniques such as planned grazing regimes over wider spatial and timescales. The planned timed grazing is slowly returning a mix of native grasses and certainly maintains improved ground cover (80–95 per cent), with additional benefits for water quality and deep soil moisture (Earl and Jones, 1996; Savory, 1999). Input costs have been greatly reduced and production increased.

Clear *triple-bottom-line* benefits have therefore arisen from the Tilbuster Commons innovation. In addition to considerable environmental and grazing resource improvements, the system appears better at managing production *risk*, as evidenced by the resilience of the collective grazing resource during the recent drought. There has been a considerable *freeing* up of time and labour as well as reduction in financial costs, and each landholding family's dividend also represents a better (farm) income than they had been able to achieve individ-ually. The company business structure contributes robustness to the day-to-day operational rules, collective decision-making and risk management (e.g. to destock early through the recent drought), and the sharing of benefits and responsibilities.

Furracabad Valley group farming initiative

A further initiative concerned with exploring the potential of a common prop-erty regime to enhance the economic, social and environmental sustainability of rural land use has been underway since 2000. It is focused on the Furracabad Valley some five to seven kilometres from Glen Innes (also within the New England Tablelands). The valley consists of about 25–30 farms, vary-ing from 10 to 1,500ha in size. This initiative arose from the experiences of the valley's Landcare group, who have worked together successfully for over a decade in addressing their common environmental and natural resource management problems. These successes led the group's members to become interested in exploring how they might enhance their economic and social sustainability by building on the platform for collective action they had estab-lished (Marshall, 2004a; Marshall et al, 2005).

Driven by this interest, they completed a Farming for the Future programme offered by NSW Agriculture (now Department of Primary Industries). The programme highlighted the economies of scale that smaller farms in the valley were missing out on. The view was formed that all farms in the valley could gain economically by pooling their resources into a *group farming* operation, perhaps structured similarly to the Tilbuster Commons, and share the resulting economies of scale. Compared with the alternative where some farmers buy others out in order to capture these economies for themselves, it was anticipated that the group approach would better maintain the district's social fabric.

At a meeting of landholders held in May 2000, it was agreed that implementation of the concept would best occur as a formal project involving professional support and a staged consultation process. The ensuing application to the Commonwealth Government's Regional Assistance Program for project funding justified this approach as follows: 'Farmers have traditionally operated in management isolation, making their own decisions and rarely having to make joint decisions that directly influence their financial future. It is here that the greatest challenge lies in ensuring that stakeholders fully understand the concept and the impact on them.' The funding application was approved in early 2002. The aim of the project was to develop the group farming concept to the stage of a business plan and achieve sign-off from a critical mass of landholders on implementing the concept in accordance with that plan.

The landholders originally expressing interest in the group-farming concept were interviewed in early 2003, to determine whether there was sufficient serious interest to justify preparation of a business plan. While virtually all the landholders interviewed acknowledged the concept to be good in principle, for most it was *too much, too soon*. Of the 18 farm businesses interviewed, five indicated a serious interest in leasing their land to the proposed group farming arrangement within the reasonably near future. While this level of interest was less than hoped for originally, it was judged sufficient for starting to consider how the group farming enterprise might be structured, and to assess the financial implications of such a structure for participating landholders. It was noted that the 2,454ha of land held in aggregate by these five farm businesses compared favourably with the combined landholding of around 1,300ha upon which the Tilbuster Commons had been founded.

A workshop was held in July 2003, attended by representatives of four of the five farm businesses that had indicated serious interest in implementing the concept. Although each of these individuals stressed the perceived social and environmental advantages of joining a group farming arrangement, they agreed that their decisions to join would depend ultimately on evidence that they would benefit in economic terms. The workshop was facilitated by a consultant with knowledge of group farming enterprises established elsewhere in New South Wales. He explained that his experiences in this field had taught him the importance of apportioning economic rewards within a group farming enterprise in line with two key principles:

1   all contributions of inputs to the group farming enterprise should be remunerated commercially; and
2   all remuneration should occur transparently.

The workshop facilitator suggested to the landholders present that joining a group farming enterprise would involve them contributing one (or more) of land, labour and working capital to a company that would run the affairs of the collective enterprise (hereafter referred to as *the company*). Under this structure, the resources contributed by the participating farm businesses would generate a single pool of gross income to be shared between them. Deducting from this pool the variable costs of the various enterprises utilized to generate income would yield the gross margin to the company. Deduction of the overhead costs of the company, (i.e. those not specific to particular enterprises) and the reward paid for labour and management would give the gross profit available for rewarding the land and working capital contributed by the participating businesses. The reward for the working capital contributed (net profit) would be given by deducting from gross profit the reward allocated for land. This net profit would be available for some mix (decided by the company directors) of paying dividends to the participating businesses and reinvesting in the company.

The landholders present at the workshop agreed that this structure was appropriate, and that the reward paid for labour and management should be based on commercial rates matched to the levels of skill and responsibility required. They agreed further that the reward paid for land leased to the company by the participating businesses (that would retain individual title to this land) would need to offer adequate incentive for those businesses to themselves incur the expenses of pasture maintenance and improvement, fencing, and so on. For this reason, it was agreed that land rental rates should be based on the productivity of land parcels (measured by livestock carrying capacity).

It was anticipated by those present that individual farm businesses would contribute to the start-up working capital of the group farming company pro rata to their shares of the total carrying capacity of the land run by the company. Shares in the company, and thus in the total dividends remitted to shareholders, would be allocated in proportion to the working capital contributed by each participating business. Subject to the company's constitution, the potential would exist for individual businesses to vary their investment of working capital in the group farming company by trading or gifting shares.

Based on a budget identifying the financial advantages for the individual farm businesses from joining a group farming enterprise structured as outlined above, the farm business representatives present at the workshop indicated interest in proceeding towards a business plan for such an enterprise. Nevertheless, by the time that a further meeting was convened a month later, one of these businesses had lost interest in joining a group farming arrangement. This meant that the combined land area potentially available for such an arrangement had declined to 1,741ha. Moreover, concerns were expressed that the arrangement might become *unbalanced* with this level of participation, given that one of the remaining businesses would be contributing three quarters of this area. It was decided that a group farming enterprise was not viable with this reduced level of committed interest, and consequently that the project could not be progressed to development and sign-off of a business plan.

The source of many of the obstacles to gaining the commitment of farmers to the group farming concept can be traced to time. This factor was critical in two ways. First, circumstances need to be such that a *critical mass* of farm businesses are ready to embrace the concept at the same time. Such a favourable situation seemed to prevail around early 2000, when the concept was conceived and the funding application was submitted. By the time that the project commenced, however, the situation had become less propitious. Some landholders committed to the concept had left the district. In a few other cases it seemed that the earlier enthusiasm for the concept had simply dissipated with the passage of time, perhaps due to the morale-sapping effects of the drought, or disappointment at loss of interest from others they had looked forward to working with in the group farming arrangement.

The second way that time presented an obstacle arose from the conservatism of most farmers. Due to this conservatism, considerable time is often needed to change their attitudes. Probably the most formidable attitudinal obstacle in this respect derived from the widespread *rugged individualist* self-image of many Australian farmers. Changes to attitudes of this nature do not occur overnight. In retrospect, it was optimistic to expect that the attitudes of farmers unfamiliar with the group-farming concept at the beginning of field-work for the project could be shifted sufficiently by its end (i.e. within three quarters of a year) that they would give up their independence to join such an arrangement. As mentioned above, it took nearly two years of discussions before the four farm businesses now involved in the Tilbuster Commons agreed to form an informal arrangement (i.e. from 1997 to 1999). It was not until January 2001 that a private company structure was registered for the Commons, and not until the next financial year that the company began operating. Indeed, there are grounds for optimism that the seeds planted by the Furracabad Valley group farming project will bear fruit within a few years. Between circulation of the project report in early 2004 and the time of writing, there have been a further three meetings of representatives from farm businesses in and around the Furracabad Valley who are interested in the concept, and more are planned for the future.

Although the detailed structure of the company that would manage the affairs of the Furracabad group farming enterprise remained to be finalized, prospective landholder participants in the enterprise were clear they would not be satisfied with a business arrangement for which their only protection against future non-compliance was upfront promises and handshakes. Their proposed common property regime would include finer-scale institutions defining their common property rights (e.g. relating to the kinds of internal mechanisms for conflict resolution highlighted as important in the sixth feature of a robust common property regime listed in the previous section) and individual property rights (e.g. in respect of transferring access rights to descendants, apropos of the first listed feature). The structure and associated institutional arrangements finally adopted, it followed, would need to be enforceable with affordable transaction costs if necessary through avenues under relevant law and government administration. Several of the elements, described earlier (e.g. common property regime features 1, 2, 4, 5, 8, and 9 listed in the previous section), important to potential success of the Furracabad common property regime would therefore be supported by a legal structure for their business arrangement.

If implemented, the common property regime arrangements associated with the group farming concept promise to deliver significant advantages in and around the Furracabad Valley over the longer term by increasing opportunities for multiple use of the land coming under these arrangements. For some landholders interviewed during the project, a perceived advantage of such arrangements was that they would allow pooling of land with similar non-agricultural qualities, such that the combined area of land with such qualities becomes sufficient for commercial exploitation (e.g. hunting, ecotourism, etc.). Potential for specialization from the pooling of labour was also identified as a possible advantage. Some labour may then become available for non-agricultural activities, such as running farmstays or supervising wildlife tours. A further advantage identified along these lines was that group farming enables the participating individual businesses to share the risks of moving into non-agricultural uses of their resources, and thus may facilitate evolution of multiple use of rural land over the longer term. For these benefits the elements of feature nine above could be provided through collectively agreed rules and operational plans within a legal business structure such as a company or trading cooperative.

Structures and Entities to Support Cross-Tenure Common Property Regimes for Resource Management

Design features of successful common property regimes include clear boundaries around both the resource(s) and membership of user rights, as well as capacities to distribute benefits, manage external perturbations, and protect their decision-making autonomy. Various forms of structures and entities are available to help groups of resource users design such features into arrangements for contemporary common property regimes. The above examples of contemporary common property regimes in rural Australia are, or envisage, using structures similar to those found in most countries. Farm families are generally used to such entities and will feel comfortable with them. There are a variety of structures that might be useful for development of common property regimes in different contexts and circumstances, as well as for counterpart organizations (e.g. Landcare groups or non-profit organizations) that are purpose-designed for specific functions (including, as in the case of Bookmark and Tilbuster, for resource management and restoration). This section provides a brief outline of potentially useful structures. It is summarized from work undertaken for the (Australian) Rural Industries Research and Development Corporation (RIRDC) that examined potential institutional and business structures for multiple use of natural resources, such as associated with wildlife and ecotourism cooperative ventures in outback Australia (Brunckhorst et al, 2004).

In Australia, Landcare groups have been the main form of collective action across land holdings to undertake specific environmental rehabilitation works. For the most part, over the *Decade of Landcare* during the 1990s, they were

informal unconstituted groups with seed funds from an incorporated association at a regional level. There is now an increasing trend (and requirement from
government) for Landcare groups themselves to be Incorporated associations,
although many still operate under a regional Landcare organization or government agency. A limited range of formal structures exist for managing collective
land management activities of non-profit entities that are created for the specific
purpose of undertaking charitable or environmental activities by a group of
members. Non-profit status is a prerequisite for registration on the Registry of
Environmental Organizations (Federal) and for tax purposes, such as
deductibility, goods and services (GST) rebate, exemptions from various duties
and bank charges. Such structures include *Trusts* as non-profit foundations
(such as the Australian Landscape Trust). They also include incorporated associations (under state government legislation), as many independent Landcare
groups are constituted. The purpose and strengths of these types of structures
in a resource management context lie in their ability to attract funding to undertake environmental activities, while adequately representing the interests of
their members in these endeavours. In this role, such a structure can be a useful
counterpart organization to a structure formalizing a cross-tenure resource
management enterprise. We return to a consideration of this role later.

Table 10.1 provides a comparative summary of the features of three entities (partnership, trading cooperative, and company). This information might
be useful for cross-tenure enterprises, such as grazing, wild harvest or other
wildlife enterprises, and ecotourism (see Brunckhorst et al, 2004).

Organizational structures or business entities suitable for conduct of
enterprises supporting cross-property title, multiple resource uses (e.g. livestock grazing, hunting tourism, commercial wildlife harvesting, and
ecotourism) include private companies, partnerships and cooperatives. Due
to space limitations, a limited number of the most appropriate structures are
examined here. These are based on federal or New South Wales (state) legislation and requirements that are similar across other Australian states and
territories.[1]

Partnership

The partnership form of business involves an association between at least two
persons carrying on business in common with a view to profit. Like the incorporated association and cooperative, it is the partnership agreement that states
partner responsibilities and reduces potential disputes.

Unlike the incorporated association and cooperative, the establishment of
a partnership does not create a separate and distinct structure. Profits and
losses generated by the partnership activities are distributed to the partners,
who are individually responsible for paying income tax. At the death of a partner, the partnership is dissolved and a new partnership comes into existence –
unless the partnership agreement provides otherwise. There is no flexibility to
easily transfer membership in the partnership. Reflecting the absence of a separate partnership structure, this business arrangement does not provide a risk
management structure. Hence, partners face unlimited liability for losses

Table 10.1 *Summary of features of corporate structures that might be suitable for wildlife enterprise business entities*

Feature	Partnership	Company	Cooperative (Trading)
Potential Role of Entity	Primary trading entity	Primary trading entity	Primary trading entity
Establishment Costs (for NSW; other states might vary)	$126	$1,200–1,600	$171
Represents Collective Interests in Decision-making	Yes	Yes – through entitlement, and number of voting rights is issued via voting share	Yes – rule of one vote per member Relationship between Cooperative and its members
Primary Guiding Instrument	Partnership agreement	Constitution	Rules
Risk Management	Provides no risk protection to partners. Liability of venture capital partners is limited to their investment	Limited liability	Limited liability
Membership	Minimum 2, maximum 20	No upper limit	Minimum 5, no upper limit
Governing Legislation	Partnership Act [in each state]	Corporations Act 2001 (Commonwealth)	Co-operatives Act 1992 (NSW) [similar for other states]
Taxation Implications	Each partner responsible for own tax. Losses unable to be distributed.	Company pays tax on its profits. Dividends issued to shareholders, able to be franked.	Cooperative pay tax on profits, and may frank dividends. Dividends tax deductible.
Management by	Partners	Board of Directors	Members

incurred by the partnership. In addition, a partner may bind the other partners to a contract without their authority. This characteristic of partnerships raises doubts regarding their usefulness for application in a collective decision-making context.

Recent legislative reform by the Federal Government provides the option of a limited partnership. This structure distinguishes the general partners with unlimited liability and the investing partners with limited liability. This reform sought to provide partnerships with enhanced opportunities to access venture capital.

Company and trust

The company structure is a popular and flexible corporate form through which commercial activities may be undertaken. The company exists as a separate legal entity in perpetuity. It provides limited liability to its members and interests in a company are easily transferred.

There are several types of company structures, including companies limited by shares, and those companies limited by guarantee. Companies limited by shares include proprietary companies (Pty Ltd), unlimited proprietary (Pty), and limited companies (Ltd). In addition, there are no liability (NL) companies. The company is responsible for paying income taxes assessed on the taxation of its profits. Shareholders receive their entitlements to profits by way of dividends. Tax paid by the company can be passed to the shareholders by way of franked dividends.

For the purposes of supporting a group of landholders or other rightsholders interested in developing a common property regime for more sustainable rural resource enterprises such as those being considered here, the proprietary company might be appropriate and familiar to landholders. Proprietary companies can provide shareholder flexibility, as well as allow for participative decision-making, ease of transfer of membership, and limited liability. The company structure achieves flexibility in ownership and decision-making by the collective shareholders through the ability to issue a range of shares that contain various characteristics. For example, voting may or may not be attached to financial interests of shareholders in the organization. Management of the company is the responsibility of the directors or elected board.

A trust can be defined as an arrangement binding a person or corporation (the trustee) to administer an asset (land, money, some object, a business, etc.) for the benefit of a person or corporation (the beneficiary). A trust asset is owned dually. The beneficial owner is the real owner and gets the *benefit of ownership*. However, the trustee is the legal owner. For community organizations, this might take the form of the local council (as trustee) holding a building (asset) in trust for the benefit of a specific community group.

Consequently, there are special requirements in establishing a trust. There must be a difference between the legal ownership of the asset and the beneficial ownership. There must be property for which the trust exists, and all parties to the trust must know and understand the obligations regarding the trust. The trustee is usually subject to trustee legislation, and the beneficiaries are subject to the trust deed.[2] There are three kinds of trust arrangements (fixed, discretionary, unit), each having a different way of managing entitlements, and sometimes assets.

There is potential for conflict with common property regime principles that require the beneficiaries (members) to be involved in the decision-making of the enterprise – a role normally confined to the trustee who cannot be a beneficiary member. On the other hand, a trustee that is well trusted by the members might contribute other valuable elements, such as monitoring and conflict resolution. Overall, the trust is not considered a structure that is readily flexible for supporting cross-property enterprises (Brunckhorst et al, 2004).

Cooperative

The cooperative is a business form that exists to deliver benefits to members, usually co-owners. Cooperatives are distinctive for fostering a democratic style of work, pooling of resources to be more competitive, buffering external risks or perturbations, and sharing skills. The trading cooperative is a particular type of cooperative, structured so that the profits can be distributed to members. This type is suitable for commercial organizations, and would appear to support many of the design features of long-enduring common property regimes as discussed earlier.

The formation of a cooperative requires a minimum of five members. Trading cooperatives are more similar than other cooperatives in form to the company business structure. Like a company, there are no restrictions on trading. In contrast to the company, however, the trading cooperative distinguishes between the shareholding and voting rights of members. Each member of a trading cooperative is entitled to a single vote regardless of his or her financial interests in the cooperative represented by shareholdings.

The rules of the cooperative establish and define the relationship between members and the cooperative structure. The rules therefore provide an effective description of the requirements and expectations of membership. Such rules might be an advantage over other business forms in that the institutional culture and the responsibilities of members are clearly defined from the outset rather than assumed. Nevertheless, institutional evolution can still occur since the cooperative's rules can be altered over time.

The ongoing costs associated with maintaining the cooperative include fees that apply when amending these rules. The administration requirements of a cooperative are otherwise similar to those for a company. The Australian Taxation Office views a trading cooperative as a *cooperative company* and assesses these entities by the same taxation regime that they apply to a company. Unlike a company, however, the dividends paid to members are tax deductible. This provides an incentive to distribute all profits to members. More recently, cooperatives have been granted the opportunity to frank part of their dividends, thereby assisting taxation planning of members.

An overhaul of the cooperative legislation in the State of New South Wales in 1992 made it possible for cooperatives to raise additional capital from non-members. Investment can be made through purchase of a special kind of *share* called Cooperative Capital Units (CCU). These CCUs are flexible instruments that allow them to be designed to contain elements of both equity (representing ownership in the cooperative) and debt.

The cooperative structure appears to combine the provision of equity in decision-making processes with the flexibility needed to support multiple property (land title) resource use by the collective owners as members. While a company can be structured in a way to provide participatory decision-making by shareholders (as with Tilbuster Commons), it is the responsibility of the company board to undertake the management of the company activities. A cooperative can have a management board (a subset of members), but the relationship of members with the cooperative automatically includes *ownership* rights and responsibilities (which a company shareholder may not have). This formal recognition of member responsibility is likely to enhance the social capital aspects of collective decision-making. Both the company and trading cooperatives provide similar advantages for risk management (e.g. limited liability for members).

Business structures for enterprise collaboration across landholdings

A company structure will work well for development of cross property enterprises involving grazing or a variety of other diversifications; for example, wildlife harvest and/or ecotourism. Through such a structure, different resource rights and responsibilities can be decided along with operational rules, and arrangements for reporting and monitoring, governance, trading and profit distribution. It can also have a trust or incorporated association allied with it providing non-profit charitable or environmental activities, or it can act as a corporate trustee. Company structures have worked well for the Bookmark Biosphere Reserve enterprises and the Tilbuster Commons model, both of which utilize an allied non-profit environmental organization.

The trading cooperative business structure appears to have been underutilized in recent years. Cooperatives appear to provide the same benefits as a company structure, but offer additional flexibility. A cooperative together with an incorporated association for environmental restoration and conservation could provide an efficient vehicle for sustainable wildlife enterprises and reduced cattle or sheep stocking rates. A collective of ecotourism operations (a common property regime) could be nested within such a cross-property primary production enterprise having differentiated resources and access (perhaps farm based, but with multiple property access enjoyed only by members of the cooperative).

General considerations for development of wildlife and ecotourism enterprises

Ecotourism tours, farm-stays and various wildlife harvest and value adding enterprises have potential to provide improved environmental and socio-economic returns for outback Australia. Harvesting of wildlife, such as kangaroos or emus, is likely to qualify as a primary production activity as it might be interpreted under a management plan as 'maintaining animals for the purpose of selling them or their bodily produce' (Income Tax Assessment Act ITAA 97 s995–1 1). In this regard, the *management* of animals is likely to be interpreted in a similar manner to fisheries.

Importantly, the wildlife harvest business structure is likely to maintain a primary producer status rather than the members or shareholders of the entity. There are several concessions provided to primary producers through the taxation system. Of these, the two that are likely to provide benefits for wild harvest activities are the Energy Grant Credit Scheme, and the Deductibility for Environmental Protection programmes. These are not described here. A variety of farm diversification taxation issues related to the commercial use of wildlife, tourism hunting and ecotourism are discussed in the RIRDC report *Taxation of Primary Producers and Landholders* (Ashby and Polkinghorne, 2004).

Future developments of government policies for outback enterprises, such as value added products from wildlife harvest, are likely to be based on fisheries and the existing kangaroo industry. However, regulations regarding the kangaroo industry require some considerable overhaul in order to allow easier flows of wildlife products from harvest through value adding activities to markets.

Collective enterprises beyond the farm gate

For products that are completely new to the marketplace, a processing, distribution and marketing system beyond the farm gate (the *value adding* or supply chain) will not exist. It can be a difficult, time consuming, expensive and risky exercise for farmers to undertake value-adding activities by themselves. The array of skills and motivations required may not be shared by many landholders (see Stayner and Doyle, 2003). After all, farmers' special skills and interests lie in raising and growing things and in land management, rather than in off-farm business and marketing. Stayner and Doyle (2003) found that post-farm gate activities often ended up being hived off into separate businesses that have flexibility to respond to the competitive pressures of their own markets and than can be operated at arm's length from farming operations. Indeed, in order to achieve the objectives of diversified enterprises it will be important for landholders to continue to focus primarily on designing and managing the multiple farm level production systems.

These findings, together with an appreciation that better returns can come to an agricultural community through participating in value-adding activities (e.g. additional employment and services), indicate that an appropriate way forward will often be for landholders to establish one or more cooperative businesses for value-adding activities that are separate from, but operate locally alongside, a common property regime established for running agricultural and associated resource management activities. Cooperating farmers or landholders should closely consider the sorts of relationships they will have with other participants in the value chain beyond their farm gates. In these cases, landholders or other community members might need to become involved as a collective to create such a value chain. A collaborating group of farmers might provide primary produce to a local community owned cooperative that undertakes processes, value adding and marketing. For example, an additional collaboration of two or more collectives with different business focus linked through resource value adding benefits such as a small abattoir producing meat and other products for a cross-tenure wild harvest of kangaroos and feral goats. Nesting of institutional arrangements, and possibly business entities, with a particular focus and role (for clear boundaries of operations and interactions) could be useful. Such relationships could require the negotiation of supply contracts or agreements with producer collectives, processors, wholesalers, retailers or exporters. Benefits might include reduced uncertainty and risks associated with producing a novel commodity. Landholders have, in recent years, experimented with various forms of producer alliances that establish relationships of one sort or another with the supply chain. Some beef producer alliances have been quite successful in value adding, providing lessons that could be useful to other enterprises of farmer collectives (see Pinnacle Management, 2000).

Counterpart organizations and combinations

In order to gain synergies for both economic and environmental benefits, it can be useful for a group of farmers to establish a variety of organizational and institutional arrangements to undertake different activities, whether agricultural production, ecosystem conservation and restoration, natural resource management, ecotourism, value adding, or marketing.

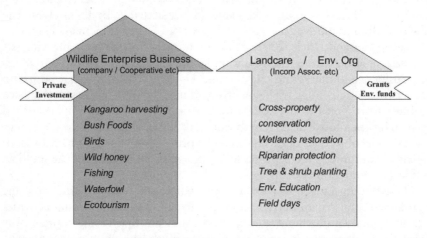

Figure 10.3 Complementary parallel arrangements to maximize synergies between wildlife enterprise businesses and environmental outcomes

Separate but complementary organizations can provide some advantages for co-owners or members in integrating wildlife or ecotourism enterprises (across land titles) with environmental rehabilitation and education (Figure 10.3). Incorporated association arrangements that some Landcare groups work under, or other non-profit environmental organizations that are registered under the Commonwealth Government's Register of Environmental Organizations (e.g. a foundation such as the Australian Landscape Trust supporting Bookmark collectives), could play a valuable role and contribute additional benefits to landholder collectives (Brunckhorst et al, 2004).

Complementary or counterpart Landcare/business organizations, such as those used by the Tilbuster Commons and Bookmark Biosphere common property regimes, reinforce the close relationship between the environment, resource base and enterprises in the minds and actions of participants (Figure

10.3). In turn these relationships support capacities in robustness and resilience within and across the socio-ecological system. While these relationships are not analysed further here, we believe this is a considerable and potentially fertile topic deserving increased research effort (see Brunckhorst 2000, 2001; Anderies et al, 2004).

Lessons for Designing Robust Cross-Tenure Collaboration towards Sustainable Rural Development

Common property regimes have significant potential to bring about the cooperation across landholdings needed to achieve sustainable futures for outback Australia. Nevertheless, a group of landholders who decide to combine their resources in order to realize the advantages of this cooperation will probably find advantages in using a business structure recognized under law to lower the transaction costs involved in facilitating enterprise efficacy, distributing responsibilities and rewards, maintaining legal stability, and making and enforcing collective decisions.

McKean (2000a, b, 2002) identified several important features of enduring common property regimes that contributed robustness in terms of relationships of co-owners or collaborators with the world external to their common property regime. One is that members of the collaboration, as a group, have independent jurisdiction or autonomy (design feature number nine above). Government instruments, such as statute business structures, help defend and support a group's independence to design and implement their own institutional arrangements. The use of a structure in development of a common property regime that is supported by law will also reduce greatly the transaction costs for the common property regime in dealing with issues like liability, insurance, asset and financial accounting, labour and taxation. In this chapter, we have explored how different kinds of corporate structures and entities recognized by Australia's legal system can assist common property regimes to fulfil more closely the design features that history shows are important for their enduring success. These features can contribute robustness to the common property regime institution, without compromising self-organizing capacities for monitoring, flexible reorganization, and adaptation that contribute to resilience.

A company or trading cooperative can provide appropriate structures for supporting the operation of a common property regime, including by protecting its autonomy. These structures allow landholders to retain individual title to their properties. They provide a mechanism whereby natural resource systems spread across individually owned properties can be managed as single units, while at the same time setting clear boundaries around the group of landholders with rights to appropriate the benefits arising from more integrated management of those systems. They can serve as vehicles for diversification into enterprises for which success requires access to large-scale resource systems, such as wildlife, ecotourism and cultural tourism enterprises. They may also be useful to Indigenous peoples seeking to *reassemble* property and tenure systems for natural resources in ways that increase their opportunities to pursue new enterprises without detracting from existing ones (e.g. benefiting from differentiated resource access across multiple land tenures). Building on existing efforts, further *on-ground experiments* could be devised to build further understanding of such collectives; for example, a group of tour guides in a region working as a collective to secure and distribute returns from providing access to an ecotourism experience spread across multiple landowners' properties. The landowners may or may not also be a collective for this purpose or for other larger scale resource use enterprises having collective benefits.

We conclude that adoption of business structures can appreciably enhance the robustness of common property regime arrangements in rural contexts for sustainable use of resources at larger scales – across the boundaries of individual land titles. Like Australia, many countries have legislation that recognizes and provides support for particular kinds of corporate structures that might be useful in contributing robustness to common property regime institutional arrangements and operations. This advantage arises to the extent that adoption of a structure allows a common property regime to more effectively fulfil the 11 design features for long-enduring common property regimes discussed at the beginning of this chapter. It could be expected that adoption of an appropriate business structure for a common property regime would strengthen fulfilment of the following design features in particular:

- clearly defining the boundaries (number 1 in our list);
- clear definition of collaborating members or co-owners for self-governance (2);
- inclusion of locally designed rules (4);
- equitable distribution of responsibilities and benefits (5);
- provisions for conflict resolution (6);
- authentication and support for the autonomy and independence of the group (9); and
- capacity to achieve appropriate scales (10).

Acknowledgements

We have greatly benefited from discussions with many colleagues, including Phil Coop, Steve Dovers, Robert Dulhunty, Eric Freyfogle, Simon Fritsch, Dale Goble, Gerry Kelly, John Malcolm, Margaret McKean, Elinor Ostrom, Pamela Parker, Richard Price, Ian Reeve, Alice Roughley, Mike Scott, Margaret Shannon, George Wilson and Sima Williamson. Thank you to the Tilbuster Commoners, communities of Bookmark Biosphere Community Trust, the Australian Landscape Trust, and participants in the Furracabad Valley group farming project for *having a go* so that we can all learn together. Land and Water Australia, the Rural Industries Research and Development Corporation, the Australian Research Council and the Commonwealth Department of Transport and Regional Services have funded different elements of this work.

However, the opinions and conclusions expressed herein remain our interpretations.

Notes

1   It should be noted that this work is a generalized summary to provide background on structural arrangements for enterprises to operate across multiple landholdings of tenures, such as wildlife utilization or ecotourism, and is not to be construed as legal, accounting or investment advice. Other considerations not dealt with extensively and requiring further consideration include corporate governance, property law and possible licensing issues. In the final analysis, it will be up to individual landholder groups to seek such professional advice and to adopt a structure with which they are personally comfortable and which meets the particular requirements of their common property regime's context and domain of operation.
2   Obligations may differ across state jurisdictions, so detailed advice regarding a particular state's legal requirements should be sought from a corporate accountant and solicitor.

References

Anderies, J., Janssen, M., and Ostrom, E. (2004). A framework for the robustness of social-ecological systems from an institutional perspective. *Ecology and Society*, 9(1), 18. Online: www.ecologyandsociety.org/vol9/iss1/art18

Ashby, R. G. and Polkinghorne, L. N. (2004). *Taxation of Primary Producers and Landholders: Improving Natural Resource Management Outcomes*. Rural Industries RandD Corporation, Canberra: RIRDC Publ. No. 04/026.

Berkes, F. and Folke, C. (1998). Linking social and ecological systems for resilience and sustainability. In F. Berkes and C. Folke (eds.), *Linking Social and Ecological Systems: Management Practices and Social Mechanisms for Building Resilience*. New York: Cambridge University Press.

Bromley, D. W. (1992a). *Making the Commons Work: Theory, Practice, and Policy*. San Francisco: Institute for Contemporary Studies.

Bromley, D. W. (1992b). The commons, property, and common-property regimes. In D. W. Bromley (ed), *Making the Commons Work*. (pp3–15). San Francisco: ICS Press.

Brunckhorst, D. J. (2000). *Bioregional Planning: Resource Management Beyond the New Millennium*. Amsterdam: Harwood Academic.

Brunckhorst, D. J. (2001). Building capital through bioregional planning and biosphere reserves. *Journal of Ethics in Science and Environmental Policy 2001*, (1), 19–32.

Brunckhorst, D. J. (2002). Institutions to Sustain Ecological and Social Systems. *Journal of Ecological Management and Restoration*, 3 (2), 109–117.

Brunckhorst, D. J., Bridgewater, P. and Parker, P. (1997). The UNESCO Biosphere Reserve program comes of age: Learning by doing, landscape models for sustainable conservation and resource use. (pp. 176–182). In P. Hale and D. Lamb (eds), *Conservation Outside Reserves*. Brisbane, QLD: University of Queensland Press.

Brunckhorst, D. J. and Coop, P. (2003). Tilbuster commons: synergies of theory and action in new agricultural commons on private land. *Journal Ecological Management and Restoration*, 4 (1),13–22.

Brunckhorst, D., Coop, P. and Malcolm, J. (2004). *Structures for Wildlife Enterprises*. Refereed report to the Rural Industries RandD Corporation on Project UNE 92A,

Wildlife Management Conservancy Structures. Institute for Rural Futures: University of New England.

Commons, J. R. (1968). *Legal Foundations of Capitalism*. Madison: University of Wisconsin Press.

Commonwealth of Australia, (2000). *Prime Minister's National Action Plan for Salinity and Water Quality*. Canberra: Commonwealth of Australia.

Coop, P. and Brunckhorst, D. J. (1999). Triumph of the commons: age old lessons for Institutional Reform in the Rural Sector. *Australian Journal of Environmental Management,* 6 (2), 23–30.

Coop, P. and Brunckhorst, D. J. (2001). Old practices building new institutions: a commons approach to the rural crisis. In G. Lawrence, V. Higgins and S. Lockie (eds), *Environment, Society and Natural Resource Management: Theoretical Perspectives.* UK: Edward Elgar Academic Press.

Dahlman, C. J. (1980). *The Open Field System and Beyond: A Property Rights Analysis of an Economic Institution*. Cambridge: Cambridge University Press.

Dovers, S. (2000). *Environmental History and Policy: Still Settling Australia*. Melbourne: Melbourne University Press.

Earl, J. M. and Jones, C. E. (1996). The need for a new approach to grazing management – is cell grazing the answer? *Rangeland Journal*, 18, 327–350.

Hanna, S., Folke, C. and Mäler, K.-G. (1996). *Rights to Nature*. Washington, DC: Island Press.

Lee, K. N. (1993). Greed, scale mismatch, and learning. *Ecological Applications*, 4, 560–564.

Marshall, G. R. (2005). *Economics for Collaborative Environmental Management: Renegotiating the Commons*. London: Earthscan.

Marshall, G. R., Fritsch, S. J. and Dulhunty, R. V. (2005). Catalyzing common property farming for rural sustainability: Lessons from the Furracabad Valley. *Australian Agribusiness Review*, 13, paper 17. Online: http://www.agrifood.info/review/2005/Marshall_et_al.html

Marshall, G. R. (2004a). *Furracabad Farm Cluster Project. Final Report, Institute for Rural Futures*. Armidale: University of New England.

Marshall, G. R. (2004b). From words to deeds: enforcing farmers conservation cost-sharing commitments. *Journal of Rural Studies*, 20, 157–167.

Marshall, G. R. (2004c). Farmers cooperating in the commons? A study of collective action in salinity management. *Ecological Economics*, 51, (3–4), 271–286.

Marshall, G. R. (2002). Institutionalising cost sharing for catchment management: lessons from land and water management planning in Australia. *Water, Science and Technology*, 45 (11), 101–112.

McKean, M. (1992). Management of traditional common lands (Iriaichi) in Japan. In D. W. Bromley (ed). *Making the Commons Work: Theory, Practice and Policy.* (pp 63–98). San Francisco: Institute for Contempory Studies.

McKean, M. (1996) Common property regimes as a solution to problems of scale and linkage. Chapter 11. In S. Hanna, C. Folke, and K.-G. Mäler (eds), *Rights to Nature*. Washington DC: Island Press.

McKean, M. (1997). Common property regimes: moving from inside to outside. Proceedings of the Workshop on Future Directions for Common Property Theory and Research. (cited 21/07/98). Online: www.indiana.edu/~iascp/webdoc.html

McKean, M. (2000a). Designing new common property regimes for new landscape futures. In D. Brunckhorst and D. Mouat (eds). *Landscape Futures.* (Refereed proceedings of international symposium on Landscape Futures, Sept. 1999. UNESCO Institute for Bioregional Resource Management and University of New England

McKean, M. (2000b). Common property: what is it, what is it good for, and what makes it work? (pp.27–55). In C. Gibson, M. McKean, and E. Ostrom, (eds). *Keeping the*

Forest: Communities, Institutions, and the Governance of Forests. Cambridge: Massachusetts Institute of Technology Press.

McKean, M. (2002). Nesting institutions for complex common-pool resource systems. In J. Graham, I. Reeve, and D. Brunckhorst, (eds). *Landscape Futures: Social and Insititutional Dimensions.* Proceedings of the 2nd International Conference on Landscape Futures, 4–6 December, 2001, Armidale. Institute for Rural Futures. Armidale: University of New England.

Netting, R. (1976). What Alpine peasants have in common: observations on communal tenure in a Swiss village. *Human Ecology*, 4, 135–146.

North D. C. (1990). *Institutions, Institutional Change and Economic Performance.* Cambridge: Cambridge University Press.

Ostrom, E. (1990). *Governing the Commons: The Evolution of Institutions for Collective Action.* Cambridge: Cambridge University Press.

Ostrom, E. (1992). *Crafting Institutions for Self-governing Irrigation Systems.* San Francisco, California: Institute for Contemporary Studies Press.

Ostrom, E; Dietz, T., Dolsak, N,; Stern, P., Stonich, S. and Weber, E., (eds). (2002). *The Drama of the Commons.* Washington, DC: National Academy Press.

Pinnacle Management, (2000). *BeefNet Alliance Handbook: Guidelines for Forming and Operating Effective Beef Alliances.* North Sydney: Meat and Livestock Australia.

Reeve, I. J. (1998). Commons and coordination: towards a theory of resource governance. In R. Epps, (ed). *Sustaining Rural Systems in the Context of Global Change.* Proceedings of the Conference of the Joint IGU Commission for the Sustainability of Rural Systems and the Land Use – Cover Change Study Group. Armidale: University of New England.

Reeve, I. J. (1997). Property and participation: an institutional analysis of rural resource management and landcare in Australia. In: S. Lockie, and F. Vanclay (eds). *Critical Landcare.* Charles Sturt University, Australia: Centre for Rural Social Research.

Reeve, I. J. (1992). Sustainable agriculture: problems, prospects and policies. In G. Lawrence, F. Vanclay and B. Furze (eds.). (pp208–223). *Agriculture, Environment and Society: Contemporary Issues for Australia.* Melbourne: MacMillan.

Schlager, E. and Ostrom, E. (1992). Property-rights regimes and natural resources: a conceptual analysis. *Land Economics,* 68, 249–262.

Schmid, A. A. (1972). Analytical institutional economics: challenging problems in the economics of resources for a new environment. *American Journal of Agricultural Economics*, 54, 893–901.

Singleton, S. (1998). *Constructing Cooperation: The Evolution of Institutions of Co-Management.* Ann Arbor: University of Michigan Press.

Stayner, R. and Doyle, B. (2003). Adding value to your farm products. Ch. 2 In Richard Meredith (ed). *Options for Change: New Ideas for Australian Farmers.* Canberra: RIRDC Publication No. 03/030.

Watson, J. (1993). Fostering community support for the Fitzgerald River Biosphere Reserve, Western Australia. *Nature and Resources,* 29 (1–4), 24–28.

Williamson, S. Brunckhorst, D. J. and Kelly, G. (2003). *Reinventing the Common: Cross-Boundary Farming for a Sustainable Future.* Sydney: Federation Press.

Wondolleck, J. M. and Yaffee, S. L. (2000). *Making Collaboration Work: Lessons from Innovation in Natural Resource Management.* Washington DC: Island Press.

11

The Need to Consider the Administration of Property Rights and Restrictions before Creating them

Ken Lyons, Kevin Davies and Ed Cottrell

Objectives and Operational Model for the Administration of the Property Rights and Markets

The term *property rights*, as discussed by Smajgl and Larson in Chapter 1 of this book, is also used in this chapter in its fullest generic sense. It is used synonymously with *property RORs* where ROR is an abbreviation for rights, obligations and restrictions. The term *property rights* can have many different meanings to different groups. Some take the term *property* to only relate to *real property*, or definitions of property in particular legislation. Some consider property rights and land rights to be the same. Some view property rights as a generic term encompassing, or synonymous with, some or all of the following: access rights, use rights, entitlement rights and similar terms. Some consider the generic term also includes obligations, restrictions, controls and similar expressions. Others view *rights* as being solely restricted to rights and not to include obligations, restrictions, etc. Some consider the terms *access rights* and *use rights* to have specific meanings. Access and use rights can be considered as modifying restrictions to, or obligations on, rights held by another.

Objectives for the Operational Administration of the Property Markets

In their work with the emerging land markets in former socialist East European countries, Dale and Baldwin (1999) considered the land market to be composed of the following elements: the legal basis; the regulating institutions; the participants; the goods and services; and the financial institutions. The conceptual model Dale and Baldwin (1999) developed has been expanded and is presented in Figure 11.1. The conceptual model shows unbundled rights and includes links to social stability, capital formation and natural resource sustainability. Each individual property rights pillar can be considered as having three integral parts: a policy and regulator part; an administering institutions part; and a services, process and data part (Figure 11.1). Each of these parts can be examined in terms of its structural completeness and its operational efficiency.

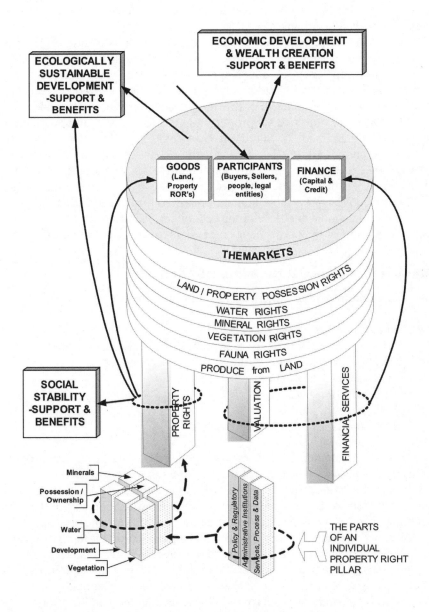

Figure 11.1 Conceptual model of the land market structure

While much has been written about land and property markets, there appears to have been little work done on what constitutes an effective and efficient land market and how to measure that. Dale and Baldwin (1999) provide a list of characteristics and elements of efficient and effective land markets, which are indicators of market activity. International initiatives, such as LARI (Land and Real Estate Initiative), a multi-sectored association of partners convened by the World Bank to help realize the full benefits of land and real estate to the economy and to specifically extend those benefits to the poor, have also developed diagnostic tools for assessing land and real estate markets (Pamuk, 1999; World Bank, 2001).

One of the stated objectives of land administration is to support markets in property rights. To measure this objective it is necessary to assess the effectiveness and efficiency of the respective markets, to determine if the performance is contributing adversely (and if so, where and how?), and then determine how to improve. All of this requires measures of performance.

The suggested objectives of property rights and markets, and the qualities that should be attained, are summarized in Table 11.1. The objectives in the table are intended as a starting point for the debate on the final set of objectives. However, existence of the comprehensive set of measures and their characteristics is prerequisite for the development of effective indicator sets.

The objectives in the Table 11.1 are presented for land and real estate, with a focus on transitional and developing economies. Additionally, there is a need for development of the performance measurements for land administration.

An operational model for administration

The major administration functions surrounding property rights are:

- a statutory and regulatory framework;
- the determination of property rights, legal declaration, guidelines;
- application processing for dealings, permits/licences etc;
- the provision of information;
- compliance checking;
- appeal processes; and
- a viable and orderly market for trading.

Analysis of the main departments responsible for the administration of property rights in Queensland indicates that there is little difference between the administration of the various types of property rights (Figure 11.2). Each requires the macro functions of policy and legal formation, determination and declaration, handling of transactions/dealings, information, compliance and appeals.

A report developed by Lyons et al. (2002a) presents an in-depth discussion and debate on the various issues of the property rights management and administration. The report proposes a number of 'why not' questions, and brief 'pros' and 'cons' to foster debate and discussion. The main aim of the discussion is to promote property rights management and administration that meets its objectives, effectively and efficiently.

Table 11.1 *Suggested objectives for property rights and markets*

Objectives	Qualities to be Attained
1 To ensure all property rights are clearly defined, secure in law and in practice.	Property rights are clear, certain, unambiguous, exclusive, legally enforceable, tradable; the area/spatial extent to which each specific property right applies is clear, certain, and unambiguous.
2 To support the operation of markets in the various property rights.	Markets operate effectively, efficiently, and in accordance with good governance, international best practice, with the Australian Charter of Regulatory Principles for Small Business; no unnecessary inter-jurisdictional impediments (such as non-harmonized regulatory regimes)
3 To ensure that transactions and trading in property rights can be carried out.	Dealings are simple, transparent, certain in outcome, easily accessible, affordable, conducted expeditiously, with no disincentives.
4 To provide legally correct composite/integrated information on all property rights that apply to or affect any area of land.	Composite/consolidated/integrated information on all property rights applying to any land parcel(s) or selected area(s) is quickly and easily obtainable at low cost.
5 To enable property rights to be used as a source of capital/credit and economic development	In the world's 'best' 10 for efficiency of capital-raising from property rights and their markets.
6 To support government revenue raising/taxation based on land.	Property right valuations (assumed as a basis of taxation) are current, fair, transparent, information readily available.
7 To contribute to social stability.	The community has confidence in and respect for the land administration. Independent dispute resolution/decision challenge is available quickly, is accessible and affordable, matters are resolved expeditiously. Dispute rates are among the lowest 10 in the world; public confidence and the application of good governance is among the world's top 10.
8 To contribute to natural resource and environmental sustainability.	Efficient and effective management of property rights to further sustainability objectives.
9 To operate effectively and efficiently, with a service philosophy, with public confidence and stringent accountability.	In the world's top 10 for efficient and effective administration, service, public confidence, and accountability.

Source: Lyons et al (2002b)

Suggestions for Improvements

During 2002 to 2004 the authors conducted two consultancies dealing with the efficiency and effectiveness of property rights administration. The first consultancy was conducted in 2002 for the Queensland Government Department of Natural Resources and Mines and focused on Queensland. The second was conducted in 2003 for the same Department together with the Western Australia Department of Land Information, under the auspices of SCOLA (Standing Committee on Land Administration) of ANZLIC (Australian New Zealand Land Information Council) (Lyons et al, 2002a, b, 2004a, b).

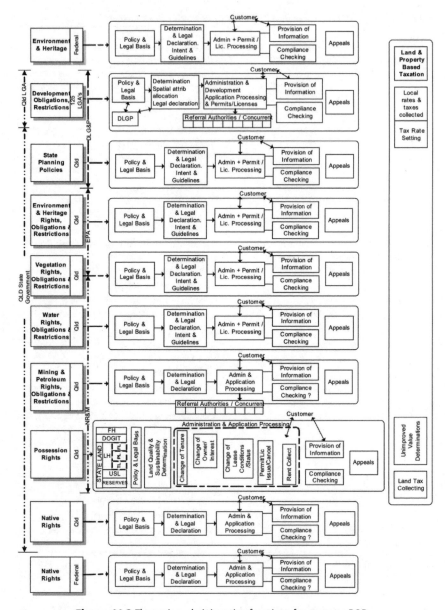

Figure 11.2 The major administrative functions for property RORs

Source: Lyons et al (2002b)

DGLP:	Department of Local Government and Planning	LGA:	Local Government Area
DOTIT:	Deed of Grant in Trust	LH:	Leasehold
EPA:	Environmental Protection Agency	NR&M:	Natural Resources and Mines
FH:	Freehold	Qld:	Queensland
FL:	Freehold lease	USL:	Unallocated State Land

Lessons learnt during the work conducted in 2002 and 2004 were presented at the National Summit on Improving the Administration of Property Rights and Restriction, held in Brisbane in 2004 (ANZLIC, 2004). The focus of the National Summit was on operational and administration issues. The authors have presented 13 suggestions for improvement of effectiveness and efficiency of the property administration. The need for the improvements is based on three main propositions:

- There is a need to reengineer traditional land administration so that it can more effectively, efficiently and holistically administer all property rights, obligations and restrictions, and the markets associated with them.
- There is a need to establish and implement best practice for the definition, creation, and administration of property rights, obligations and restrictions that is binding on all stakeholders, including the creators and administrators.
- There is a need for easy, quick and cheap discovery of *all* details of *all* rights, obligations and restrictions (RORs) that affect the use, enjoyment and value of any land or property, or part thereof, and for there to be certainty associated with the results.

The main suggestions for improved effectiveness and efficiency of the property administration were:

1   Agree explicit objectives, supported by models, for the administration of property rights and markets.
2   Achieve and provide reliable comprehensive information on all rights, obligations and restrictions (RORs) from a single point of enquiry.
3   Formulate a standard or best practice for the definition and creation of an ROR which is binding on all creators of RORs.
4   Address the erosion of Torrens Principles to regain the application of its principles to all RORs.
5   Instigate national benchmarking to measure the effectiveness and efficiency of ROR creation and administration.
6   Foster a national summit to address the overall topic of Property RORs, their creation, markets and administration.
7   Acknowledge 'there is a serious problem' as well as recommending approaches 'to address the issue'.
8   Seek a regulatory impact assessment on the amount of legislation and the number of agencies involved.
9   Strive for greater coordination between agencies.
10 Rationalize a whole of government approach in each jurisdiction.
11 Achieve greater harmonization between jurisdictions.
12 Seek a fundamental reassessment of what property RORs are to achieve and the most effective and efficient way (systems, administration etc.) to achieve the aim.
13 Seek a compliance audit (assuming 2 above implemented) of all existing RORs with the aim of rectifying those that don't comply.

The following subsection discusses in detail some of those proposed improvements.

Reliable comprehensive information on all rights, obligations and restrictions (RORs) from a single point of enquiry

The prime objective of this proposed improvement would be to make it possible to quickly and easily discover all RORs that affect the use, enjoyment and value of any segment of land or property or part thereof.

It is recognized that several initiatives and proposals under discussion deal with the provision of information on the most common RORs. However, the goal should be to cover all RORs. It is also considered of prime importance that there be a single point of enquiry, and that information provided is reliable and authoritative.

The Parliamentary Report of the Western Australian Public Administration and Finance Committee (2004) presents three recommendations relevant to this issue (recommendations R34– R36):

- R34 – that, the Department of Land Information maintains a comprehensive and publicly available list of all policies, strategies and plans which impact on administrative decision-making pertaining to land use.
- R 35 – that, in the short term, the Department of Land Information continues to implement its aim of establishing itself as a 'one-stop shop' database of all interests affecting land, as an urgent priority.
- R36 – that, for the long-term, the Department of Land Information, introduces, as soon as practical, an electronic three-dimensional certificate of title which records all interests affecting the parcel described on the certificate of title.

An example of the recent controversial court decision is the case of *Hillpalm v Heaven's Door* (2002, NSWCA 301). The NSW Court of Appeal upheld the Land and Environment Court's decision that council's consent created a right which, although not registered, could be relied on by all later transferees and the owner of Lot one could force the owner of Lot two to grant the right of way. The Environmental Planning and Assessment Act 1979 (under which the 25 year old condition of consent was enforced) was held to take precedence over the system of title registration of the Real Property Act 1900, not only because it is a later act but also because it 'partakes more of a public law enactment compared to the Real Property Act's private law complexion' (NSWCA *Hillpalm v Heaven's Door*, 2002). This alters what had previously been understood to be the law; that a certificate of title could be relied upon as recording all interests in land with which a purchaser need be concerned. It places a difficult new burden on purchasers who should now ensure no outstanding development consent conditions might affect the title to land they intend to buy.

Standard or best practice for the definition and creation of a ROR register

At the core of this proposal are assumptions that every ROR must:

- be defined and created in some standard way, or conform to some best practice criteria;
- be no less rigorous than that required for land registration and entering on a Certificate of Title (CT);
- be unable to be legally brought into force unless (a) it complies with the standard; (b) is registered with a single Government Agency; and (c) the information is open to all.

It is recognized that it will be no small matter to gain acceptance from the great variety of agencies that create and administer particular RORs to the principle, agreement and implementation of a single standard. However, the need for a standard is considered to be of fundamental importance, so as to overcome one of the major sources of the problem of uncertainty in RORs. It may be necessary for coordinating bodies such as the Council of Australian Governments (COAG) to concur on the importance of this area.

There is no shortage of articles in the literature that deal with property rights, and they cover myriad views and philosophies. There are far fewer articles that deal with suggestions of a practical nature concerning how to define these rights. Three excellent articles are by Scott (1999), Young and McColl (2002), Sheehan and Small (2002). The focus of these three articles is essentially on the characteristics of natural resources, such as water and fish.

Given the intense debate in Australia over water rights and vegetation clearing, it is clear that, from the Australian perspective, the focus is on *rights*. However, the definition and extent of *obligations* and *restrictions* are of equal importance. There are myriad restrictions that can apply, and they can affect the use, enjoyment and value of a property, and they assume a great importance when purchasing a property. However, it appears that the same amount of thought on what constitutes the essential characteristics of a property obligation and restriction has not been given as that afforded to the essential characteristics of a property right.

Table 11.2 lists some possible characteristics that RORs should exhibit. It is not meant to be exhaustive; it merely aims to set the scene for discussions as to what might be a suitable set of essential characteristics.

Regaining the application of Torrens principles to all RORs

In 1858 Torrens introduced the system named after him to overcome the weakness of the English Property Law then operating in Australia. The weaknesses of the pre-existing system were perceived as: complexity, cost, uncertainty, slowness and creation of a low credit value against the land (Lyons et al, 2002b).

It is interesting to speculate how Torrens would rate the regulatory regime existing now, nearly 150 years after his simplifications. Public Adminstration and Finance Committee (2004) references Butt's (2003) comments on that aspect:

Table 11.2 *Possible characteristics that RORs should exhibit*

Characteristic	Comment
Duration	The period for which the interest is defined
Flexibility	The extent to which the interest can be modified or altered without consent
Exclusivity	The degree to which the holder receives all the benefits
Transferability	The extent of freedom to trade (level of constraints)
Divisibility	Whether or not the interests can be subdivided into parts or each part held separately
Universality	Entitlements (rights over how they can be used) are completely specified
Enforceability	Property assets and rights are secure from involuntary seizure and encroachments
Quality of title	The extent of protection from fraud, opportunity to use as collateral, etc.
Spatial Extent	The exact geographical extent where any particular ROR has force
Clarity of Definition	To be couched in such a way that there is no uncertainty as to the meaning of the particular ROR
Discoverability	All information on every ROR to be on a public register, which is easily accessible
Consistence	Every ROR to be consistently defined, created and information about it available
Security	The degree of security afforded by a right to be very clearly defined, together with higher-ranking securities/interests that may be in place
Right of Appeal to Independent Body	A right of appeal to an independent body as distinct from that which defined and granted the ROR

> *Indefeasibility of title is the great catchcry of the Torrens system. It is what distinguishes that system so clearly from other registration systems. Without it, the Torrens System would be a mere shell. Both are inimical to the philosophy behind the Torrens system. Sir Robert Torrens would not have been pleased.*

Table 11.3 lists some explicit and implicit principles and characteristics of the Torrens system, and provides comments on how well these are being met when considering all RORs.

Table 11.3 indicates that several original intents of the Torrens system have been eroded, such as the principle of holding in one place all information necessary to take into account in a transaction. It also appears that some of the original defects the Torrens system was established to overcome, such as complexity, uncertainty and cost, have crept back in.

It could be argued that the Torrens Register handles several RORs well. It could also be argued that it should handle all RORs, as its original purpose was to include all RORs that affected tradability.

It is essential that Environmental Protection Agencies (EPAs) in all jurisdictions become part of the reform process, as they are, and are likely to be for some considerable time, a major creator of obligations and restrictions.

Table 11.3 *Explicit and implicit principles of the torrens system*

Principle	Aim	Current Situation
Mirror	Certificate of Title (CT) and the Register contain all interests	Does not contain all RORs
Curtain/Completeness	No searching behind the register required; contains all required information (i.e. a one stop shop)	Many locations need to be searched; never sure that all locations have been searched.
Conclusive/ Indefeasibility	Title is correct and paramount	Not 100% reliable
Openness/ Transparency/ Discoverability	The Register is open to all to inspect and obtain information	Still applies to the RORs held on the Torrens Register. Does not seem to apply well to many other RORs not held on the Torrens Register
Indemnity	Recompense for those who suffer loss from relying on title information	Applies in certain circumstances

National benchmark for ROR creation and administration

The creation of a national benchmark for measuring effectiveness and efficiency of ROR creation and administration was also recommended. This benchmark system could be similar to inter-jurisdictional performance measurement system currently implemented by the Productivity Commission over complex areas of government service delivery such as health, police, and justice.

The Development Assessment Forum (DAF) (Department of Transport and Regional Services (2005), Walsh Consulting and UTS Centre for Local Government (2002)) has undertaken comprehensive work on performance measurement and its application in the area of public administration. The systems diagram and discussion in Lyons et al, (2004b) identify costs as one of the main factors needing benchmarking and systematic evaluation. The cost increase affects both the government running these systems and the user complying with them.

There appears to be a consensus among users of the system that cost and complexity of the system have increased, and are continuing to increase (Lyons et al, 2004b). A comprehensive framework considering cost measurement for both the supply and demand sides and a performance comparison methodology, applied in and between jurisdictions, would be a valuable tool for the assessment of effectiveness and efficiency of RORs administration.

Conclusions

This chapter reports on a range of suggestions to improve the effectiveness and efficiency in the administration of property rights in Australia, with the aim of starting the discussion on administration of the rights, obligations and restrictions (RORs) after their inclusion into the legal framework. Hopefully, sometime in the future, there will be a binding best practice for the definition and creation of RORs.

A total of 13 suggestions are made for improvement of the effectiveness and efficiency of the system governing administration of the RORs. The main rationale for improvement can be summarized as follows:

- It is becoming difficult and costly to determine exactly what all the rights, obligations and restrictions (RORs) are that affect any particular piece of land.
- The costs of administering and complying with the myriad legislation and resultant administrative procedures and systems are very high and uncertainty is being produced.
- The uncertainty of what RORs apply, and where they apply, is beginning to have an adverse impact on security – in some cases this is affecting property value and the amount of capital that can be raised using land as collateral. Private Title insurance is now available in some states of Australia.

References

ANZLIC, (2004). *National Summit on Improving the Administration of Property Rights and Restrictions*, ANZLIC and the Queensland Government Department of Natural Resources and Mines, Brisbane in 2004. Online: www.ANZLIC.org.au/events_landsummit_nov04_program.htm.

Butt, P. (2003). Indefeasibility Overridden – Significantly. *ALJ*, 77 (88), 88–89.

Dale, P. and Baldwin, R. (1999). *Development of Land Markets in Central and Eastern Europe*. Final Report. Project P2128R of the European Action for Cooperation in the Field of Economics Program.

Department of Transport and Regional Services, (2005). Australian Government. Online: www.daf.gov.au/Index.aspx

Mayers, J. (2005). *The '4 R's': Rights, Relationships, Responsibilities and Revenues.* Online: www.iied.org/forestry/tools/four.html

Lyons, K.; Davies, K. and Cottrell, E. (2002a). *On the Efficiency of Property Rights Administration in Queensland*. Report to Queensland Government Department of Natural Resources and Mines. Online at: www.ANZLIC.org.au/events_land summit_nov04_program.htm.

Lyons, K.; Cottrell, E. and Davies, K. (2002b). The Case for Refocusing and Re-Engineering Land Administration to Better Meet Contemporary Needs. In *Property Rights and Markets*. Proceedings of the Joint AURISA and Institution of Surveyors Conference, Adelaide, November 2002. Online: www.ANZLIC.org.au/ events_landsummit_nov04_program.htm.

Lyons, K.; Cottrell, E. and Davies, K. (2004a). *On the Efficiency of Property Rights Administration*. Report to Queensland Government Department of Natural Resources and Mines. Online: www.ANZLIC.org.au/ events_landsummit_nov04_ program.htm.

Lyons, K.; Cottrell, E. and Davies, K. (2004b). On the Efficiency of Property Rights Administration. Paper to *the National Summit on Improving the Administration of*

Property Rights and Restrictions. Brisbane: November 2004. Online: www.ANZLIC.org.au\events_landsummit_ nov04_program.htm.

Pamuk, A. (1999). *Tools for a Land and Housing Market Diagnosis.* http://info.worldbank.org/etools/docs/library/115504/toronto99/assets/t-pamuk-mod06.pdf

Public Administration and Finance Committee Parliament of Western Australia (2004). *The Impact of State Government Actions and Processes on the Use and Enjoyment of Freehold and Leasehold Land in Western Australia.* Report. Online: www.parliament.wa.gov.au/Parliament/commit.nsf/(ReportsAndEvidence)/D89047DADC4CF0C48256E9100809C9A?opendocument

Rigsby, B. (1998). A Survey of Property Theory and Tenure Types. Marine Tenure in Australia. *Oceania Monograph* 48. N. Peteraon and B. Rigsby, University of Sydney. *Ocenia Monograph* 48, 22–46.

Scott, A. 1999. Fishermen's Property Rights. In Arnason, R. and Gissurarson, H. H. (eds). *Individual Transferable Quotas in Theory and Practice.* (pp15–30). Reykjavik: University of Iceland Press.

Sheehan, J. and Small G. (2002). Towards a Definition of Property Rights. *Pacific Rim Real Estate Society (PRRES) conference.* Christchurch New Zealand. Online: http://business2.unisa.edu.au/prres/Proceedings/ Proceedings2002/Sheehan_Towards_a_definition_of_property_rights.pdf

Walsh, P. and A. Consulting Pty Ltd and UTS Centre for Local Government (2002). *A National Development Assessment Forum Study*: Comparative Performance Measurement and Benchmarking of Planning and Development Assessment Systems. Online: www.daf.gov.au/reports/daf_benchmarking_final_1202.pdf

World Bank (2001). *Diagnostic Tool for Assessing Land and Real Estate Markets.* Unpublished.

Young, M. and McColl, J. (2002). *Robust Separation – A search for a generic framework to simplify registration in trading of interests in natural resources.* Adelaide: CSIRO Land and Water, Policy and Economic Research Unit.

12

Building Institutional Incentives in Dying Communities

Alex Smajgl, Melissa Nursey-Bray,
Karen Vella and Alexander Herr

Introduction

Australia's *outback* regions have become the focus of renewed development interests from industry and political spheres, which include, for example, more intensive agricultural and irrigation development and managed population growth. There is mounting pressure for outback regions to explore options for diversifying the use of natural resources (Holmes, 1996) and their portfolios of products; in particular, diversifying into growing service industries such as tourism and potential new international markets for environmental services. Outback regions have a potential to provide environmental services such as carbon sequestration and biodiversity credits to prospective international markets (Faith et al, 2003; Williams et al. 2004). These regions also face increasing demands by society for tourism, recreation and biodiversity conservation and by traditional owners for additional use and access rights.

Natural resource use and management in Australia is governed by a complex system of laws, policies and guidelines, instituted by governments and organizations at a range of scales, from local to state and federal. Institutional arrangements regulate land use and management through a combination of broad overarching rules, such as environmental duty of care, and numerous specific arrangements targeting the management of specific issues or land features. In practice, institutional arrangements are administered through compartmentalized and fragmented management structures at various juris-dictional levels and with differential power and capacity for implementation. Misunderstanding and ignorance of ecological principles, policy frameworks that are fragmented and compartmentalized by separate government depart-ments and inappropriate institutional arrangements have often led to management decisions that have had serious implications for ecosystem health and biodiversity preservation (Holling, 1995; Picket et al, 1997).

It is increasingly evident that fragmented ad hoc institutional arrangements and formal government decision-making processes are having serious implications on the social and economic conditions in towns and communities in rural and outback Australia. The erosion of social and economic conditions appears to have an impact on the vulnerability of rural towns and communities and on the capacity of rural populations to participate in institution building and re-design.

This chapter presents the *key* findings from research that identified institutional arrangements at a community level and considered how they interacted and influenced human behaviour. The study concentrates on the institutional arrangements in the outback community of Etheridge Shire. The study combined in-depth qualitative research with quantitative modelling approaches.

The Region: Etheridge Shire

Located within the Savanna Region of Northern Australia, the Etheridge Shire spans 39,308km², extending across parts of the Einasleigh Uplands and Gulf Plains Bioregions (Thackway and Cresswell, 1995) (Figure 12.1). The administrative centre of the shire is Georgetown.

The physical landscape of the Etheridge Shire is characterized by gently sloping hills and wooded savanna grasslands. The Etheridge Shire local government area covers the upper part of the Gilbert River Basin, which forms the beginning of the Einasleigh, Etheridge and Gilbert Rivers.

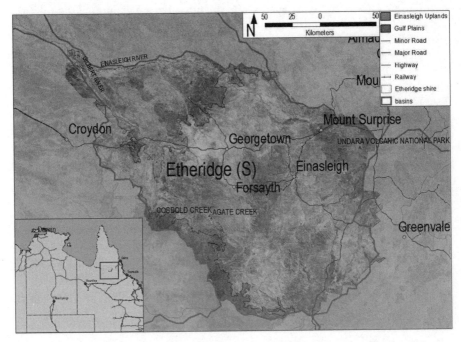

Figure 12.1 Location of the Etheridge Shire in Northern Australia

The Etheridge Shire was once an important mining region for gold, copper, silver, lead and tin. However, the mining boom has now subsided and there is only one remaining active mine in the Shire (QLD NRM, 2004).

Cattle grazing dominates land use in the Shire and occurs predominately on leasehold land. A small proportion of freehold land exists within the Shire (one per cent of Shire area) and national parks also occupy a small land area (three per cent of Shire area). Other important land uses include tourism, and horticulture and hay production primarily along the Gilbert River. Access to water for irrigation and development is a limiting factor for the further expansion of these uses (Northern Gulf Resource Management Group 2001 in McDonald and Dawson, 2004).

Etheridge Shire is the traditional country of the Ewamian people. The Ewamian people have long-standing cultural connections to the area and have been active in engaging with pastoralist, mining, tourist and local government interests to ensure Indigenous participation in decision-making. Indigenous involvement in the area has resulted in the establishment of a number of Indigenous Land Use Agreements (ILUAs) and Memoranda of Understanding (MOUs) between traditional owners and local government that have been negotiated independent of tenure. The ILUA process has been acknowledged by parties to the agreements as very successful: 'The negotiations have all been on a voluntary basis with long term benefits emanating for both Traditional Owners and local government/graziers' (NGRMG, 2001).

Based on Australia Bureau of Statistics (ABS, 2001) census data for the Etheridge shire indicates a resident population of approximately 1,000 persons in 2001, two per cent of whom were Indigenous. Forecasts show an aging population (52 as median age in 2026) and only small annual population growth of 0.3 per cent between 2001 and 2026 (Queensland Government Planning, Sport and Recreation, 2004; OESR, 2003).

Major employment in the region comes from Agriculture, Forestry and Fishing (41 per cent) followed by Accommodation, Cafes and Restaurants (nine per cent), Mining and Government Administration (8.4 per cent) and Defence (8.2 per cent). Eighteen per cent of people had higher education (vocational/tertiary) qualifications and internet use was recorded at 20 per cent of population. Based on 2001 census data, the employment rate was 99 per cent with a labour force participation rate of 70 per cent. In 2001, most people (67 per cent) earned AU$160–AU$699 per week (ABS, 2001). Agricultural production in the shire was AU$44 million for the year 1998–1999 (OESR, 2003).

The Etheridge Shire is subject to a sophisticated institutional and legislative framework that exists at all levels from local to federal and a number of key arrangements govern land use, resource access, and environmental management. The Queensland and Australian Governments have implemented these legislative arrangements largely in response to broad concerns and expectations across Queensland and Australia. They provide a high degree of control over human behaviour and resource use and management in practice as a consequence.

The conditions and pressures in the Etheridge Shire epitomize those facing many outback and remote rural communities in Australia and, as such, the Etheridge Shire provides an interesting case study within which to examine the interplay between externally driven formal arrangements and locally formed informal institutional arrangements.

Present social and economic conditions in the Etheridge Shire reflect the impact of rural structural adjustment in the beef industry in the 1980s and increasing measures for environmental protection since the late 1990s.

In particular, this case study provides a good opportunity to examine the impact of formal and informal rules on the human dimensions of outback life including population, social relationships, infrastructure investment, attitudes and local rules.

Qualitative Approach

This research project applied the Framework for Institutional Analysis and Development (IAD) as the theoretical basis for collecting and analysing information and it formed a conceptual map to define the major types of structural variables present in institutional settings (Ostrom, 2003, p. 13). The framework used in this chapter is described in detail by Ostrom in Chapter 2 of this book.

According to the IAD framework, three sets of contextual attributes structure behaviour and decision-making in a natural resource system:

1   The physical attributes of the natural resource system and material conditions.
2   The attributes of the community of participants – the key stakeholders who have an interest or relationship to the institutional structures and processes operating within the situation of interest.
3   The formal and informal institutional arrangements (rules) used by participants.

To underpin the use of the IAD framework, the research team gathered information on the region and institutional arrangements via desktop analyses, fieldwork and meetings with key contacts. The case study work was conducted in four phases:

1   scoping;
2   establishment;
3   fieldwork; and
4   follow up and feedback.

The following section provides a summary of fieldwork findings, which was taken to develop an agent-based model.

Findings

The research revealed rich information about the rules governing human behaviour and relationships in the communities, and the social context of the Etheridge Shire. Overall, the research found that local social institutions have evolved uniquely in response to the specific conditions experienced in the outback. External institutional arrangements offered problems in the specific context of the Etheridge Shire mainly due to issues of scale, language, local capacity and relations of power.

One of the interesting fieldwork findings emerging from the semi-structured interviews concerned the impact of population dynamics on local investment and community attitudes and perceptions towards the future of the Shire. The remainder of this chapter will now consider the results in terms of this specific topic in further detail.

The following section explains respondent perceptions towards land use and development opportunities in the Etheridge Shire. Following on from this the chapter considers alternative development scenarios in the social context of the Etheridge Shire.

Land use

It is the broad perception that savanna regions such as the Etheridge Shire are facing increasing pressures to diversify land use but also face institutional constraints to the implementation of such changes (Holmes, 1996, 2000; Department of Transport and Regional Services, 2001; Duff et al, In Press).

The respondents in the Etheridge Shire identified attitudes and pressures for multiple-use options to be relatively relaxed or nonexistent. Although respondents identified some localized interest in diversification into uses such as tourism and cropping, most community members are uninterested in further diversifying land use in the Etheridge Shire beyond the scale of existing land use. It follows therefore that within this context, the respondents did not identify institutional arrangements as either major factors constraining or enhancing their access to multiple-use options and outcomes. This result is surprising given the broader rhetoric and interest in diversifying savanna land-use and perceptions that formal institutional arrangements pose significant impediments to multiple-use opportunities.

In addition, interviews revealed that there is little perceived pressure for change in the Etheridge Shire. For example, in terms of diversification into tourism, interviews identified that a couple of key tourist operators and the Etheridge Shire Council are driving new opportunities. This includes the development of tourist attractions and facilities, the Terrestrial Centre, a wash down bay and rubbish facility. In almost all cases, the scale of these operations is compatible with existing land tenure and institutional requirements. More widespread development of tourism in the region is naturally constrained by the people themselves. Respondents stated that the existing beef cattle culture underpins a general lack of interest by graziers in tourism. Respondents also identified that many members of the community possess limited skills in providing tourism experiences and limited capital to invest in infrastructure to meet tourism demands. Within this context, formal institutional arrangements are not perceived by respondents to be a key determinant for diversification.

People and community

Respondents identified that building and maintaining community capacity (for example, concepts of place, community and lifestyle) is the predominant driver for decision-making in the region. This is guided by much of the lived experience in the Shire and respondents identified that it governs decisions about future business directions, land use, settlement, lifestyle and recreation.

Respondents identified that the lack of opportunities available for education and training are key disincentives for retaining people in the Etheridge Shire. This was also a concern expressed by community respondents in relation to their experienced reality that once children leave the Shire, they often do not return. This was succinctly captured by one respondent:

> *Because you don't have any high schools, you send them away to boarding schools, so if your kids do go to uni there is very little for them to do coming back here, so they go elsewhere.*

Employment, education, community capacity and leadership, social and family relations, sense of community and place were all factors raised as needing injection and impetus within the community. As captured by one respondent:

> *There is very little to attract young people to stay in the region. It goes hand in hand with economic development, it is a low economic development area, it is hard to attract young people to stay in this region.*

Shire residents frequently characterized the region as 'dead or 'dying', a social vacuum, a place where one could feel socially alienated. One respondent identified:

> *One of the pressures that gets me down every now and again, is the negativity in the town. … This town is depressed I think, emotionally, people just aren't positive. They have just run out of energy I suppose, and it is really unhealthy here.*

Many respondents perceived that the challenges of building community could be addressed through capacity building strategies. These strategies were presented as options that would enable the community to become more resilient. In particular the study found that there was a need to build community leadership, capacity, skills and the inclination of residents to stay and contribute to the community.

In this context respondents highlighted the need to find and support local leaders as a possible mechanism for enhancing social cohesion and economic development. As noted by one:

> *There are no drivers in there that can help to develop it. Even the local government struggles with promoting and marketing tourism here.*

In addition, improved access to tourism attractions was identified as a key development obstacle:

> *Roads, end of story, roads. Our biggest problem out here is ... roads.*

Future opportunities

In summary, interviews revealed that people within the local community perceive that Georgetown, the regional centre of Etheridge Shire, is dying because of:

* an ongoing difficulty in recruiting local people into local government and regional leadership positions;
* youth exodus from the Shire to attend schooling and later employment;
* economic depression in Georgetown;
* stagnation of the urban centre, principally as a result of the inability to stimulate residential or other urban (e.g. industrial) development owing to a lack of available freehold land in Georgetown and other infrastructure such as roads or schools; and
* limited ability in the past to attract income from traffic en-route to Karumba (e.g. tourism and transport).

Some respondents expressed frustration that Georgetown residents were not more proactively involved in supporting the survival of their town. The respondents themselves were quite heavily involved in community and development activities within the Shire and identified that they had a strong sense of place attachment to the Shire and a deep interest in its longer term viability. This contrasted with their perception of many of the other town residents who were identified as being transient and less interested in the long-term survival of Georgetown. Other respondents identified a general lack of interest in diversifying land use further into uses such as tourism, and an inability to invest further in public good activities because of the demands of their own family life and family businesses.

Interviews also revealed local government aspiration to see Georgetown develop into a regional 'hub' of services for the wider Southern-Gulf region. Development into a regional service centre would involve new business development both to capture passing custom as well as meet the broader regional service demands (for services such as mechanics for example) currently provided out of major regional centres such as the Atherton Tablelands or Cairns. However, in order to implement these aspirations institutional arrangements need to create enabling opportunities.

These qualitative findings have been translated into a model structure to assess whether local development aspirations can be met by investment in roads and to investigate the impact of migration dynamics under alterative circumstances. Crucial for the modelling exercise is a structured view on explaining variables for community capacity. This step leads to the concept of social cohesion.

Quantitative Approach

The modelling exercise aimed to translate the results of the qualitative analysis into a modelling structure, thus combining real-world data with assumptions. As such, potential drivers for change in the community were examined in order to predict which future conditions may lead to positive outcomes in response to concerns identified by community members in previous sections.

In the context of institutional arrangements, simulation tools are mainly based on game-theoretical approaches (Ostrom et al. 1994) and agent-based models (Smajgl, 2004). This section presents an agent-based model for the Etheridge Shire. The following sections will:

1   describe the empirical and theoretical goals of this modelling work;
2   define the institutional focus for the model application;
3   explain the methodology; and
4   apply the model to two policy scenarios to explain the output side of this approach.

Modelling goals

The modelling exercise integrates an empirical and a theoretical goal. The empirical goal of the agent-based model is to assess the contribution of different policy options to a political goal. Our field work identified a variety of public goals at different scales, one notable goal being the aspiration to see Georgetown as the administrative centre of the Etheridge Shire developed into a regional centre (or a so-called *hub*). Consultations with the community identified a clear underlying perception that Georgetown is a *dying town*. Earlier in this chapter it was shown that current projections for population and average age of residents underscore the dying town scenario.

The theoretical goal of this model is to simulate the evolution of informal rules. We aim to simulate the dynamics of interactions between behaviour at an individual level, where decisions are made under a set of perceived rules, and at the community level, where (informal) rules emerge. Previous work by Smajgl et al, (2003) indicated that the success of an investment that targets a significant population growth depends on the existing informal institutional arrangement. Investments in social infrastructure, such as a community centre or road, might trigger a significant response at the individual level because individuals perceive the change as an improvement. If the investment occurs in a situation where the main attitude towards the future of the community is negative, the response might be negligible.

In order to implement the link between the individual's perception of community needs and communication, individual learning has to be simulated. The next section explains how learning is implemented and develops the model structure of this agent-based approach.

Social cohesion and the institutional impediment

In this model we implement social cohesion as a common-pool resource. As with traditional common-pool resources, individuals can extract or add a certain level of social cohesion. In this case, extraction occurs in the form of not contributing to the process of creating trust and bondage within the township. Conversely, individuals benefit because a high level of social cohesion is likely to lower transaction costs.

In an in-depth empirical study in several small towns in northern Canada Blishen et al, (1979) identified that social cohesion is a core variable for community capacity. It was also found that social cohesion is fundamental for the two other important factors, political efficacy and economic vitality. Social cohesion is defined in various disciplines (Friedkin, 2004). Berger-Schmitt (2002, p. 405) defines social cohesion as 'a characteristic of a society dealing with the connections and relations between societal units such as individuals, groups, associations as well as territorial units'. More specifically the Social Cohesion Network of the Policy Research Initiative of the Canadian Government defines social cohesion as 'the ongoing process of developing a community of shared values, shared challenges and equal opportunity within Canada, based on a sense of trust, hope and reciprocity among all Canadians'. (Jackson et al, 2000).

In order to formulate the institutional link between individual behaviour and social dynamics, the responses of community members were analysed to discover the origin of the low social cohesion. An informal rule was formulated to define the underlying attitude of people in the Etheridge Shire towards the community and social cohesion. This rule impacts on how people reward other's efforts to participate in collective actions for the benefit of the town's interests, as opposed to individual interests. The rule is not restricted to altruistic behaviour as decisions that seek to improve an individual's situation with obvious benefits for the community also fall into this category. Nevertheless, as it also includes altruistic behaviour we will refer to it as the rule for altruistic behaviour. It can be expected that, formulated as an informal rule (Crawford and Ostrom, 1995), this institution would take the following form in the Etheridge Shire:

> *Every resident shall invest effort in improving public goods, which will be rewarded by an increasing social acceptance in the community or otherwise the person will be increasingly alienated by the township.*

Instead of finding this informal rule in place in our case study community, the fieldwork in the Etheridge Shire showed that altruistic effort does not appear to be rewarded by most members of the community. In other words, there is no institutional incentive for individuals to contribute to social cohesion through exhibiting altruistic behaviour. Although most residents in the Shire rank landscape amenity high and list it as a reason to live in the area, they rank the perceptions of the township and the community as low. Furthermore, individual investment in a public good might also be low because harsh conditions dominate outback life, and it requires a lot of time to run individual businesses.

In the context of fieldwork findings and the concept of social cohesion we developed a simulation tool as part of the application of an agent-based model. The agent-based model was applied to analyse dynamics within the scope of individual and community scales in order to focus on the evolution of the rule of rewarding altruistic behaviour.

Following Blishen et al, (1979), strong social cohesion enables a community to communicate needs more efficiently, which will lead to increased ability to secure funding for better roads or other services.

Methodology

The model development analyses the evolution of the rule on rewarding altruism in the context of social cohesion, which we define as a common-pool resource, and adds a learning mechanism for agents. Learning takes place as reinforcement dynamics and as fictitious play. Reinforcement learning describes the process of memorizing pay-offs linked to the own strategy choice (Holland and Miller, 1991) while fictitious play includes the observation of pay-offs other agents receive from their strategy choice and the placing of this into the context of one's own decision (Young, 1993). The combination of both approaches is important because it is more likely that people learn from more than just their own experience (Camerer and Ho, 1999; Brenner, 2004).

Similar to the typical prisoner's dilemma situations with public goods, individuals do not receive direct rewards from investment in the public good (Fudenberg and Tirole, 1991). The rational choice between investing in a public good and in a private good always prefers the private option if communication and collaboration is not allowed. Outside of the rational choice paradigm many cases show that altruism exists (Henrich, 2004).

In this specific case we model social cohesion as the public good. Strong social cohesion allows the effective prioritization of community needs and its effective communication in the policy and planning process. Social cohesion increases if individuals contribute time for the needs of the community, which ranges from talking to other community members to active participation in policy. Social cohesion would be zero if all individuals in a group lived in absolute isolation neglecting the existence of the group.

The model assumes that a low number of persons in the Etheridge Shire are very active in improving the situation of the community, which matches our field data. Another group of people experiments with the impact of such an investment. We define the agents' attitude to the community as the distinguishing attribute. If effort by experimenting individuals is rewarded by the rest of the community, their activity level remains high or rises. Quantitatively, social cohesion is modelled as the sum of time all individuals spend on community needs.

The agent-based model defines each person in the Etheridge Shire as an agent. Each agent is defined by the following attributes: age, family membership, location (rural or town), income, status (student, working adult, retired), residential status (living in community, boarding school, moved out, newborn, died, or immigrating).

This framework defines the capacity for simulations of individuals that are connected in a township. The main decisions that agents make within this framework are:

1   whether to return to the local community after having spent years (normally four years) at boarding school; and
2   whether income is sufficient to support the size of the family.

It was shown that nearly all children from the Shire move to the east coast after boarding school and most of the children from the rural area in the Etheridge Shire return if the property allows an income above the poverty line. Families leave the Shire if they lived for two years under the poverty line: social security payments give an indication for a lower level that triggers the decision to move out. We assume for the poverty line a lower level of annually AU\$5,800. As stochastic elements we implement varying rainfall that impacts the income situation of rural families and varying tourism numbers and spending of local customers that changes the income of local business owners in the township.

Two major expectations can be identified based on the Qualitative Approach section presented above:

1   that Georgetown is a *dying* town; and
2   the aspiration that Georgetown should be a so-called hub that provides all needed services to the surrounding outback region.

This makes it necessary to shift the main focus to the township of Georgetown and less on the rural parts of the Etheridge Shire. However, as the main tourist attractions are in the rural regions surrounding Georgetown, decision-making processes in these regions are crucial. Additionally, the economic situation of the rural and the town residents influence the income situation of town people.

Heterogenous agents make their decisions about how much of their spare time they spend investing in civic activities. *Investment* can vary from articulating a positive attitude towards the community with optimistic expectations to the organization of community meetings. The agents learn, in a reinforcement process, if it is worth bearing the opportunity costs of investing in the community. Opportunity costs can be either financial benefit, through additional effort in individually owned business, or non-financial benefit at an individual or family level (e.g. personal satisfaction, pride). Agents experiment randomly with investing effort in the community and they gain knowledge

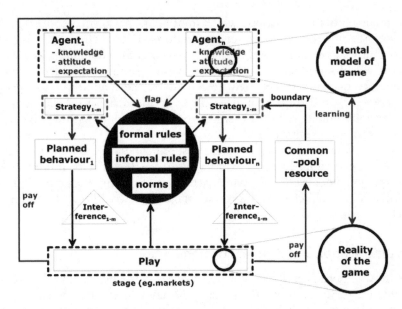

Figure 12.2 Conceptual model for learning and evolving institutions in agent-based model

about the decision-making situation. Figure 12.2 shows the underlying concept of learning.

The strategy choice in the model is restricted by the existing institutional setting because the informal rule for rewarding social engagement does not exist. At the same time social cohesion, as the common-pool resource, bounds the strategy choice of individuals as we assume a medium or high level of social cohesion to be necessary for effectiveness in political and planning processes. A township with strong social cohesion is very likely to be effective in demanding more resources, or collectively organizing themselves to provide more resources for community needs.

The Qualitative Approach section above identified two major community assets that are missing or underdeveloped: schools and roads. Although the size of a community is an important factor for external investment in both of these assets, there are communities in the outback smaller than Georgetown with better roads and a high school. The road conditions in the Shire are set in the model as a limiting factor for diversification into tourism activities, restricting access especially for buses. Provision of a local high school, as a second example, is dependent not only on the number of students in the Shire but also on effectiveness of the community in demanding a high school.

Because of different attitudes and changing expectations, agents experiment within their capacity, as defined by their mental model of the situation. Agents are also able to perceive the fact that they may not receive rewards for their contributions to the community. If there are enough people that perceive the negative influence of the institutional arrangement, they may flag their discontent with this situation, which represents an agent expressing their displeasure with the outcomes of their efforts. If enough people flag their discontent we assume that a change occurs within the community as a whole, and individual social behaviour towards investing in the social cohesion of the community becomes increasingly rewarded by the majority of the people. Furthermore, we assume that over time, as social cohesion increases, the demand for community infrastructure (roads and high school) will be articulated at a broader political level.

Such a dynamic can lead to increased social cohesion and improved conditions in the community without external influence. If stochastic influences lead to a situation where suddenly many agents put effort into the community, the informal rule would change at a certain stage. This would be captured by the baseline scenario.

Baseline scenario and policy options

The most important indicator for our analysis is the population. In order to develop a baseline scenario, the model calibration attempted matching population projections cited above. These seem very optimistic as most community members communicated a much more pessimistic view on future developments. The development of a reference case within the agent-based model showed that the predictions of a dramatically aging population (52 as median age in 2026) is unlikely to happen within the population numbers (between 954 and 1258 persons in 2026). Such a decrease would be linked to a much lower population path. As the projections are based on unpublished ABS data and methodological aspects are not published, the path cannot be reconstructed.

The reference case is based on different population dynamics. We assume that up to two children from a rural family return after receiving education to run the property. The return of students from town families is ruled by earning potential on the coast versus in the local township, and therefore occurs only rarely. The *return* feature is combined with a changing income situation and the assumed poverty line, which triggers decisions of residents to move out.

At the same time, increasing income in the township defines an incentive for people to move into Georgetown. The highest income in the community is chosen as a base for the decision-making as it is assumed that the highest income receives greater community attention than averages. The highest income means that a local business owner hires more staff or that a new entrepreneur is attracted. Additionally, the model assumes random death with a rising likelihood from age 50 to 100. No agent can be older than 100 years. Births occur randomly in families that can afford another family member. Community wide, we assume a natality rate of seven per 1,000 of population. Given these projection conditions, we see that the population in Etheridge Shire decreases slightly to 887 people in 2030. As mentioned above, the median age is unlikely to increase to 52. Instead, in this baseline scenario, the median age increases from 37 to 43 in 2030. Figure 12.3 shows the resulting reference path for the population size.

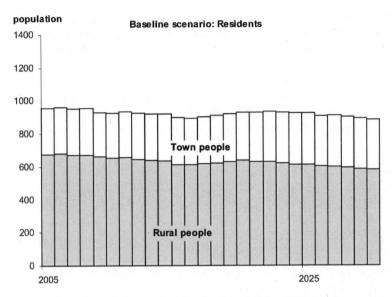

Figure 12.3 Population projection for Etheridge Shire, 2005 to 2030, baseline scenario

The Qualitative Approach section above explained that two indicators are important for this analysis of migration decisions of individuals: social cohesion as a non-market value and the number of tourists as an important factor for income. Figure 12.4 shows the change in social cohesion and the fluctuation of tourists visiting the shire for the baseline case.

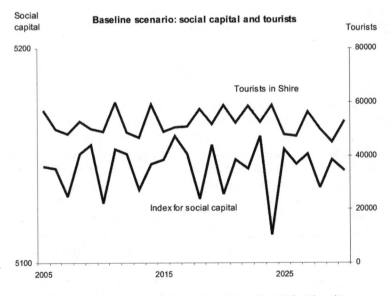

Figure 12.4 Index for social cohesion and tourists in Etheridge Shire, 2005 to 2030, baseline scenario

Both figures make it clear that the aspiration of a growing town will not be met. In other words, the social cohesion as an endogenous potential to trigger an increasing population is too low. Given the internal dynamics of the community, it appears that Georgetown does not have the internal capacity to realize its growth expectations. This means that aspirations to see a much bigger Georgetown providing services to the surrounding areas can not be met unless external investment improves the situation. The following scenarios analyse the potential of such investments in the context of social cohesion.

Scenarios

In this section we analyse two scenarios: road upgrade with community engagement process, and without.

Scenario 1: Road upgrade with community engagement process

The first scenario is focused on the impact of upgraded roads as a response to community demands. We assume an investment in roads to an extent that most regional attractions, such as Cobbolt Gorge, are accessible by all types of vehicles. This would, for instance, grant access for big buses from Cairns to bring potentially bigger tourist groups to the whole Shire. Currently, only one regional tourist attraction, Undara Lava Tubes, is open without access restrictions.

Additionally, we assume that if not only one but three or four attractions are easily accessible, longer trips could be offered for tourism markets. We assume that increasing the number of tourists leads to increased incomes for town people and the owners/managers of tourist attractions. We assume that the average spending of tourists in Georgetown is AU\$40. Additionally, based on similar outback locations we assume that the number of tourist nights will double in average if roads were upgraded. The change in available income positively impacts the income situation in Georgetown and creates a migration incentive.

This scenario links the increasing income to migration dynamics and analyses how the informal rule of rewarding individual contributions to community needs evolves. We assume for Scenario 1 that many community members perceive the external investment as an external reward for the efforts of community members. This triggers the realization of other agents that there might be a positive pay-off for individual contributions to community benefits. As better roads mean higher revenue for tourism operators and lower transportation costs for cattle stations, we assume agents in these businesses will reward the community members who were actively involved in creating better road conditions. As fictitious play takes place, other agents observe the reward mechanism and engage themselves in community processes. This means that they want to be rewarded for their effort (and will indicate their unhappiness when not rewarded), which means that step by step the informal rule changes at the community level.

Figure 12.5 shows a significant population increase under the modest assumption that a maximum of 25 families could move per year to Georgetown. As the external investment to upgrade roads occurs in reaction to the rising demand of an active group of community members, other agents learn. We assume that in five years the negotiations lead to a finalized upgrade of roads. This means that the income situation for most families improves and the incentive for other families to move into the region increases.

Crucial for this analysis is the change of informal institutions due to the incline in social cohesion. As explained above the indicator for the informal rule on investing in the community is the demand for the second community need, a school with high school features. The opening of such a school indicates that demands were successfully articulated. The major change in population dynamics occurs in 2013 when a high school is opened. The stars in Figure 12.5 indicate when the investment is finalized.

The regional description earlier in this chapter showed that Georgetown has no high school and responses listed made clear that the absence of a high school is an important factor for population dynamics. Often whole families leave the area because they cannot pay for the boarding fees for several children at the same time. Several other places in North Queensland, for instance Charters Towers, showed that a high school can attract families from other rural places that have no high school.

The opening of a high school has to be seen in the context of how social cohesion evolves. The positive result of negotiations as an external reward for altruistic behaviour and the fictitious play-based learning of other community members increased the ability of a greater number of people to reward altruism. We still assume that, depending on their attitude, agents experiment with altruistic responses. Community members themselves reward positive attitude towards the community, which leads to positive reinforcement learning of agents. This learning process leads within three years, 2011–2013, to a massive

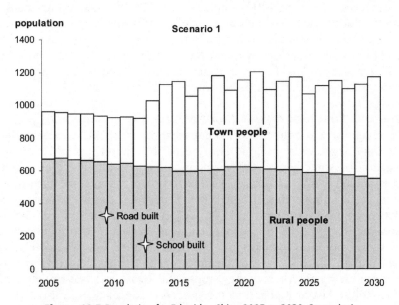

Figure 12.5 Population for Etheridge Shire, 2005 to 2030, Scenario 1

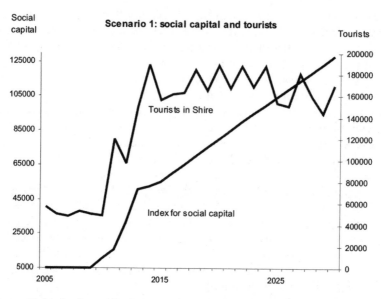

Figure 12.6 Index for social cohesion and tourists, Etheridge Shire, 2005–2030, Scenario 1

increase of social cohesion. Figure 12.6 shows the increasing social cohesion, which is based on the time that people invest in the community.

Within this phase, the community formulates a strong demand for a high school, which is granted in 2013. This initiates a strong population growth as families, attracted by available schooling, move into town. The Shire population stabilizes at around 1200 people. After 2026, the community does not generate enough income for all town families and some families leave again. However, the high school also improves the education in the Shire, initiating skills and business development, and the creation of employment opportunities. This is likely to lead to a second step upwards in the population dynamics but is outside of the scope of this chapter.

Scenario 2: Road upgrade without community engagement process
In the second scenario the model assumes that roads are upgraded without the community negotiation process. This means that the community cannot see that action by some community members made any difference to achieving their aspiration of upgraded roads, so there is no activation of the altruism rule.

Figure 12.7 shows that although improving road conditions led to much higher income for most town people, the general attitude towards the town remains negative. Social cohesion remains at the levels seen in Figure 12.4 while tourist numbers increase in a similar fashion to Figure 12.6. The weak social cohesion means that no dynamics occur to flag demand for a high school, which means that young people still leave and occasionally whole families follow. Even higher income does not trigger significant migration dynamics.

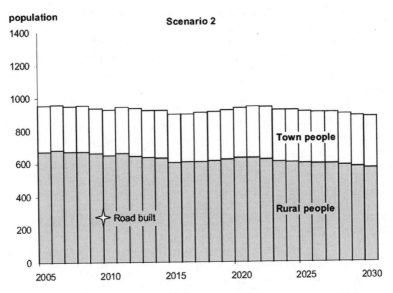

Figure 12.7 Population for Etheridge Shire, 2005 to 2030, Scenario 2

Results of the Scenarios 1 and 2 indicate that the process of including community members in the planning and decision-making process is crucial for endogenous processes to trigger a build-up of social cohesion.

Limitations

These modelling results have to be treated cautiously because of a limited understanding of underlying individual attitudes. The timeframe of the research project did not allow an analysis of institutional arrangements to the depth that is required to rigorously calibrate the rules of the agents. The actual decision-making process of the Department of Education in regard to opening a high school is also hypothetical rather then representing true population requirements.

A properly calibrated model is able to visualize and quantify policy options influencing social change and can therefore be used as an effective tool for proactive decision-making. However, if the application of the model is to have a meaningful policy-making role, the underlying calibration of the artificial agents has to be based on time and space specific background information.

Conclusion

Fieldwork conducted in the Etheridge Shire found weak social cohesion and out-migration dynamics. Core reasons underpinning out-migration include a lack of schooling, which forces children and many families to leave the region, and a lack of income possibilities. Most residents do not identify formal institutions as restricting their land use aspirations. However, they do perceive that formal institutional arrangements have contributed towards prevailing local social and economic conditions including those of de-population and loss of social capital, and loss of community. In this broader institutional environment created by formal arrangements, informal institutions serve to further weaken social cohesion.

Social cohesion is an important driver for Etheridge Shire and it has implications for institutional arrangements and planning processes. The Etheridge Shire faces community capacity issues relating to language, community information flows and communication structures, and attitudes of lethargy, particularly within urban communities. Issues of governance, political cognition and political socialization are additional capacity issues facing the Etheridge Shire community not discussed in this chapter.

The modelling exercise shows how models can be used in analysing the impact of informal institutions on social cohesion and thereby on the trajectory of development. The contrasting results from the two scenarios make clear the importance of community participation in planning and negotiations about external investment, thereby quantifying the importance of the process through which community aspirations are achieved.

References

Australian Bureau of Statistics (ABS), (2001). *Census Usual Residents Profile, LGA33100 Etheridge (S) (Local Government Area)*. Canberra: Commonwealth of Australia.

Berger-Schmitt, R. (2002). Considering Social Cohesion in Quality of Life Assessments: Concept and Measurement. *Social Indicators Research,* 58, 403–428.

Blishen, B. R., Lockhart, A., Craib, P. and Lockhart, E. (1979) *Socioeconomic Impact Model for Northern Development, Volumes 1 and 2*, Ottawa: Canadian Department of Indian and Northern Affairs.

Brenner, T. (2004). *Agent Learning Representation*. Unpublished manuscript. Jena: Max Planck Institute.

Camerer, C. and Ho, T.-H. (1999). Experienced-weighted Attraction Learning in Normal Form Games. *Econometrica*, 67, 827–874.

Crawford, S. E. and Ostrom, E. (1995). A Grammar of Institutions. *American Political Science Review*, 89, 582–600.

Department of Transport and Regional Services, (2001). *Investing in Northern Australia: More than Outback – More Upfront*. Canberra: Department of Transport and Regional Services.

Dore, J. and Woodhill, J. (1999). *Sustainable Regional Development: Final Report*. Canberra: Greening Australia.

Duff, G.; Jacklyn, P.; Landsberg, J.; Ludwig, J.; Morrison, J.; Walker, D. H. and Whitehead, P. In Press. *Managing Pluralism in North Australian Natural and Cultural Resource Management: Reflections on a Decade of Cooperative Activity*. Canberra: Land and Water Australia.

Faith, D. P.; Carter, G.; Cassis, G.; Ferrier, S. and Wilkie, L. (2003). Complementarity, Biodiversity Viability Analysis, and Policy-based Algorithms for Conservation. *Environmental Science and Policy*, 6, 311–328.

Friedkin, N.E. (2004). Social Cohesion. *Annual Review of Sociology*, 30, 409–425.

Fudenberg, D. and Tirole, J. (1991). *Game Theory*. Cambridge: MIT Press.

Henrich, J. (2004). Cultural Group Selection, Coevolutionary Processes and Large-Scale Cooperation, *Journal of Economic Behaviour and Organization*, 53, 3–36.

Holland, J. H. and Miller, J. H. (1991). Artificial Adaptive Agent in Economic Theory. *American Economic Review*, 81, 365–370.

Holling, C. S. (1995). What Barriers? What Bridges? In Gunderson, L.H.; Holling, C. S. and Light, S. S. (eds). *Barriers and Bridges to the Renewal of Ecosystems and Institutions.* (pp. 3–34). New York: Columbia Univeristy Press.

Holmes, J. (1996). Changing Resource Values in Australia's Tropical Savannas: Priorities in Institutional Reform. In Ash, A. (ed.). *The Future of Tropical Savannas.* (pp28–43). Collingwood: CSIRO Publishing.

Holmes, J. (2000). Balancing Interests Through Land Tenure Reform: Regional Contrasts Between the Barkly and the Gulf. In Dixon, R. (ed.) *Business as Usual? Local Conflicts and Global Challenges in Northern Australia.* North Australia Research Unit. (pp. 134–154). Darwin: The Australian National University.

Jackson, A., Fawcett, G., Milan, A., Roberts, P., Schetayne, S, Scott, K. and Tsoukalas, S. (2000) *Social Cohesion in Canada: Possible Indicators*, Quebec: Department of Canadian Heritage.

McDonald, G. T. and Dawson, S. J. (2004) *Northern Gulf Region: Natural Resource Management Plan*, Georgetown, Qld: Tropical Savannas Management CRC and NGRMG Ltd.

NGRMG, (2001). *Northern Gulf Regional Strategy*. Georgetown, Qld: Northern Gulf Resource Management Group.

OESR (2003) *Population Projections to 2051*, Brisbane: Queensland Government.

Ostrom, E. (2003). *Doing Institutional Analysis: Digging Deeper than Markets and Hierarchies*. Workshop Readings in Political Theory and Policy Analysis series. Bloomington: Indiana University.

Ostrom, E.; Gardner, R. and Walker, J. (1994). *Rules, Games, and Common-pool resources*. Ann Arbor: The University of Michigan Press.

Picket, S. T. A.; Ostfled, R. S.; Shachak, M. and Likens, G. E. (eds). (1997). *The Ecological Basis of Conservation: Hetrogeneity, Ecosystems and Biodiversity*. New York: Chapman and Hill.

QLD NRM, (2004). *Interactive Resource and Tenure Maps (IRTM)*. The State of Queensland (Department of Natural Resources, Mines and Energy). Online: http://www.nrme.qld.gov.au/science/ geoscience/tenure_maps.html

Queensland Government Planning, Sport and Recreation, (2004). *Population and Housing Fact Sheet – Etheridge Shire*. Brisbane: Queensland Government.

Smajgl, A. (2004). Modelling Evolving Rules for the Use of Common-pool Resources in an Agent-based Model. *Tenth Biennial IASCP Conference Oaxaca.* Digital Library of the Commons, Indiana University. Online: http://dlc.dlib.indiana.edu.

Smajgl, A.; Vella, K. and Greiner, R. (2003). Frameworks and Models for Analysis and Design of Institutional Arrangements in Outback Regions. *IASCP Pacific Regional Meeting – Traditional Lands in the Pacific Region: Indigenous Common Property Resources in Convulsion or Cohesion.* Digital Library of the Commons, Indiana University. Online: http://dlc.dlib.indiana.edu.

Thackway, R. and Cresswell, I. D. (Eds), (1995). *An Interim Bioregionalization for Australia. A Framework for Setting Priorities in the National Reserve System Cooperative Program*. Version 4. Canberra: Australian Nature Conservation Agency.

Williams, R. J.; Hutley, L. B.; Cook, G. D.; Russel-Smith, J. and Edwards, A. (2004). Viewpoint: Assessing the carbon sequestration potential of mesmic savannas in the Northern Territory, Australia: Approaches, uncertainties and potential impacts of fire. *Functional Plant Biology,* 31, 415–422.

Young, H. P. (1993). The Evolution of Conventions. *Econometrica*, 61, 57–84.

13

The Potential for Market Mechanisms to Achieve Vegetation Protection in the Desert Uplands

John Rolfe

Introduction

Resource economists have three functions in dealing with natural resource management issues: analysing the reasons why environmental problems occur, evaluating whether it is worthwhile to address the problems, and designing mechanisms to help solve these problems. These steps have been applied to the issue of vegetation management in the Desert Uplands bioregion, an area approximately the size of Tasmania in central-western Queensland.

In rangeland areas of extensive pastoral operations, environmental losses may be associated with the loss of vegetation from clearing activities, as well as the introduction of artificial water points and alteration of vegetation from intensive grazing pressure, changed fire management and the introduction of exotic species. Many of these development activities lead to increases in agricultural production, particularly in the beef industry, but with associated negative impacts on biodiversity and land condition (Rolfe, 2000). In the cases where environmental damage is closely associated with production losses, there is little disagreement about the need for remedial action, but wider disagreement about who should bear the costs. There are other cases where there are direct tradeoffs between production and environmental factors, and often more substantial disagreements about resource use.

In economic terms, the major reason why such disagreements arise is that the costs and benefits arising from development fall unevenly across different groups in society. The production benefits are largely private benefits that accrue directly to landholders. In making choices to increase development or intensify operations, landholders balance these benefits against the financial costs that they will incur directly, as well as their own perceptions about factors such as salinity risks and biodiversity loss.

Many of the potential losses that result from development and intensification accrue to other groups in society, and can be viewed as social costs. If activities result in indirect losses, such as land degradation and salinity, these costs tend to be borne by future generations of landholders and by downstream or neighbouring properties. If activities result in biodiversity loss, the impacts will tend to be borne by the wider state and national community who place a value on preserving such factors. If clearing results in increased levels of greenhouse gas emissions, these impacts may be spread more globally.

Landholder activities that impose social costs on wider communities are usually presented as examples of externalities (AFFA, 1999). In making the decision to develop or intensify, landholders are not always taking into account the consequences for the broader community. Governments generally have a role in correcting externality problems where it is worthwhile (after transaction and administration costs have been taken into account). There is a variety of mechanisms available for this purpose, but regulation is often the dominant policy approach. An example of this comes from the vegetation clearing debate, where the Queensland State Government has increased regulatory controls over the past decade with the aim of halting all broadscale clearing by the end of 2006.

These issues may also be viewed from a Coasian viewpoint, where the externality problem is understood as arising from missing property rights. Landholders receive signals from society to produce more beef and wool, and clear land to meet those needs, but do not receive corresponding signals about the wishes of society to preserve biodiversity and reduce greenhouse gas emissions. If property rights could be established to register those demands, then the market mechanism would operate to produce both commercial and environmental outcomes. In cases where landholders hold explicit or implicit property rights over production choices, the use of a Coasian framework rather than an externality framework may be a more appropriate choice (Anderson, 2004).

The production benefits that can be gained from development or intensification are rarely uniform. The best quality agricultural land, with high production benefits per hectare, tends to be developed first. As this land becomes scarcer, it becomes more economic to develop lesser quality land. This pattern can be seen in Queensland, where clearing activities have moved from high rainfall and fertile soil areas westwards into the scrub and then the woodland vegetation types. Falling real costs of machinery, as well as new development techniques (e.g. introduced pastures), have also aided in this process.

The preservation values per hectare of native vegetation are also rarely uniform. People in society generally place most importance on unique and/or endangered species and ecosystems. As a species or ecosystem moves from being plentiful and widespread towards being restricted and endangered, the preservation values attached to an average unit or hectare are likely to rise substantially. Many of these values are classified as non-market values, and more specifically as non-use values, which make them difficult to assess. Specialized non-market valuation techniques can be employed to estimate these non-use values.

Rolfe, Blamey and Bennett (2000) report some estimates for non-market values within an economic analysis of tree clearing in the Desert Uplands region. They used the choice modelling technique to estimate the non-use values held by households in Brisbane for protecting both environmental factors and the livelihood of people in rural communities in that region. This involved surveying households and offering them a series of choices where environmental protection options were offset with employment losses in the region and increased taxes to the householder. The results were analysed in a logistic regression model to identify how respondents traded off the various attributes that made up the choice sets.

The results indicate that there were substantial non-use values associated with options that give greater protection to biodiversity in the Desert Uplands region. The authors compared these non-use protection values with the production opportunities in the Desert Uplands to conclude that for slight to modest increases in vegetation protection, the values of biodiversity protection would outweigh the sum of potential employment and production losses. For more substantial levels of protection, the latter tended to outweigh the former, although the value of possible greenhouse gas emissions (unaccounted for in that analysis) may still make many tree clearing activities in the region uneconomic from the viewpoint of society as a whole.

Given this background, the focus of interest in the project reported here was on designing mechanisms to ensure that the benefits of landholder activities (increased agricultural production) are not outweighed by the costs (impacts on biodiversity). While government regulation is often used in Australia to address environmental problems, it can involve substantial costs. These include transaction costs (including administrative and compliance costs) and opportunity costs (the costs of subsequent production losses). As a consequence, there is developing interest in the use of market-based instruments to address land management issues because of the potential cost efficiencies involved. The best example of this comes from the BushTender programme in Victoria, where a competitive tender mechanism was used to allocate public funds to enter into conservation agreements with landholders (Stoneham et al, 2003).

In this chapter, the use of a potential market mechanism to achieve a balance between production and environmental outcomes in the regional area is explored. An auction (competitive tender) mechanism was trialled for the purposes of establishing vegetation corridors to determine if this is an appropriate and cost-effective way of achieving a balance between environmental and production outcomes. The use of the mechanism represents a *mediated Coasian* approach to environmental protection issues, because it establishes property rights for management activities and provides a framework for negotiation. In particular, the mechanism represents acceptance of the existing distribution of property rights, and then negotiation with landholders to achieve better environmental outcomes.

In the next section, an overview of the case study of interest is presented, followed by an outline of the methodology used in the project. Following from there, results of the project are summarized, and discussion and conclusions are presented in the final section of this chapter.

Case Study of Interest

The Desert Uplands bioregion is an area of acacia and eucalypt woodlands covering 6.88 million hectares in central-western Queensland. The bioregion is classified in the rangeland zone of Australia. The region is used primarily for beef cattle, with some sheep run on the western side. It is less productive for pastoral purposes than regions to the east and south because of its relatively low rainfall and poor soils, and vegetation that is reasonably unpalatable to domestic stock. While development in the region is limited and the integrity of most ecosystems remains high, trends in management and development appear to be impacting on biodiversity (Rolfe et al, 2000). The most visible impact is tree clearing, but overgrazing, land degradation and weed invasion are also problems in some areas.

While the vegetation clearing issue has been addressed with regulatory tools, other management issues may still need to be addressed in the region. An example is the potential establishment of landscape linkages across the bioregion to be primarily managed for their biodiversity values. These would run east–west to minimize risks of long-term biodiversity losses, especially if major climate changes occur. Landscape linkages are important because there are still substantial pressures to further increase the intensive agricultural management of this bioregion as land prices escalate and cell grazing practices are in vogue (Rolfe and McCosker, 2003).

In the southern Desert Uplands, where more clearing activities have occurred, a landscape linkage would need to be about 120 to 150 kilometres in length to cross the region. Agreements with 10 to 12 landholders would be needed to establish a landscape linkage corridor, with only a proportion of each property being involved in a corridor. A linkage zone could be in a standard corridor shape across the region, or it could be a number of blocks of vegetation with some connecting strips and corridors.

The focus of a linkage corridor would be to achieve dual production and conservation outcomes at minimal cost. This means that cattle could still be produced in linkage areas, but there would be some reduction in grazing pressure and limits on further development to ensure biodiversity outcomes are achieved. The key challenge in designing a linkage corridor is to identify the most cost-effective corridors across the region given that a number of potential routes exist and landholder choices are inter-related. Market-based incentives (MBIs) offer a potential cost-effective means of establishing corridors.

The market-based instrument analysed in this case study was a conservation auction (commonly referred to as a competitive tender mechanism). This instrument frames the conservation solution in terms of landholders supplying management actions over parts of their properties in return for incentive payments through a regional natural resources management group. The framing accords with perceptions that landholders have about their property rights, and the political reality that regulation is very unlikely to be used to achieve those goals because of the potential administration costs and complexity of information involved. The key research question was how to design a conservation auction process where landholders were expected to compete on price, but where cooperation was also needed to ensure that corridors linked at property boundaries.

Methodology

The methodology used in the project involved a series of field experiments, where landholders from the Desert Uplands participated in a conservation auction *game* specifically designed for this project. Although it is more common to conduct experiments in a laboratory environment, a workshop setting was considered more appropriate when landholder participation was being sought (Rolfe et al, 2004). The use of landholders in the region as workshop participants has potential advantages in terms of:

- identifying the opportunity costs (and heterogeneity in costs) faced by landholders;
- identifying likely participation rates in an auction system, across different auction formats; and
- identifying the transaction costs and potential administration costs associated with a competitive tender mechanism.

The experimental workshop was a new hybrid model developed for this project to explore issues of auction design. It represents a synthesis between experimental economics and a field pilot without being easily classified into either group. Like experimental economics, it utilizes a simulated environment to test how people would form bids. However, it is not as tightly controlled as a normal experimental procedure. It is like a field pilot in that it focuses on a real-world application with actual landholders, but does not go beyond hypothetical scenarios in a half-day workshop.

The workshops were designed around the use of an experimental *game* developed specifically for the project. A series of *dummy* properties were developed that were realiztic for landholders while minimizing the number of variables that could affect participants' bid behaviour. The *dummy* properties looked different in terms of size and layout, but were designed to be consistent in terms of underlying characteristics. Each had five different vegetation types in equal proportions across properties, a similar number of waterways, fences and waters, and a house and access road.

The workshops involved up to 12 landholder participants, and lasted for approximately three to four hours. Each participant was randomly allocated to one of the 12 properties available. Using their knowledge of the region, each participant had to design a corridor across his or her dummy property, and then identify what annual payment would be needed before he or she would enter into a five-year conservation agreement. Different mechanisms were tested for participants to link their corridors at property edges, and incentive prizes were awarded to encourage cost-effective bids. A simple metric was employed to evaluate bids according to the environmental benefits generated.

Participants were asked to develop their bids based on their experience

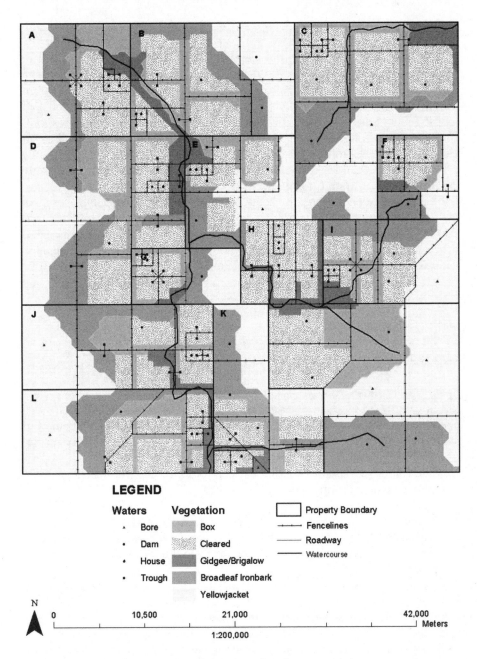

LEGEND

Waters		Vegetation			
▲	Bore		Box		Property Boundary
•	Dam		Cleared	—•—•—	Fencelines
•	House		Gidgee/Brigalow	——	Roadway
•	Trough		Broadleaf Ironbark	——	Watercourse
			Yellowjacket		

N

0   10,500   21,000   42,000
                                                      Meters
                    1:200,000

Figure 13.1 Landscape map of 12 dummy properties

with their own properties. Full details of, and results from, the workshops are presented in Windle et al, (2004). The planning issues involved in designing the workshops and auction design are presented in Rolfe and McCosker,

(2003) and Rolfe et al. (2004). A copy of the maps of the 12 properties is shown in Figure 13.1.

The experimental workshops were designed primarily to test different bidding mechanisms when landholder cooperation is required for vegetation corridor linkage across the region. However, the structure of the game meant that it was possible to ask for individual bids from participants that modelled a BushTender type of system. The workshops were separated into two sessions. In the first part, multiple individual bidding rounds were held to test the efficiency of multiple round auctions and to familiarize participants with the process. In the second part, the focus was on testing bidding formats to ensure landholder cooperation for the formation of a corridor.

For management actions, bid complexity was reduced by specifying a simple management action that landholders could consider. The main condition was that landholders would have to ensure a minimum level of biomass was maintained throughout the year. In a region where extensive grazing is the main land use, maintenance of a threshold level of biomass is likely to be associated with:

- improved levels of ground cover;
- reduced runoff and associated movement of sediments and nutrients;
- continued plant diversity;
- protection of habitat for small biota; and
- habitat for larger biota in periods of climatic variation.

Specifying the management action required meant that all participants were bidding to provide the same service, although they were free to design the area and shape of nominated vegetation on their dummy property. This made bid assessment more manageable in the workshop and allowed the heterogeneity in opportunity costs between landholders to be explored.

The following baseline conditions were outlined for the management of nominated areas on properties:

- Commitment to retain a certain amount of pasture at the end of the dry season annually – about 1500kg/ha (pasture photographs were provided).
- Fire is allowed but the area must be destocked until minimum biomass is reached.
- No additional exotic plant species can be introduced deliberately.

Contract design issues were important in the workshop because these identified the *rules of engagement* and assured participants that their property rights were not being affected without voluntary agreement. Simplicity was achieved by specifying a contract process that was simple to understand and familiar to landholders. There were three key components of the agreements specified:

- They would be for a five-year period with annual payments;
- They would be in the form of a contract; and
- They would include a monitoring process based on an annual visit, with two weeks' notice.

The length of period was an important issue. If the period is too long, then it may be a major disincentive for landholders to be involved. A shorter period has advantages in terms of making it easier for landholder to *trial* the mechanism. In cases where only limited opportunity costs are involved and the issue is more about changing behaviour patterns, then a short time period may be all that is necessary. However, if time periods are too short, then the payments to landholders may not cover the transaction costs involved. The five-year period was seen as being a good compromise between these objectives.

The annual payment mechanism was chosen to reinforce the message about an annual provision of services, as well as providing leverage for contract compliance. In cases where it is important to attract participation and/or to meet capital costs, it is common to have some or all of the payment as an initial lump sum. In the workshops, participants were told that all capital costs involved (for providing fencing and watering points) would be met separately. This made an annual payment stream more plausible.

Contracts were chosen as being the least threatening binding mechanism. The main alternatives were covenants, or, in the case of leasehold land, some revision of lease conditions. Both have problems in terms of plausibility or acceptability, so simple contracts were chosen. A monitoring system was presented that would allow inspections to occur with minimum disturbance. These conditions were generally well accepted in the workshops, indicating that the contract details were unlikely to be a major deterrent for participants.

To select the most cost-effective bids, it is normal to assess the bids gained in a conservation tender process against some measure of the biodiversity gains achieved (Stoneham et al, 2003). The assessment instrument is known as the metric, and can range from very simple ones, which are easy to use but may not be very accurate, to more complex ones. These are much more precise, but come at a cost of being more difficult to construct and perform.

There were three broad components of a metric identified for this project: the biodiversity score, the management actions and the corridor score. In this case study, the use of a specified management action has avoided the need to have a separate score for this issue, reducing the metric to a biodiversity score and a corridor score.

The biodiversity score was calculated for each property by five main vegetation types or classifications. Weights were assigned to each vegetation type, based on relative scarcity in the region (Table 13.1). General estimates (inversed) were made of the percentage of each broad vegetation type that remains in the Desert Uplands area. For example, a rating of ten for Brigalow/Gidgee means that there is about 90 per cent cleared in the region (the real figure is in the high 80 per cent range), while a figure of five for Box means that about 80 per cent has been cleared (the real figure is probably slightly lower). A weighting of 0.5 was adopted for cleared country on the basis of expert opinion to identify that while it has some value for conservation purposes (perhaps to allow regrowth in connecting strips), it has a much lower benefit than the vegetated areas.

The corridor score related to the percentage of east–west linkage in the offered bid area on the property. In effect, relative bid values were not altered

Table 13.1 *Weightings for different vegetation types in the biodiversity index*

Vegetation Type	% Cleared	% Remaining	Weight (Inverse of % Remaining)
Brigalow/Gidgee	90	10	10
Box	80	20	5
Silver-leaf ironbark	60	40	2.5
Yellowjacket	30	70	1.5
Cleared land			0.5

The biodiversity score was assessed by adding the relative contribution of each vegetation type:

Biodiversity Score (BS) = (Brigalow area × 10) + (Box area × 5) + (Ironbark area × 2.5) + (Yellowjacket area × 1.5) + (Cleared area × 0.5)

if the offered bid area formed a corridor across the property, but were reduced if the bid area did not form a corridor. For example, if a submitted bid only represented 80 per cent of a corridor linkage, the relative bid value was reduced accordingly:

Corridor score (CS) = percentage of corridor across the property

The relative value of the bids was assessed in the following stages:

1   Assess the biodiversity score (BS).
2   Include the corridor score adjustment (BS×CS).
3   Assess relative bid value ([BS×CS]/$ bid offer).

Key results of the project

Two workshops were run within the region in April 2004 at Barcaldine and Jericho respectively. Each workshop lasted for half a day, with several bidding rounds conducted. The first part of the workshop involved bids for management agreements on individual properties, while the second part involved bids for corridor establishment across properties. The average area offered by participants was 13,861 acres, or 64 per cent of the average property size of the dummy properties used in the workshops.

A summary of the bid information for all bids is shown in Figure 13.2. This illustrates that while the bulk of bids received were below AU$0.50/biodiversity unit, there was also a substantial group of bids between AU$0.50 and AU$1.50 per biodiversity unit, and some bids up to AU$3.50/biodiversity unit. The results demonstrate that opportunity costs vary across landholders, and that some bids are much more cost-effective than others. A very similar pattern can be seen when the bid information is presented in cumulative form (Figure 13.3). This demonstrates that as the total amount of funding to be allocated rises, the bid prices accepted in terms of AU$/biodiversity unit will also rise.

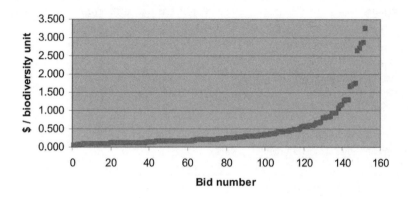

Figure 13.2 Summary of bid information at both workshops (relative value)

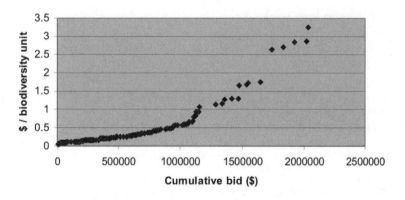

Figure 13.3 Summary of bid information at both workshops (cumulative bid)

The bids received were analysed statistically to identify what were the key drivers of bid amounts. Bids from the individual bidding rounds (no corridor formation tested) at both workshops were pooled in a multiple regression model. The results are shown in Table 13.2.

The model shows that the areas of the three most productive country types (cleared, Gidgee and Box country) were very important in predicting the values of individuals' bids, but areas of low productivity (Ironbark and Yellowjacket) were not. The coefficients for vegetation type show that respondents wanted on average: AU$11.62 for each acre of Gidgee, AU$2.77 for each acre of Box, and AU$5.31 for each acre of cleared country that was involved.

Table 13.2 *Predictors of bid value in individual rounds at workshops*

Coefficients	Coefficent	Std. Error	Significance
Constant	−17793.26	3657.38	.000
Gidgee scrub (acres)	11.62	2.21	.000
Box (acres)	2.77	.86	.005
Broadleaf Ironbark (acres)	−.06	.67	.931
Yellowjacket (acres)	−.11	.31	.727
Cleared (acres)	5.31	.52	.000
Enterprise size (dummy)	3549.27	1091.21	.004
% of property developed	−331.48	116.88	.011
Interested in being paid by govt (dummy)	8355.42	1684.95	.000
BID ROUND	−2814.92	427.07	.000

Notes: Dependent Variable: Bid amount

Model fit: Adjusted r-square = .973

The model results also indicate that:

- bids are strongly influenced by factors apart from the areas of vegetation involved;
- bids are positively linked with enterprise size (participants from smaller properties tended to make more competitive bids);
- bids are negatively linked to development level (indicating that landholders on more developed properties have less to offer – and perhaps don't need the money as much); and
- bids are linked to individuals' level of comfort in being paid by government for ecosystem services (those not comfortable need to be paid more money).

The model has high explanatory power (Adjusted r-square = 0.973) but there is a very large constant, indicating that other variables not in the model may also be important. The dominance of factors other than vegetation type in the model suggests that a number of factors not related to opportunity costs were driving bid formation, indicating that high transaction costs were associated with these bids. This is not surprising given the relative novelty of these types of concepts and mechanisms to landholders in the region.

The results of the two groups of tests conducted at the workshops also demonstrated some important outcomes. The first session involved bids for management actions on individual properties, with the process repeated across three or four rounds in each workshop. Significant efficiencies in bid formation were identified with the use of multiple round auctions. The average bid price fell under the competitive pressure of successive bidding rounds (Figure 13.4), while the amount of biodiversity credits that could be purchased for a fixed budget allocation rose (Figure 13.5). There was substantial statistical evidence that bids became more cost-efficient as successive auction rounds were held (Windle et al, 2004).

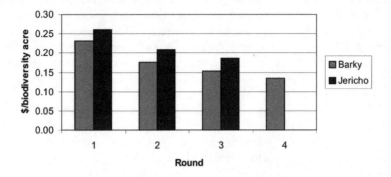

Figure 13.4 Average relative bid values for successful bidders

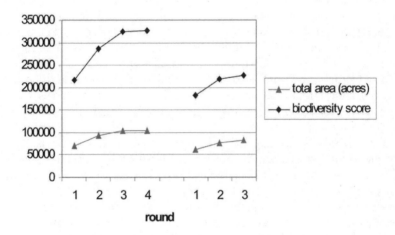

Figure 13.5 What could be purchased from landholders for AU$50,000

Reductions in bid prices are likely to be generated from a number of sources, including adjustments for uncertainty and rent seeking as learning effects occur and competitive pressure is recognized. However, there are also likely to be increased transaction and administration costs associated with multiple bid rounds, suggesting that only a small number of rounds will be efficient in conservation auction systems. The number of rounds necessary to generate efficient bids may be reduced if participants are familiar with the process prior to a *live* auction.

The second session in each workshop involved bids for corridor establishment across properties. Two main formats for corridor formation were tested.

One of these was a *limited cooperation* approach, where participants in the workshops were organized into groups to design joining linkage zones across properties, and then were asked to submit individual sealed bids for their component. The other format tested was a *bid/rebid* approach, where participants lodged individual bids for corridors across their properties, and then were offered incentives to adjust their bids to take account of the designs on neighbouring properties.

The *limited cooperation* approach was found to be practical in designing corridors with a small number of participants. This model involved the cooperation of neighbouring landholders to plan a corridor location, and then submission of sealed bids for individual components. Participants in the workshops seem to prefer this model because of the social interactions involved and the confidential nature of the bids lodged. The key advantages identified by workshop participants for the *limited cooperation* model were that participation and compliance rates were likely to be higher than in an *individual bid* model. It appears likely that the social interaction, peer pressure and information exchange associated with involvement in small groups helps to encourage participation and compliance. This means that where low participation rates are a potential problem, some aspects of this model may provide real benefits.

There are three key potential disadvantages of the *limited cooperation* model. The first is that transaction and administration costs can be expected to rise as a factor of the number of participants involved because the number of potential interactions that are possible will increase. This means that direct negotiation between all participants may only be feasible in relatively small groups.

The second disadvantage with the *limited cooperation* model is that only a very small number of corridor options are likely to be generated, which may reduce competitive pressures. The third disadvantage of this model is that bid prices are likely to be higher. One reason is that, even though bids are sealed, participants with lower marginal opportunity costs are likely to raise bid prices towards those with higher opportunity costs. It will be very difficult for negotiations over corridor location to occur without some information about bid prices also being transmitted. The other reason is that under this model there is more incentive to include some rent component in bid prices (because bidders think their bids are disguised in the larger group bids).

There was anecdotal evidence that a *full cooperation* model, where landholders plan corridors together and then submit open bids, would not be viable. This is because there is a strong preference in rural areas for bids to be sealed, and because an open bidding format would encourage all bids to be set at the level of landholders with the highest opportunity costs. The first factor would reduce participation rates, while the second would reduce the economic efficiency of the bidding process.

The *bid/rebid* model was found to be practical in designing corridors, with some evidence that the model was more cost-efficient than the *limited cooperation* approach (Figure 13.6). An *individual bid* approach to corridor formation only works with multiple bidding rounds. In the experimental workshops, landholders were asked to submit a bid for a corridor across their

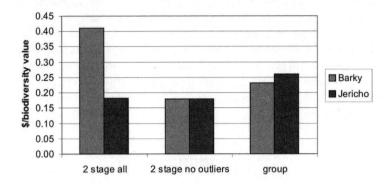

Figure 13.6 Average relative bid values for corridor formation in workshops

property, with the knowledge that a full corridor would need to be achieved before any individual bids could be successful. After the first round, bids were assessed and the location of each property corridor was drawn on a large map for all participants to view. As expected, the number of individual bids generated a series of discrete links that rarely happened to join at property boundaries. Participants could then see where potential corridors could be formed across the area covered by the 12 properties. It was also apparent that a number of options existed to form a corridor, and it was not clear from a bidder perspective (seller) where the buyer might choose to locate the corridor and if their bid would be successful.

Participants were then informed that their first bid would remain *live* but they could put in another bid if they wished. They would only win an incentive prize if they were part of the most cost-efficient corridor bid, giving clear incentives for participants to be part of one or more corridors linking across their dummy property. There are several potential strategies landholders might adopt in the second round to increase their chance of success. For example they could:

- relocate their first bid to link with one or more neighbours;
- provide an additional area to link to a different corridor option; or
- reduce their bid price.

This bidding format was very successful. Many landholders bid for multiple corridor locations across their property, with the result that many options for different corridor linkages were identified (a total of 18 in Barcaldine). Some landholders preferred this approach to that of working in a group, particularly those who had been placed in a group with people who had contrasting viewpoints. However, some of them did consult and negotiate with their neighbour in developing a second bid.

This *bid/rebid* model was efficient in that there were incentives for individual behaviour that led to group outcomes. A key advantage of the *bid/rebid* model is that it allows a large number of potential corridors to be identified (thus enhancing the competitive process). Another key advantage is that there is more competitive pressure on individual participants (leading to more cost-efficient bids). However, in the workshop results there were no significant differences in the bid values between the two corridor formation processes tested (Windle et al, 2004).

Conclusions

The results presented in this chapter suggest that there is potential for conservation tender processes to be used to achieve some environmental outcomes more cost-effectively in rangeland areas than would be possible with regulatory processes. The key advantages of conservation tender processes are that they allow for the simultaneous pursuit of production and conservation outcomes at varying levels across different properties, and they increase cost-effectiveness through the use of competitive mechanisms. There is evidence that these efficiencies may be enhanced by design mechanisms such as repeated auction rounds in the tender process, and the use of incentives to generate cooperative behaviour from landholders.

At the broader level though, the key advantage of these competitive tender mechanisms is that they recognize current allocations of property rights, and any changes are negotiated voluntarily. Other solutions to environmental problems, such as government regulation, often involve some coercive reduction in the explicit or implicit property rights held by farmers. This makes it difficult in a political economy sense to negotiate changes, and can generate inappropriate (and unexpected) incentives. These include changes in perceptions of sovereign risk and reductions in private incentives to recognize and care for environmental assets.

These competitive tender mechanisms have more relevance to a Coasian view of environmental problems, where the policy maker is non-judgemental about the causes of the problem, but analytical about the most efficient ways of achieving desired changes. By working with existing property right structures, policy makers have opportunities to achieve change with minimal protest or negative impact. As well, it becomes easier to tailor programmes for different issues and scales, and to involve a range of different change agents. When property rights need to be adjusted, this normally involves government and a political process, meaning that change is often slow and difficult. Acceptance of existing property right structures creates a great deal more flexibility for different engagement and management processes to be trialled. A range of non-government agencies can also be engaged with landholders to negotiate changed environmental management, and more innovation in management arrangements can be explored.

There is also a range of challenges involved in adapting competitive tender mechanisms to rangelands issues. Particular challenges relate to contract design, auction design and metric design issues, the problem of achieving high participation rates from landholders, and identifying funding sources. Despite these issues, there appears to be great potential for conservation tenders to be designed for Australian rangelands areas.

Acknowledgements

The research reported in this chapter is based on a research project funded by a partnership of the Commonwealth and State Governments through the national Market Based Instruments programme. The contribution of Jill Windle, Juliana McCosker, Stuart Whitten and members of the Desert Uplands Buildup and Development Committee to the project and the results presented in this chapter are gratefully acknowledged. The comments of Graham Marshall and Jim Binney on earlier drafts of this chapter are much appreciated.

References

Agriculture, Forestry and Fisheries – Australia (AFFA) (1999). Managing Natural Resources in Rural Australia for a Sustainable Future. Canberra: Discussion Paper.

Anderson, T. (2004). Donning Coase-coloured glasses: a property rights view of natural resource economics. *Australian Journal of Agricultural and Resource Economics,* 48(3), 445–462.

Rolfe, J. C. (2000). Broadscale tree clearing in Queensland. *Agenda,* 7(3), 217–236.

Rolfe, J. C., Blamey, R. K. and Bennett, J. W. (2000). Valuing the preservation of rangelands: Tree clearing in the Desert Uplands region of Queensland. *The Rangeland Journal,* 22(2), 205–219.

Rolfe, J. C. and McCosker, J. C. (2003). Overview of the Issues in Planning a Corridor Tender Process, Establishing East-west Corridors in the Southern Desert Uplands. *Research Report No.* November 1, 2003. Emerald: Environmental Protection Agency and Central Queensland University.

Rolfe, J. C., McCosker, J. C., Windle, J. and Whitten, S. (2004). Designing Experiments to Test Auction Procedures, Establishing East-west Corridors in the Southern Desert Uplands. *Research Report No.* 2. Emerald: Environmental Protection Agency and Central Queensland University.

Stoneham, G., Chaudhri, V., Ha, A. and Strappazzon, L. (2003). Auctions for conservation contracts: an empirical examination of Victoria's BushTender trial. *Australian Journal of Agricultural and Resource Economics,* 47(4), 477–500.

Windle, J., Rolfe, J. C., McCosker, J. C., and Whitten, S. (2004). Designing Auctions with Landholder Cooperation: Results from Experimental Workshops, Establishing East-west Corridors in the Southern Desert Uplands. *Research Report No.* 4. Emerald: Environmental Protection Agency and Central Queensland University.

14

A Metaphysical Grounding for Ecologically Sustainable Property Rights

Garrick Small

Introduction

The burden of this book is to explore the potential and appropriateness of using property rights as a tool in the realization of sustainable land use. Ken Lyons et al have shown in Chapter 11 of this book the historical connection between rights and obligations within land title and the way that a community's formulation of its property title should be prudently informed by the prevailing understanding of what constitutes the best mix of rights and obligations. Spike Boydell has likewise illustrated in Chapter 6 the complexity of rights and obligations within Fijian property. The authors generally agree on the potential for well-considered obligations, crafted into the very foundations of property, to provide desirable outcomes for the community. While these claims are well articulated and recognized as an obvious necessity by many in the environmental movement, they press for changes in the institution of property that are outside the modern conception of private property. For centuries property has been formally understood to be a private right whose erosion would be a major civil attack on the rights of the individual. Richard Weaver (1948) described obligation-free private property as a 'metaphysical right' that was being attacked in his country and its demise would spell the end of his nation. His view was an extension of the English Lord Blackstone who earlier described property as:

> *that sole and despotic dominion which one man claims and exercises over the things of the world, in total exclusion of the right of any individual in the universe.* (Blackstone, 1769)

Blackstone was commenting on the laws of England, and his account indicates that private property is based on the total exclusion of the rights of others or the community. While English law has diluted this despotic dominion somewhat, it remains as the fundamental principle for private title. It throws into question whether communities should use the overarching power of the state to alter what are ultimately private rights.

This question can be approached from two directions. First, whether the proposed benefits will be realized more effectively using this approach and second, whether it is proper for the state to intervene in this way.

Ronald Coase (1960) argued that property rights were irrelevant in attaining ecologically sustainable outcomes in property use. Coase claimed that as long as property rights were private and clearly defined, the free market would eliminate inappropriate land uses without the need for government intervention. Where one party believed another was engaged in activities that produced offensive externalities, they could buy the rights to perform those activities and shut them down. The elegance of Coase's hypothesis was that it required no state intervention and no loss for any party: the offended party could freely choose either the disutility of tolerating the offending activity, or the financial cost of shutting it down; the property holder did not lose any rights, but rather traded them away for a fair price. The only role for the state was perhaps to represent the community in buying out the private property right to offensive activities. It would be just one more market participant. Similar mechanisms would operate where the property rights were initially in the hands of the party offended.

While some may object to paying polluters to stop polluting, others maintain that existing property rights to non-sustainable property uses are licit and complain that the removal of property rights amounts to theft from private owners. At the base of this argument is the premise that all existing private property rights are licit, and as such should not be dissolved without compensation. Implicitly this position rests on the belief that property rights have no meaning beyond their positive content. The fact of legal existence is being held to be sufficient reason for their acceptance by the community and compensation for removal.

Coase's position appears to make discussion of property rights as a vehicle for ecologically sustainable development superfluous. However, much relies on the assumption that particular current property rights regimes have no normative content or significance. Coase is content to have the community compensate property owners for being stopped from non-sustainable activities. Even worse, he would militate against future revisions of property rights aimed at dissolving private rights for non-sustainable practices. The obvious beneficiaries of the Coase position are current property owners who enjoy rights to engage in non-sustainable practices.

Rolfe, in Chapter 13, presents an example of the proposed 'mediated Coasian approach'.

Environmentalists tend to believe that non-sustainable practices should never have been permitted in the first place and hence compensation for their discontinuation is inappropriate. Given the necessity of sustainability for humanity's long-term viability, it follows that the discontinuation of non-sustainable practices is a normative good. This leads to recognition that there exist fundamental qualitative differences between property rights that facilitate non-sustainable practices and those that do not. Given these fundamental differences, some property rights may not warrant the same legal support as others. As science reveals the dimensions of sustainable land use, previously permitted activities may be assessed in terms of their underlying suitability for the community in terms of long-term responsible environmental stewardship.

Coase tends to bring an economic paradigm to bear on what is essentially a physical issue pertaining to human life and its management. Positive economics, as currently practiced, is formally value-free; it eschews normative directives in pursuing its object of optimal resource allocation. Environmentalists also seek optimal resource allocation, though economics tends to be focused more on allocations between current actors, whereas environmentalism, especially in the areas of sustainable resource management, is concerned with inter-generational allocation, or equity. Economics allows current economic actors to value inter-generational allocation and it is the strength of this value that is the dynamic in Coase's theorem. For Coase, present economic actors will buy ecological sustainability from those with the property rights to damage the environment. He relies on action groups to be highly motivated to pay for inter-generational equity and leaves irresponsible property rights-holders free of any overarching sanction against denying future generations an equitable participation in environmental resources. While this may work within economic theory, the psychological drive required is questionable in practice.

The environmentalist's approach implicitly recognizes the fundamental importance of working within physical realities when framing human conventions. This would attach values to particular options that are denominated in terms of the common good. Environmentalism, at least in terms of its value structure organized towards the material support of the environment, is necessarily premised on qualitative distinctions that lead to normative policy principles. Ecological sustainability recognizes that knowable negative outcomes will result from particular human behaviours and is orientated towards establishing principles for appropriate behaviour by humans with respect to the environment, so as to preserve the environmental patrimony passed on to future generations. Ultimately, it can be seen as grounded on beliefs in the appropriate relations between this generation and those in the future. This fundamental obligation for equity is the dynamic for the notion of property as an amalgam of rights and responsibilities that lies behind existing environmental planning legislation and the view of property outlined by Lyons and others (Chapter 11).

The logic of Coase's position earned him a Nobel Prize and considerable acclaim despite the failure of empirical tests of his theory (Hylan, Lage et al, 1996) and detailed theoretical rebuttals (Canterbury and Marvasti, 1992; Mishan, 1993). The failure of empirical tests has never been a problem to the discipline of economics. E. J. Working (1927) demonstrated why empirical studies of demand would always be necessarily flawed, but the discipline continues to use them. Richard Jones (1976) enumerated the failure of empirical tests of the theory of supply before advocating its continued adoption, and Samuelson similarly did so concerning the perfect market, showing that the depiction of the functions of supply and demand in a perfect market situation were different to that commonly portrayed but then proceeded to adopt the common portrayal for the rest of his text (Samuelson, 1975). There is a raft of disaffected economists who recognize the weakness in the discipline, such as Lawrence Boland who has devoted considerable attention to the internal contradictions in the basic set of theories that comprise positive market economics (Boland, 1982, 1988, 1992). Boland's demonstration that positive market economics cannot be a true representation of what happens in the economy is also not important to economists. Milton Friedman, another Nobel Prize winning economist, set out the position that economic theory does not have to correspond to the causal relationships that actually exist in the economy, but only that the theory must be tolerably effective at predicting policy outcomes to warrant acceptance (Friedman, 1953). Jones followed this methodological approach though Morris Altman is representative of the many who consider it to place economics in a peculiar position with respect to other sciences (Altman, 1999). Since Coase is based on the premises of positive market economics, these methodological problems do not auger well for his prescriptions and go some distance towards explaining the empirical shortcomings of his theory, despite its celebrated endorsement.

Property tends to be closely related to economics. When Freidman (1980) and Novak (1982) argued for liberal capitalism they included defences of unrestrained private property. Marx and the socialists based much of their economics on an alternative form of property first expounded by Proudhon when he asserted 'Property is theft' (Proudhon, 1840). Both ideological extremes deal with private property as a set of rights, not obligations, with the socialists not revising private property but eliminating it. The use of property rights in the management of sustainable resource management therefore requires an approach to property that is different to both of these.

The focus on obligations, especially obligations based on scientific factors, marks a distinct departure from the thinking on property in recent centuries. Property theory has been linked with law and economics by thinkers such as Thomas Hobbes, John Locke, William Blackstone and Adam Smith. It has not been linked to notions of obligation as these connote an ethical element very different to the despotic rights observed by Blackstone. Within a democratic culture, for a state to impose obligations on property owners, there must be broad support. As property owners are also voters, and often influential voters, recognition of the importance of obligations attached to property must be also embraced in some measure by property owners as well. Broadly accepted obligations between persons who influence action beyond the requirement of the law (and in fact have the force to give rise to supporting legislation) are ethical obligations. What is being suggested then is that the insertion of obligations into property requires recognition that property is an ethical institution. Modernity has been singularly against this trend, both in property and in economics in general (Boettke, 1998), though there have been several attempts to reverse this trend (Boulding, 1969; Crespo, 1998).

Simply arguing for ethical environmental obligations within property is not sufficient, as there is a range of ethical systems. Notionally, market economics are based on the ethical system of utilitarianism, though Meikle noted that this was circular and ineffective (Meikle, 1995). Twentieth century ethical systems are also problematic. Warnock reviewed three approaches that dominated the past century (Warnock, 1967). Of these, emotivism is often cited in contemporary texts and consists of the claim that moral statements are no more than a grammatical form intended to influence the behaviour of the hearer. This position fits well into the postmodern claim that relationships are grounded on power alone (Grosz, 1990). While Grosz traces this belief to a reading of Hegel, it is better located as coming from the thought of Neitzsche who considered that the '… aim of knowledge is not to know, in the sense of grasping absolute truth for its own sake, but to master' (Copelston, 1965). If knowledge, and in fact all human interaction, is motivated by a contest to dominate, then human utterances are not related to anything more than the personal will to power. This means that there is no robust objective meaning to human discourse (Casey, 2001), leading postmodern theorists to treat all discourse with suspicion (Currie, 1998). While this belief is particularly associated with post-modernity, it can be traced back to Machiavelli (d.1527) at the dawn of modernity who claimed that pragmatic influence was more important than truth (Machiavelli and Mansfield, 1985).

The environmental sustainability project is radically opposed to this approach. It is based on recognized objective scientific conclusions concerning the implications of some physical land uses and a belief regarding how these should impact on future people. It is based on some level of confidence in science delivering a true understanding of objective realities. While this is generally understood with respect to natural sciences, it is less certain for the applied sciences that implicitly include ethical components such as economics. It is closely connected with the belief that ethical principles have no objective content.

In the case of environmental sustainability, this is not the case. Two premises are required in order to deduce the objective necessity of environmental action. The first is the natural science pertaining to the particular environmental issue, and the second is the notion that humans are equal. While both of these premises may be debateable, if they are acknowledged, then unsustainable resource use becomes violence against those humans, largely in the future, who will be disadvantaged without compensation. Moreover, the two premises may be thought of as objective statements about the world. As such, their validity is not a matter of popularity, but the fact that they reflect the world as it is, regardless of their acceptance by those in positions to act on their recognition. Assuming they relate to states of the world that do not change (e.g. human nature is constant and the environmental science is valid) human action that seeks to violate them will always cause harm, even if it is not apparent to those who do it at the time. If human actions do harm to innocent persons, they have no ethical claim for support and those in the habit of performing them have no grounds for compensation. This argument rests on the possibly of moral thought having knowable objective foundations.

The Metaphysics of Morals

Emmanuel Kant attempted to set out a system of judging moral action by focusing initially on the metaphysical foundations for moral action (Kant,

1785). He did this in an attempt to moderate some of the flaws in thought of David Hume. Hume had earlier sought to excise metaphysics from philosophy and morals when he argued 'All this is metaphysics… That is enough; there needs nothing more to give a strong presumption of falsehood.' (Hume, 1777, p. 289). Overall, it was Hume who was the more successful. Metaphysics has dropped out of general view to the point that few people are even aware of what it is. Metaphysics is the study of being, or more specifically of what is fit to be. Metaphysics examines the construction of natures, what things have to be in order to be what they are. At one level metaphysics is obscure because it deals with the obvious, but its conclusions give direction to all of the other sciences.

Metaphysics is built into every human utterance and its conclusions enable humans to meaningfully communicate and pursue science. Every noun denotes a specific thing and the necessary characteristics for a thing to be labelled with a particular noun are necessary elements in the thing's being. If a thing has characteristics that are different to those necessary to the named by one noun, it will be called by another. In addition to necessary characteristics, things also have accidental particular characteristics. A chair may be made of wood, but it would still be a chair if it were made of metal. The way that characteristics are attributed to things is a major part of the object of metaphysics, to the point that most sentences that contain the verb 'to be' are metaphysical statements. A major object of most science can be described as extending the accuracy and precision of human understanding of the necessary and accidental characteristics of things. That is, the object of most science is the development of the precision of the metaphysical understanding of natures.

A major premise in metaphysics is that the essential meaning pertaining to particular nouns does not change, even though it may be refined. For example, if a chair was so constructed that it had the characteristics of a wardrobe, it would no longer be a chair, even if it were possible for humans to sit on it. This general position is adopted by everyone who uses speech sensibly as a necessity of speech itself.

When applied to human nature, metaphysical enquiry examines what exactly is meant by human nature. While there may be some debate as to the validity of particular statements about human nature, some things must be constant in order to be able to speak of it at all. Essentially, humans are social creatures with intellect who have common physical needs, such as food, clothing and shelter. It is commonly accepted that humans possess free will. From this comes a widely held view that humans deserve some level of freedom as a basic human right. Other human rights that are widely accepted can also be traced back to the metaphysical construction of human nature. Human rights are fundamental ethical principles and it can be seen that both trace their origins to human nature that is understandable through metaphysical enquiry.

This approach to the sciences and metaphysics can be seen to align well with common experience and the way that humans refine their knowledge, it is sometimes referred to as naïve realism. Though naïve realists do not use the terminology of philosophy and science, they believe that that the external world exists, that it is essentially consistent and knowable. They refine their knowledge by learning more about the things that are important to them, believing that essential knowledge has a stability and accessibility that makes the enterprise of enquiry worth pursuing. The classical Greeks, Socrates, Plato and Aristotle, systematized realist thought to the point that Aristotle left a system of understanding that has formed the basis of contemporary science, ethics and philosophy. This system of thought is known as classical realism and has been refined by various thinkers over the intermediate centuries, despite being criticized by philosophers such as Hume and those in his wake.

Classical Order of the Sciences

Classical realism organized all sciences into an interrelated hierarchy as shown in Figure 14.1, based on Ashley (2003). An understanding of the relationships between the sciences in the classical scheme is useful for exploring the potentials for property as a vehicle for promoting ecological sustainability. In the classical schema there are three basic groups of sciences: the natural sciences, the practical sciences and the queen sciences. The natural and practical sciences are familiar, but, with the exception of mathematics, few people take much interest in the queen sciences, and even less in their unusual title. The queen sciences are sciences of review; their objects are methodological tools used by the other sciences. Pure mathematics is of little use to the real world, except that it is a key to developing our understanding of natural sciences such as physics and astronomy. The various sub-disciplines within philosophy have this same quality. Every human enquiry implicitly relies on logic, and the fundamental importance of metaphysics, regardless of whether these are explicitly recognized. Other branches of philosophy are similar.

Applying the title science to these disciplines is also unfamiliar in recent times. Sociologists and economists are familiar with the debate over whether their disciplines are genuine sciences, but to call metaphysics and mathematics sciences betrays the popular understanding of what constitutes science. The classical definition of science is *the pursuit of certain knowledge through cause.* By this is meant that any endeavour that aims to replace opinion with certain knowledge may be a science. This definition is adopted in this chapter. Various sciences may be identified according to the particular aspects of understanding that are being pursued, so an understanding of physical things comes within physics, an understanding of chemicals and their behaviour is achieved through chemistry and so on. The environmentalist pursues certain knowledge of the mechanisms that affect the stability of the environment. While the environmentalist may use physics and chemistry, the object of environmental science is distinct, just as anatomy also uses physics and chemistry to understand living bodies.

The importance of the queen sciences can be seen fairly easily in terms of their relationship to the natural sciences. It also explains why natural scientists, such as Stephen Hawking (1988), or Thomas Kuhn (1970), sometimes stray into writing on philosophical topics such as metaphysics and epistemology, despite having little formal training in these areas. Their scientific work already

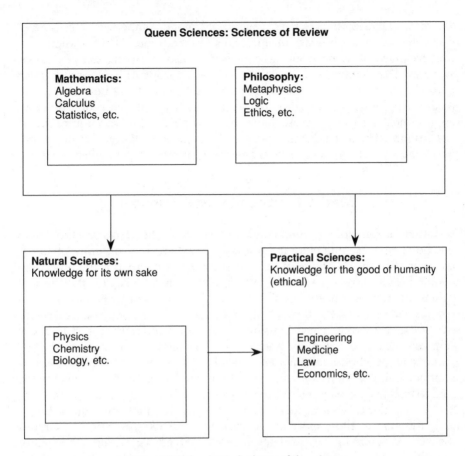

Figure 14.1 The classical schema of the sciences

has had them working with these more esoteric sciences and they have recognized that some of the most interesting questions that appear in their respective disciplines have their origins in the queen sciences.

This problem is nowhere more pointed than in the practical sciences. The practical sciences are distinct from the natural sciences because their objects are connected with human goods. The objects of natural sciences pertain to knowledge for its own sake, whereas the application of knowledge for the good of humanity is the characteristic of the practical science. Strictly speaking, the physicist pursues a certain understanding of physical bodies for its own sake, just as the chemist is attracted to deeper knowledge of the nature and behaviour of chemicals for no more than the satisfaction of understanding chemistry better. When the insights of physics or chemistry are applied to some human purpose they become structural or chemical engineering. The practical sciences are sometimes called applied sciences, a title that explicitly recognizes their objects as applications of knowledge that would otherwise be merely theoretical.

Most practical sciences have a significant moral component. This is especially obvious in law, but also plainly evident in medicine. The professions that practice practical sciences, such as engineering, also tend to have ethical codes. If a moral is defined as a principle for the appropriate relations between persons, the extent of the importance of moral thought can be better recognized. Applying the insights of science is fraught with questions of appropriateness. To meet these questions is the object of moral enquiry and its applications. The many distinct systems of morals have all been developed out of attempts to satisfy this question. Some appear more capable than others.

Method in the Classical Sciences

It is not uncommon to find confusion between the terms 'method' and 'methodology' in contemporary research. Nowhere is this confusion more common than the discipline of property economics. Method is the procedure adopted for a particular research exercise, while methodology is the study of which methods are best suited to particular topics and situations. Natural science is dominated by so called scientific method that uses empirical methods of data gathering, reviewed using mathematical and statistical tools. Social sciences, such as sociology, use a wider variety of methods that are informed by social and psychological theories. Sociologists recognize that the narrow methodological assumptions that suit the natural sciences do not necessarily lead to effective development of social science.

Among these, feminist methods stand out as both effective and substantially different to those more appropriate to physics (Gross, 1992). Feminist theorists recognize human diversity and the apparently capricious behaviour of the will and reject a view of human nature that emphasizes narrow rationality and the assumption of determinism. Feminists are suspicious of the epistemological and even logical assumptions of scientific empirical method, recognizing instead that human behaviour follows patterns that are not narrowly logical and deterministic. Feminists are also suspicious of many social data gathering methods, such as set questionnaires, preferring instead in-depth interviews and narrative. They argue that these are more likely to capture an understanding of the dynamics of the human person as they are encountered in a way that standardized questioning cannot. While sociology still grounds its methods on fundamental empirical premises, it illustrates that the study of method is more involved than variations on quantitative scientific method.

The methods appropriate to mathematics are radically different to those of the natural and practical sciences. Very little development in mathematics is based on empirical exploration. While calculus has manifold applications in the natural world, it is intelligible independent of it. Likewise the behaviour of large numbers and some mathematical functions are impossible for humans to observe, yet humans can understand them with certainty. Generally the best mathematics is achieved with the least empiricism, as higher mathematics students learn when mastering topics such as the behaviour of surfaces in n dimensional space or the transcendental nature of e. Despite these mathematical notions being extremely useful in physics and engineering, they are impossible to discover using empirical scientific method.

The other queen sciences are similar to mathematics. Each has a particular suite of methods that are appropriate for extending the science, and empiricism has little importance. This means that empiricism is only useful to certain sciences and then only to some degree. Moral philosophy is a particularly contentious queen science methodologically. David Hume was explicit in setting out to '... attempt a like reformation in all moral disquisitions; and reject every system of ethics, however subtle or ingenious, which is not founded on fact and observation' (Hume, 1777, n.138, p. 175). His moral sentiment theory represented the height of the Enlightenment moral thought and can also be found almost identically in the moral writings of the Father of modern economics, Adam Smith (1759). Both claimed that moral values had no basis in knowable cause, but could be only learned through observation of people's reactions to particular moral actions. From this position have come both the belief that moral values are purely subjective, or relative, and the tendency to explore moral questions through empirical methods such as opinion polls.

Enlightenment thought was the systematic articulation of the modern position as it had been evolving over the previous two centuries and formed the basis for subsequent developments in modernity and eventually the premises for postmodernity. Applied to moral philosophy, it led Alasdair MacIntyre to conclude that 'The problems of modern moral theory emerge clearly as the product of the failure of the Enlightenment project' (MacIntyre, 1985 p. 62). Immanuel Kant (d.1804) sought to moderate Hume's position and more obvious shortcomings while retaining the fundamental premises of modernity. He did this by arguing that there was a moral imperative to only act in such a way that the underlying principle could be applied universally (Kant, 1785). This suggests objectivity, but since Kant did not advocate actual objective moral universals, his system collapses into whatever the moral actor decides would make an effective moral universal, which is a far more flexible creature. Kant did advocate certain aspects of moral action that suggested conclusions drawn from objective metaphysical premises. These included his emphasis on duty as a necessary condition for moral action and his insistence on respecting the dignity of persons as always deserving respect as subjects and not objects in moral acts. Implicitly his suggestion that there existed a categorical imperative that was always and everywhere necessary for deciding moral action recognizes the need for objective unchanging constants and hence submits to the classical metaphysics that modernity seeks to refute.

Economics remains as a casualty of this premature rejection of metaphysics and goes some distance to explain the success of the Coase hypothesis as a theory. Adam Smith followed David Hume in rejecting metaphysics, and built his economics on empirical foundations. However, metaphysical assumptions still form the foundations of the science. Lawrence Boland reviewed the consistency of contemporary economic theory and its premises and concluded that economics is built on very doubtful metaphysical and moral premises. Of these, the best known is the definition of the economic actor (*homo economicus*) who is supposedly a rational self-interested utility maximizing individual.

While economics works for these creatures, the difference between *homo economicus* and flesh and blood human persons is enormous. Boland observed that 'Fifty years ago metaphysics was considered a dirty word but today most people recognize that every explanation has its metaphysics' (Boland, 1997, p. 81). If the metaphysics is wrong, the moral implications will be faulty and the strength of the science will be compromised. Economics has adopted utilitarianism as a way of sidestepping this problem, but the problems within utilitarianism itself are considerable.

Utilitarianism was developed by Jeremy Bentham (d.1832) and John Stuart Mill (d.1873) as a positive scientific system of morals consistent with Hume's claim that moral systems should adopt the methodology of the natural sciences. Utilitarianism provides the moral actor with a quasi-mathematical algorithm that is ultimately applied subjectively by the moral actor without objective moral values (Bentham and Lafleur, 1781; Mill, 1859). Utilitarianism finds contemporary application in the formulation of public policy and has an intimate relationship with economics (Mirrlees, 1982). Modern students of economics are introduced to the economic actor (*homo-economicus*) as a rational utility-maximizing individual, mirroring almost exactly the Benthamite construction of human nature. Despite utilitarianism's current popularity, Scott Meikle demonstrated 'how little utilitarianism does of what an ethics is supposed to do' (Meikle, 1995) when contrasting Aristotle's economics with the current discipline and their respective moral foundations. Bernard Williams explicitly recognized the flaws that emerged from utilitarianism's subjective foundations when he noted 'they [utilitarians] are committed to something which in practice has those implications: that there are no ultimately incommensurable values' (Williams, 1972).

If there are no objective standards available for judging the merits for appropriate relations between people, then all that remains is anarchy. This was one of Peter Kreeft's arguments against the moral relativism that he found dominant in the western world in recent times (Kreeft, 1999). For environmental sustainability, this anarchy would be devastating because it implies that natural science knowledge regarding the impacts of certain human acts has no objective merit as principles for human action. Coase implicitly accepts this anarchy by seeing no intrinsic principle for sanctions against unsustainable behaviour.

The Metaphysics of Environmentalism

Natural science normally accepts implicit metaphysical assumptions of constancy and rationality in the natural world. The natural scientist proceeds with the confidence that insights that are gained in one circumstance may be transferred to all other comparable circumstances, and that the natural world follows intelligible logical laws. The environmental scientist straddles the natural and practical sciences. The natural side of environmental science concerns the physical, chemical, biological and other effects of various human acts. The practical science side of environmental science concerns the direction of human action, through both freely chosen behavioural change and public policy by distilling from natural environmental science directives for appropriate human action.

In order for the practical side of environmental science to be more than the arbitrary exercise of power, it must be grounded in a robust objective moral order. There are several channels through which this objective moral order can be investigated. All begin with an understanding of the human person, or human nature, and some include implications that follow from the relationship between humans and the external world. Two will be explored here.

Humans are members of a single biological species. As well as the general attributes of their biological classification, they have the distinction of living their lives through willed, rather than instinctive, action. They also have a sense of aesthetic that appears to be unparalleled in other living things. Their biological and aesthetic needs are partially met by their access to the external world, for food, clothing, shelter and aesthetic experience. They are also social creatures, and this adds yet another dimension to their needs for complete fulfilment. As creatures with intellects and wills they require freedom to make decisions as a fundamental condition in order for them to fully realize themselves. As members of the same species, all humans have the same dignity as persons. For a person to act in a way that causes harm to an innocent other person is for them to violate the fundamental metaphysical equality that exists between them. Aristotle argued that much of ethics can be related to philosophical proportion (Aristotle, 1976). If humans are connected by fundamental equality, then to act so as to create inequality is to violate the objective metaphysical relationship between particular human persons. This is the case regardless of the relationship between them, in terms of amicability, space or time.

From this can be deduced that if natural science ascertains reliably that current human actions will advantage a current human actor but harm innocent future persons, then the acts have no legitimacy. In this way natural science supplies objective principles for appropriate actions between persons, especially persons separated by time. As such they are instances of moral principles. If the acts have no legitimacy, they have no grounds for continuance and their cessation warrants no compensation. In this way the moral principles may inform the law and economics. This is totally consistent with the classical realist relations between the sciences.

A second aspect of human nature is that humans have the capacity to understand the order that is found in the material world. Humans are also capable of appreciating the goodness and beauty of the world. This understanding represents a knowable truth about the world. For humans to so act as to cause harm, ugliness or disorder is for them to violate their understanding of the world and its potentials. While circumstances may arise where these unfortunate outcomes may be necessary to some degree, it violates the actor's own humanity to will them without serious need. Cruelty to animals or wanton destructiveness to the landscape are inhuman because they are the result of human decisions to unnecessarily will suffering and disorder onto the external world.

Property Rights as Moral Institutions

With a focus on human nature, it is easy to understand why classical realists considered property as a social convention only. Humans, like other animals, have a need of the things of the world for survival, but the idea of ownership is an artefact of human social relations, not human nature. Aristotle recognized that humans managed things more responsibly when they had personal responsibility for them, but he also recognized the more fundamental universal necessity for inalienable access to the resources of the world (Aristotle, 1981). His dual theory of property, often summarized as private ownership with common use, reflects this complexity regarding property.

The notion of property as naturally an amalgam of rights and responsibilities is a recent revival of this theme that goes back to classical times and is philosophically intelligible only within classical realism. Both sides of the duality proceed from human nature and the nature of the external world. The construction of the institution is ultimately grounded on metaphysical insights that lead to moral principles. The principles are not the institution, but only fundamental requirements that any particular institution must embody in some way. The property institutions of some cultures display these dual aspects quite evidently. Many high context Indigenous cultures permit private ownership of land for personal livelihood, but retain rights for the tribe. Ancient feudal property as evident in many parts of the world allocated private rights but moderated obligations to the community in the form of rents to the lord of the land, sometimes in goods and sometimes in human service. Contemporary Australian property is a mixture of private ownership rights with responsibilities, or obligations, to the community through a variety of channels including land use restrictions and land taxes.

Whatever the form, the property convention that a society adopts reflects the understanding of appropriate relations between persons that is dominant at the time. In some cases this understanding changes over time, but in all cases it is ultimately moral. This does not mean that the institution will always be an embodiment of sound morality, only that it may be judged in moral terms. The German dispossession of Jewish owners from property under Hitler was legal, but immoral. Other cases may not be so clear cut. Some thinkers have argued for totally unrestrained private property free from state sanction (Friedman, 1980; Novak, 1982; Bethell, 1998; DeSoto, 2000), while others have contended private property is theft (Proudhon, 1840; Marx, 1867). Karl Zimmerman concluded that something closer to Aristotle's moderate middle position has greater historical support in terms of cultural outcomes (Zimmerman, 1947; Small, 1997).

In Australia the resumption of property rights by the states must be compensated under the constitution, but this underscores the importance of getting the right balance of private rights in the first place. State leasehold offers greater flexibility at the time of renewal, but it is subject to political pressures. In a democracy, when the state grants leasehold, there is an incentive to vote in a party who will be a compliant landlord. This may benefit current occupants at the expense of future generations. Given that this is not unknown in practice (Brennan, 1971), although morally flawed, reveals a flaw in the mechanics of democracy.

It remains incumbent on the environmental movement to convince the community as a whole, and not least those with current property rights, that there are knowable objective moral principles that guide human action, and these should inform the construction of the institution of property beyond current partisan self-interest. By focusing on the metaphysical foundations that underlie the environmental position a methodology is available that explains why compensating for lost property rights is not only inappropriate but may also be employed to explain why the Coase hypothesis has failed in practice.

References

Altman, M. (1999) 'The methodology of economics and the survival principle revisisted: some welfare and public policy implications of modelling the economic agent'. *Review of Social Economics*, 57 (4), 427–449.

Aristotle (1976) *Ethics*. London: Penguin.

Aristotle (1981) *The Politics*. London: Penguin.

Ashley, B. (2003) 'Dominican guide for sharing our secular resources for the study of theology for preaching in the twenty-first century'. www.op.org/domcentral/study/ashley/guide/dominicanguide.pdf. 2005.

Bentham, J. and L. J. Lafleur (1781) *An Introduction to the Principles of Morals and Legislation*. New York: Hafner Pub. Co.

Bethell, T. (1998) *Noblest Triumph: Property and Prosperity Through the Ages*. New York: St. Martins Press.

Blackstone, W. (1769) *Commentaries on the Laws of England: A Facsimile of the First Edition of 1765–69*. Chicago: Chicago University Press.

Boettke, P. J. (1998) 'Is economics a moral science? A response to Ricardo F. Crespo'. *Markets and Morality*, 1 (2), 212–219.

Boland, L. A. (1982) *The Foundations of Economic Method*. London: Allen and Unwin.

Boland, L. A. (1988) *The Methodology of Economic Model Building : Methodology after Samuelson*. London; New York: Routledge.

Boland, L. A. (1992) *The Principles of Economics: Some Lies My Teachers Told Me*. London: Routledge.

Boland, L. A. (1997) *Critical Economic Methodology: A Personal Odyssey*. London: Routledge.

Boulding, K. (1969) 'Economics as a moral science'. *American Economic Review*, LIX.

Brennan, F. (1971) *Canberra in Crisis*. Fyshwick, ACT: Dalton.

Canterbury, E. R. and A. Marvasti (1992) 'The Coase Theorem as a Negative Externality'. *Journal of Economic Issues*, 26 (4), 1179–1189.

Casey, M. A. (2001) *Meaninglessness: The Solutions of Nietzsche, Freud, and Rorty*. North Melbourne: Freedom Publishing.

Coase, R. (1960) 'The Problem of Social Cost'. *Journal of Law and Economics*, 15.

Copelston, F. (1965) *A History of Philosophy*. New York: Image.

Crespo, R. F. (1998) 'Is Economics a Moral Science?' *Markets and Morality*, 1 (2), 201–211.

Currie, M. (1998) *Postmodern Narrative Theory*. New York, Palgrave: St. Martin's Press.

DeSoto, H. (2000) *The Mystery of Capitalism: Why Capitalism Triumphs in the West and Fails Everywhere Else*. New York: Basic Books.

Friedman, M. (1953). *The Methodology of Positive Economics. Essays in Positive Economics*. (pp3–43). Chicago: The University of Chicago Press.

Friedman, M. (1980). *Free to Choose*. Harmondsworth, England: Penguin.

Gross, E. (1992). 'What is feminist theory?'. In S. Himmelweit and H. Crowley (eds) *Knowing Women: Feminism and Knowledge*, Cambridge, England: Cambridge, MA, USA, Polity Press in Association with the Open University. vi, 396 pp.

Grosz, E. (1990). *Sexual Subversions*. Sydney: Allen and Unwin.

Hawking, S. W. (1988) *A Brief History of Time: From the Big Bang to Black Holes*. London: Bantam.

Hume, D. (1777) *Enquiries Concerning Human Understanding and Concerning the Principles of Morals*. Oxford: Clarendon.

Hylan, T. and Lage, M. et al. (1996) 'The Coase theorem, free agency, and major league baseball: a panel study of pitcher mobility from 1961 to 1992'. *Southern Economic Journal*, 62 (4), 1030.

Jones, R. (1976) *Supply in a Market Economy*. London: Allen and Unwin.

Kant, I. (1785) *Grounding for the Metaphysics of Morals*. USA: Hackett.

Kreeft, P. (1999) *A Refutation of Moral Relativism: Interviews with an Absolutist*. San Francisco: Ignatius Press.

Kuhn, T. (1970) *The Structure of Scientific Revolutions*. USA: University of Chicago Press.

Machiavelli, N. and H. C. Mansfield (1985) *The Prince*. Chicago: University of Chicago Press.

MacIntyre, A. (1985) *After Virtue*. London: Duckworth.

Marx, K. (1867) *Das Kapital*, first volume, English translations widely available.

Meikle, S. (1995) *Aristotle's Economic Thought*. Oxford, England: Oxford University Press.

Mill, J. S. (1859) *On Liberty*. London: Fount.

Mirrlees, J. A. (1982). 'The economic uses of utilitarianism'. In A. Sen and B. Williams *Utilitarianism and Beyond*. (pp. 63–84). Cambridge, Cambridge University Press.

Mishan, E. J. (1993). 'Economists versus the greens: an exposition and a critique'. *The Political Quarterly*, 64 (2), 222–42.

Novak, M. (1982) *The Spirit of Democratic Capitalism*. New York: Madison.

Proudhon, P. J. (1840) *What is property? An Inquiry into the Principle of Right and of Government*. London: W. Reeves.

Samuelson, P. A. (1975) *Economics*. Sydney: McGraw Hill.

Small, G. R. (1997) 'A cross cultural economic analysis of customary and Western land tenure'. *The Valuer*, 34 (7), 617–625.

Smith, A. (1759) *The Theory of Moral Sentiments*. New York: Garland.

Warnock, G. J. (1967) *Contempory Moral Philosophy*. London: McMillan.

Weaver, R. M. (1948) *Ideas Have Consequences*. Chicago, IL: University of Chicago Press.

Williams, B. A. O. (1972) *Morality: An Introduction To Ethics*. New York: Harper and Row.

Working, E. J. (1927) 'What do statistical "demand curves" show?' *The Quarterly Journal Of Economics*, Vol. XLI (1927), 212–235.

Zimmerman, C. C. (1947) *Family And Civilization*. New York: Harper.

Contributors

Alex Amankwah, LLM (Cornell) SJD(NYU), Associate Professor, James Cook University School of Law, Townsville, Queensland, Australia. Email: alex.amankwah@jcu.edu.au

Spike Boydell, Professor of Built Environment, School of Construction, Property and Project Management, Faculty of Design, Architecture and Building, University of Technology, Sydney, NSW, Australia. Email: spike.boydell@uts.edu.au

Katrina Myrvang Brown, Macaulay Land Use Research Institute, Craigiebuckler, Aberdeen, AB15 8QH, UK. Email: k.brown@macaulay.ac.uk

David J. Brunckhorst, Institute for Rural Futures, University of New England, Armidale, NSW, Australia. E-mail: dbrunckh@une.edu.au

Ed Cottrell, Cottrell, Cameron and Steen Pty Ltd, Cleveland, Queensland, Australia. Email: ccssurveys@oznetcom.com.au

Donna Craig, Chair of Desert Knowledge, Charles Darwin University; and Professor of Law, Director, Indigenous Rights Program Centre for Environmental Law, Macquarie University, Sydney, NSW, Australia. Email: donna.craig@law.mq.edu.au

Kevin Davies, Digital Strategies Pty Ltd, St Lucia South, Queensland, Australia. Email: daviesk@ds.au.com

Rolf Gerritsen, Director, Economic Policy Unit, Department of the Chief Minister, Northern Territory Government, Darwin; Project Leader Tropical Savannas Cooperative Research Centre, Australia. Email: rolf.gerritsen@nt.gov.au

Alexander Herr, Spatial Analyst, CSIRO Sustainable Ecosystems, University Drive, Townsville, Queensland, Australia. Email: alexander.herr@csiro.au

Michael Jeffery, Q.C., Director, Centre for Environmental Law, Macquarie University, Professor of Law and Director of the Centre for Environmental Law, Macquarie University, Sydney, NSW, Australia and recently, Deputy Chair, IUCN Commission on Environmental Law. Email: michael.jeffery@law.mq.edu.au

Silva Larson, Socio-economic Researcher, CSIRO Sustainable Ecosystems, University Drive, Townsville, Queensland, Australia. Email: silva.larson@csiro.au

Ken Lyons, Spatial Information Services Pty Ltd, Montville, Queensland, Australia. Email: klsis@attglobal.net

Graham R. Marshall, Institute for Rural Futures, University of New England, Armidale, NSW, Australia. Email: gmarshal@pobox.une.edu.au

Melissa Nursey-Bray, Institutional Analyst, CSIRO Sustainable Ecosystems, University Drive, Townsville, Queensland, Australia.
Email: melissa.nursey-bray@csiro.au

Elinor Ostrom, Workshop in Political Theory and Policy Analysis, Indiana University, Bloomington, Indiana, USA. Email: ostrom@indiana.edu

John Rolfe, Associate Professor in Regional Economic Development, Faculty of Business and Law, Central Queensland University, Rockhampton, Queensland, Australia. Email: j.rolfe@cqu.edu.au

Alex Smajgl, Environmental Economist, CSIRO Sustainable Ecosystems, University Drive, Townsville, Queensland, Australia.
Email: alex.smajgl@csiro.au

Garrick Small, Associate Head of the School of Construction, Property and Project Management, University of Technology, Sydney, NSW, Australia. Email: garrick.small@uts.edu.au

Anna Straton, Environmental Economist, CSIRO Sustainable Ecosystems, Darwin, Northern Territory, Australia. Email: anna.straton@csiro.au

Karen Vella, Institutional Analyst, CSIRO Sustainable Ecosystems, University Drive, Townsville, Queensland, Australia. Email: karen.vella@csiro.au

Tyron J. Venn, College of Forestry and Conservation, The University of Montana, Missoula, Montana, USA. Email: tyron.venn@cfc.umt.edu

Index